# Watching the Watchers: Corporate Governance for the 21st Century

# Watching the Watchers: Corporate Governance for the 21st Century

Robert A.G. Monks
Nell Minow

The most comprehensive examination and commentary on corporate governance that I have yet seen . . . If I had to choose one book among the dozens available to explain and illuminate the complexities of corporate governance, this definitive treatise would be it.

*Hugh Parker*

*Corporate Governance* is a lucid and comprehensive introduction to a subject that is of critical importance to anyone interested in business. Everyone, from student, to scholar, to corporate employee, officer, director, or shareholder, will find it valuable.

*Donald Jacobs, Dean, Kellogg School of Business, Northwestern University*

This is what we've needed – a solid text on corporate governance written by two of the real stars in the field.

*D. Jeanne Patterson, Associate Professor of Public and Environmental Affairs, Indiana University*

. . . a fresh, thoughtful, and timely look at the problem of corporate governance . . . a little gem.

*Joseph A. Grundfest, Professor of Law, Stanford Law School*

. . . authoritative and informative, with some fascinating case vignettes . . . A monumental work.

*Bob Tricker, Editor, Corporate Governance*

. . . carefully blends economic and legal aspects of corporate governance. Highly recommended for use in seminars on board practices, MBA programs, and corporate governance forums.

*Cornelis A. de Kluyver, Dean, School of Business Administration, George Mason University*

Highly useful . . . illuminates the current issues facing managers, boards of directors, and shareholders, as well as explaining their respective roles in the corporation.

*Ira M. Millstein, Weil, Gotshal & Manges; Lester Crown Visiting Faculty Fellow, Yale School of Management*

Provides a strong theoretical framework for the subject. It gives meaning to the important public policy issues by numerous examples, case studies, and policy statements.

*Professor J. Fred Weston, UCLA*

# Watching the Watchers: Corporate Governance for the 21st Century

Robert A.G. Monks
Nell Minow

BLACKWELL
*Business*

First published 1996

Blackwell Publishers, Inc.
238 Main Street
Cambridge, Massachusetts 02142

Blackwell Publishers Ltd.
108 Cowley Road
Oxford OX4 1JF
UK

*Library of Congress Cataloging-in-Publication Data*

Monks, Robert A. G., 1933–
  Watching the watchers: corporate governance for the 21st century/Robert A. G. Monks, Nell Minow.
    p.   cm.
  Rev. ed., with new chapter added and some deletions, of: Corporate governance. 1995.
  Includes bibliographical references and indexes.
  ISBN 1-55786-866-2 (hb)
  1. Corporate governance—United States. I. Minow, Nell, 1952–   . II. Monks, Robert A. G., 1933–   . Corporate governance. III. Title.
HD2745.M66   1996
658.4—dc20                                                                96-16619
                                                                               CIP

*British Library Cataloguing in Publication Data*

A CIP catalogue record for this book is available from the British Library.

Typeset by AM Marketing

Printed in the United States of America

This book is printed on acid-free paper

To the future: Max, Mariah, and Megan
R.A.G.M.

To David, Benjamin, and Rachel
N.M.

# Contents

# List of Cases in Point

# Foreword
# by B. Minoru Makihara,
# CEO of Mitsubishi Corporation

The term "corporate governance" is fairly new in the vocabulary of management science in Japan, but it is quickly increasing in importance. Japan's major manufacturing and trading corporations are experiencing a substantial downturn in profitability that has pushed returns on investment to their lowest levels in the postwar era. One cause of such declines can be found in the inability of the existing framework of corporate management – the structure of corporate governance – to cope with recent changes in the business environment. The much-admired and often exaggerated *keiretsu* system of cross-ownership and close monitoring by banks and big block holders has become less effective, and no new structure has been developed to replace it. In this sense, the current recession gripping Japan can be described as a "governance recession."

As governments throughout the world reduce barriers to trade, and as investors insist on being able to purchase securities in any company, regardless of its domicile, understanding and evaluating corporate governance systems is absolutely essential. The European Community was successful in adopting consistent standards for some aspects of governance; others are still being debated. The emerging economies in eastern Europe are trying to re-invent capitalism and avoid the mistakes other economies have made in the past. In the United States, shareholder activism, sparked by the excesses of the takeover era, has itself sparked a new era of activism by boards of directors, with an astonishing series of CEO firings in 1992 and 1993. The successful shareholder initiatives at companies like Sears, American Express, ITT, and Westinghouse demonstrated that, effectively, informed owners can add value.

With much less fanfare, but no less importance, Daimler-Benz, the "crown jewel" of the German industrial establishment, was willing to change its long-time accounting and disclosure practices to be eligible to list its securities on the New York Stock Exchange. This shows that even major corporations will make governance changes in order to have access to capital. It also shows that the markets reflect the advantages of at least some governance provisions, for example, the additional transparency afforded by the disclosure requirements of the New York Stock Exchange and the U.S. Securities and Exchange Commission. And the recent rejection of Rupert Murdoch's proposed listing by the Australian Stock Exchange, because he wanted to sell non-voting shares, demonstrates that governance considerations are crucial in competing for capital.

Those who plan a career in international business must understand corporate governance, both its historical context and its current controversies. The field draws from law, economics, ethics, politics, management, finance, and several other categories. Understanding the issues raised by corporate governance requires familiarity with the concepts, assumptions, and vocabulary of each of these fields, plus a willingness to synthesize and even transcend them. The book authored by Bob Monks and Nell Minow is a comprehensive and insightful analysis that should be required reading for anyone entering the world of business.

I have known and worked with Bob Monks for almost half a century, since we were roommates at Harvard College. Bob served on the Advisory Board of Mitsubishi International Corporation when I was its Chief Executive Officer. I like to say of Bob that he is never in doubt and occasionally wrong. It may be a function of our aging, but I find him less wrong in recent years, and, in the area of corporate governance, he has been a prophet in the United States, Japan, the United Kingdom, Australia and the continent of Europe. Bob and his long-time partner, Nell Minow, have established themselves throughout the world as the leading authorities in this field, and as active and effective participants in it as well. I urge the reader to pay careful attention to what they have to say.

# Acknowledgements

First and foremost, we want to thank Kit Bingham, our Director of Research, without whom this book would still be just a dream. His tireless, thorough, creative, and even cheerful diligence provided most of the case studies and supporting material, and he made even the more tedious aspects of research and writing a genuine pleasure.

We are very grateful to the heroic scholars whose work instructed and inspired us, especially Jonathan Charkham, Sir Adrian Cadbury, David Walker, Robert Clark, Alfred Conard, Peter Drucker, Melvin Eisenberg, Betty Krikorian, Jeanne Patterson, Margaret Blair, Adolf Berle and Gardiner Means, and James Willard Hurst.

We have also learned a great deal from our colleagues, clients, and friends, including the widely disparate group of institutional investors all joined together by their commitment to the beneficial owners they serve as fiduciaries and the corporate managers they monitor as shareholders. These are also our heroes. They include Olena Berg, Dale Hanson, Rich Koppes, Kayla Gillan, Ned Regan, Tom Pandick, Harrison J. Goldin, Carol O'Cleireacain, Patricia Lipton, Nancy Williams, Ned Johnson, Dean LeBaron, Dick Schleffer, Janice Hester-Amey, Joe Grundfest, Martin Lipton, Ira Millstein, Luther Jones, Roland Machold, Michael Jacobs, John and Lewis Gilbert, Peg O'Hara, Mort Kleven, Alan Lebowitz, Karla Scherer, Abbot Leban, Bill Steiner, Tom Flanagan, Bill McEwen, David Greene, Alan Towers, and Alan Kahn. We are also especially grateful to our dear friends Sarah A.B. Teslik, Executive Director of the Council of Institutional Investors, and Ralph Whitworth, of the United Shareholders Association, who provided the leadership, support, and intellectual foundation for most of the developments in this area over the past few years. We have also learned a great deal from Bernie Black, Mark Roe, and Jack Coffee. John M. Nash and Jean Head Sisco of the National Association of Corporate Directors deserve thanks for their labors in the field of governance.

We are grateful to those who permitted us to use their material in this book, which added inestimably to its value. Thanks to Chancellor William Allen, Ira Millstein, Martin Lipton, Jay Lorsch, Cyrus F. Freidheim, Hugh Parker, Shann Turnbull, Oxford Analytica, Joe Grundfest, Jamie Heard, Howard Sherman, Bruce Babcock, and Geoff Mazullo. Cathy Dixon guided us through the thorny securities law issues with patience, good humor, and unbounded expertise. Gary Lyons was very kind in supplying us with the data for many of our charts. Mitchell Fromstein was most generous not only with useful material but also his own time. Newton Minow and Stanley Frankel sent us constant clippings and gave us thoughtful advice. Thanks especially to Virginia Smith and HarperBusiness for allowing us to adapt and update some of the material in our first book, *Power and Accountability*. And our deepest gratitude to Ben Makihara for his thoughtful foreword.

There is a special section of heaven for those who are willing to trudge through early drafts and provide comments. Thanks very much to Margaret Blair, Alfred Conard, Wayne Marr, Jane Zanglein, and Stu Gillan.

We want to thank our colleagues, including Jamie Heard, Howard Sherman, Francis Corcoran, Jill Lyons, Gary Lyons, Yvonne Payne, and Amy Nadel of Institutional Shareholder Services and Jim Pannell, Adrian Gould, Pat Thompson, and Cory Caouette of LENS. Barbara Sleasman is the finest professional with whom we have ever worked. We would also like to thank the people at Blackwell, including Richard Burton, who got us started, and Rolf Janke, Paul Stringer, and Roger Jordan who kept us going. Alexandra Lajoux was a brilliant (and tactful) editor. Hugh Parker did a graceful edit to transform this edition from its original design as a textbook, and contributed a splendid new chapter.

*Note from Bob Monks:* I sometimes feel like Samuel T. Coleridge's famed wedding guest "who grabbeth one of three" and proceeds to regale each with his memorable tale. In view of my utter preoccupation with this book and its subject matter, I am profoundly grateful for the civility and forebearance of friends and family and the love and understanding of my wife – Milly – and partners – Barbara and Nell.

*Note from Nell Minow:* Thanks and love to my extended family, including all of the Minows and Apatoffs; my friends Kathy and Andrew Stephen, Kristie Miller, Jesse Norman, Tom Dunkel, Judy Viorst, Sarah Teslik, Nadine Prosperi, Debbie Morris, John Adams, Shannon Hackett, David Drew, Terry Savage, Bill Pedersen, Gary Waxman, Sarah Hadley, Matthew Frost, Amy Schaul, Steve Wallman, Sam Natapoff, Michael Kinsley, Parvane Hashemi, Ellen Twaddell, Steve Friess, Yusef Harden, Duncan Clark, Peter Bernstein, Ellen Burka, Michael Deal, and Stuart Brotman. Thanks to Bob Monks, the perfect partner. Most of all, I want to thank my family – my children, Benjamin and Rachel, and my husband, David, still the best person I know.

# Introduction

What is corporate governance? It is the relationship among various participants in determining the direction and performance of corporations. The primary participants are (1) the shareholders, (2) the management (led by the chief executive officer), and (3) the board of directors. In this book, we will devote a chapter to each leg of this corporate "tripod." Other participants include the employees, customers, suppliers, creditors, and the community. Their interests and impact are reflected in this book as well.

In the following pages, we will set forth the rights, the obligations, and the impact of all of these direct participants in corporate governance. We will explore in detail the roles that the various "corporate constituents" can, do, and should play in determining corporate direction, strategy, and performance. But in order to understand these players, we must first understand the play – What is a corporation for? Who should provide its direction? We have to establish where we are trying to go before we can figure out how much progress we have made in getting there and what we need to do to go further.

Therefore, we begin with an examination of the theory, the myth, the reality, and the future of the corporate structure. We will start off with three brief examples that illustrate some of the most important issues facing those who invest in, work for, and direct corporations. The questions to keep in mind, as we examine the issues that corporations face, are "Who is in the best position to make this decision, and does that person/group have the authority to make it?" Each of the cases in point in this section and throughout the book highlights decisions by corporate management that were challenged in court by one or more of the other "corporate constituents." They each raise questions about whether management made the right decision about what the business should do with its resources and whether the court made the right decision about what the law should permit. While there are no clear answers for any of these cases, we try to consider both the substance and the process of the decisions being challenged. In other words, we ask not only whether this was the correct decision from the perspective of the future competitiveness and vitality of the business, but also whether the process for identifying and evaluating the options available was the one most likely to produce the right answer.

## Case in Point: Should the Chicago Cubs Play Night Games?

Can CEOs decide not to pursue opportunities that will increase revenues? In 1968, some shareholders of the Wrigley Corporation sued the company and its directors for failing to install lights in Chicago's Wrigley Field. The shareholders claimed that the company's operating losses for four years were the result of its negligence and mismanagement. If the field had lights, the Cubs could play at night, when revenues from attendance, concessions, and radio and television broadcasts were the greatest. The shareholders argued that the sole reason for failing to install the lights was the personal opinion of William Wrigley, the president of the company, that baseball was a daytime sport, and that night games would lead to a deterioration of the neighborhood. "Thus," the complaint concluded, "Wrigley and the directors who acquiesced in this policy were acting against the financial welfare of the Cubs in an arbitrary and capricious manner, causing waste of corporate assets. They were not exercising reasonable care or prudence in the management of the corporation's affairs."[1]

The court ruled against the shareholders. As long as the decision was made "without an element of fraud, illegality, or conflict of interest, and if there was no showing of damage *to the corporation,* then such questions of policy and management are within the limits of director discretion as a matter of business judgment," the court ruled (emphasis added).

## Case in Point: Should AT&T Owners Pay for Propaganda?

Is a corporation entitled to free speech? A Massachusetts statute prohibited corporations from making expenditures to influence the vote on "any questions submitted to the voters, other than one materially affecting any of the property, business, or assets of the corporation." The law made it clear that this prohibition extended to all tax issues, even those that did "materially affect" the company. The statute was declared unconstitutional because it infringed the First Amendment rights *of the company* to freedom of speech.[2]

Two justices of the Supreme Court who heard a case raising some similar issues had opposite reactions.

Justice William Brennan did not want corporate management to use the shareholders' money to promote their ideas: "The State surely has a compelling interest in preventing a corporation it has chartered from exploiting those who do not wish to contribute to the Chamber's political message. 'A's right to receive information does not require the state to permit B to steal from C the funds that alone will enable B to make the communication.' "[3]

Justice Antonin Scalia thought it was worthwhile to bring ideas to the marketplace, and he did not worry that the extra support for those ideas from the corporate bank account would sway anyone otherwise unwilling to buy them: "The advocacy of [AT&T or General Motors] will be effective only to the extent that it brings to the people's attention ideas which – despite the invariably self-interested and probably uncongenial source – strike them as true."[4]

## Case in Point: Who Pays the Penalty When Babies Drink Sugar Water?

How do you punish a corporation? The president and vice president of Beech-Nut admitted that they knowingly permitted adulterated apple juice to be sold for babies. The babies who drank the juice, of course, had no way of knowing that the juice was not right, and no way of communicating it if they did. The company pled guilty to 215 counts of violating federal food and drug laws, and paid a $2 million fine. According to the *New York Times,* its market share dropped 15 percent. The president and vice president were not fired. On the contrary – the company paid all of their legal fees and their salaries until their appeals ran out. No one from the company ever went to jail or paid a fine out of his own pocket. On the witness stand, one of the executives explained his decision to continue to market the adulterated juice: "What was I supposed to do? Close down the factory?"

There is one theme to all three of these examples, and indeed to all problems of corporate governance, and that is the issue of agency costs. The price we all pay for the benefits of the corporate structure is our loss of control. Investors lose control over the use of their capital. Managers lose control over their sources of funding. Other participants in the corporate structure – employees, creditors, and so forth – also lose some measure of control. The board has the oversight responsibility. They monitor the extent to which the various corporate participants retain control, the costs and benefits of their attempts to do so, and the resulting balance of powers among them.

In this book, we will focus on the three most significant players in the corporate process: shareholders, managers, and directors. Together, these forces shape a corporation's focus, its direction, its productivity and competitiveness, and ultimately, its viability and legitimacy. First, however, we will begin with an inquiry into the nature of the corporation itself.

## Ideas about Corporations

Concentration of economic power in all-embracing corporations represents a kind of private government which is a power unto itself – a regimentation of other people's money and other people's lives. *Franklin Roosevelt*

The myth that holds that the great corporation is a puppet of the market, the powerless servant of the consumer, is, in fact, part of the doctrine by which its power is perpetuated. *John Kenneth Galbraith*

Merchants have no country. The mere spot they stand on does not constitute so strong an attachment as that from which they draw their gains. *Thomas Jefferson*

By making ordinary business decisions [corporate] managers now have more power than most sovereign governments to determine where people will live; what work they will do, if any; what they will eat, drink, and wear; what sorts of knowledge, schools, and universities they will encourage; and what kinds of society their children will inherit. *Richard J. Barnet and Ronald Mueller*

Corporations, especially the large and complex ones with which we have to live, now appear to possess some of the qualities of nation states including, perhaps, an alarming capacity to insulate their members from the moral consequences of their actions. *Paul Eddy, Elaine Potter, and Bruce Page*

## NOTES

1. *Shlensky v. Wrigley,* 95 Ill. App. 2d 173, 237 (1968).
2. *First National Bank of Boston v. Bellotti,* 435 US 765 (1978).
3. *Austin, Michigan Secretary of State, et al. v. Michigan State Chamber of Commerce,* Brennan, concurring opinion, p. 7.
4. Id., Scalia's dissent, p. 5.

# 1

# What Is a Corporation?

Definitions of the term *corporation* reflect the perspectives (and the biases) of the people writing the definitions. Those who have tried to come up with a definition end up like the blind men who tried to describe an elephant, one feeling the tail and calling it a snake, one feeling the leg and calling it a tree, one feeling the side and calling it a wall. Similarly, some lawyers and economists describe the corporation as simply "a nexus (bundle) of contracts," arguing that the corporation is nothing more than the sum of all of the agreements leading to its creation.[1]

## DEFINITIONS

"A corporation is an artificial being, invisible, intangible, and existing only in the contemplation of the law. Being the mere creature of the law, it possesses only those properties which the charter of its creation confers on it, either expressly or as incidental to its very existence. These are such as are supposed best calculated to effect the object for which it was created. Among the most important are immortality, and, if the expression be allowed, individuality; properties by which a perpetual succession of many persons are considered the same, and may act as a single individual." *Chief Justice John Marshall*

"A body of persons granted a charter legally recognizing them as a separate entity having its own rights, privileges, and liabilities distinct from those of its members." *American Heritage Dictionary*

"An artificial person or legal entity created by, or under the authority of, the laws of a state. . . . The corporation is distinct from the individuals who comprise it." *Black's Law Dictionary, 6th ed., 1990*

"An ingenious device for obtaining individual profit without individual responsibility." *Ambrose Bierce, The Devil's Dictionary*

All of these definitions have some validity, and all, including the one from *The Devil's Dictionary,* reflect the corporation's key feature – its ability to draw its resources from a variety of groups and establish and maintain its own persona separate from all of them. As Henry Ford once said, "A great business is really too big to be human."

In our view, a corporation is a mechanism established to allow different parties to contribute capital, expertise, and labor, for the maximum benefit of all of them. The investor gets the chance to participate in the profits of the enterprise without taking responsibility for the operations. The management gets the chance to run the company without taking the responsibility of personally providing the funds. In order to make both of these possible, the shareholders have limited liability and limited involvement in the company's affairs. That involvement includes, at least in theory, the right to elect directors and the fiduciary obligation of directors and management to protect their interests.

This independent entity must still relate to a wide variety of "constituents," including its directors, managers, employees, shareholders, customers, creditors and suppliers, as well as the members of the community and the government. Each of these relationships itself has a variety of constituents. The corporation's relationship to its employees varies, for example, depending on the circumstances: whether or not they are members of a union, whether or not they are pension plan participants. And each of these relationships affects the direction and focus of the corporation. The study of corporate governance is the study of the connection of those relationships to the corporation and to one another.

## EVOLUTION OF THE CORPORATE STRUCTURE

While in law, corporations are, at least for some purposes, considered to be a fictional "person," at its core each corporation is in fact a structure. The corporate structure was developed to meet particular needs that were not being met by earlier forms available to business. It evolved through a Darwinian process in which each development made it stronger, more resilient, and more impervious to control by outsiders.

As we examine that evolutionary pattern, it will become clear that every change the corporate form has undergone has been directed toward the corporation's own perpetuation and growth. The advantages and disadvantages of this fact of business life are discussed throughout this book.

In their earliest Anglo-Saxon form, municipal and educational corporations were granted perpetual existence and control over their own functions as a way of insuring independence from the otherwise all-encompassing power of the king. By the seventeenth century, corporations were created by the state for specific purposes, like the settlement of India and the American colonies. Their effectiveness is credited as one of the principal explanations for Europe's half millennium domination of the globe. Limiting investors' liability to the amount they actually invested was a critical factor in attracting the necessary capital for this unprecedented achievement.[2]

Even as recently as 1932, US Supreme Court Justice Louis Brandeis argued that, "The privilege of engaging in such commerce in corporate form is one which the state may confer or may withhold as it sees fit."[3] He emphasized the importance of making sure that states conferred the privilege of the corporate structure only in those cases where it was consistent with public policy and welfare, for example, "as a means of raising revenue; or, in order to procure for the community a public utility, a bank, or a desired industry not otherwise attainable; or . . . an instrumentality of business which will facilitate the establishment and conduct of new and large enterprises deemed of public benefit."[4] He noted that

The prevalence of the corporation in America has led men of this generation to act, at times, as if the privilege of doing business in corporate form were inherent in the citizen, and has led them to accept the evils attendant upon the free and unrestricted use of the corporate mechanism as if these evils were the inescapable price of civilized life, and hence, to be borne with resignation. Throughout the greater part of our history, a different view prevailed. Although the value of this instrumentality in commerce and industry was fully recognized, incorporation for business was commonly denied long after it had been freely granted for religious, educational, and charitable purposes. It was denied because of fear. Fear of enchroachment upon the liberties and opportunities of the individual. Fear of the subjugation of labor to capital. Fear of monopoly. Fear that the absorption of capital by corporations, and their perpetual life, might bring evils similar to those which attended mortmain.[5] There was a sense of some insidious menace inherent in large aggregations of capital, particularly when held by corporations. So at first the corporate privilege was granted sparingly; and only when the grant seemed necessary in order to procure for the community some specific benefit otherwise unattainable. The later enactment of general corporation laws does not signify that the apprehension of corporate domination had been overcome.[6]

Brandeis points out that the decision to remove the strict requirements imposed on corporations was not based on the legislators' "conviction that maintenance of these restrictions was undesirable in itself, but to the conviction that it was futile to insist on them; because local restriction would be circumvented by foreign incorporation."[7] In other words, the characteristics of the corporate form were so important to people in business that legislators recognized that they could not beat them, and therefore might as well join them, or at least permit and then tax them.

What made the corporate form so appealing, so essential? According to Dean Robert Clark, of Harvard Law School, the four characteristics essential to the vitality and appeal of the corporate form are:

- limited liability for investors;
- free transferability of investor interests;
- legal personality (entity-attributable powers, life span, and purpose); and
- centralized management.[8]

He adds that three developments, starting in the late nineteenth century, made these attributes particularly important. The *first* was the need for firms far larger than had previously been the norm. Technological advances led to new economies of scale. For the first time it made sense to have firms of more than a dozen people, and suddenly there were companies employing hundreds, then thousands. The *second* was the accompanying need for capital from a range of sources broader than in the past, when the only game in town was a small group of wealthy individuals who had previously invested by private negotiation. The *third* condition was that private ownership of investment property had to be "accepted as a social norm." The concept hardly seems revolutionary now, but it was radical, even a century ago, when it was widely assumed that most property would belong to the state, the church, or a select number of wealthy people. While this tradition was challenged from time to time, as, for example, during the Colonial and Revolutionary period of US history, the idea of widespread private property is essentially a modern one.

Let's look at Clark's four characteristics.

1. *Limited liability* The notion of limited liability goes back to at least 2000 BC, when merchants provided the financing for seagoing vessels. But it was first spelled out by the English courts during the fifteenth century. This means that the corporation is separate from its owners and employees; what is owed to the corporation is not owed to the individuals in the group that make up the corporation; and what the group owes is not owed by the individuals that make it up. Hence, if a corporation goes bankrupt and is sued by its creditors for recovery of debts, the individual members of the corporation are not individually liable. The US Supreme Court, in the 1886 case of *Santa Clara County v. Southern Pacific Railroad,* refined this notion by ruling that a corporation is to be regarded as a person.

If a dozen people pool their funds to create a partnership, they risk losing not just their stakes, but everything they have. Partners who operate a restaurant are personally liable for debts to unpaid creditors and employees, for any injuries to a patron who sues after falling down the restaurant stairs, and for the misconduct of fellow partners, even for which they had no knowledge or control. Investors in a corporation that operates a restaurant have no such risk. If Beech-Nut had been a partnership, all of the partners could have been liable to pay the fine as well as for any damages the court could might award to the consumers who purchased the adulterated juice.

This kind of shared liability may work well when the partnership is small enough to enable everyone to keep an eye on each other and share in all decisions, and when the personal investment of each partner is big enough to give each one the same incentive for low risk and high returns.[9] But this oversight and incentive would be impossible in a setting of not just dozens, but millions of "partners" investing in a company. No one would buy stock in a large corporation if his risk of loss were unlimited. One of the primary advantages of investing in stock is the certainty that whatever happens, the risk of loss is limited to the amount of the investment.

Note that revisions in bankruptcy law and practice in the United States during the 1980s gave shareholders a second chance to profit from failing enterprises. Airline companies were able to avoid union contracts and asbestos companies were able to avoid tort liability. Most prominently of all, Texaco was able to negotiate down the damages assessed against it arising out of the Pennzoil acquisition. It became expedient even for companies with substantial assets to declare bankruptcy because of the protections – and the extra time – it gave them. Ultimately, many of these companies emerged from bankruptcy with their liabilities better organized, and the shareholders – whose downside liability was always limited – were given a second chance to profit.

There is a catch here, however. With limited liability comes limited authority. A partner has a co-equal right to run the company with all of the other partners (unless the parties have agreed to another arrangement by contract). It is the partner's high level of control that makes his high level of liability acceptable. And it is the shareholder's low level of risk that makes his low level of control acceptable.

2. *Transferability* Just as important as limited liability in achieving an acceptable level of risk is the free ability to transfer one's holding. A partnership interest is complicated and difficult to value, and there is no stock exchange where partnership interests can be traded. By contrast, stock is almost as liquid as cash. A shareholder who is concerned that his stock may be losing value can sell almost immediately.

Transferability is also a function of limited authority. It is as though the shareholder says, "I will put my money at risk, with little authority to control the enterprise, as long as I can control my own risk by selling out any time I want to."

3. *Legal personality* A partnership dies with its partners. Or it dies when one partner decides to quit (unless there are explicit contractual provisions to the contrary). Continuing after the death or resignation of the partners can be complicated and expensive. A corporation lives on for as long as it has capital. This is a fairly recent development. Business corporations in the United States during the nineteenth century usually had a life limited to a term of years. As Justice Brandeis wrote in *Liggett v. Lee,* only in the most recent times have people assumed that perpetual existence was a necessary – to say nothing of a desirable – attribute of corporations.

Legal personality has other benefits as well. One is demonstrated by the Beech-Nut example, where actions that would result in a penalty for an individual, perhaps even a jail sentence, have no such result when the individual commits them as part of a corporation. Another is in the First Amendment example, where corporate management is allowed to use investors' money to promote a political agenda with which they may not agree. Another is ownership. It is because corporations are defined as legal persons that they may own property, including real estate, copyrights, and other assets.

This aspect, too, depends on limited authority by investors. To the extent the investors do have authority, they jeopardize the company when they are unavailable to exercise it. Legal personality allows the corporation to act, to own, and to continue past the life span of any individual or group.

4. *Centralized management* Partnerships are managed by consensus or majority vote (unless partners explicitly agree otherwise). The point is that every partner has, if he wants it, a co-equal say in the affairs of the company. In a corporation, the power to determine the company's overall direction is given to the directors and the power to control its day-to-day operations is given to the managers.

This is another aspect of the limited authority given to investors. In order to allow the company to operate with maximum efficiency, the shareholders give up the right to make decisions on all but the most general issues facing the company.

Initially, a corporation was not permitted to engage in any activity unless it was specifically approved by the state in granting its charter. The original rule was based on the state's presumption *against* corporate activity; every undertaking had to be explicitly justified and approved. But as the corporate form became increasingly popular, the presumption shifted. By the late nineteenth century, business corporations were permitted to organize for any lawful purpose, without requiring the prior approval of the government.

Just as dramatic – and just as important – as this shift in the relationship between the corporation and the government was the shift in the relationship between the corporation and its shareholders. As corporations grew in size and age, their ownership became increasingly fractionated and markets developed to assure almost total immediate liquidity. This increased their strength and scope, but it reduced their accountability. In the early days, when the directors sat around a real board, they represented the shareholders because they *were* the shareholders. As corporations grew in size and complexity, the law tried to develop a standard of performance for directors that would encourage the same sense of duty and care that they would naturally use when they were representing themselves.

## THE PURPOSE OF A CORPORATION

Corporations are such a pervasive element in everyday life that it is difficult to step back far enough to see them clearly. Corporations do not just determine what goods and services are available in the marketplace, but, more than any other institution, corporations determine the quality of the air we breathe and the water we drink, and even where we live. It helps to spend some time talking about the purposes that corporations serve.

### Human Satisfaction

Business corporations provide an outlet for the satisfaction of essential human drives – quests for fulfillment, success, and security. The corporate structure allows value to be placed on differing contributions that, taken alone, would have only a fraction of their aggregate value, so that the whole is greater than the sum of its parts. Through corporations, skills and experience can be competitively marketed and rewarded according to their contribution to value. Corporations have provided a means for the ambitious to achieve, the enterprising to prosper, and the ingenious to be enriched beyond their fondest expectations – the role played by the church or the military at other times and in other cultures. Money invested buys perpetual ownership in a cornucopia of self-renewing abundance. Only the amount invested is at risk, and, if an investor buys ownership in several companies, he can spread that risk, and a portfolio corporation can be divested at any time to reduce significantly the possibility of loss.

Above all else, creating a structure for the agglomeration of talent and capital has permitted an increasing number of individuals the opportunity to create wealth for themselves and their descendants.

### Social Structure

Corporations offer lasting and resilient social structures. Human beings have created social structures since their cave days, in order to foster cooperation and specialization. For centuries, these structures were devoted to goals that were not (necessarily) financial. For example, during the Dark Ages and the Middle Ages, western man was organized under the single church. Toward the end of the medieval era, signs of this "church triumphant" system abounded. Under its banner, whole populations committed themselves for decades to Crusades. The gross national product of the continent was devoted to construction of magnificent houses of worship. Then, in a remarkable turn of events aided by religious protest, Henry VIII abruptly asserted the primacy of civil authority. For several centuries, right to the end of World War I, civil order based on hereditary rulers dominated the West.

At about this time, power in the form of ability to create wealth through goods and services desired by a population willing to pay passed to an entirely new type of entity, the huge worldwide corporations.

### Efficiency and Efficacy

Corporations enable people to get things done. The words "businesslike," "professional," and "enterprise" are synonymous with "beneficial efficiency" and "efficacy." The translation of an idea into a product; human ingenuity into bricks, mortar, and equipment; and savings into "growth stocks," has materially enhanced the lives of many people in democratic capitalist societies.

The challenge has been to adapt the corporate form to the needs of society. To this end, the state has maintained the original corporate model, chartering special purpose corporations to achieve a particular objective. For example, in order to assure better control by America of its fuel needs, the US Congress created the United States Synthetic Fuels Corporation in 1980 and attempted to use private sector personnel and techniques to solve a public problem. Similarly, organizations such as the Federal National Mortgage Association show the government's recognition that if it is going to compete with Wall Street, it must be through a private, for-profit organization.

This works both ways, of course. It is an understatement to say that the government does not hesitate to regulate corporations for a variety of reasons, some tangential to the corporation's activities. Society can induce or restrain particular corporate activities through tax and regulatory "fine tuning." For example, much New Deal legislation attempted to achieve social goals while pursuing economic ones. The Davis-Bacon Act of 1931 is one of three labor statutes passed in the 1930s to protect workers employed on government contracts. Davis-Bacon provides minimum wage requirements and fringe benefits for government-employed construction workers. More recent examples include laws and regulations prohibiting discrimination on the basis of age, race, gender, and disability, and a Clinton Administration proposal, enacted in 1993, requiring companies of more than 15 employees to grant "family leave" to those who required it.

## Ubiquity and Flexibility

Corporations give individuals a greater and more lasting sphere of action. Corporations have no boundaries in time or space. A corporation continues despite the death or retirement of its highest officers. A corporation that is chartered in Delaware can do business anywhere in the world. Corporations can be moved. They can be transformed by a revision to their legal or financial structure. A corporation's officers and directors can change its place of incorporation, close existing places of business and open new ones virtually without restraint, and reallocate investment capital. American companies change their state of incorporation to receive the benefits of favorable laws, or reincorporate offshore for tax reasons. The free trade agreements in Europe and Northern America are creating a "borderless world" in which a company's legal domicile relates to nothing but its own convenience.

An individual may decide to refrain from certain risky actions for several reasons. He may fear blame, shame, liability, even prison. But corporations, though they may be fined, cannot be jailed. This makes the corporate form a way of transferring enterprise liabilities to society as a whole. With their ability to provide jobs, corporations are aggressively courted by competing locations and states and countries "race to the bottom," imposing fewer and fewer constraints on profit potential. The state anti-takeover laws enacted hastily to protect local companies from the prospect of a contest for control (sometimes, as in Massachusetts, signed by the governor in the headquarters of the company in question) are just one example.

## Identity

Indeed, corporations have a life, and even citizenship, of their own, with attendant rights and powers. They appear to have personalities. We speak of "Ma Bell" and "Big Blue." Corporations are "persons" within the meaning of the United States Federal Constitution and Bill of Rights. They are entitled to protection against the taking of their property without due process of law. They are entitled (at least to some extent) to freedom of speech.

They can contribute money to political causes and campaigns, though some restrictions apply, due to post-Watergate reforms.

As the source of jobs, and therefore of the livelihood for people who vote, they have significant political capital. Corporations, therefore, are powerful participants in the deliberations of our lawmakers.

Corporations also decide what products and services will be available. This applies not just to laundry soap and toothpaste, but also to medications and safety equipment. They decide investment priorities. They establish workplace conditions. They set prices.

## THE CORPORATION AS A "PERSON"

Author and reporter William Greider describes the development of corporate "personalities."

> The great project of corporate lawyers, extending over generations, has been to establish full citizenship for their business organizations. They argue that their companies are entitled to the same political rights, save voting, that the Constitution guarantees to people. In 1886 the Supreme Court declared, without hearing arguments, that corporations would henceforth be considered "persons" for purposes of the 14th Amendment – the "due process" amendment that was established to protect the newly emancipated black slaves after the Civil War. Fifty years later, Justice Hugo Black reviewed the Supreme Court's many decisions applying the 14th Amendment and observed that less than one half of one percent invoked it in protection of the Negro race, and more than 50 percent asked that its benefits be extended to corporations. . . .
>
> In the modern era of regulation [corporate lawyers] are invoking the Bill of Rights to protect their organizations from federal laws. . . . Corporations, in other words, claim to be "citizens" of the Republic, not simply for propaganda or good public relations, but in the actual legal sense of claiming constitutional rights and protections. . . . Whatever legal theories may eventually develop around this question, the political implications are profound. If corporations are citizens, then other citizens – the living, breathing kind – necessarily become less important to the processes of self-government."[10]

## THE CORPORATION AS A "MORAL PERSON"

Thomas Donaldson provides an analytical structure within which this question can be addressed:

In order to qualify as a moral agent, a corporation would need to embody a process of moral decision making. On the basis of our previous discussion, this process seems to require at a minimum:

1. The capacity to use moral reasons in decision-making.
2. The capacity of the decision-making process to control not only overt corporate acts, but also the structure of policies and rules.

[The first] is necessary to raise the corporation above the level of a mere machine. To be a moral agent, something must have reasons for what it does, not simply causes for what it does, and for something to be a moral agent, some of those reasons must be moral ones. Obviously, corporations are unable to think as humans, but they can employ reasons of a sort, and this is shown by the fact that they can be morally accountable. That is, with the proper internal structure, corporations, like humans, can be liable to give an account of their behavior where the account stipulates which moral reasons prompted their behavior.[11]

Can business "do well by doing good?" This is a perennial question. On one end of the scale, companies such as The Body Shop and Ben and Jerry's have made social responsibility (or, at least, their view of social responsibility) part of their marketing strategy. Consumers can feel less guilty about buying arguably decadent products like makeup and ice cream if they know that by doing so they are supporting good causes. But can companies thrive when the cost of social responsibility raises prices too high, instead of making the products more marketable, making them less so? Clearly, there is some point past which the company's goods and services will become too expensive.[12]

At one end of the scale are the most basic aspects of social responsibility, like compliance with the law. At the other end of the scale are activities so unrelated to the goods and services sold that pursuing them is considered by the marketplace to be irrelevant, even detrimental to the company's productivity.

Look again at the very first example in this book, the lawsuit challenging the decision not to put lights in Wrigley Field. This decision, which deprived the fans of night games and the investors of a substantial source of revenue, was made on the basis of management's notion of social responsibility. Later we will consider the example of Stride Rite, which profited from its (well-deserved) reputation for commitment to the community, while it was making the (economically justified) decision to move jobs out of the community.

The key question here, one of the core issues of corporate governance, is "Who decides?" A CEO can decide that the company's social responsibility is best met by making a substantial donation to his alma mater, which then shows its gratitude by giving him an honorary degree and a box at the school's football games. It also gives him a very happy and congenial member of his board of directors when he invites the university's president on his board. But is this "social reponsibility?"

## Case in Point: Imperial Chemical Industries Plc

In 1993, Sir Denys Hendersen explained to his shareholders why he was proposing to downsize Imperial Chemical Industries (ICI), a dominant company in one of the most important worldwide industries – the chemical and pharmaceutical business. ICI had sales in the tens of billions of dollars, earnings in the billions and employees in the hundreds of thousands. Yet in 1993, it proposed a "demerger" of a major unit, Zeneca.

A detailed proposal was sent to shareholders to explain the move. The company cited "important, broader trends," including "intensified competition in industrial chemicals, most notably from the Middle East and Asia Pacific, increased costs of maintaining and developing new technology, especially in the bioscience areas, together with the adverse effects of the worldwide economic recession which began in 1990" as reasons for the demerger. In response to these trends, ICI pledged "to reshape its operations . . . focusing on those businesses and territories where it enjoyed strong market positions, reducing costs in order to remain competitive and disposing of non-strategic operations. These measures continue to be vigorously implemented, although the profit improvement benefits to date have been more than offset by the impact of the economic recession."

Henderson continued in the traditional language of business and finance, explaining, "In recent years, ICI's bioscience activities have expanded rapidly and have become increasingly distinct from its traditional chemical operations, and both face very different opportunities and challenges in the years ahead. The bioscience activities employ different technologies, are more R&D intensive and serve a largely separate customer base. The Chemicals businesses are, in contrast, for the most part capital intensive, volume driven and based on large scale process technology."

What was more important, however, was what Henderson left out. He did not mention Hanson Industries, whose purchase of a significant stock position in ICI was widely credited with being the prime cause of the demerger. ICI had performed poorly for some years, and its stock price had become heavily discounted as a result. Hanson was a known raider, and when the company announced its substantial holding in ICI, commentators asked when, not if, Hanson would attempt to take over the chemical giant.

The ICI demerger preempted the possible bid. Hanson, had he taken over ICI, would almost certainly have completed a similar break up. The fact that ICI restructured on its own volition made the company a far less tempting target, since the company was able to realize the kinds of values that a raider would look to achieve. Thus, the threat of takeover forced ICI to split itself into two smaller, leaner, more competitive companies.

Not that Hanson Industries applauded the demerger. As Lord White, Hanson's chairman said: "If ICI had not spent so much time during the last year fighting a bid that was never made and spent it on seeing how it could improve shareholder value it might have come up with a better solution a lot earlier."[13]

Even the largest and richest of corporations need constantly to assess their position and to make whatever changes are necessary to be competitive. The basis of a corporation's existence is wealth maximization – this is its reason for being. There is no such thing as a "good" corporation that is not competitively profitable. Corporations live in a world where the market determines what people will buy and what they will pay. A corporation that does not produce goods that people want at a price they are willing to pay has no reason to exist.

## THE CORPORATION IN SOCIETY

Before we evaluate the effectiveness of the major players in corporate governance, we should look at corporations from the perspective of what our society wants and needs from them. From this perspective, the answers are fairly clear. We want jobs that pay a decent wage and goods and services that meet our needs. We want challenges to our creativity and ingenuity, and when we meet those challenges, we want to feel proud of the results, and we want to be rewarded. We want corporations to work with us to keep the workplace and the environment healthy. We want a continual sense of progress and growth from our corporations. We want our interest in the company – whether as employee, shareholder, customer, supplier, creditor, or neighbor – to be designed for the long term.

Two connected sets of laws govern the relationships of these constituent groups to the corporation. One is comprised of the laws imposed by the legislature. Ideally, these laws would exist only as a kind of floor or backstop to establish minimum standards, permitting maximum flexibility for the corporation and its governing entities. In other words, the government should step in only when the system of corporate governance cannot be assured of producing a result that is beneficial to society as a whole. To go back to our original criteria for determining who is in the best position to make a particular decision, the government should set the standards when it has better information and fewer conflicts of interest than any (or all) of the other parties who play a role in setting the course for the corporation.

In practice, however, corporations have influenced government at least as much as government has influenced business. The corporate "citizen," with the right to political speech (and political contributions) has had a powerful impact on the laws that affect it. In theory, corporations support the free market, with as little interference from government as possible. In reality, whenever corporations can persuade the government to protect them from the free market, by legislating barriers to competition or limiting their liability, they do so.

> People of the same trade seldom meet together but the conversation ends in a conspiracy against the public, or in some diversion to raise prices. *Adam Smith*

To the extent that corporate governance standards are established by law, one could argue that these provisions' greatest value is in providing the illusion of accountability. For example, an article written by two thoughtful observers of corporate governance, one a law professor, one a judge, points to mandatory corporate governance provisions to support their argument that these rules provide a solid foundation for real (and informed) freedom of choice for investors. The rules which inspire this confidence are:

> States almost uniformly forbid perpetual directorships; they set quorum rules, which typically require a third of the board and sometimes half of the investors to participate on critical decisions; they require "major" transactions to be presented to the board (occasionally shareholders too) rather than stand approved by managers or a committee; they forbid the sale of votes divorced from the investment interest and the accumulation of votes in a corporate treasury; they require managers to live up to a duty of loyalty to investors.

Federal law requires firms to reveal certain things when they issue securities, and public firms to make annual disclosures.[14]

The authors go on to acknowledge that, "Determined investors and managers can get 'round many of these rules, but accommodation is a sidelight."[15] Throughout this book, there are examples of "get(ting) 'round" these rules. It does not mean much to "forbid perpetual directorships" if management continues to renominate the same people. The GM board, in the middle of the company's troubles in 1992, had one member who had been on the board for 20 years, and two who had served for 15. Requiring the approval of a third of the board or half the shareholders does not mean much if the board is entirely selected by and beholden to management and the shareholders do not have the ability to overcome the obstacle of collective choice to make informed decisions. Chapters 2 and 3 have further discussion of these issues, as well as the "duty of loyalty" the one share, one vote issue, and the relevance of required disclosures.

Much of the law affecting corporations is designed to benefit them, whether directly or indirectly. These laws vary from state to state and country to country, in part because of the famous "race to the bottom" competition between states in the United States, who compete for corporate chartering business through increasingly diluted provisions for oversight.[15]

## The Marketplace

Corporations also operate under the laws of the marketplace. While these laws can be influenced to some extent by the legislature, the marketplace is the ultimate arbiter of corporate performance. No matter where a company is located and what it produces, these laws affect, even determine, every decision made by its directors and officers. We would call this the law of economics, if we could use that term without then limiting ourselves to the narrow vocabulary and assumptions of that academic specialty.

This set of laws reacts to and influences the first set. When a company changes its state of incorporation for tax reasons, for example, that is a function of economics. So too is a company's consideration of the differing social laws of states and nations, such as varying regulations governing occupational safety and environmental standards. Like a consumer selecting a car, the corporation's choice of domicile is based on an evaluation of the costs and benefits of all of the options. The same kind of evaluation applies to decisions about whether to invest in research and development or whether to update a local factory (or retrain local workers) versus reducing costs by moving the operation abroad.

## A PROPOSAL FOR CHANGE

As corporations expand their operations and markets into virtually all parts of the world, we must begin to develop a more consistent and coherent approach. In order to do that, we must, whenever possible, integrate the most important legislated standards with the realities of the economic laws, so that all incentives promote the five overall goals outlined above, or at least so that they do not conflict with them. The law should be process oriented, not substantive. Its focus should be the relationships between the corporation and its constituents, to reduce conflicts of interests (agency costs) and make sure that the right people are making the decisions (or at least are able to monitor the results of the decisions) that affect them most.

One of the problems that is presented by this task is finding some way to balance the need for long-term planning with the need for present-day assurances that whatever is planned for the long term is indeed likely to happen. Corporations must have as their primary and overriding goal the generation of long-term value. A commitment to the satisfaction of employees, suppliers, customers, and the community is essential for achieving this goal. But calibrating that commitment to achieve maximum value in the long term is a daunting task. No one can predict the future. In the last decade alone we have seen both new and long established corporations achieve market dominance and extraordinary growth and vitality, only to fall into disaster, sometimes beyond recovery. How do we know that today's commitment to a long-term research and development project is going to produce a Mustang instead of an Edsel? More important, how can our laws best be designed to increase the likelihood that it will be the former instead of the latter?

## CORPORATE POWER AND CORPORATE PERFORMANCE

We grant legitimacy and authority to the exercise of public (government) power through accountability. We are willing to defer to the authority of elected officials because we put them there, and if we do not like what they do, we can replace them. In the United States, the checks and balances of the three branches of government add to the credibility and legitimacy of the government. Any of the three branches that goes too far can be curbed by one of the others.

In theory, the legitimacy and authority of corporate power is also based on accountability. Corporate governance also has its checks and balances (including the government). In order to maintain legitimacy and credibility, corporate management needs to be effectively accountable to some independent, competent, and motivated representative. That is what the board of directors is designed to be.

Corporations exercise vast power in a democratic society. In a thoughtful and enduring essay, *The Corporation; How Much Power? What Scope?*, Carl Kaysen outlines the various alternative modes for containing corporate power,[16] asking whether and how corporate power can be "limited or controlled."

> Broadly, there are three alternative possibilities. The first is limitation of business power through promoting more competitive markets; the second is broader control of business power by agencies external to business; the third, institutionalization within the firm of responsibility for the exercise of power. Traditionally, we have purported to place major reliance on the first of these alternatives, in the shape of antitrust policy, without in practice pushing very hard any effort to restrict market power to the maximum feasible extent. I have argued elsewhere that it is in fact possible to move much further than we have in this direction, without either significant loss in the overall effectiveness of business performance or the erection of an elaborate apparatus of control. While this, in my judgment, remains the most desirable path of policy, I do not in fact consider it the one which we will tend to follow. To embark on a determined policy of the reduction of business size and growth in order to limit market power requires a commitment of faith in the desirability of the outcome and the feasibility of the process which I think is not widespread. What I consider more likely is some mixture of the second and third types of control.[17]

Kaysen is pessimistic about the prospects for corporate self-regulation. "The development of mechanisms which will change the internal organization of the corporation, and define more closely and represent more presently the interest to which corporate management should respond and the goals toward which they should strive is yet to begin, if it is to come at all."[18]

How do we make sure that corporate power is exercised in the best interests of society? How do we measure corporate performance? How should society measure corporate performance? Those two questions are closely related, but their answers are worlds apart. For example, imagine a company that has record-breaking earnings and excellent shareholder returns. This is in part made possible by a rigorous cost-cutting campaign which includes illegal dumping of toxic waste materials, thereby saving the money that had been used to meet environmental standards for disposal. The company's balance sheet and other financials will look very good. But the cost to society, in damage to the health and property of those affected by the illegal dumping, will not be factored in. Neither will the cost of investigating and prosecuting the company, which will be borne by the taxpayers. (The cost of defending the company, and any fines imposed, will of course be borne by the shareholders.)

## Cases in Point: Corporate Crime

- **Alleco** The company's CEO, Morton M. Lapides, was convicted of a price-fixing scheme that resulted in record-breaking fines. The judge found the facts of the case so disturbing that he took the unprecedented step of issuing a prison sentence to the corporation. The judge said, "I cannot imagine any company being more tied up with illegal activity." Four of its top managers were directed to spend up to two years in community service. The conviction notwithstanding, Lapides was permitted to take the company private.

- **General Electric** In 1992, GE settled with the government over charges that the company had been falsely billing the federal government for military sales to Israel during the 1980s. Company employees had conspired with an Israeli air force general to divert the money to their own pockets. GE's jet engine division was suspended from bidding for future Pentagon contracts, and the company agreed to pay fines of $69 million. GE's shares dipped to $0.87 on the news.[19]

- **Drexel Burnham Lambert** In December 1988, the securities house pleaded guilty to six felony charges alleging widespread securities fraud and inside dealing. Drexel agreed to pay a fine of $650 million. The following March, the US Attorney's office in New York issued a 98-page indictment charging Michael Milken with similar crimes. Milken had single handedly made Drexel successful via his aggressive hawking of junk-bonds, a security that financed most of the takeovers of the 1980s. So central was

Milken to Drexel's success that the firm paid Milken compensation of as much as $550 million in one year alone. Roiled by the charges of fraud, and damaged by the increasing collapse of junk-bond financed firms, Drexel filed for bankruptcy protection in February 1990. Just two months later, Milken agreed to plead guilty. In November 1990, he was sentenced to a prison term of ten years. The sentence was later reduced, and Milken was eventually released in the summer of 1993. He subsequently taught a finance course at the University of California at Los Angeles.

- **A. H. Robins** The company marketed an intra-uterine contraceptive device called the Dalkon Shield, despite the fact that the company had over 400 unfavorable reports from physicians. The device was eventually recalled after the deaths of 17 women. By mid-1985, over 14,000 product liability suits had been filed against the company, forcing it into bankruptcy. In 1987, a court ordered the company to set aside $2.4 billion in a trust fund to compensate women injured by the shield. Later, the company also agreed to pay out nearly $7 million to stockholders.[20]

- **Gitano Group** In December 1993, three Gitano executives pleaded guilty to charges that they had sought to circumvent customs duties on imported clothes. Following the charges, Gitano's largest customer – Wal-Mart Stores – announced that it would cease to do business with Gitano, adhering to strict company standards regarding vendor partners. In January 1994, Gitano's board of directors concluded that it was unlikely that the company could continue to operate without Wal-Mart's support, and the board voted to put the company up for sale.

All the stakeholders in these companies lost as a result of these actions. Corporations are supposed to be governed by a system of checks and balances to make sure that these disasters do not happen. Who failed? Who paid the price? If it is not the same people, why not?

Accountability requires not just a mechanism, but a standard. That standard is usually described as "maximizing long-term returns for the owners." (Milton Friedman adds, "within the limits of the law," but we assume that compliance with the law is assumed as a part of value maximization.) The relationship of any particular corporate action to shareholder returns does not have to be immediate or direct. Corporations can give away money, voluntarily increase their workers' compensation over required, or even competitive, levels, spoil their customers and act as benefactors in the communities where they function, all to the extent that these activities can be credibly related to increasing the long-term value of the enterprise. To the extent that they drive up costs to make the company's products and services less competitive, they cannot be credibly related to profit maximization.

The extent to which corporations can pursue objectives that are by definition not related to value generation must be severely limited, both as a matter of legislated and economic rules. Compare the current corporate system to the prevailing western system of political legitimacy and accountability. We allow the legislature to make economic tradeoffs. We give this level of authority to the government, which derives its legitimacy from its accountability through the political process.

As in the political domain, in the corporate domain accountability should be based on a comprehensible standard that is widely understood. It can be argued that employees, customers, suppliers, and the residents of host communities should share with owners the entitlement to hold corporations accountable. Yet to date, no one has developed a language of accountability that would be equally acceptable to all of these constituencies; indeed, no one has succeed in conceiving of acceptable quantifiable standards. As Milton Friedman said, "Few trends could so thoroughly undermine the foundations of our free society as the acceptance by corporate officials of a social responsibility other than to make as much money for their stockholders as possible."[21] Friedman is too often cited in a simplistic way. There is no need to accept the most narrow definition of profit as defined by accountants as the ultimate rudder for corporate direction, and there is need to understand that the size and power of the corporate system tends to dominate the language of accountability.[22]

> I submit that you can not abandon emphasis on the view that business corporations exist for the sole purpose of making profits for their shareholders until such time as you are prepared to offer a clear and reasonably enforceable scheme of responsibilities to someone else.[23]

## CORPORATE CRIME: "WITHIN THE LIMITS OF THE LAW"

> "Did you ever expect a corporation to have a conscience, when it has no soul to be damned and no body to be kicked?" *Edward, First Baron Thurlow, Lord Chancellor of England*

By classifying particular conduct as "criminal," government gives its most unequivocal signal that particular activities are intolerable. That seems simple enough when applied to armed robbery or assault, but criminal law and corporate activity seem to exist in different media, like oil and water. Understanding the difficulty that society encounters in trying to communicate absolute standards of conduct to corporations is an essential beginning to the study of governance.

Why do corporations engage in criminal behavior? It has to be because, at some level, they find that the benefits outweigh the costs. Or, more likely, the managers who take the risk of criminal behavior decide that the benefits accrue to the corporation, while the costs are borne elsewhere. And these costs are enormous. A single price-fixing case was found to cost the affected consumers more than all of the robberies of that year. Shareholders in particular pay the costs on all sides: as members of the community, they pay the costs of the crime itself; as taxpayers, they pay the costs of the prosecution; as shareholders, they pay the costs of the defense and any penalties.

The people who decide to violate the law, however, pay very little. There is a great disparity between the way individual criminal offenders and corporate criminal offenders are treated. One reason for this is society's perception of the crimes. We are more likely to imprison violent offenders than white collar criminals, despite the fact that the white collar crime, in absolute terms, is more expensive. The business judgment rule and the limitation on director liability restrict the shareholders' ability to get the courts to order reimbursement for the payment of these expenses or the loss in share value. Corporate managers rarely go to jail; indeed, they seldom even lose their jobs. The company pays the fines, which are seldom high enough to offset any gains, and the company pays the legal fees.

Corporations have limited economic liability, as described above and at one time this extended to criminal activity. In modern times, at least in theory, corporations do have criminal liability. Originally, the standard for determining that a corporation (and its officers) was liable for criminal activity was *respondent superior,* vicarious liability by the corporation for the acts of its employees, as long as those acts were (1) within the scope of the employment and (2) with the intent of benefiting the corporation. This required knowledge (willfulness) on the part of the employee. He had to know what he was doing and know that it was illegal. Recently, however, there has been a trend to criminalize a broader category of behavior, often for political reasons. This began in the health and safety area, regulations established a new standard in holding corporations liable for "flagrant indifference," "neglect," "failure to perceive a substantial risk," etc. And ignorance of the law is no excuse. Courts have held that corporate officers are presumed to know certain things, just because of their position. And the knowledge of *any* employee can be attributed to the company as a whole, even if the employee did not inform anyone else.

The primary justifications for penalties are deterrence, incapacitation from further crimes and rehabilitation. All of these depend on some degree of moral culpability. It is easy enough to apply them to an individual who commits a crime (assuming that there is no problem of proof). A thief is sent to jail to deter him (and others) from future crime, to keep him away from society so that he cannot commit further crimes, and to give society a chance to teach him to do better. Some systems also try to incorporate compensation of some kind for the victims as well, though this has been less a priority of the criminal justice system than of the civil justice system; and in the criminal system such compensation is more likely to take the form of community service than direct payment to the affected individuals.

The failure of our efforts to rein in criminal corporate conduct stems from trying to treat artificial entities as if they were natural persons. Legal scholar John C. Coffee, Jr., of Columbia University has stated the problem succinctly: "At first glance, the problem of corporate punishment seems perversely insoluble: moderate fines do not deter, while severe penalties flow through the corporate shell and fall on the relatively blameless."[24]

## Probation of Corporations

In March 1986, the US government prepared a "sentencing memorandum" recommending "probation" and a fine for the Bank of New England, following the bank's conviction on 31 counts. The crime involved repeated failure to file Currency Transaction Reports (CTRs), a requirement imposed in an effort to track financial transactions that may be related to illegal activities. In this case, although the bank admitted to its failure to file thousands of these forms, the prosecution centered on a bookie named McDonough, whose failure to file CTRs for his dealings with the bank made it impossible for the government to prosecute McDonough for tax and gambling offenses.

The memo pointed out that "the (bank's) misbehavior was truly institutionalized, having been engaged in by numerous employees and officers on repeated occasions over a four-year period. . . . The failure to file the required CTRs involved not one, but at least ten bank employees. . . . The failures to file were aggravated by the fact that some of the employees knew McDonough was a bookie and that he was trying to circumvent the CTR law. . . . The bank's culpability as an institution was compounded . . . when [the] Branch Manager . . . was informed of repeated failures to file and deliberately chose not to file the forms even though she admitted to fully knowing that they were required by law. . . ." Furthermore, said the memo, the bank's internal fraud officer and other senior officials were also made aware of the problems.

How can a corporation be sentenced to probation? The "probation" requested by the government in this case required regular reporting by the bank on its program (including the names of personnel assigned) to comply with CTR requirements.

After emphasizing the law's clear message that failure to file CTRs is a serious crime and that fines should be "severe" enough to have "some real economic impact," the memo recommended a fine that amounted to less than 0.0002 percent of the bank's asset base and two percent of its net income. The comparable fine for an individual would approximate that portion of the individual's salary earned in one week *after* all living expenses have been paid and taxes withheld.

In 1986 testimony before the US Sentencing Commission, Douglas H. Ginsburg, then Assistant Attorney General for Antitrust (now judge on the DC Circuit Court of Appeals) bemoaned the inadequate penalties for individuals convicted of price-fixing. "There can be no doubt that price-fixing is a serious crime. It cannot be inadvertently committed, it causes substantial social harm, and it creates no redeeming social benefits." He noted that the average time served for the small percentage of defendants who actually went to prison was only about 30 days. Fines for individuals averaged less than $16,000. The average fine for a corporation was about $133,000.

The failure of our sentencing system to achieve deterrence is evident from our continuing discovery of significant numbers of price-fixing conspiracies each year. The explanation for this is also obvious. Price fixing offers the opportunity to extract huge sums from consumers, and there is a good chance that price fixers will escape detection despite our best efforts. To deter so potentially lucrative an enterprise requires much higher levels of fines and imprisonment than are currently imposed.

Before addressing fines and imprisonment, however, I would like to explain why four kinds of alternative sentences or sanctions – community service, probation, debarment, and restitution – are not adequate substitutes for imprisonment and heavy fines. Such alternative sentences or sanctions often impose little hardship on offenders, and their very availability leads all too often to their substitution for more meaningful sentences, thus undermining deterrence.

First, many of the community service sentences imposed in recent years were not punishment at all. One defendant's community service involved coordinating an annual rodeo for charity. A defendant in another antitrust proceeding was required to organize a golf tournament fund raiser for the Red Cross. The experience proved so pleasant that he quickly agreed to organize the golf tournament again the next year! In yet another case, the defendant was sentenced to give thirty hours of speeches explaining the economic effects of his criminal activities – punishment that in practice is more likely to frustrate than to advance the purposes of the antitrust laws. Such penalties can do nothing but trivialize the offense in the eyes of the business community and the public.[25]

Judge Ginsburg went on to explain that probation had little deterrent impact and "implies unwarranted judicial regulation of the defendant's business activities." Debarment (making the company ineligible to sell to the government) was also ineffective. "Ironically, by eliminating competitors, it can impose on society the same harm as does the crime it is designed to punish. Indeed, there could be situations in which all potential suppliers might be debarred, making the product, at least for a while, totally unavailable."

Many ingenious solutions have been suggested, including the "equity fine."[26] But all face the same obstacle: cooked books. As John Braithwaite explains in his study of the pharmaceutical industry, ". . . companies have two kinds of records: those designed to allocate guilt (for internal purposes), and those for obscuring guilt (for presentation to the outside world). When companies want clearly defined accountability they can generally get it. Diffused accountability is not always inherent in organizational complexity; it is in considerable measure the result of a desire to protect individuals within the organization by presenting a confused picture to the outside world. One might say that courts should be able to pierce this conspiracy of confusion. Without sympathetic witnesses from within the corporation who are willing to help, this is difficult."[27]

Despite various efforts to place corporations "on probation," to require payments to causes that benefit society, and even to jail executives, it is plain that nothing being done at this time is effective and that the problem is becoming more acute. In 1980, *Fortune* magazine surveyed 1,043 large companies and concluded that a "surprising" and "startling" number (about 11 percent) of them had been involved in "blatant illegalities." Two years later, *US News and World Report* conducted a similar survey of America's largest 500 companies, and found that, in the preceding decade, 115 had been convicted of at least one major crime.[28] In 1990, the *New York Times* found that 25 out of the 100 largest Pentagon contractors had been found guilty of procurement fraud in the preceding seven years.[29]

There will always be a need for legal sanctions, but the job of meting out punishment should not belong to the government alone. Indeed, without self-regulation by private industry, government's power to deter crime will decline further. As Braithwaite observes, "[S]ome executives abstain from bribery because they are afraid of being punished. Most abstain from bribery because they view it as immoral. One reason that they view it as immoral is that executives who bribe are sometimes punished and held to public scorn. Do away with criminal punishment and you do away with much of the sense of morality which makes self-regulation possible. Self-regulation and punitive regulation are, therefore, complementary rather than alternatives."[30]

Self-regulation is the responsibility of all participants in the corporate governance system. Unfortunately, under the current system, the risk of engaging in criminal behavior is evaluated by corporate managers who have very little to lose, even if the company is prosecuted. The criminal justice system has not been able to provide the appropriate level of deterrence, incapacitation, and rehabilitation for white collar offenders or compensation for their victims.

Corporate crime is not victimless. Those adversely affected include the shareholders, often thousands of them. Long-term shareholders certainly have an interest in making societal and corporate interests compatible, but they are not likely to have the resources to be able to make that interest felt throughout the company, either before or after the fact. They can, however, take steps to make sure that the other parties in the corporation have the right incentives and authority.

How can shareholders make this system work? They have no interest – much less competency – in developing or prescribing internal corporate procedures. Yet they do have some responsibility for this area. Shareholders expect managers to run their business in a way that will encourage a supportive governmental and societal climate to capitalist enterprise, and that means that the shareholder's concern is to hold managements accountable for their conduct of the business "within the rules." Shareholders expect some of the responsibility for failing to establish mechanisms for preventing and responding to corporate crime in the past. In the future, shareholders need to make unmistakably clear that continued corporate crime will not be tolerated. They do not and should not determine how a corporation devises information flows to assure that notice of potentially criminal activity is received at the appropriate level, how a company develops incentive systems to assure that compliance with law has the clear and undivided attention of appropriate personnel, or what review structures are established to monitor, review, document, and validate compliance with law. As Judge Ginsburg said,

> Shareholders should no more be insulated from the gains and losses of price fixing than from the gains or losses from any other risky management decision. Indeed, it is essential that shareholders have the incentives to institute appropriate safeguards to prevent criminal behavior.[31]

Shareholders, along with directors and officers, must see to it that companies have information systems to expose, not cover up, wrong-doing. One way to do this is by setting forth the conditions of eligibility for service on the board of directors. Unquestionably, the board of directors has the authority, indeed the responsibility, to promulgate basic corporate policies.

> More active stockholder participation might force greater corporate compliance with the law in some areas, although, as we have pointed out, their primary concern is often corporate stock growth and dividends. . . . Far reaching corporate reform, however, depends on altering the process and structure of corporate decision making. Traditional legal strategies generally do not affect the internal institutional structure. . . . At present few clear functions are usually specified for corporate boards of directors; they frequently have

served as rubber stamps for management. If a functional relationship and responsibility to actual corporate operations were established, directors would be responsible not only for the corporate financial position and stockholder dividends but also for the public interest, which would include the prevention of illegal and unethical activities undertaken in order to increase profits.[32]

Directors have the authority to establish policies requiring management to implement obedience to the law as a corporate priority. And shareholders have the authority and the means to make directors do just that. By amending the by-laws to make compliance with the law a condition of eligibility for service on the board, they ensure that the buck will stop somewhere. Directors are highly motivated to continue to be eligible to serve as directors of public companies.

One way in which boards can exert its authority is described by long-time consumer advocate, Ralph Nader: "[T]he board should designate executives responsible for compliance with these laws and require periodic signed reports describing the effectiveness of compliance procedures."[33] Other reformers recommend mechanisms to administer spot checks on compliance with the principal statutes should be created. Similar mechanisms can insure that corporate "whistle blowers" and nonemployee sources may communicate to the board "in private and without fear of retaliation knowledge of violations of law."

Professor Christopher Stone's *Where the Law Ends*[34] is perhaps the best known work on corporate criminal liability. He concludes that the suspension of directors is the most effective way of dealing with the problems of corporate criminality. He says,

> In general, though, I think it would be best if for all but the most serious violations we moved in the opposite direction, relaxing directors' liability by providing that any director adjudged to have committed gross negligence, or to have committed nonfeasance shall be prohibited for a period of three years from serving as officer, director or consultant of any corporation doing interstate business. Why is this better than what we have now? For one thing, the magnitude of the potential liability today has become so Draconian that when we try to make the law tougher on directors the more likely effects are that corporate lawyers will develop ways to get around it, judges and juries will be disinclined to find liability, and many of the better qualified directors will refuse to get involved and serve. The advantages of the "suspension" provision, by contrast, are that it

is not so easy to get around; it is not so severe that, like potential multi-million-dollar personal liability, it would strike courts as unthinkable to impose; but at the same time it would still have some effective bite in it – the suspendees would be removed from the most prestigious and cushy positions ordinarily available to men of their rank, and would, I suspect, be object of some shame among their peers.

An alternative model appears to exist in Japan. In 1981, after a series of leakages from a nuclear power station owned and operated by the Japan Atomic Power Company, the chairman and president of the company resigned in the hope that trust in nuclear power stations would be restored under new leadership.[35]

## CORPORATIONS AND GOVERNMENT: CO-OPTING THE MARKET

Many observers have argued that corporate power has created a framework within which only the illusion of free choice exists. One example is that of the Chrysler Corporation.

### Case in Point: Chrysler

In 1977, Chrysler was the tenth largest US company, and 14th largest in the world. Within two years, however, the company was in serious trouble. In 1979, Chrysler's new boss, Lee Iacocca, told the federal government that without huge, federally guaranteed loans, the company would almost certainly fold.

Loan guarantees were a familiar element of US economic policy. In 1970, the Penn Central Railroad requested a $200 million loan under the Defense Production Act of 1950, a measure that allowed public corporations to borrow from the Treasury if the national defense was at stake. Congress refused Penn Central's request, and only after the railroad filed for bankruptcy was it granted $125 million in loan guarantees. One year later, Congress narrowly approved (by one vote in the Senate) Lockheed Aircraft's request for $250 million in guaranteed loans. In that instance, New York Senator James Buckley sonorously warned, "If the inefficient or mismanaged firm is insulated from the free-market pressures that other businesses must face, the result will be that scarce economic and human resources will be squandered on enterprises whose activities do not meet the standards imposed by the market place." Ultimately, however, the prospect of unemployment for Lockheed's 17,000 workers and the 43,000 employees of supplier companies was enough to see that Lockheed received the loans.

Senator Buckley's arguments were revived in 1979 when a similar debate broke over Chrysler. On the one hand was America's commitment to free markets; on the other, the lives of tens of thousands of Chrysler's employees. Michael Moritz and Barrett Seaman describe the issue as it faced Congress: "The Corporation's 4,500 dealers and 19,000 suppliers were another matter. Unlike the company's, their presence was tangible and their plight immediate. There was a Chrysler dealer or supplier in every congressional district in the country. These were the merchants of the nation, men who had inherited businesses from their fathers and had, in some cases, passed them on to their sons. Family commitments stretched back to the days of Walter Chrysler, and the businesses were located in the small communities of Middle America, like Great Bend in Kansas. These weren't garish swashbucklers from Detroit, bouncing billions and tweaking communities with the flash of a calculator." The authors describe how: "the company drew up computerized lists outlining contributions in every district and showing congressmen how much local, state and federal tax was contributed by Chrysler showrooms. Working through the Dealer Councils (the officials elected by the dealers themselves), an average of two hundred dealers a day came to Washington to lobby their representatives. Coached for an hour in the early morning about what they should and should not say, the dealers spent their days roaming corridors, rapping on doors and buttonholing congressmen as well as their administrative and legislative aids. The sight of these independent small businessmen was mighty effective." As one Chrysler dealer observed: "The very survival of a lot of good people in this country and a lot of small businesses depends upon the whims . . . of the political system."

Moritz and Seaman sum up as follows: "The underlying precept of a free economy is that unsuccessful corporations do not survive. In recent years in the United States this proposition has been subjected to violent rejection. Not only are companies such as Lockheed, which were arguably essential to national defense, "bailed out" through political action, but such a quintessential consumer giant as Chrysler proved the modern axiom that no large company will be allowed to fail in the United States today. Rarely has the power of a large, if broke, corporation been so effectively and overtly employed as in Chrysler persuading the US government to provide special financial aid to insure its survival."[36]

This case shows that only the small companies are really at risk of any meaningful market test. A corporation that is large enough cannot be allowed to go broke in a "free" capitalist society. The power of larger corporations to involve themselves in the most critical decision making by citizens has been recently reaffirmed by the US Supreme Court. In *The Bank of Boston v. Bellotti,* the court upheld corporations' right to enter the arena of political advertising. The Court said that the bank must be permitted to spend whatever shareholder funds it thought appropriate to influence voting on a referendum matter that, by definition, was not related to its business. This shows that the power of corporations has advanced to the point of domination of the political process. It is power – political power – and not the workings of the marketplace that determines corporate survival.

Not only have corporations succeeded in dominating the executive and legislative branches of government in the United States, but they have made substantial inroads on the judicial branch as well. As discussed earlier, in the "race to the bottom" for corporate chartering and related legal fees, the various states have competed to be the most congenial to corporate management, who choose the place of domicile. During the takeover era of the 1980s, the courts seemed to do the same (see the discussion in chapter 3). The Delaware "factor" is the underlying rationale for many of the decisions of its Chancery and Supreme Courts.

### Case in Point: "Delaware Puts Out"[37]

Although Delaware is one of the smallest states in the union, more companies are incorporated there than any other state. Joseph Nocera explains why: "The degree to which Delaware depends upon its incorporation fees and taxes is really quite extraordinary: It's a $200 million a year business, comprising nearly 20 percent of the state budget."

During the 1980s, when a vigorous market for corporate control developed, managements appealed to the Delaware courts for protection. What became apparent was that large corporations would do whatever it took to ensure that the Delaware courts would continue to issue opinions favorable to management. In 1990, a number of pro-shareholder decisions began emerging from the Delaware Chancery court, forcing companies "in play" to entertain hostile bids. These decisions aroused a tough response from Martin Lipton, a corporate lawyer who made his name defending companies from takeover in the 1980s. In Nocera's words: "Marty Lipton went nuts. He lashed out at the [Delaware Chancery] court, sending scathing notes to his very long list of major corporate clients, most of whom were incorporated in Delaware. In one conspicuously leaked memo, he wrote ominously, 'Perhaps it is time to migrate out of Delaware.' Lipton acted the way bullies always act when they know they have someone by the balls: He squeezed."

## MEASURING PERFORMANCE

We cannot tell what the future impact of corporate strategy will be on shareholder value. Will spoiling the customers produce devoted loyalty or will it drive up prices too high? Will a long-term research and development project pay off? Will cost-cutting measures expose the company to future liability claims? Will the acquisition of a new business provide synergy or cause loss of focus? How can anyone – shareholders, directors, or managers – evaluate a company's performance if they cannot predict its future?

In order to establish a context for the evaluation of a company's performance, it makes sense to define the ultimate purpose of a corporation as long-term value creation. This creates a framework for defining the rights and responsibilities of shareholders and directors and therefore for determining how they should be organized, how they should be motivated, and how they should be evaluated. For example, it does not mean much to set long-term value creation as the goal if we allow the people who have primary responsibility for meeting the goal to be the ones who define it; that would be like allowing students to grade their own exams.

The expressions "long term" and "value" are subject to many interpretations. Anyone who is being evaluated has an incentive to define "long term" as "after I am gone." Anyone who is being evaluated has an incentive to define "value" as "results from whichever financial formula makes us look most appealing this year." While far from perfect, there is an entire spectrum of concepts of economic performance. These traditionally include balance sheets and earnings statements prepared according to Generally Accepted Accounting Principles (GAAP), the availability of cash to meet corporate needs, and the ability to raise new cash from outside sources. The problems of evaluating corporate performance are highlighted by management expert Peter Drucker:

> One of the basic problems is that management has no way to judge by what criteria outside shareholders value and appraise performance. The stock market is surely the least reliable judge or, at best, only one judge and one that is subject to so many other influences that it is practically impossible to disentangle what, of the stock market appraisal, reflects the company's performance and what reflects caprice, affects the whims of securities analysts, short-

term fashions and the general level of the economy and of the market rather than the performance of a company itself.[38]

Drucker, along with former New York State Comptroller Ned Regan and others, has advocated periodic "business audits" by expert outside parties to provide perspective in evaluating a company's performance. But is there such a thing as "independence" in professionals, as long as they are hired by the people they are supposed to evaluate? Even if they are people of exceptional integrity and insight, by the time they do the study and produce the report, it may be too late.

"Performance measurement" must be a flexible and changing concept. What is suitable for one time or company is wrong for others. Therefore, the single most important structural requirement is that the standard be set by someone other than management. Yet it must be by some group vitally interested in what we have already said was the only legitimate goal – long-term value creation. For that reason, it cannot be the government or the community, which have other priorities they would be happy to have corporations address.

The best entity for establishing goals and evaluating the performance of any corporation is its board of directors. It is in the "creative tension" between the informed, involved and empowered monitors – the board of directors in the first instance and the owners ultimately – that the corporation's performance can best be monitored on an ongoing basis.

## BALANCING INTERESTS

At some point, any long-term strategy will seem at odds with the goal of profit maximization. The same is true of any commitment to corporate constituents beyond that required by law. It is impossible to determine whether a new benefit program for employees will be justified by the increased loyalty and enthusiasm it inspires. There are so many opportunities for mistakes and even self-dealing that this area requires oversight and accountability. The way it is handled is a strong indicator of the merits of any corporate governance system.

The key is finding the right system of checks and balances. A board that will blithely approve paying for a $120 million art museum with the shareholders' money is obviously operating without such a system. So is the CEO who will spend $68 million on developing an (ultimately disastrous) "smokeless" tobacco cigarette before informing his directors. (See discussion of both of these cases in chapter 3.)

A particular paper company may have some expertise in determining an appropriate method of – for example – storing bark or floating logs down a river. If the company makes that determination, it is likely to be designed to impose as much of the cost as possible on someone else. Society's interest demands that a publicly accountable authority make the ultimate determination of what is acceptable when the issue is not purely one of economics. Regulation by government is justified two ways. First, it is the government's responsibility, because the government is (at least in theory) uniquely able to balance all appropriate interests as it is equally beholden (and not beholden) to all of them. Second, if enough of the community objects to the action taken by the government, they can elect new representatives who will do better.

Directors who fail to consider the interests of customers, employees, suppliers, and the community fail in their duty to shareholders; a company that neglects those interests will surely decline. The danger lies in allowing corporate managers to make policy trade-offs among these interests. That should be left to those who have a more direct kind of accountability – through the political process. It is the job of elected public officials, not hired corporate officers, to balance the scales of justice.

F.A. Hayek posed the alternatives this way:

> So long as the management has the one overriding duty of administering the resources under its control as trustees for the shareholders and for their benefit, its hands are largely tied; and it will have no arbitrary power to benefit from this or that particular interest. But once the management of a big enterprise is regarded as not only entitled but even obliged to consider in its decisions whatever is regarded as the public or social interest, or to support good causes and generally to act for the public benefit, it gains indeed an uncontrollable power – a power which could not long be left in the hands of private managers but would inevitably be made the subject of increasing public control.[39]

There have been long periods in recent American economic history during which large corporation managers have viewed themselves as fiduciaries for society as a whole. Ralph Cordiner, the long-time CEO of General Electric Company, exemplified this standard. He said that top management was a "trustee," responsible for managing the enterprise "in the best balanced interest of shareholders, customers, employees, suppliers, and plant community cities."

In the recent times, more than half of the states in the United States (38 as of mid-1994) have passed "stakeholder" laws, which permit (or even require) directors to consider the impact of their actions on constituencies other than shareholders, including the employees, customers, suppliers, and the community.[40] This is in contrast to the traditional model of the publicly held corporation in law and economics, which says that corporate directors serve one constituency – their shareholders. Many people think this is a mistake. James J. Hanks, Jr., of the law firm Ballard, Spahr, Andrews & Ingersoll, has called it "an idea whose time should never have come."

Typically, these statutes "apply generally to decisions by the Board, including decisions with regard to tender offers, mergers, consolidations and other forms of business combinations."[41] Most state laws of this kind do not mandate constituency-based decision making, and just permit these provisions to be adopted by corporations, with shareholder approval. And most make it clear that the board's authority is completely discretionary, and that no stakeholder constituency will be entitled to be considered.

Companies cannot afford to ignore the needs of their constituencies. Indeed, in the past, "stakeholder" proposals have been occasionally submitted by shareholders, asking the board to undertake a more comprehensive analysis of proposed actions. But we agree with Hanks that "stakeholder" language, in legislation or in corporate charters, can camouflage neglect, whether intentional or unintentional, of the rights of shareholders.

It has always been permissible, even required, for directors and managers to consider the interests of all stakeholders, as long as they do so in the context of the interests of shareholder value. Courts have upheld a corporation's right to donate corporate funds to charities, for example, if it was in the corporation's long-term interests. As the American Bar Association Committee on Corporate Laws pointed out: "[T]he Delaware courts have stated the prevailing corporate common law in this country: directors have fiduciary responsibilities to shareholders which, while allowing directors to give consideration to the interests of others, compel them to find some reasonable relationship to the long-term interests of shareholders."[42] The Committee also noted that the Delaware Supreme Court's decision in the *Unocal* case, which enabled directors to analyze the effects of a potential takeover on a variety of factors, including constituencies, does not suggest "that the court intended to authorize redress of an adverse 'impact' on a non-shareholder constituency at the expense of shareholders."[43] While it is useful (and cost-effective) for boards to consider the best way to meet the admittedly competing needs of the company's diverse constituencies, it is imperative for them to give shareholders first priority.

The Business Roundtable seems to agree. In its 1990 report, "Corporate Governance and American Competitiveness," it contrasts political and "economic" organizations. "Legislative bodies . . . represent and give expression to a multiplicity of constituent interests. Our political system is designed to create compromises between competing interests, to seek the broad middle ground. . . . This system of governance would be fatal for an economic enterprise."

## Case in Point: Protection, Pennsylvania Style

In 1990, Pennsylvania risked the consequences F.A. Hayek warned about when it adopted the notorious Act 36 of 1990, which went far beyond other stakeholder laws in moving beyond the rather benign concept of "consideration" of the interests of others, to a standard with more legal bite: usurpation. Directors may consider "to the extent they deem appropriate" the impact of their decisions on any affected interest. They are not required "to regard any corporate interest or the interests of any particular group . . . as a dominant or controlling interest or factor" as long as the action is in the best interest of the corporation.

The previous version of the law, adopted in 1983, included a stakeholder provision similar to those adopted by many other states, but the new version went further than any other state had, so far, by expanding the list of interests that may be considered and, more important, by establishing that no interest must be controlling (including the interests of shareholders), as long as the directors act in the best interests of the corporation. Other changes to the fiduciary standard include an explicit rejection of the Delaware "heightened scrutiny" test applied to directors' actions in change-of-control situations. Note: This statute was adopted very quickly, with the strong support of a major Pennsylvania company that was then the target of a hostile takeover attempt. The attempt was ultimately unsuccessful, thanks in part to the passage of this law, which included other anti-takeover provisions as well.

The *Wall Street Journal* called it "an awful piece of legislation," and it soon became apparent that many Pennsylvania companies agreed. By October 15, 1990, 99 companies – nearly 33 percent of the state's publicly traded companies – had opted out of at least some of the provisions of the bill. Over 61 percent of the *Fortune 500* incorporated in Pennsylvania opted out, as did over 56 percent of those in the S&P 500. So massive was the stampede out of Pennsylvania Act 36 that a *Philadelphia Inquirer* editorial noted: "These business decisions make it all the more clear that the law was crafted not in the best interest of the state's businesses, but to protect Armstrong World Industries Inc. and a few other companies facing takeover attempts." A company spokesman for Franklin Electronics Publishers stated that its board "believes that the Pennsylvania legislation runs counter to basic American principles of corporate democracy and personal property rights."

Some scholars have developed what they call an "ethical contract." The ethical contract is built on the model of more traditional, operational contracts between the executives and the other stakeholders in the venture. It assumes that any executive's legitimacy can only be sustained by the interaction of these "relationships" with other stakeholders. External legitimacy of the executive and the employees must be sustained and controlled by the personal ethic of the individuals involved as well as by broader corporate and societal ethics. The personal ethic operates through conscience. The corporate and societal ethics work through the internal and external systems of scrutiny, each of which is reinforced by mechanisms for enforcement. Together, these underpin the "corporate contract" between the employee and the firm.[44]

It seems to make the most sense to envision a hypothetical long-term shareholder, like the beneficial owner of most institutional investor securities, as the ultimate party at interest. That allows all other interests to be factored in without losing sight of the goal of long-term wealth maximization. But without a clear and direct and enforceable fiduciary obligation to shareholders, the contract that justifies the corporate structure is irreparably shattered.

In our view, the arguments advancing a "constituency" or "trustee" role for corporate functioning are miscast. It is difficult enough to determine the success of a company's strategy based on only one goal – shareholder value. It is impossible when we add in other goals. There is no one standard or formula for determining the impact that today's actions will have on tomorrow's value. The only way to evaluate the success of a company's performance is to consult those who have the most direct and wide-reaching interest in the results of that performance – the shareholders. The problem is one of effective accountability (agency costs). Only owners have the motive to inform themselves and to enforce standards that arguably are a proxy for the public interest.

## GOOD AND BAD CORPORATIONS?

### Cases in Point: What Is a "Good" Corporation?

Let's begin with some examples of companies that have made economic decisions with (arguably) adverse social consequences. The first case in point is an actual case. The rest are hypotheticals, adapted from real cases.

- For several decades following World War II, the great inventor Edwin Land, chairman of Polaroid Corp., pioneered project after project to promote the public good – creating work groups to determine job characteristics, banning discrimination in employment, locating new plants in distressed areas, developing new technology. In the late 1960s, it was revealed that one of Polaroid's most versatile products was producing photo identification cards. In most cases, this was a useful technology. But a controversy arose when it was revealed that Polaroid's photo ID machines were the key to enforcement of the apartheid laws in South Africa.

- A chemical company complied with all applicable laws in the disposal of its waste chemicals, burying most of them in state-of-the-art drums in a landfill. Twenty years later, there was a statistically high rate of cancer and birth defects in the housing development located near the landfill.

- A small manufacturing company in a very competitive market is advised by its lawyer that it is not meeting federal environmental standards. The cost of bringing the company into compliance would more than wipe out the company's profits for the year and could drive up the cost of the company's products. None of its competitors is undertaking the expenses of meeting the standard. The odds of prosecution are low. The company decides not to comply.

- A newspaper company with a liberal outlook frequently publishes strongly pro-environment editorials. It is printed on paper produced outside the United States, which is cheaper than US paper, partly because the producers do not have to comply with US environmental laws.

These were companies who made arguably anti-social decisions for economic reasons. Let's look at some examples of companies who make uneconomic decisions for social reasons.

- In a landmark 1919 case, *Dodge v. Ford Motor Co.*, a Michigan court ordered Henry Ford to pay dividends to his shareholders.[45] The case arose when Ford ceased paying out a special annual dividend of over $10 million, and the Dodge brothers sued. At the time, Henry Ford owned nearly 60 percent of the company, and the Dodge brothers, 10 percent.

  Ford Motors was rich in surplus capital, and the company would have had no difficulty in paying the dividend. Henry Ford claimed, however, that he needed the money for expansion (he planned a second plant) and he didn't wish the cost of such growth to be borne by the consumer in the form of higher car prices. Indeed, because times were tough, Ford wanted to lower the price of cars. Ford argued that the stockholders had made enough money, and it was more important to help the working man through the depression. (Some suggested that Ford's reasons weren't so altruistic: he knew that the Dodge brothers planned to join the automaking business, and he didn't want to finance their expansion by paying dividends.)

  The Michigan Supreme Court reminded Ford of his duty to the stockholders. Their message was that Ford's generosity was all very proper, but not when he was being generous with other people's money. The court wrote: "There should be no confusion . . . of the duties which Mr. Ford conceives that he and the stockholders owe to the general public and the duties which in law he and his co-directors owe to protesting, minority stockholders. A business corporation is organized and carried on primarily for the profit of the stockholders."

  Compare this example with the Wrigley decision about installing lights so the Chicago Cubs could play night games in the introduction.

- A publicly held chain of restaurants is closed on Sundays, due to the religious beliefs of the management. Clearly, the company (and the shareholders) are foregoing considerable revenue.

- A publicly held oil company spends over $100 million to build an art museum for the CEO's collection.

Sometimes the conflict between economic and social goals is even more complicated:

- An oil company with lucrative operations in South Africa is scrupulous about imposing the highest standards of equal rights for its employees. It has therefore made jobs and wages available to black South Africans that are not available to them elsewhere. The company is pressured by some of its shareholders and by outside groups to withdraw from South Africa entirely, even though a sale of the division would be uneconomic for the company and would leave the black employees unlikely to do as well with the successor owners.

- A major consumer goods company includes among its many and widely varied charitable contributions a six-figure donation to Planned Parenthood. Employees, shareholders, and consumers who object to abortion protest this contribution, so the company cancels it. They are then confronted with employees, shareholders, and consumers who object to the cancellation, and demand that the company continue to support Planned Parenthood. At annual meetings ranging over a period of several years, more time is given to this issue than any other. Who should decide?

Another example of how difficult it is to use social tests of company performance is Stride Rite Corporation, as discussed by the *Wall Street Journal*: "In the past three years alone, Stride Rite has received 14 public service awards, including ones from the National Women's Political Caucus, Northeastern University, the Northeast Human Resources Association, and Harvard University, which praised it for improving the quality of life in its community and the nation."[46] And yet Stride Rite is in the process of moving shoe-making jobs outside of the slum areas of Boston, indeed outside of the United States to foreign countries where employment costs are significantly lower. Is it socially responsible to move jobs out of depressed areas? Is it socially responsible to stay in these areas if it means going bankrupt?

The former chairman, Arnold Hiatt, wanted Stride Rite to be (and be seen as) a leader in socially responsible capitalism. He passionately espoused a Jeffersonian vision linking corporate and social responsibility. When Stride Rite joined 54 other companies to form Businesses for Social Responsibility, he said, "If you're pro-business, you also have to be concerned about things like jobs in the inner city and the 38 million Americans living below the poverty line. . . . To the extent that you can stay in the city, I think you have to . . . [but] if it's at the expense of your business, I think you can't forget that your primary responsibility is to your stockholders."[47]

For the sake of this argument, let's define "social judgments" as explicit trade-offs of profit maximization in favor of social goals.

Doug Bandow, a former Reagan aide, offers a view from the supply-side:

> Corporations are specialized institutions created for a specific purpose. They are only one form of enterprise in a very diverse society with lots of different organizations. Churches exist to help people fulfill their responsibilities toward God in community with one another. Governments are instituted most basically to prevent people from violating the rights of others. Philanthropic institutions are created to do good works. Community associations are to promote one or another shared goal. And businesses are established to make a profit by meeting people's needs and wants.
>
> Shouldn't business nevertheless "serve" society? Yes, but the way it best does so is by satisfying people's desires in an efficient manner. . . . Does this mean that firms have no responsibilities other than making money? Of course not, just as individuals have obligations other than making money. But while firms have a duty to respect the rights of others, they are under no obligation to promote the interests of others. The distinction is important.[48]

Bandow goes on to say that promoting other goals (giving to charity, exceeding regulatory or industry standards for pollution control or employee benefits) is permissible if it promotes the firm's financial well-being (all of the above may create loyalty in employees and customers), or if the shareholders know (and presumably therefore approve) of the program. He uses as an example the jeans company Levi Strauss, which informed shareholders when it went public that it intended to continue its generous charitable giving program.

For another approach to charitable giving, consider Warren Buffett's Berkshire Hathaway. Each shareholder designates a charity, and Buffett contributes to that charity, proportionate to the shareholder's holdings of stock. While admitting that his approach may not be suitable for companies with institutional investors having "short-term investment horizons," Buffett believes it is a more principled approach to corporate giving.

> Just as I wouldn't want you to implement your personal judgments by writing checks on my bank account for charities of your choice, I feel it inappropriate to write checks on your corporate "bank account" for charities of my choice. . . . I am pleased that Berkshire donations can become owner-directed. It is ironic, but understandable, that a large and growing number of major corporations have charitable policies pursuant to which they will match gifts made by

employees (and – brace yourself for this one – many even match gifts made by directors) but none, to my knowledge, has a plan matching charitable gifts by owners.[49]

## EQUILIBRIUM: THE CADBURY PARADIGM

Corporations must balance many competing considerations – long- and short-term notions of gain, cash and accounting concepts of value, democracy and authority, and, as we said in the title of our last book, power and accountability.

The intricate equilibrium of corporations has been particularly well described by Sir Adrian Cadbury, following a tradition that extends for two generations before his birth – Sir Adrian's grandfather refused to provide Cadbury chocolate to British troops in South Africa in protest against the Boer War.

From his base in the United Kingdom, Sir Adrian has provided world-class leadership and guidance with respect to corporate governance. He has been the notably successful CEO, and then chairman, of Cadbury Schweppes, a non-executive director of IBM Europe and the Bank of England, and Chairman of the Cadbury Commission which in 1992 published governance guidelines for the UK.

In his classic study, *The Company Chairman,* Cadbury identified multiple levels of responsibility in the corporation:

> In practice, it is possible to distinguish three levels of company responsibility. The primary level comprises the company's responsibilities to meet its material obligations to shareholders, employees, customers, suppliers and creditors, to pay its taxes and to meet its statutory duties. The sanctions against failure to match up to these relatively easily defined and measured responsibilities are provided by competition and the law.
>
> The next level of responsibility is concerned with the direct results of the actions of companies in carrying out their primary task and includes making the most of the community's human resources and avoiding damage to the environment. . . . Beyond these two levels, there is a much less well-defined area of responsibility, which takes in the interaction between business and society in a wider sense. How far has business a responsibility to maintain the framework of the society in which it operates and how far should business reflect society's priorities rather than its own commercial ones?[50]

## Case in Point: Johnson & Johnson[51]

Johnson & Johnson faced two crises with its Tylenol product, the first in 1982 and the second just four years later. The episodes show

how a company can respond to an almost instant evaporation of consumer confidence by demonstrating to the public that it is more interested in safety than profits.

In 1982, seven people died after taking tampered Tylenol. One variety of the product was sold in capsule form, and the capsules could easily be opened. It was clear that the poison had been inserted in the capsules after they left Johnson & Johnson and before they were bought by the consumers. Sales of the product plummeted in a wave of consumer uncertainty. Johnson & Johnson recalled all of their Tylenol capsules and introduced new "tamper-resistant" packaging, so that consumers could know if a bottle had been opened prior to purchase. The company was able to regain market share despite the initial drop in sales.

By 1986 Tylenol had regained a 35 percent share of the $1.5 billion non-prescription pain-reliever market, as big a share as the product had achieved before the 1982 crisis. Tylenol was Johnson & Johnson's most profitable single brand, accounting for some $525 million in revenues in 1985. The capsule form accounted for roughly a third of that. When, in February 1986, it became known that a New York woman died of taking cyanide-laced Tylenol, those revived revenues were threatened. The incident became more serious when a second bottle of adulterated capsules was discovered in the same Westchester village.

The questions facing Johnson & Johnson were these: Should the company launch another all-out offensive to calm consumer fears, or could the company get by with less drastic damage limitation? Did a pair of contaminated bottles in a New York suburb warrant a nationwide campaign to withdraw the capsules? According to the *New York Times,* chairman James E. Burke's aim was to strike a balance "between what is good for consumers and what is good for Johnson & Johnson."

Johnson & Johnson did indeed withdraw all Tylenol capsules from the nation's shelves, and replace them with new "caplets." These were coated tablets that were safer from contamination. The full withdrawal – which could cost the company's shareholders $150 million, or one-quarter of Johnson & Johnson's 1985 earnings – was deemed necessary in the light of bans in fourteen states on the sale of Tylenol, and a drop in sales similar to that following the 1982 crisis.

In an interview with the *New York Times,* James Burke said the company's decision making was argumentative and aggressive. Discussions were characterized by "yelling and screaming" he said. Some executives pressed for the withdrawal and discontinuation of the capsule product. Others argued that an isolated incident in a small town did not merit a national campaign.

The decision to withdraw the capsules was encouraged by a $4 fall in Johnson & Johnson's stock price in the days following the death of the Westchester woman.

The company launched a massive publicity campaign to defend the Tylenol product, led by James Burke himself. The company held three news conferences, and Burke made over a dozen television appearances, including one on "Donahue."

## MEASURING VALUE ENHANCEMENT

As we have noted throughout this book, the measure of corporate performance must be value enhancement. This is difficult, at best. If it is impossible to determine in the present what the impact of current decisions will be on future value, it is not much easier to determine after the fact what the impact of past decisions has been.

There are many measures of corporation value. While a full discussion of the range of measures could easily fill several books, it is useful to include at this stage a brief description of the pros and cons of some of the most popular measures. To stay within the context of a discussion of corporate governance, we examine these measures by asking two questions: (1) What does each of them contribute to (or how does each interfere with) the ability of the three primary parties to corporate governance to do their part in guiding the corporation? (2) Who is in the best position to decide when to apply which measures?

### GAAP

We begin, of course, with the Generally Accepted Accounting Principles (GAAP). Readers should note that the operative term here is "generally accepted," not "certifiably accurate."

GAAP is a language by which the assets and liabilities of corporations are recorded in balance sheets and their functioning is stated in income statements. Accounting purports to present performance in numbers; by the consistent use of a fixed set of quantitative techniques, accountants can accurately depict the course of a business over long periods of time.

Accounting rules are important because the Securities & Exchange Commission (SEC), the New York Stock Exchange (NYSE), and other regulatory bodies require that companies have "certified financial statements." The purpose of these rules is to assure a consistent (if minimal) level of disclosure. What they measure, they measure consistently over time and between companies, and that has some utility. But it is crucial to remember that there is enough flexibility and room for interpretation in the GAAP to permit accounting firms to compete with each other by offering more creative approaches, and there are many clients out there who will hire the firm whose creativity is most in its own favor. Accountancy is a business, indeed, a competitive business, and one of its characteristics is the willingness to find solutions to a client's problems. One accounting firm's charges against earnings are another's "charge offs" to surplus, for example. For this reason, the numbers may not be as "apples and apples" as an outsider evaluating them would wish for.

It is best to view accounting as an invented foreign language like Esperanto – useful enough for communicating across cultures, but really not particularly helpful in day-to-day business dealings. For example, accounting has always had a hard time dealing with inflation. The "nominal" or stated value of an asset departs widely from its market value. And many items that are vitally connected to the profitability of the enterprise are not carried as assets on a balance sheet: the value of a concession to drill for oil, the value of brand names, the "goodwill" associated with a new venture launched by a household name. Accounting standards are based on a time when real property, like machinery, was the most important asset. They do not reflect the value of "human capital."

But the real problem with accounting standards is that through their general acceptance, appearance becomes reality. New forms of measurement are rarely conceptualized or applied. And existing standards are too often seen as far more objective and meaningful than they are. For example, "earnings" are one of the critical components of value in the marketplace, yet essentially, earnings are what accountants say they are. Earnings are subject to manipulation. Much of it is legal and some is even appropriate, but some goes far beyond what should be acceptable. In recent years, there has been an increasing tendency towards what has been called "big bath" accounting. This is the practice when a company decides at the end of the year that it must make a one-time only "restructuring charge." This charge is not assessed against current earnings, it is levied against the accumulated earnings of the venture.

There is an *Alice in Wonderland* character to this. Imagine a company that has reported over the past five years earnings of $10 a share each year; then in year six, the company decides on a restructuring charge of $75 a share. During all of the six-year period, the company is deemed to be operating profitably from an accounting point of view. Each year has its $10 earnings; the retroactive "restructuring charge" cannot affect the five years of perceptions that have passed. Furthermore, because it is a restructuring charge, it does not alter the reported "earnings from ongoing operations" in year six, which are, let's say, $10 a share. Thus, the company has lost money over a six-year period, and yet each annual component shows a profit at the time of reporting. This trick is especially popular for new CEOs, as it enables them to start with, if not a clean slate, a cleaner one.

The numbers make more sense if you keep in mind that accounting earnings are not economic earnings. Accounting standards are like a maze through which to work one's way. A concept as simple as "costs" can be interpreted a dozen different ways. If the CEO is a veteran who wants to show steady progress, costs may be reported one way. If she is a restructurer to be compensated according to new reported earnings, costs may be calculated another way. And if she is top gun of a defense firm that is paid only a "cost plus" percentage, costs will be calculated another way.

Consider the situation of Westinghouse Corporation, which by 1993 had taken six restructuring charges over the previous seven years. It got to the point that the "operating earnings" figures were meaningless; most analysts disregarded the company's figures and developed their own understanding of Westinghouse operations.

In many instances, the accounting conventions have material impact on the company's decisions. For example, in the late 1980s, Westinghouse decided to expand its real estate financing business very substantially. In order to motivate the executives, they devised a compensation package that provided incentive for an improved return on the equity invested (ROE). The executives were so motivated that they dramatically improved the ROE by the fastest method available – they borrowed. This leverage brought increased earnings (and, hence, compensation) to the bottom line. Everyone was happy, until Westinghouse became overwhelmed by its new debts. When the real estate commitments proved to have been carelessly assumed, the entire company (not just the real estate division) almost went bankrupt – and all because of an accounting formula to create incentives for salespersons.

The different accounting practices in different countries have produced some grotesque consequences. Until recently, in the United States, the "goodwill" arising out of an acquisition – meaning the extent to which the purchase price exceeds the value of the tangible assets – could not be charged off against the ongoing earnings of the enterprise.[52] In the UK goodwill arising out of acquisitions has been amortizable. Thus, the celebrated Blue Arrow scandal involved the acquisition by a small UK company of a much larger American one on terms with which other potential American acquirers could not compete. Blue Arrow was able to take on a level of debt that could be buried in its balance sheet over a period of years; an American firm, by contrast, would have to take a hit to its profits. As John Jay wrote in *The Sunday Telegraph:* "Thanks to the disparity between United States and British accounting rules over the treatment of goodwill, an American white knight was out of the question and Fromstein [Manpower's CEO] was reduced either to contemplating some kind of poison pill acquisition or suing for peace."[53] Arbitrary accounting rules thus generate uneconomic corporate decisions.

The long-time controversy over the best way to value stock options is a good illustration of many of the issues relating to corporate governance, including executive pay and measuring both performance and value, and the relationship of business, shareholders, government, the press, and the community in resolving these questions.

## Case in Point: FASB's Treatment of Stock Options

A stock option grant is the right to buy a company's stock at a fixed price for a fixed period. That usually means that an executive is granted the right to buy the company's stock at today's trading price for a period of ten years. If the stock goes up over that period, the executive can "cash out" the increase in the stock's trading price.

Stock option grants usually account for the multi-million-dollar executive pay packages. For example, at the end of 1992, Disney CEO Michael Eisner reaped profits of $197 million from his options. Eisner's gains were huge because he held options on a large number of shares, and because Disney's stock price had improved dramatically.

The 1990–92 recession caused an intense spotlight to be cast on the issue of executive compensation – how could executives be earning extraordinary fortunes while laying workers off and closing down plants? While we will address the executive compensation issue in greater depth elsewhere, we will focus here on one element of the controversy: the accounting for stock option grants.

Stock options offered a unique advantage. They were not charged to earnings, and yet were tax deductible. In other words, companies could issue stock options without recording them as an expense on the income statement, while, at the same time, deducting their cost from taxes paid to the federal government.

When a company pays a CEO in cash, that payment is treated as an expense: it is deducted from company earnings on the earnings statement, and the company claims that expense as a tax deduction. But when a CEO exercises an option – let's say on 10,000 shares, at $15 a share – and sells the shares at $35 a share, the company generally does not show any expense on its earnings. Yet the company may deduct $200,000 (the difference between $15 and $35 times the 100,000 shares) as a business expense.

When this anomaly attracted the attention of the press, shareholders, and Congress, all looked to the group responsible for setting accounting standards for US corporations – the Financial Accounting Standards Board (FASB). FASB is not a government organization, but the Securities and Exchange Commission (SEC) takes its recommendations into account when issuing accounting regulations.

Through FASB, corporate managers and accountants are self-regulating. That is, FASB (made up of a board of trustees taken from managerial ranks and the accounting profession) issues accounting rules and the private sector agrees to abide by them. Historically, Congress has never legislated accounting practices. Because FASB and the corporate world have been able to agree on accounting standards, the government has never thought it necessary to become involved.

The issue of accounting for option grants gave rise to a controversy that threatened to destroy this status quo. Two US senators issued conflicting bills that would put Congress in the position of legislating accounting rules for the first time.

The difficulty of the issue is due to the fact that it is notoriously hard to determine the value of options. An option grant becomes valuable only if (and to the extent that) the stock goes up; if the stock drops in value over the term of the grant, the option grant is worthless. Thus, if a company issues its CEO an option grant of 10,000 shares, the grant may, in ten years, be worth millions of dollars or it may be worth nothing. The value is determined by the performance of the stock over this term. However, the right to buy stock at a fixed price in the future clearly has value.

This was the conundrum facing FASB: How do you account for something of undetermined value? Obviously, it is impossible to predict precisely the growth or depreciation of stocks over a ten-year period. However, it is possible to factor in various known elements – the stock's historic performance, its volatility, and company earnings estimates – into an option pricing model. Such a model gives an estimated, though far from guaranteed, idea of what an option is worth. Two models currently favored by regulators are the Black-Scholes model developed by financial economists Fischer Black and Myron Scholes in the early 1970s, and the binomial pricing model.

The question before FASB was whether it should require companies to use an option pricing model as the basis for charging the cost of the option to earnings. In other words, if a company issues an option grant to its CEO of 10,000 shares, should it produce an estimated value of that option and enter that sum as a liability on the balance sheet?

The issue of accounting for options is not a new one. FASB first proposed that the cost of options be deducted from earnings in 1984. The response from corporate America was so fierce, however, that FASB tabled it indefinitely. Eight years later they found that the debate had turned 180 degrees – FASB was criticized for its inaction. At the forefront of the critics was Senator Carl Levin (D-Michigan), who sponsored a bill that would require companies to charge option grants to earnings. Levin criticized options as "stealth compensation" because they transferred enormous wealth to executives without ever appearing on the income statement.

Once again, the business community opposed possible changes to the accounting rules. Business leaders argued that a balance sheet should record known costs and expenses; it should not cover estimated sums that might or might not be a cost to the company in years to come. Companies which used options widely to compensate thousands of employees complained that they would no longer be able to be so generous with their grants. Startup companies said that options were a vital means of compensating key employees when there was insufficient cash flow to pay regular salaries and bonuses and warned that accounting for options would render them bankrupt.

In April 1992, to Senator Levin's delight, the FASB board voted unanimously to change its rule on accounting for stock options. It proposed that options were valuable at the time of grant, that this value could be estimated, and that the cost of such options should therefore be deducted from corporate earnings. All that remained was to write this proposition into a rule that the business world would accept. FASB put together a 15-member task force, representing corporations, institutional shareholders, accounting firms, investment managers, compensation consulting firms, and venture capitalists. The task force was charged with finding a method of accounting for stock options that all sides could agree on.

But while the FASB task force might have reached agreement among its members, it had not convinced the outside world. Much of the criticism of FASB's decision was based on the fact that the rules would not affect senior executives so much as middle management. Companies with broad-based options schemes involving many employees asserted that they would have to scale back their programs. They argued that while it was likely that senior executives would still receive large grants, employees further down the ladder would be unable to share in the company's growth. Companies such as PepsiCo, Wendy's, and Merck & Co. could see their pretax earnings decline up to 10 percent, according to one compensation analyst. A Wendy's official told the *Wall Street Journal* that if such an estimate were correct, the company would be forced to drop its stock option scheme which currently extends to an eighth of the company's workforce.

The Business Roundtable (BRT), a group representing 200 chief executives of the nation's largest corporations, launched a forceful campaign to stop FASB's rule change. A BRT spokesman said the group favored "disclosure rather than distortion of financial statements."

Shareholder groups also opposed the rule change. The Council of Institutional Investors (CII), representing pension funds and other major stockholders, argued against a charge to earnings. Sarah Teslik, executive director of the Council, agreed that option grants are valuable but said they weren't "dollars out of a company's coffers." CII agreed that investors had a right to an accurate picture of what options were being granted to executives, and the cost to shareholders of such grants. However, CII believed that it was not necessary for companies to take a charge to earnings to reflect the cost of options granted. Rather, "we believe that expanded disclosure is the best assurance that shareholders can have that their interests are being served. It therefore should eliminate the need for other potentially harmful governmental interference in shareholders' relationships to the companies they invest in."

CII recommended disclosing:

- the number of options outstanding, their exercise price, remaining terms, and the number of option holders they affected;
- the number of options exercised, forfeited, and expired;
- the number of new options granted, including exercise price, terms, and vesting requirements.

The Council's recommendations were supported by numerous groups. Corporate support came from General Electric, AT&T, and Apple Computer, among others. Six major accounting firms also supported CII's initiatives. They were also joined by the United Shareholders Association, the National Association of Corporate

Directors, and Peter Lynch, former portfolio manager of Fidelity's Magellan Fund.

But as Senator Levin sought to have FASB's rule changes incorporated into law, he ran into opposition within the Senate itself – Joseph Lieberman (D-Connecticut) sponsored a bill opposing FASB's rule change, which was passed by a vote of 88–9 in May 1994. FASB capitulated.

## MARKET VALUE

*Fortune* magazine has developed and perfected the concept of annually ranking the nation's (and, in later years, the world's) companies by their size. They calculate size by volume of sales, by net earnings, and – most significantly – by the market value of their equity capitalization. What is the largest company in the world? According to *Fortune,* it is the one that is worth the most. Being considered a "Fortune 100" or "Fortune 500" company has long been considered an untarnishable badge of honor. But this is changing.

Market value has statistical interest, but to whom is it really meaningful? The public's valuation of a company in the marketplace has unique value, because it is the only judgment that cannot be manipulated. Various notions of value based on concepts like earnings per share, book value, rate of return on reinvested capital, and the like are based on accounting principles that are so highly flexible that they have limited significance. But the fact that the market valuation is independent does not make it accurate in absolute terms. Fair market value doesn't tell you everything about what a company is worth. We are all familiar with the Dutch tulip bulb mania and "Popular Delusions and the Madness of Crowds." The public can value companies on bases that in retrospect appear idiotic. Examples include conglomerates in the 1960s, the "nifty fifty" in the early seventies, and possibly television cable companies in the 1990s. The greater the price a company can command for its shares on the market, the greater is its power to raise future capital through equity sales. But even strong current market value provides little insurance against its own future decline. That insurance must be provided by good planning on all fronts.

Conglomerates face special obstacles to traditional notions of head-to-head free market competitiveness, as shown by the following case in point.

## Case in Point: The Battle of the Theme Parks

Six Flags theme park began an aggressive ad campaign emphasizing what it saw as its primary advantage over Disney World; its geographic convenience. The message of the ads was that people could go to Six Flags and have a wonderful time, and still be home in time to feed the dog. Both theme parks were held by massive conglomerates, Six Flags by Time Warner and Disney World, of course, by Disney. Instead of responding with its own ads responding to Six Flags, Disney went to Time Warner, pulling its advertising from Time Warner publications and threatening to pull out of a joint venture for video distribution. What impact does this kind of response have on competitiveness and the efficiency of the market?

Ultimately, what is important is the company's continuing ability to obtain the capital necessary for the profitable production of goods and services that can be sold at a profit, and there is no magic monitor of this ability. More important than the worth of a company, which measures (imperfectly) today's value is the health of a company, which can predict tomorrow's.

## FRANCHISE
## "ISN'T IT MORE IMPORTANT TO GO FROM #5 TO #4 EN ROUTE TO #1 THAN TO INCREASE EPS BY 5 PERCENT OR 10 PERCENT THIS YEAR?"

Cyrus F. Freidheim, Jr., vice-chairman of Booz-Allen & Hamilton, made a provocative presentation at a conference on corporate governance sponsored by Northwestern University's Kellogg Graduate School of Management.[54] Acknowledging that there are "a number of CEOs who won the compensation battle (by hitting specified performance formulas) but whose companies lost the competitive war," he went on to attack the popular measuring stick, earnings per share (EPS), echoing the critiques of 1980s valuation gurus like Northwestern's Alfred Rappaport (now with LEK/Alcar) and Joel Stern of the New York consulting firm Stern Stewart. Friedheim said EPS has the advantage of simplicity and clarity, but is of questionable value in determining the health of an enterprise because it is too susceptible to manipulation. EPS can be driven up by liquidating the franchise, by restructuring and weakening the balance sheet, by playing "the accounting game with acquisitions, convertible securities, switching conventions. And none of those things would improve the value of the enterprise a wit." Freidheim is similarly skeptical of "the 'Rs' – ROI, ROE, ROCE, ROA, ROS, ROT. They all have a place in managing the business . . . but each can pay off without performance if followed as the measure."

Using stock price as the measure puts too much emphasis on the short term, Freidheim says:

> Let's stipulate that the return on shareholders' investment is maximized if the enterprise leads its industry in growth, profitability, and competitiveness over the long-term.
>
> Let's now reduce that to a framework for evaluating the performance of the CEO and the enterprise. Performance equals:
>
> • building the franchise, and
>
> • achieving long-term financial results and strength . . .
>
> The three financial categories that should be measured are:
>
> • Earnings
>
> • Growth in the financial base
>
> • Financial strength
>
> In measuring earnings, what should we use if not earnings per share? We should pick ones that demonstrate the effectiveness of the CEO in directing all of the companies' capital without the muddying effects of accounting changes . . . and which produce what we want: cash.
>
> The best of these could well be cash flow on investment. . . . The second financial measure is simply growth in equity before dividends. . . . The final financial measure focuses on financial strength . . . the balance sheet.

Coca-Cola CEO Roberto Goizuetta has a pillow embroidered, "The one with the biggest cash flow wins."

## EVA™: ECONOMIC VALUE ADDED

A 1993 cover story in *Fortune* magazine called EVA (economic value added) "today's hottest financial idea and getting hotter." The cover headline said EVA is "the real key to creating wealth . . . and AT&T chief Robert Allen and many others use it to make shareholders rich." Stern Stewart, which *Fortune* calls EVA's "preeminent popularizer," says that "quite simply, EVA is an estimate of true 'economic' profit after subtracting the cost of capital." EVA is commonly defined as (ATOP − WACC) × TC (where

ATOP is after-tax operating profit, WACC is the weighted average cost of capital, and TC is total capital). It cannot be reduced to a simple formula, however. As Ernst & Young EVA expert David Handlon (based in Washington, D.C.) advised us in a recent conversation, "the applied meaning of EVA varies tremendously from company to company, so each company should tailor it carefully to fit its own circumstances." Despite EVA's complexity, however, it has become very popular because its impact at major companies like Coca-Cola, CSX, and Quaker Oats has been galvanizing. *Fortune* noted that stock prices track EVA more closely than earnings per share or operating margins or return on equity. "That's because EVA shows what investors really care about – the net cash return on their capital – rather than some other type of performance viewed through the often distorting lens of accounting rules." By analyzing at the division level, managers can see if they are making more than their cost of capital. And since implementing EVA also includes a compensation plan, managers not only know it, they feel it.

## Case in Point: Quaker Oats

Until Quaker adopted the EVA concept in 1991, its businesses had one overriding goal – increasing quarterly earnings. To do it, they guzzled capital. They offered sharp price discounts at the end of each quarter, so plants ran overtime, turning out huge shipments of Gatorade, Rice-a-Roni, 100 percent Natural Cereal, and other products. Managers led the late rush, since their bonuses depended on raising operating profits each quarter.

This is the pernicious practice known as trade loading (because it loads up the trade, or retailers, with product), and many consumer products companies are finally admitting it damages long-term returns. An important reason is that it demands so much capital. Pumping up sales requires many warehouses (capital) to hold vast temporary inventories (more capital). But who cared? Quaker's operating businesses paid no charge for capital in internal accounting, so they barely noticed. It took EVA to spotlight the problem . . .

Quaker employs a version of EVA it calls controllable earnings . . . Free from the quarterly scramble, the Danville plant is whittling away at working capital and pays a stiff capital charge in the accounts for stocks of raw materials and finished goods.

The company was able to close down five of its 15 warehouses, and its stock is up 30 percent. It's no wonder Quaker CEO William Smithburg says EVA "makes managers act like shareholders."[55]

Not everyone is as enthusiastic, however. John Balkcom and Roger Brossy of Sibson & Co. warn of the "hidden traps in EVA-based incentives – value increments depend on the cost of capital, which can change materially if interest rates rise or fall or if the company changes its capital structure. Our experience suggests that the combination of EVA, organizational refinement, and customized incentives unlocks value. But no one of these three elements works by itself. Many monolithic companies have introduced EVA without the complementary organizational changes enacted by the likes of AT&T and Quaker, and the result has been a new, more cumbersome 'value bureaucracy' that impedes decision-making, misallocates capital, and destroys value."[56] Another way of thinking about this critique is in corporate governance terms. No matter how valid the method for evaluating the company's performance and direction, it cannot work itself. It must be applied within an organizational structure permitting decisions to be made by those with the best information and the fewest conflicts.

## HUMAN CAPITAL: "IT'S NOT WHAT YOU OWN BUT WHAT YOU KNOW"

Lawyer and Darden School of Business professor Richard Crawford, in his book, *In the Era of Human Capital,* documents the movement from an industrial society to a "knowledge society." As the economy shifts from "production of standard, tangible things with a split between production and consumption," to an "integrated global economy whose central economic activity is the provision of knowledge services with more fusion of producer and consumer," the primary resource shifts from physical capital to human capital. How does this affect the way we quantify value? The GAAP still assume that physical capital is the company's most important asset, even though overall investment in human capital has been higher for almost 30 years. Standard accounting rules assign no value to human resources, although they account for about 70 percent of the resources being used by US businesses, according to Crawford. He suggests "putting human capital on the balance sheet," including "off-balance-sheet intangible assets and human capital assets."

## THE VALUE OF CASH

Ultimately, a company is valued because of analysts' conviction that it can generate certain levels of positive cash flow from present and future operations. Any calculation of company value necessarily is based on "guesses" as to what will happen in the future. Some of the guesswork is taken out of the projections by taking into account the strength of its past performance, the quality of its products, the positioning of its niche within its industry, the competitiveness of its technology, its ability to sustain margins, and, most critically, the vision and competence of its management. For example, when an under-performing company replaces its CEO, the market's reaction can be highly positive. as shown by the market's response when Goodyear and Allied Signal replaced poorly performing CEOs with well-regarded outsiders. Similarly, Lord Weinstock's announcement in July 1994 that he was extending GEC's retirement age so that he could stay on for two more years sent the company's value down significantly.

The market's valuation of human capital extends beyond the CEO slot. Eastman Kodak's market value went up $2 billion on the hiring of Christopher Steffen – the highest ranking outsider appointed at Kodak since 1912 – and then lost $1.6 billion on the day that Steffen resigned twelve weeks later. This kind of reaction shows that the market's valuation of a company depends not just on the value of the company's assets, but also very much on the market's perception of the management's ability to manage those assets.

A company's capacity to survive and prosper is based on its ability to obtain the capital necessary to conduct its business at a competitive price. No matter how famous a company, no matter how admired its products, ultimately its worth lies in its ability to raise capital at a cost significantly less than the increase in earnings resulting from the new investment. Someone with a lower cost of capital can always buy goods, build plants, and finance sales cheaper than the competition. Business is done on the increment; a new entrant into the business creates a new reality by its cost of capital. This becomes the competitive bogey which the rest of the industry has to meet regardless of their actual costs.

As Michael Jacobs argued persuasively in *Short Term America*,[57] the international competitiveness of a country – the United States in his account – rests on its ability to provide capital to domestic companies at a rate that is internationally competitive. The perceived threat that Japanese industry would simply take over the rest of the world in the 1980s was largely based on their having virtually a zero cost of capital. Companies can survive from the earnings generated from operations in excess of depreciation and dividends. But, as even the Japanese have learned, markets change.[58] Debt that was attractive one year suddenly is non-competitive the next. Even the most financially secure company must continually have access to capital markets in order to assure that it is using the most cost effective capital at all times.

The definition of a financially successful company might be this: the ability on a continuing basis to generate returns from new investment in its business that are substantially greater than the cost of obtaining the funds.

## Case in Point: Daimler-Benz and the New York Stock Exchange[59]

On March 30, 1993, Daimler-Benz announced that it would list its shares on the NYSE, making it the first German company listed on a US exchange. The move was highly significant because it showed that Daimler-Benz was prepared vastly to improve its financial disclosure in return for access to the United States' large and liquid capital markets.

The move was the result of lengthy discussions between Daimler-Benz management, NYSE chairman and CEO William Donaldson, and SEC chairman Richard Breeden regarding disclosure requirements for the listing. And while the final agreement involved compromise on all sides, it appears that the SEC for the most part held sway over the other two parties.

In order to list its shares on the NYSE, Daimler-Benz will be required to provide greater financial disclosure than is required under German law. Breeden stressed that the SEC has not changed US policy regarding disclosure requirements for foreign companies seeking listings on US stock exchanges. In fact, he referred to the agreement as a "complete rejection of the approach suggested by the [New York] stock exchange." For years, the NYSE has advocated that the SEC relax some disclosure requirements in order to attract foreign companies but the SEC has remained steadfast.

Key aspects of the agreement included:

- Daimler-Benz AG, the parent company, proposed to adjust its earnings upward by DM4 billion ($2.42 billion) in 1992, by claiming hidden reserves of this amount as "extraordinary earnings." This move highlights one of the most controversial aspects of German company law and accounting practices, whereby companies may accumulate large hidden reserves, thereby artificially deflating the company's value. The result of this practice is that most German companies, including Daimler-Benz, are undervalued on the stock exchange. The decision to allocate these reserves

indicates that the disclosure regime demanded by the SEC will
provide greater transparency regarding the company's financial
situation.

- Daimler-Benz will have the choice of one set of financial data for
  German investors and another set for US investors in accordance
  with SEC requirements, or a single set complying with requirements of both jurisdictions. It is not yet clear how Daimler-Benz's
  listing on the NYSE will affect the disclosure of information
  related to the company's annual general meeting. It will be interesting to see how the listing will affect disclosure in this respect.
  (While German disclosure requirements are quite high in compari-
  son with other continental European jurisdictions, they are not
  as stringent as SEC requirements.)

- Daimler-Benz will be required to present cash flow statements in
  accordance with US accounting principles.

- Daimler-Benz will not be required to offer financial information
  on previous years in accordance with US accounting principles.

According to the SEC, more than 200 foreign companies have listed
on the US exchanges over the past three and half years; however,
no German company had ever done so. Several years ago, six of
Germany's largest listed companies (Daimler-Benz AG, BASF AG,
Bayer AG, Hoechst AG, Siemens AG and Volkswagen AG)
approached the SEC as a united front, attempting to forge a compromise whereby German companies would not be subject to the complete SEC disclosure regime. This approach failed, and Daimler-
Benz decided to "go it alone." In a March 1993 press release,
Gerhard Liener, Daimler-Benz's chief financial officer, said: "We
were on the way to becoming a global company and I realized that
I might have been caught in an anachronistic way of thinking. Just
as English has become the language of international business, Anglo-
Saxon accounting has become the accounting language worldwide.
I thought it was foolish to go on trying to play Don Quixote tilting
at windmills."

Recent developments, both financial and regulatory, may explain
why Daimler-Benz decided to make the move alone at this time.
The company's financial difficulties may have contributed to a decision to seek capital abroad.

Factors affecting the German economy as a whole may also have
influenced Daimler-Benz's decision. In the March press release cited
above, Liener said: "[T]he agreement we have reached with the
SEC gives us access to the world's largest and most dynamic stock
market."

The Daimler listing carries implications for corporate governance worldwide. A recent study by the Oxford Analytica group predicts that as competition for global capital increases, corporations will be forced to make concessions to the providers of capital.[60] Daimler, by its NYSE listing, has shown that it is willing to make significant governance concessions in the quest for new and cheaper investment sources. Other companies said to be interested in following Daimler's lead in the United States include Germany's Deutsche Bank and Switzerland's Nestlé group.

These examples show that transparency (disclosure) and good governance can produce a lower cost of capital, as equity markets increasingly recognize the value of reduced agency costs.

## CORPORATE "EXTERNALITIES"

Each business imposes costs that are not usually reflected in its profit and loss statements. Some of this is tradition, some of it reflects the difficulty of valuing intangible elements, and some of it reflects the success of companies in having governments, regulators, and professional auditors make accommodating rules. These are "externalities," costs incurred by business but paid for elsewhere.

The quotation from Adrian Cadbury on page 42 speaks of a second level of company responsibility – considering the implications of a corporation's operations on the rest of society. Certainly, some corporate operations may have an adverse impact on society. In some cases, corporations pay for this cost; in others, society as a whole absorbs the cost. This is referred to as a "corporate externality." Examples include the EPA standard setting an acceptable level for the odor of emissions from paper mills and the wrongful death statutes limiting the amount of recovery for human lives in coal mining accidents.

In theory at least, the government is in the best position to decide which aspects of corporate cost should be charged to the enterprise. The two examples in the last paragraph illustrate this point. In the United States environmental and occupational safety standards are set by the legislature and regulatory agencies.

Some companies have made significant, if sporadic, efforts over the last decades to reflect the "real" (in contrast to GAAP) cost of their operation. During the administration of US President Jimmy Carter, Commerce Secretary Juanita Krepps actually proposed a formal methodology for "social accounting." The report declared that "changing public expectations of business" demanded that corporations reveal such information as: "the impacts of day-to-day business activities on the physical environment, on employees, consumers, local communities and other affected interests."[61]

One attempt to design a "social responsibility accounting" proposes the following characteristics of a social report:

1. Each report should include a statement of its objectives which allows *(inter alia)* the assessment of the:
   • grounds for data selection
   • reasons for form of presentation chosen.
2. The objective of a social report should be to discharge accountability in the spirit of improved democracy.
3. The information should be directly related to the objectives held for the particular groups to whom it is addressed.
4. The information should be unmanipulated and readable by a non-expert. It must be audited.[62]

Note that in item 2, the report is to a broad "democracy" rather than to shareholders, directors, employees, the government or any other specific group. The authors themselves acknowledge that there may be some internal inconsistency between these requirements (item 4 alone seems to us to be internally inconsistent), and indeed some conflicts of interest between the intended readers of such a report. But, they conclude that "These are matters outside the model itself. We seek information to discharge accountability, what society does with that information has to be society's concern."[63]

In late 1993, Time Warner published a "Social Responsibility Report" that documents the company's view of itself as "a company of ideas . . . a company of conscience." The report explicitly ties Time Warner's "determination to make a difference as well as a profit" to the company's financial performance: "Our position as the world's leading media and entertainment company could not have been achieved – and could not be sustained – solely from business success. It rests equally on Time Warner's traditions of social responsibility and community involvement." Activities documented in the report include programs for literacy (involving Time Warner's publications, cable, and other products as well as 200 employees), voter education, environment education, minority business support and development, equal employment opportunity, sponsorship of community programs and art programs, and health education and research. The company's involvement ranged from employee volunteers to grants to provision of products and services, including space in the company's publications.

Perhaps wisely, Time Warner did not try to quantify the costs, the benefits, or the net of these endeavors. Attempts to do so have looked like financial economist Ralph Estes' "comprehensive social accounting model," which follows:

$$SS = \sum_{i=1}^{n}\sum_{t=1}^{\infty}\frac{B_i}{(1 + r)^t} - \sum_{j=1}^{m}\sum_{t=1}^{\infty}\frac{C_j}{(1 + r)^t}$$

where $SS$ = social surplus or deficit
$B_i$ = the $i$th social benefit
$C_j$ = the $j$th social cost
$r$ = an appropriate discount rate
$t$ = time period in which benefit or cost is expected to occur.

## Case in Point: Social Accounting at ARCO

Atlantic Richfield (ARCO), under the leadership of chairman Robert O. Anderson and president Thornton F. Bradshaw, included social consequences as a part of the formal annual report to shareholders:

> Corporate responsibility is easier to discuss in generalities than in specifics. Inevitably, it becomes a matter of management judgment. Atlantic Richfield chooses to believe that it is acting responsibly in the most essential sense when discharging the traditional functions of a corporation with care and dedication. . . .
>
> Beyond these fundamentals, however, is the even broader world where there are opportunities and challenges whose ultimate impact on the bottom line can no longer be denied. They provide an accurate measurement of the humanity – and social desirability – of this company.

## Case in Point: Eastern Gas & Fuel Associates

An even more imaginative effort was made by the late CEO of Eastern Gas & Fuel Associates, Eli Goldston, who actually attributed dollar values to particular "social" consequences of his corporation's actions:

> *To our shareholders:*
> There has been much talk in recent years of corporate social responsibility and of the need to develop some sort of social

accounting to gauge how well a given firm is performing – not just as an economic unit but as a citizen. Indeed, some have suggested that these measures of corporate performance beyond net profit should be subjected to an independent social audit.

This insert for the 1972 Annual Report of Eastern Gas & Fuel Associates has been designed as an experimental exploration of two aspects of social accounting for "self-auditing" purposes:

(1) What are some internal topics on which management can presently assemble and organize reasonably accurate and coherent data?
(2) Which issues of social accountability are of external interest and to what extent are shareholders in particular interested, if at all?

To explore the first of these aspects we have gathered statistical information that covers four topics from among the many that are currently of concern to those studying corporate social responsibility:

• Industrial safety
• Minority employment
• Charitable giving
• Pensions

The topics for this first report were not chosen because they are necessarily the most important ones, or the ones that might make us look good, but because they are the most readily measurable, because our goals with respect to them are comparatively simple and clear, and because they lie in areas where management can rather directly influence results. In addition, managerial decisions on these topics can have a significant impact on earnings per share.

In the process of making this first consolidation of social data from our various operations, we found that our records were less complete and less certain than we had believed. We also found that even inadequate disclosure begins to exert a useful pressure on management to comply with new public expectations as to the conduct of large corporations. It may also be some of the best evidence that management is sincerely concerned and making an effort to meet proper expectations.

Four major recurring principles for the quantification of social responsibility have been suggested:

The first is that our priorities have been changing with some rapidity. Many of our political, economic, and commercial measures of progress have become obsolescent. We need a new kind of social accounting that goes beyond GNP for the nation and goes beyond net profit for the firm.

Second, while we think of our current economic and accounting measure of GNP and net profits as very precise when you really get into the nitty gritty of how they are put together, their certainty is delusive.

Third, many proposed imprecise measures of social accounting can be sufficiently accurate to be instructive. They are not hopelessly less accurate than GNP or net profit, and so they can be quite useful, even though they lack precision, for many purposes for which we cannot use GNP and net profit.

And finally, while our efforts to calibrate our concerns by social accounting will reflect this new sense of priorities, without personal observation in the field and a weighing of the figures that we create with moral concerns, social accounting itself becomes only a new numbers game.

As we proceed with these early attempts to develop some form of internal social accounting, we should acquire additional useful insights into this new art.

*Eli Goldston, President*

## NON-ECONOMIC CONSIDERATIONS IN CORPORATE MANAGEMENT

When should corporate management pursue objectives that are not directly correlated with profit maximization? This is the third level of corporate responsibility mentioned above by Adrian Cadbury: "How far has business a responsibility to maintain the framework of the society in which it operates and how far should business reflect society's priorities rather than its own commercial ones?"

David Engel has provided a magisterial analysis of the answer to this question.[64] In the "balancing interests" section above, we discussed the limits to the scope of corporate managers' discretion. Nobody elected them to make social decisions. The legitimacy of corporate power requires that it be limited to business and not extend to the trade-offs necessary to balance competing social goals. Engel concludes that there are four general areas where extra value maximization objectives are justifiable.

### 1. *Obey the law*

This may appear to be a relativistic command, but Engel argues that it is absolute. In many instances, a corporation can make a cost/benefit calculation and conclude that it is cheaper to break the law than to obey it. This involves weighing the costs of compliance against the probability of getting caught, plus the costs of attorneys' fees, lost time, and damages that would be awarded. Engel argues that corporations, in using such analysis, will ultimately run the risk of subverting the "legitimacy" of the societal base that is, in turn, a necessary precondition for profitable corporate operations.

The "law" underlying the legitimacy of capitalism is the existence of competition. To the extent that markets are not free, prices fixed, or territories divided, the justification for the profit structure of business disappears. The ultimate crime in recent times was the so-called electrical price-fixing scandal of the late 1950s. It was unusual in its scope, and even more unusual because several executives of General Electric and Westinghouse went to jail.

## Case in Point: Price Fixing

In the years 1959–60, government investigators unraveled the largest price fixing and market rigging conspiracy in the 50 year history of antitrust law. The conspiracy aimed to divide up the $17 billion market for power generating equipment and electrical goods. Among the indicted companies were the two giants of the industry, Westinghouse Electric Corp. and General Electric Corp.

In 1959, the Tennessee Valley Authority (TVA), which operated the largest electrical generating capacity in the United States, asked for bids on a hydroelectric turbine generator for its Colbert Steam Plant. General Electric and Westinghouse offered (secret and sealed) bids of over $17.5 million. To the fury of those two companies, TVA awarded the contract to a British firm that bid a little over $12 million. GE and Westinghouse sought to have the award overturned as prejudicial to "national security" since they would be unable to repair foreign equipment in times of national emergency.

TVA explained why it had gone abroad for the contract: "For some time, TVA has been disturbed by the rising prices of turbo generators. There are only three American firms which manufacture large turbo generators. Since 1951, the prices charged by these manufacturers for such equipment have increased by more than 50 percent while the average wholesale price of all commodities has increased only 5 percent."[65] Between 1950 and 1956, GE and Westinghouse had increased prices on power transformers six times, one firm copying the other's price increase within days. Between 1946 and 1957, prices on large turbines had been raised ten times.

The story instantly aroused the interest of Tennessee Senator, Estes Kefauver, chairman of the Senate Subcommittee on Antitrust and Monopoly. He quickly announced an investigation into the pattern of identical bidding. An investigation into TVA's records found 24 instances of matched bids in just over three years. Some of these bids were the same down to the nearest hundredth of a cent. These were all secret, sealed bids.

The examination of TVA's records also found:

- Circuit breakers: Identical bids of $21,000 were submitted by GE, Westinghouse, Allis-Chalmers, and Federal Pacific.

- Suspension circuit breakers: Eight identical bids of $11,900.

- Condenser tubing: Eight identical bids quoting prices down to the last thousandth of a cent.[66]

TVA was not the only organization to complain. Many local, state, and other federal agencies backed up TVA's complaint, saying they had also received a series of similar bids.

In July 1959 the Justice department announced that a federal grand jury in Pennsylvania was investigating the bidding for possible antitrust violations. In February 1960, the jury handed down the first seven of what would amount to 20 indictments. By the end of the summer of 1960, 29 electrical manufacturers and 45 of their executives had been indicted. The government alleged that the effect of the conspiracy had been to raise the power of electrical equipment throughout the country to high, fixed, and artificial levels, as price competition was restrained, suppressed, and eliminated.

As antitrust law had developed until this point, corporations generally offered one of two responses to an antitrust indictment. First, they could plead guilty and pay the fine. As one author describes, "Between 1890 and 1959, whenever a fine was imposed, it was paid, almost happily and cheerfully, as a cost of doing illicit business. Prison sentences were seldom imposed and usually suspended. Somehow the violation of the antitrust law never was considered more than a gentleman's misdemeanor – and a gentleman was never sent to jail for violating the antitrust law. Being indicted under the Sherman Act was regarded as nothing more than a bad corporate cold, which could be shaken off by the payment of a nominal number of dollars."[67]

Second, corporations could plead *nolo contendere,* literally, "I do not contest." Because this plea did not admit guilt, any party seeking damages would have to prove wrongdoing. In other words, a *nolo* plea put the burden of proof on the damaged parties. As a result, *nolo* pleas were common in antitrust cases.

Initially, Westinghouse and General Electric did not feel they had too much to worry about – just a "bad corporate cold." They had violated antitrust laws before, and would no doubt be accused of doing so in future. As the evidence grew in 1959, however, the giant electric companies began to get worried.

In March 1960, the companies were arraigned on the first seven charges, considered by the government to be the most serious. Westinghouse and GE pleaded not guilty; every other company pleaded *nolo*. The government believed the charges were too severe for a *nolo* settlement, and took the unusual step of asking the judge not to accept such pleas. Assistant Attorney General, Robert Bicks, head of the antitrust division, told the judge: "The Attorney General states his considered judgment that these indictment charges are as serious instances of bid-rigging and price-fixing as have been charged in the more than half-century life of the Sherman Act."[68] In other words, the government wasn't charging the electric companies with mere technical violations of the act, as was usually the case. They had evidence of serious and sustained criminal activity.

The judge granted the government's request to throw out the *nolo* pleas, leaving the corporations wondering if they could possibly win at trial. As the number of indictments increased through 1960, the corporations found themselves looking at a series of trials that could last five years. Allis-Chalmers decided not to fight the battle and pleaded guilty to all charges. This undermined the defenses of the remaining companies. After the nineteenth indictment was handed down, Westinghouse and GE approached the government with a possible settlement. The companies would plead guilty on the most serious charges in exchange for a *nolo* plea in the remaining cases. After long negotiations, the government agreed, but insisted on guilty pleas in the seven most serious charges.

General Electric chairman, Ralph Cordiner, learned that GE was going to be deeply involved in the scandal in September 1959. The next January, he addressed GE's annual management conference on the subject of Business Ethics in a Competitive Enterprise System. He said: "The system will remain free and competitive only so long as the citizens and particularly those of us with responsibilities in business life, are capable of the self-discipline required. If we are not capable of self-discipline, the power of the government will be increasingly invoked as a substitute, until the system is no longer free or competitive."[69]

In 1961, GE's stockholders met for their first annual meeting since the indictments. The next day, the *New York Times* editorial page carried the following comment. "Unhappily, little recognition of this responsibility [to inspire public confidence] manifested itself at the annual meeting of GE stockholders . . . For a company with nearly half a million share owners, the meeting had too much of a rubber-stamp quality to provide an inspiring demonstration of democracy at work in the corporate field. It merely supplied fresh ammunition for those who doubt the moral underpinnings of our industrial society."[70]

The Westinghouse annual meeting was not so uneventful. A shareholder made a motion from the floor for the company's three top executives to resign. A second proposal called for a committee of directors to determine if management should have known what was going on. The resolutions were defeated by overwhelming margins.

By the end of 1964, GE had settled about 90 percent of its lawsuits, paying out about $200 million. Westinghouse settled about the same for $110 million. The total settlements for the industry were about $500 million.

## 2. *Disclose information about social impact beyond the minimum requirements of law that relate to the impact of corporation on society*

Full disclosure at the outset may result in fewer sales in the short term, but it will contribute to a society in which the legitimacy of corporate power is more generally conceded than when there are surprises. There are many recent examples of companies that learned the hard way that it is cheaper to disclose negative information than to suppress it: Dow Corning's research on the health hazards of its breast implants, A.H. Robins' research on its intra-uterine contraceptive device, tobacco companies' research on the harmful effects of tobacco, and Beech-Nut's evidence that it was manufacturing adulterated apple juice.

## 3. *Dramatically reduce corporate involvement in politics*

In the past decade, we have witnessed the consequences of incest between the state and its corporations with the virtual collapse of the Italian state and economy and the humiliating defeat of the LDP party in Japanese elections. In the United States, the problem is demonstrated by the level of political action committee campaign contributions, the increase in the expense and use of lobbyists, and the perception that government lacks the will and capacity to deal effectively with large companies. Corporations need to have some say in the government process affecting them, but not so much that they undercut the popular support for government in the process. Engel's point is echoed by Andrew B. Schmookler:

> The protection of that equality, therefore, should be our first priority, even if that requires some sacrifice of other important rights. Two general principles would advance our democracy.
>
> First, access to political speech must not be apportioned according to wealth, at least in the publicly licensed broadcast media. If a corporation like Exxon buys time to broadcast a message with

political import, there should be equal time provided (perhaps at Exxon's expense) for an opposing point of view. Defining political speech might not be easy, but it should not be impossible. Our legal system continually solves definitional problems of this nature. The right of free speech is sacred, but there is no reason it should be defined in a way that subverts one of its primary purposes: the protection of democracy. Exxon has the right to be heard. But let us hear also the voices of other people, though they lack Exxon's billions, on the same policy-related questions.

Second, our political campaigns need to be completely insulated from private wealth. This is not easily achieved, but this, too, should be possible. Perhaps it could be achieved with some combination of free air time, public financing in proportion to registered voters signing petitions, and automatic public financing. In any event, it is incompatible with the principle of democracy for a candidate to have an advantage over an opponent because the supporters of the one are rich and those of the other are poor.

Let us not despair of the possibility of democracy. We have yet fully to try it.[71]

### 4. Adhere to the "Kew Gardens" principle

In the late 1960s, a young woman named Kitty Genovese returned to her apartment in the Kew Gardens section of New York City and was stabbed in broad daylight in the courtyard in full view of her neighbors, none of whom did anything to save her as she slowly bled to death. She became a symbol of the tragic consequences of failing to act. Engel argues that corporations should act when failing to do so would certainly create serious damage for society.

These four "Engel principles" form the critical basis for developing a theory of performance measurement for corporations because they reveal the need to limit corporate power to a known, definable, and limited sphere. With these principles in place, it is time to turn to the people who are responsible for monitoring corporate performance, the shareholders and the board of directors.

## NOTES

1. See, for example, Ronald Coase, "The Nature of the Firm," *Economica*, 4, 1937, p. 386 and Frank H. Easterbrook and Daniel R. Fischel, "The Corporate Contract," *Columbia Law Review,* 7, Nov. 1989, p. 1416. "The corporate structure is a set of contracts through which managers and certain other participants exercise a great deal

of discretion that is 'reviewed' by interactions with other self-interested actors" (p. 1418).

2. A 1993 *Wall Street Journal* article noted that a variation on the corporate structure, the limited-liability company (LLC), was "arguably the hottest thing in business start-ups today." A hybrid, which offers owners "the liability protections of a traditional corporation and the tax advantages of a partnership," was, at the time of the article, permitted in 35 states, up from only 8 in 1991. A 1988 IRS ruling that permitted LLCs to be treated as partnerships, so that each owner's profits are taxed only on his or her personal returns, and not double taxed, as with corporations, gives LLCs the advantages of partnership, and the limited liability provides the advantages of incorporation. This has not been lost on entrepreneurs or on "scam artists." Regulators have claimed that fraudulent communications technologies firms have used the LLC to avoid state and federal securities laws. *Wall Street Journal,* Nov. 8, 1993, p. B1.

3. Opinion in *Louis K. Liggett Co. v. Lee,* 53 S. Ct. 487 (1932).

4. Id.

5. Mortmain is a legal term indicating concern that rules or restrictions established by a "dead hand" (a previous generation) would impede trade or capital allocation. Brandeis speculates in a footnote that this concern was the reason for limiting corporations to fixed terms of 20, 30, or 50 years in the early statutes.

6. *Liggett Co. v. Lee,* p. 490. Citations omitted.

7. Id., p. 493.

8. Robert C. Clark, *Corporate Law* (Little, Brown & Co, Boston, 1986), p. 2.

9. Note, though, the widespread practice today of partners in professional firms (doctors, lawyers, etc.) each individually incorporating as a mechanism for minimizing both liability and taxes.

10. William Greider, *Who Will Tell the People? The Betrayal of American Democracy* (Simon & Schuster, New York, 1992), pp. 348, 349.

11. Thomas Donaldson, *Corporations & Morality* (Prentice-Hall, Englewood Cliffs, NJ, 1982), p. 30.

12. See, for example, Anne Murphy, "Too Good to be True?" *Inc.,* June 1994, p. 34.

13. Paul Abrahams and Roland Rudd, "ICI to float drugs unit in break-up of group interests," *Financial Times,* July 31, 1992. p. 1.

14. Easterbrook and Fischel, supra, pp. 1417–18.

15. Some sources argue that there cannot be a "race to the bottom" because if Delaware, for example, permitted laws that benefited management to the detriment of shareholders, then companies incorporated in Delaware would be at a competitive disadvantage in the capital market, and ultimately in the product market. See Ralph K.

Winter, "State Law, Shareholder Protection, and the Theory of the Corporation," *Journal of Legal Studies*, 6 (1977), p. 251. This argument would have more weight if shareholders were able to change the state of incorporation, instead of just refraining from investing in companies incorporated in a particular state, or selling out once the state has adopted unacceptable new legislation.

16. Carl Kaysen, "The Corporation; How Much Power? What Scope?," in *The Corporation in Modern Society*, ed. Edward S. Mason (Harvard University Press, Cambridge, 1959), p. 103.

17. Id., pp. 103, 104.

18. Id., pp. 104–5.

19. Martin Dickson, "GE shares dip on fraud allegation," *Financial Times*, June 3, 1992, p. 17.

20. See John Braithwaite, *Corporate Crime in the Pharmaceutical Industry* (Routledge & Kegan Paul, London, 1984), p. 258; and Marshall B. Clinnard, *Corporate Corruption: The Abuse of Power* (Praeger, New York, 1990), p. 103.

21. Milton Friedman, *Capitalism and Freedom* (The University of Chicago Press, Chicago, 1962), p. 133.

22. A.B. Schmookler, *The Illusion of Choice: How the Market Economy Shapes Our Destiny* (State University of New York Press, Albany, 1993), pp. 24, 25.

23. A.A. Berle, Jr., "For Whom Are Corporate Managers Trustees?," *Harvard Law Review*, 45 (1932), pp. 1365, 1367.

24. John C. Coffee, Jr., "No Soul to Damn: No Body to Kick: An Unscandalized Inquiry into the Problem of Corporate Punishment," *Michigan Law Review*, 79 (1981), pp. 386, 387.

25. Statement of Douglas H. Ginsburg, Assistant Attorney General, Antitrust Division, before the United States Sentencing Commission, Hearings Concerning Alternatives to Incarceration, July 15, 1986.

26. "When very severe fines need to be imposed on the corporation, they should be imposed not in cash, but in the equity securities of the corporation. The convicted corporation should be required to authorize and issue such number of shares to the state's crime victim compensation fund as would have an expected market value equal to the cash fine necessary to deter illegal activity. The fund should then be able to liquidate the securities in whatever manner maximizes its return." John C. Coffee, Jr., "No Soul to Damn," p. 413, citations omitted.

27. Braithwaite, *Corporate Crime in the Pharmaceutical Industry*, p. 324.

28. Russell Mokhiber, *Corporate Crime and Violence: Big Business and the Abuse of the Public Trust* (Sierra Club Books, 1988), p. 19.

29. Richard W. Stevenson, "Many are Caught but Few Suffer For US Military Contract Fraud," *New York Times*, Nov. 12, 1990.

30. Braithwaite, *Corporate Crime in the Pharmaceutical Industry*, p. 319.

31. Douglas H. Ginsburg, Testimony presented to the US Sentencing Commission, July 15, 1986.
32. Marshall B. Clinnard, *Corporate Corruption: The Abuse of Power* (Praeger, New York, 1990), p. 307.
33. Ralph Nader, Mark Green, and Joel Seligman in *Taming the Giant Corporation* (W.W. Norton, New York, 1976), p. 120.
34. Christopher D. Stone, *Where the Law Ends, The Social Control of Corporate Behavior* (Harper & Row, New York, 1975), p. 148.
35. "Nuclear Executives in Japan Resign over Recent Mishaps," *New York Times,* May 14, 1981.
36. Michael Moritz and Barrett Seaman, *Going for Broke – The Chrysler Story* (Doubleday, New York, 1981).
37. Joseph Nocera, "Delaware Puts Out," *Esquire,* Feb. 1990, p. 47.
38. Private letter from Peter F. Drucker to Robert Monks, June 17, 1993.
39. F.A. Hayek, *Law, Legislation, Liberty, Volume 3: The Political Order of a Free People* (University of Chicago Press, Chicago, 1979), p. 82.
40. James J. Hanks in "From the Hustings: The Role of States With Takeover Control Laws," *Mergers and Acquisitions,* 29, 2, Sept.– Oct. 1994. This was part of the protectionist surge that followed the 1987 US Supreme Court decision in *CTS Corp. v. Dynamics Corp. of America,* which permitted certain kinds of state anti-take- over statutes.
41. Ga. Code Ann. Sec. 14–2–202.5.
42. The American Bar Association on Corporate Laws, "Other Constit- uency Statutes: Potential for Confusion," *The Business Lawyer,* 45, 4, Aug. 1990, p. 2261.
43. Id., p. 2259.
44. Tom Cannon, *Corporate Responsibility* (Pitman Publishing, Marsh- field, MA, 1992), p. 79.
45. James Willard Hurst, *The Legitimacy of the Business Corporation in the Law of the United States:* 1780–1980 (University of Virginia Press, Charlottesville, 1970), pp. 82–3. "[I]n *Dodge Brothers v. Ford Motor Company:* Management's prime obligation was to pur- sue profit in the interests of shareholders and not to adopt pricing policies designed to promote the interests of wage earners or to effect wider sharing of the gains of improved technology."
46. Joseph Pereira, "Split Personality: Social Responsibility And Need for Low Cost Clash at Stride Rite," *Wall Street Journal,* May 28, 1993, p. A1.
47. Id.
48. Doug Bandow, "Social Responsibility: A Conservative View," *Utne Reader,* Sept.–Oct., 1993, pp. 62–3. Reprinted from *Business and Society Review,* Spring 1992.
49. 1989 Berkshire Hathaway annual report, pp. 52–3.

50. Sir Adrian Cadbury, *The Company Chairman* (Fitzwilliam Publishing, Cambridge, 1990), p. 149.

51. Steven Prokesch, "How Johnson and Johnson Managed the Tylenol Crisis," *New York Times,* Feb. 27, 1986.

52. Prior to passage of the 1993 Omnibus Budget Reconciliation Act (OBRA), only some types of intangibles could be written off, and of these, some had to be written off over a period of no less than 28 years. This conservative approach began to change in 1993. First, the US Supreme Court declared in *Newark Morning Ledger v. US* that if the value of an acquired asset can be measured and will appreciate over time, it can be depreciated. Then the US Congress passed OBRA, which set a maximum of 15 years for amortization of intangibles, some formerly considered non-amortizable goodwill, with even shorter periods allowed for some categories.

53. John Jay, *The Sunday Telegraph,* Feb. 4, 1990. See also Bob Hagarty, "Differing Accounting Rules Snarl Europe," *Wall Street Journal,* September 4, 1992; and "Foreign Firms Rush to Acquire U.S. Companies," *Wall Street Journal,* July 1, 1994. The last article notes that the International Accounting Standards Committee issued a new rule that will force European companies to deduct the value of goodwill from their profits, as in the United States.

54. Jan. 13, 1992. All quotes in this section from that paper.

55. Shawn Tully, "The Real Key to Creating Wealth," *Fortune,* Sept. 20, 1993, p. 38.

56. Letter to the Editor, *Fortune,* Oct. 18, 1993, p. 34.

57. Michael Jacobs, *Short-Term America* (Harvard Business School Press, Cambridge, MA, 1991).

58. For an in-depth study of growing Japanese need for equity-based capital, see Howard D. Sherman and Bruce A. Babcock, "Redressing Structural Imbalances in Japanese Corporate Governance: An International Perspective," *The Corporate Governance Advisor,* 1, 8, Dec. 1993, p. 28.

59. This case in point has been reproduced from Geoffrey P. Mazullo, "Germany's Daimler-Benz First To List Shares on New York Stock Exchange," *ISSue Alert,* VIII, 4, April 1993. Used with permission.

60. "Board Directors and Corporate Governance: Trends in the G7 Countries Over the Next Ten Years," Oxford Analytica, Oxford, England (Sept. 1992).

61. *Corporate Social Reporting in the United States and Western Europe,* Report of the Task Force on Corporate Social Performance, US Department of Commerce, July 1979, p. 3.

62. Rob Gray, Dave Owne, and Keith Maunders, *Corporate Social Accounting: Accounting and Accountability* (Prentice Hall International, Englewood Cliffs, NJ, 1987), p. 89.

63. Id. For the findings of a global group that explored these and other fundamental questions in governance, see the Caux Round Table

report on Principles for Business, the Caux Round Table Secretariat, the Hague, The Netherlands, 1994.

64. David Engel, "An Approach to Corporate Social Responsibility," *Stanford Law Review,* 32, 1, Nov. 1979.

65. John Herling, *The Great Price Conspiracy: The Story of the Antitrust Violations in the Electrical Industry* (Robert B. Luce Inc., Washington, 1962), p. 3.

66. Id., p. 5.

67. Id., p. 9.

68. Clarence C. Walton and Frederick W. Cleveland, Jr., *Corporations on Trial, The Electric Cases* (Wadsworth Publishing Company Inc., Belmont, CA, 1964), p. 34.

69. Herling, supra, p. 97.

70. Id., p. 109.

71. See Schmookler, *The Illusion of Choice,* pp. 93–4.

# *2*

# Shareholders: Ownership

---

Shareholders are often referred to as the "owners" of the corporation, but the corporation's "legal personality" raises questions about whether it can be "owned" in any meaningful and effective way. There will always be agency costs in any corporate structure in which someone other than management owns equity. Public companies will continue to have managers with agendas different from their owners'; the governance challenge is to require that the resolution of conflicts be an open process between entities that are informed, motivated, and empowered.

In order to put this issue into context, we will spend a short time on the overall issue of "ownership" before discussing its application to stock in public corporations.

## DEFINITIONS

Generally, we think of "ownership" of "property" as including three elements:

- O has the right to use P as he wishes. If it is food, he can eat it or sell it. If it is land, he can build on it or grow crops on it.
- O has the right to regulate anyone else's use of P. If it is food, he can share it or not, as he pleases. If it is land, he can decide who may step over its boundaries.
- O has the right to transfer rights to P on whatever terms he wishes. If it is a product, he can limit the use of what he sells or loans. For example, he might stipulate that it may not be resold, or restrict not just the purchaser but all future purchasers from using the land for some purpose he does not wish. If it is land, O can keep the land while he gives or sells the right to take a short-cut across it or the right to extract natural gas or oil from it. This means that O's property may be subject to restrictions when he receives it, or later as a result of rights he grants or sells while he owns it. If there are apple trees on his property, and he sells to a local farmer all the produce from the trees, he may no longer pick off an apple whenever he is hungry. He may not be able to cut a tree down if it blocks his view or he needs the wood.

There is less general agreement on a fourth component of ownership:

- O is responsible for making sure that his use of P does not damage others. As one Supreme Court justice put it: "My freedom to move my fist must be limited by the proximity of your chin."[1] If P is a dog, O is responsible for taking reasonable precautions for making sure P does not bite anyone. There are often specific statutory requirements limiting the use of property. Zoning laws may provide that O may not operate a business on his property, if it is in a residential district. Other restrictions may mean that he cannot build a structure that will block his neighbor's access to sunlight, play his radio so loudly that it disturbs his neighbors' peace, or create a dangerous "attractive nuisance" that will entice children onto his property. Environmental laws restrict O's ability to dump chemicals in a river that crosses his property. Balancing the right of O to use P with the rights of the rest of O's community has challenged the imagination of lawyers and lawmakers from the earliest notions of property.

Ownership is therefore a combination of rights and responsibilities with respect to a specific property. In some cases those rights and responsibilities are more clearly defined than in others. Much of the complexity that arises from ownership comes from the responsibility side of ownership. There is little ambiguity in "owning" a dollar bill or a loaf of bread, for example. Neither imputes much in the way of responsibility to the owner (though O is not permitted to use the dollar to buy drugs or hire a hitman and is expected to give some of it to the Internal Revenue Service).

What does it mean to own part of something? Stockholders, for example, are deemed to "own" the company in which they invest. But a share of stock does not translate into a specified segment of the company's assets, at least not unless the company dissolves and there is something left over after the creditors get what they are owed.[2] And shareholders have limited liability, limiting their responsibility to prevent or redress the corporation's wrongs.

## EARLY CONCEPTS OF OWNERSHIP

The central tenet of the Western concept of ownership is that to the extent that individuals own property, they will have the incentive to manage that property in a manner that is compatible with the interests of society as a whole. Adam Smith wrote that even if a businessman "intends only his own gain, he is . . . led by an invisible hand to promote an end which is not his intention." Indeed, Smith believed, "by pursuing his own interest, he frequently promotes that of society more effectively than when he really intends to promote it."[3] This argument is still the foundation of government policies the world over, including recent privatization drives in such diverse countries as the United Kingdom and Chile. Former British Prime Minister Margaret Thatcher privatized state-owned UK industries for the same reason that Chilean Labor Minister Jose Pinera privatized Chile's social security system:[4] namely, that the best way for a nation to achieve prosperity is to create a society of individual property owners pursuing their own interests.

Some cultures and some political systems are not based on ownership of property by individuals. Ownership has often been criticized throughout history as the expression of inequality in a world where fair treatment should be the highest priority. Karl Marx's *Communist Manifesto* memorably declares, "The theory of Communism may be summed up in one sentence: Abolish all private property." There is a natural tension between freedom and equality. On one hand, human beings must be free to express their individuality, and in so doing their differences – their inequality. On the other hand is the view that only equality is an acceptable basis for a civilized state. The conflict between these two views produces uncertainty about the value of individual contributions. Should people own according to their ability to pay or according to their need? The extreme at one end is shown by the failure of communism in eastern Europe. The extreme at the other end is epitomized by Marie Antoinette who said that if the poor had no bread, they should eat cake.

## EARLY CONCEPTS OF THE CORPORATION

The corporation could not exist without a notion of private property. If everything is owned by the king, it does not matter whether the ownership is direct or indirect, or whether it is possible for many people to share in the ownership of one entity. But the corporation is a unique subset of the category of ownership, created for unique reasons, and having a unique character. It was created as a way of resolving some of the challenges presented by private ownership; it then created a new set of challenges of its own.

The first corporations were more like municipalities than businesses. They were towns, universities, and monastic orders founded in the Middle Ages. These were collective organizations – sometimes in corporate form – as a protection against the centralized power of autocrats and as a way to create a source of wealth and power that was free from royal domination. The key elements that made them corporations were that they existed independently of any particular membership, and all assets and holdings belonged to the corporation itself, distinguishing them from partnerships.

John J. Clancy, in his thoughtful book about the language we use to talk about business, noted that the development of double-entry bookkeeping in the late Middle Ages "first developed to check errors in accounts, became a technique to separate a man's business from his private life. The firm could then be seen as a separate entity, with an existence beyond the life of the owner/operator."[5] Sir William Blackstone, the great legal scholar, made his earliest reference to corporations in a judgment that the charter of the City of London could not be unilaterally abrogated by King Charles I.

The first joint-stock companies emerged in Britain and Holland during the early seventeenth century, in response to the rapidly emerging markets of the East Indies and West Indies. In 1602 the Dutch East India Company was granted a royal charter, with permanent capital and shares of unlimited duration. The British East India Company had received its charter from Queen Elizabeth I two years earlier. A little over a century later in response to a speculative crash in the East Indies – known as the South Sea Bubble – the British Parliament passed a law (the Bubbles Act of 1720) which forbade unchartered companies to issue stock. This meant that all commercial enterprises that wished to raise capital from stock issues had to acquire a certificate of incorporation.

Corporate organization thus meant that property could be held subject to rules that transcended royal prerogatives and power. This kind of collective establishment of an entity that could limit interference by the monarch was the basis for the modern corporation. Corporate power – although limited in time, scope, and purpose – was designed to counter the otherwise unlimited centralized authority of government.

This posed a serious threat to government. Through the ownership of corporations, individuals acquired wealth, which gave them an independent source of power. The emergence of a "private sector" threatened not only the hereditary power of princes but also the wealth of the established church. The preponderance of gross national product would no longer automatically be available for the ruler's pet projects, whether the building of great cathedrals or the launching of Crusades.

Although the independence of the corporate structure was a threat in the short term to a powerful centralized government, ultimately the corporate form became the government's ally. (If it had not, it probably would not have been allowed to continue.) The level of independence the corporate form provided made the government's authority more acceptable. Indeed, it made it more necessary: a state in which people can give those citizens needed protection in the useful enjoyment of that property – the "civil magistrates" Adam Smith said owners needed to slumber peacefully.

## A DUAL HERITAGE: INDIVIDUAL AND CORPORATE "RIGHTS"

The struggle to hold property free from the demands of the state inspired European migration to the new world of the Americas, and helped to inspire the Revolutionary War for independence there. Property rights were specifically protected by the United States Constitution and its Bill of Rights. "Property" replaced the Declaration of Independence's "Pursuit of Happiness" as an "inalienable" (impossible to lose or take away) right that was protected and enforced by the state. The Constitution promised "life, liberty, and property" to every (white male) citizen of the new nation.

Over time, at least a part of this guarantee was extended to corporations as well, despite the fact that while "property" is prominently mentioned in the Constitution, the word "corporation" does not appear. Over the last century, the US Supreme Court has repeatedly ruled that certain Constitutional protections – such as "freedom of speech" and the right to the protections of "due process" in the taking of its property – extend to corporations (creatures of law) as they do to natural persons. As noted in the opening section of this book, corporations have at least some of the same inalienable rights as people.

Owners of corporations are thus heirs to a two-fold tradition: on the one hand, they personally have rights as individuals and as owners of shares in a corporate entity. On the other hand, they receive the benefits of the rights extended to that entity. In this section of the book, we will explore this dual heritage. Alfred Conard points out that the development of this dual tradition has been far from straightforward.

"[F]or a hundred years after the Constitution was written, Congress showed little interest in exercising its commerce power. Meanwhile, throughout the nineteenth century, the states built up their idiosyncratic patterns of legislation, their separate bureaucracies for dealing with corporation documents, and their addictions to tax revenues exacted for corporation privileges."[6]

Ownership in general – and share ownership in particular – is necessary for the organization of talent, money, and other energies critical to technological and industrial progress. Allowing fractionated "ownership" through public offerings of stock enabled the access to capital that funded modern industry. The corporate structure was as important in transforming commerce as the assembly line. Both were based on the same principle, specialization. You didn't need to know how to make a chair to work in a chair factory; all you needed to know was how to put the chair leg into the chair seat. And you didn't need to know how to make a chair to invest in a chair company. All you needed to do was buy some stock.

This notion of stock ownership has been indispensable in the extraordinary rise of western Europe and the United States over the last half millennium. With the opportunity through ownership to achieve wealth and independence, western man was able to successfully motivate, discipline, and organize himself in competition with other cultures. Before we continue further with the western model for corporations in modern times, we will take a brief look at the way that the corporate ideal is being re-invented as eastern Europe tries to build it from scratch.

## THE RE-INVENTION OF THE CORPORATION: EASTERN EUROPE IN THE 1990S

Some argue that the "progress" that made bigger, more complicated organizations possible produced bigger, more complicated problems. This debate is being carried on today in eastern Europe and the component states of the former USSR. Their approach to property over the past three-quarters of a century was based on the communist ideal, which denied individuals most rights of ownership, leaving nearly all property in the hands of the state. The social, political, and economic failures of this system have presented the new leaders with an historic challenge – to examine the best and worst effects of the western model of ownership and corporation laws and to devise a new system, improving it.

## Of Vouchers and Values

I visited Finance Minister Vaclav Havel of then Czechoslovakia in February 1992 to discuss his program of privatization of the nation's economy. It was an exciting time. People spoke constantly about the details of vouchers and bids, various levels of value setting and, most important, a complete change in their way of life. They aimed to convert their economy from a system of public ownership of the factories and stores in their traditionally wealthy country to one in which individuals for the first time in over half a century would become stockholders. In the West, the corporate structure evolved over time. The Czechs were starting a capitalist system from scratch. This was a moment truly worthy of the term "revolution."

The obstacles were enormous. All the incumbent bureaucratic managers were opposed; there was no way to set the value of the enterprises; nobody knew whether a particular business was profitable or not. How could an individual afford to investigate and make the kind of informed decision that markets depend on?

They couldn't. Instead, each Czech citizen was issued for a nominal amount a voucher book containing certificates entitling the bearer to an aggregate number of "points." This entitled him to "bid" for ownership in one or more of the corporations to be privatized. Over a series of bids, values would be determined by the marketplace – supply and demand, the more "bid" the higher the value, and vice-versa.

The details were overwhelming. Ultimately, in true free-market fashion, a class of "fund managers" developed who would offer to buy the vouchers from individuals for many times their cost; the managers ultimately acquired a substantial portion of all the outstanding vouchers, giving them enormous leverage in the privatization process. All of this became clearer as events unfolded; little was known in advance. By the time of my visit, it was plain that there simply wasn't enough time or wisdom in the world to assure that the privatization process would be both "fairly" and "economically" administered.

I asked Minister Havel, "But how can you assure that the process will be fair?"

He replied, "I have had to get beyond fairness. I can only hope that nothing too unfair occurs. What I have to accomplish is to get ownership into the hands of the Czech people within these precious days that my political support remains steadfast. *Once the people*

*have become owners, nothing can stop the democratic revolution."*
Robert A.G. Monks

## THE EVOLUTION OF THE AMERICAN CORPORATION

We need to go back more than 200 years before Havel's revolution to understand the way that the corporate structure evolved. America was born with a profound mistrust of power and an even more profound commitment to making sure that power drew its legitimacy from a system of checks and balances. One initial controversy that arose in the early 1830s concerned the charter of the Bank of the United States. The Bank, as originally chartered, was a private corporation though it had the power to issue notes of exchange. The Bank was not taxed, and Congress was not allowed to charter any similar institution. In return for these favors, the government was allowed to appoint five of the Bank's 25 directors. The Bank's powers shocked democrats. Roger B. Taney, Congressman and later Chief Justice of the Supreme Court, said: "It is this power concentrated in the hands of a few individuals – exercised in secret and unseen although constantly felt – irresponsible and above the control of the people or the government ... that is sufficient to awaken any man in the country if the danger is brought distinctly to his view."[7] This was a typical view of private, unchecked power.

In the early days of the United States, corporate charters were granted by special acts of the state legislatures. Applicants for corporate charters had to negotiate with legislators to arrive at specific charter provisions, notes Harvey H. Segal, including "the purpose of the enterprise, the location of its activities, the amount of capital to be raised by stock sales, and the power of its directory."[8] The theory was that the state should separately and specifically approve each new corporation, to guard against improper activity. But, as Segal noted, instead of oversight, this process "invited bribery and corruption." So, in 1811, New York enacted a general incorporation statute (though restricting it to manufacturing enterprises), and other states followed suit. But the state was still deeply involved.

> Applications had to be approved by the state secretary, or by some other high official, who enforced firm rules such as the requirement that a minimum of capital had to be paid in before an enterprise could be launched and that delinquent shareholders would be held personally liable – up to the unpaid balances on their stock subscrip-

tions – for any corporate debts. High taxes were levied, and there were also severe constraints on the kinds of securities – common stocks, preferred stocks, and bonds – that a corporation could issue.[9]

After the Civil War, companies began to form "trusts." It was clear that if competitors in the same line of business worked together instead of separately, they could control prices. This was not illegal or even disapproved of at the time. Indeed, the directors of these new entities were called "trustees," a term that still lives on in the nonprofit, banking, and securities sectors. Segal points out that, "In wielding such broad discretionary power, the trustees established important precedents for the control of corporations by professional managers rather than dominant shareholders."[10] The first antitrust laws ended the trusts, but the professional managers were there to stay.

## Case in Point: Standard Oil and the Arrival of Big Business

In the 1870s and 1880s, several companies achieved spectacular size, not by internal growth, but by merger. Perhaps the most famous example is the Standard Oil Company. Initially, Standard Oil was less a company than a cartel – a group of smaller, separate companies under the guidance of the largest refiner of them all, John D. Rockefeller's Standard Oil Company of Ohio.

Rockefeller initially created a trade association of refiners, and became its first president. Ultimately, this association became a massive, vertically integrated, centralized corporation. By 1880, the Standard Oil "group" or "alliance" numbered 40 separate companies. In 1882, the shareholders of these companies exchanged their stock for certificates in the Standard Oil Trust. The trust authorized an office of nine trustees to "exercise general supervision over the affairs of the several Standard Oil companies." Moreover, the trust chartered local subsidiaries to take over Standard's operations in each state. This allowed Standard to avoid taxes owed by "out of state" corporations. The effect of the coordination was to allow Standard Oil to tighten its already vice-like grip on the mushrooming oil industry. By the early 1890s, Standard Oil was extracting 25 percent of the nation's crude.

Though Standard Oil was broken up by a Supreme Court order in 1891, other conglomerates avoided the antitrust axe. The United States Steel Corporation, for example, created by Andrew Carnegie in 1901, created close to 60 percent of the industry's output.[11]

The next stage in the evolution of the corporate structure was widespread (and therefore diffuse) ownership. Look at the description of the first public offering of Ford Motor Company stock in David Halberstam's book, *The Reckoning*:

> It made ordinary citizens believe that buying stock – owning part of a giant company – was a real possibility in their lives. By purchasing stock, they became participants in American capitalism, owners as well as workers, junior partners of Henry Ford II. . . . The news generated excitement rarely seen on Wall Street. Everyone wanted in on the issue. . . . Early in the negotiations the principals had agreed that $50 per share would be satisfactory. But the fever kept building. The actual price turned out to be $64.50. Some ten million shares were sold, and it took 722 underwriters to handle them. At a time when $100 million was considered a handsome result from a public offering, this one brought $640 million – the sheer scale of it was staggering. The fever continued, greatly inflating the stock, but though it briefly surged up near $70 it soon hit a plateau near $50. The Ford family had been joined by some 300,000 new co-owners of their company. It was, said Keith Funston of the New York Stock Exchange, "a landmark in the history of public ownership." It was a landmark in tax avoidance, too; estimates were that Eleanor Clay Ford and her four children saved some $300 million in taxes while keeping control of the company.
>
> It also marked the beginning of a historic shift in American capitalism, a major increase in the influence of Wall Street in companies like Ford. The Street was a partner of the family now, and the family had to respond to its norms. In the old days, the Street did not demand too much of the companies whose stock it sold. But the stock market was changing now. Before the war only a small number of Americans held stocks, and they were to a large degree of the same class as the owners of the old-line companies. The market was a kind of gentlemen's club, virtually off-limits to the rest of the society. People owned stocks because their families had *always* owned stocks. They invested not so much to gain but to protect. . . . Those who were in the market were generally rich and were in for the long haul.[12]

This was the high-water mark of the old system. Ford became one of the last of the blue chips, just as blue chip stocks were becoming irrelevant. Instead of a few clubby long-term investors, the postwar era created a world where the New York Stock Exchange vowed to make every American a stockholder and where stockholders could make a lot of money fast by betting on the best of a large group of entrepreneurs. Both sides were hungry and impatient: those raising capital and those who provided it. "No one talked about safe buys; there was too much action for that. Companies like Xerox and Polaroid replaced US Steel and Ford as smart buys, and they in turn were replaced by fried chicken companies and nursing home syndicates."[13]

Mutual funds allowed investors to limit the downside and take advantage of the upside. Gerry Tsai's $250,000 fund at Fidelity reached $200 million three years later. Wall Street was no longer the exclusive enclave of young men from a tiny group of "good families;" it was open to anyone (well, any white males). "Also significant for anyone involved in business – whether the investors, the managers of the companies, or the bright young men coming out of business schools – was the effect of the talent flow. One could make far more money by playing the market on Wall Street – where cleverness was rewarded immediately – than by joining a company and getting in line to do something as mundane as producing something. The effect of this drain on ability away from the companies themselves was incalculable."[14]

One result was that companies started thinking that their product was not the product – it was the stock. Halberstam notes that at Ford, "Not only were the top people there mainly from finance, but the bias of the (stock) market invisibly but critically bore on the company's decisions. There was a great deal of talk about the effect of production decisions on the stock."[15]

Meanwhile, a different sort of "trust" was forming in one of the states, as, for corporate charters, tiny Delaware, the second-smallest state won the "race to the bottom," and became "home" to most of America's corporations, at least on paper. In 100 years, America had gone from a country where each corporate charter had to be approved by the state legislature to a country where storefronts along the streets of Delaware's capital city are covered with signs that say "Incorporate While You Wait." Woodrow Wilson, as governor of New Jersey, persuaded the state legislature to pass the nation's first antitrust laws. Once he left to become President, they were repealed.

Legal authority over corporations has always been left to the states. The federal government has very little authority over corporate governance. The theory was that the states would be "laboratories," learning from each other's successes and failures and trying to outdo each other. In reality, all of that did occur; the problem was that instead of trying to outdo each other to do what was best for the economy or the shareholders or even the community, they outdid each other in trying to attract corporations (and their tax revenues).

## THE ESSENTIAL ELEMENTS
## OF THE CORPORATE STRUCTURE

The law gives corporate managers a great deal of flexibility in determining their capital and governance structure, relying on the market for capital to create competition that will allow shareholders to "choose" the one they think is best. In our view, this power of "choice" is hardly worthy of the term, because it all but disappears the moment it is exercised. Shareholders can "choose" which companies to invest in, and companies court them on that basis. Once shareholders have invested, however, their power to influence the company is all but vestigial, as discussed throughout this chapter.

Individual ownership evolved over time into a variety of models of collective enterprise. In Darwinian terms, the corporate model has prevailed as the legal structure of choice in modern commerce because it was the "fittest." As Dean Clark's description in chapter 1 noted, corporations combine many attractive features: among them, the ability to acquire management and financial resources efficiently, the capacity to transfer holdings easily, and the ability to assert control over an underperforming venture.

Among the special attractions of the corporate form or organization are:

- A high degree of advance certitude about the ground rules of the organization. There simply isn't a lot of law on most of the other forms of doing business. In the case of entities like business trusts, the applicable law is common law, harder to determine, understand, and predict than statute.
- The financial markets have been developed to easily accommodate the mechanics of share issuance and transfer. Partnerships are more cumbersome.
- Those who put up the money can decide on the management and changes in extreme cases. In a partnership, those who put up the money cannot change the general partner.

But, as we explained earlier, perhaps the most attractive component of the corporate model is limited liability – the owner's liability is limited to the amount of his investment (or subscription).

This "limited liability" means that ventures can take very large risks and incur substantial liabilities without threatening the personal resources of their owners. Without this protection, the wealthy would be reluctant to risk their resources in risky ventures. This ability for "investors" (in contrast to active participants) to diversify their risks of investing in any single venture by investing in many is undoubtedly one of the principal reasons that capital has been available for research, innovation, and technical progress during the last two centuries.

Just because the owners have limited liability doesn't mean that the risk inherent in their investments disappears or that someone else automatically pays the liabilities. The impact of business failures hits many individuals, the community, and the government. This capacity of corporations to "externalize" the costs of their actions is a continuing problem, as explained in chapter 1.

## Case in Point: Partnership v. Corporation

Let's consider an example of two failed business enterprises, one a solely owned proprietorship (an individual) and one a corporation, both owners and operators of a modern paper mill which becomes bankrupt. Suppose that the working of the mills involved discharges of both liquid and gaseous emissions that violated environmental standards and caused great damage and financial loss to members of the community. The investigators who are responsible for enforcement of the environmental laws institute legal proceedings. So do members of the community who were damaged.

The individual owner of the mill has no alternative – he must pay the damages up to the point of personal bankruptcy. The corporation's liability is limited to the extent of its assets. If, for example, it is leasing the plant and literally "owns" no assets, then it does not have to pay damages. The benefit of this system is that the shareholders of the corporation are protected against liability. That is, they lose what they invested, but are not liable beyond that investment. On the other hand, the individual who owns the failing paper company loses almost all of his personal assets. In both cases, the community, the employees and the customers, suppliers, and other corporate stakeholders are all damaged, but in just one do they have a chance of some recourse. The corporate form of ownership does not change the cost; it just changes the extent of the owner's responsibility.

As explained in chapter 1, the corporate form limits liability, but it does not limit risk, which extends to many "corporate externalities." Nonetheless, the virtue of limited liability, combined with the benefits of investment diversification and the progress of technological innovations, have made it possible for corporations to grow to huge dimensions. Modern corporations are virtually unlimited in the scope of their enterprise, the size of their capital, the national reach of their operations, and even the span of their existence. It is not surprising, then, that they have acquired the capacity to influence the circumstances of the societies within which they operate. They have more money than individuals for financing elections (a problem of unignorable proportions in Japan, the United States, and most European countries); they have more resources to expend in influencing legislation and the administration of laws; they can hire the best lawyers, lobbyists, and media consultants. All of these costs are simply passed on to the customer – and the shareholder.

Because of this ability to influence the making, interpretation, and enforcement of laws, corporations in our time are able to "externalize" many of the consequences of their operations. In our paper company example, we assume that both the company owned by an individual and the one organized as a corporation face the same marketplace and the same obligations. But the corporation has another important advantage – it is able to participate more effectively than the individual in the process that sets the legal standards regulating permissible emission levels. It is better able to organize itself and the community to fight suits by those alleging that they have been damaged by its discharge of effluents. So ownership in a large modern corporation has come to be a one-way street – the shareholders and the managers appropriate the profits and, to the extent possible, force the costs on to society as a whole.

## THE SEPARATION OF OWNERSHIP AND CONTROL, PART 1: BERLE AND MEANS

The rights of ownership outlined at the beginning of this chapter are fairly simple when applied to a house, a car, or a herd of cattle. But the "owner" of a fractional share of a corporation has an intangible interest in an intangible entity. While the entity itself may have many tangible assets, the relation of those assets to the "owners" is questionable.

Only one of the ownership rights listed in the beginning of this chapter is unequivocally exercised by the stockholder – the right to transfer the interest. That is fairly simple; indeed, that has been the overwhelming priority in the development of the security markets. A share of stock is, above all, highly transferable, and our system puts a premium (in the most literal terms) on making sure that anyone who wants to sell (or buy) a share of stock can do so, immediately. Note, however, that during the takeover era even this paramount right was limited by corporate management and state government. Companies adopted "poison pills" and other antitakeover devices that limited the ability of the shareholders to sell to a willing buyer at a mutually agreed-upon price. And in other cases, like the Time-Warner deal, corporate management was able to prevent the shareholders from making the choice about which company was a better candidate for a business combination.

In this context, what does it mean to talk about the other two ownership rights at the beginning of this chapter? The first was the right to use the property. One does not really "use" a share of stock, beyond cashing the dividend checks or possibly using the stock to secure a loan or giving some or all of it as a gift. The shareholder does not "use" his intangible fraction of the company – even if his proportionate share of the company's assets were worth, for example, the equivalent of one desk and telephone, he cannot take it, sell it, or even use it, much less tell anyone at the company how to use it.

The shareholder-owner does not participate in the activities by which his "property" is managed. He has no relationship with the other owners; their community of interest is limited to the price of the stock.

The shareholder has the exclusive control of the stock itself. But as a condition of the shareholder's limited liability, the shareholder gives up the right to control use of the corporation's property by others. That right is delegated to the management of the corporation. Indeed, it is one of the benefits of the corporate organization to the investor; he can entrust his money to people who have expertise and time that he does not. But it is also one of the drawbacks. Thus, it is this separation between ownership and control that has been the focus of the struggles over corporate governance.

What the owner of a corporation "owns" is a certificate representing entitlement to a proportional share of the corporation. The only thing he has is the stock certificate; the corporation itself (or maybe its subsidiary) is the owner of its own property. But the certificate entitles him to particular rights and obligations, some set by federal law, some set by the state in which the corporation is incorporated. The rights of a shareholder are classically defined as (1) the right to sell the stock, (2) the right to vote the proxy, (3) the right to bring suit for damages if the corporation's directors or managers fail to meet their obligations, (4) the right to certain information from the company, and (5) certain residual rights following the company's liquidation (or its filing for reorganization under bankruptcy laws), once creditors and other claimants are paid off.[16]

Corporations today are larger and more far-reaching than anyone could have dreamed, even a century ago. In those days, industrialists such as John D. Rockefeller and Cornelius Vanderbilt and Andrew Mellon and Andrew Carnegie ruled empires that rivaled whole countries in their size and scope – and power. The companies had public shareholders, but the men who built them held huge stakes to back their stewardship. Today, with rare exceptions like Bill Gates of Microsoft and the late Sam Walton of Wal-Mart, large companies are led by men whose stakes in the company are dwarfed by the holdings of institutional investors. The shareholders who "own" the company are so diverse and so widely dispersed that it is difficult to characterize their relationship to the venture in the terms of a traditional owner.

Most people begin the study of ownership in the context of public corporations with Columbia University professors Adolph A. Berle and Gardiner C. Means, who first recognized the separation of ownership and control in the large modern corporation.

This dissolution of the atom of property destroys the very foundation on which the economic order of the past three centuries has rested. Private enterprise, which has molded economic life since the close of the middle ages, has been rooted in the institution of private property. Under the feudal system, its predecessor, economic organization, grew out of mutual obligations and privileges derived by various individuals from their relation to property which no one of them owned. Private enterprise, on the other hand, has assumed an owner of the instruments of production with complete property rights over those instruments. Whereas the organization of feudal economic life rested upon an elaborate system of binding customs, the organization under the system of private enterprise has rested upon the self-interest of the property owner – a self-interest held in check only by competition and the conditions of supply and demand. Such self-interest has long been regarded as the best guarantee of economic efficiency. It has been assumed that, if the individual is protected in the right both to use his own property as he sees fit and to receive the full fruits of its use, his desire for personal gain, for profits, can be relied upon as effective incentive to his efficient use of any industrial property he may possess.[17]

We must remember that it is not as though anyone ever made a decision that companies would work better if they separated ownership and control. There was no conscious choice in favor of treating shares of stock as though they were betting slips for races that were over at the end of each day. The wedge driven between ownership and control of American corporations was the unintended consequence of what was then thought of as progress, of the technological and procedural changes made in order to meet the needs of a rapidly expanding economy. In order to make that economy work, and in order to keep it expanding, the market placed a premium on liquidity. It was not until decades later that they began to understand that a system built around liquidity was inevitably going to be as short-sighted as a cat chasing its own tail.

## Case in Point: The Conflicted Owner

A pension fund spread its assets among six to ten different money managers at any given time, in an effort to protect itself through diversification. Each had its own formula and assumptions. On any given day, half were buying United Widget stock, and the other half were selling it to them. At the end of most days, the pension fund had the same number of shares of United Widget, but was out the transaction costs. Once a year, the three to five money managers who held the stock on behalf of the pension fund on the record date received proxies. In the year when United Widget was the target of a hostile takeover attempt by International Products, some of them voted with management and some voted with the acquirer.

Every "improvement" in the system for owning stock was designed to make it easier to trade. No one seemed to notice or care that each of these "improvements" also made it harder to exercise classic ownership rights. These rights had once been thought of as equal to the right to buy and sell freely in the "invisible hand" that kept the marketplace operating efficiently.

Shareholders' ability to perform what James Willard Hurst has called "their legendary function" of monitoring has been substantially eroded. There are two primary reasons for this. First, as noted by Berle and Means, sheer numbers rob shareholders of power. Management has every incentive to increase the number of holders.[18] It increases available capital and helps transferability by keeping the prices of individual shares comparatively low.[19]

Second, increasing the number of shares has another significant advantage for corporate management; it reduces the incentive and ability of each shareholder to gather information and monitor effectively. Even the $250 million investment in General Motors by the largest equity investor in the United States, the California Public Employees' Retirement System, is not of much significance in a company with a market value of more than $30 billion. When the number of shareholders is in the hundreds of thousands – even the millions – and each of those holds stock in a number of companies, no single shareholder can monitor effectively. How much monitoring is worth the effort when your investment (and liability) is limited and when even if you did understand the issues, there was nothing you could do about them?

Professor Melvin Aron Eisenberg writes of the "limits of share-holder consent,"[20] noting that "under current law and practice, shareholder consent to rules proposed by top managers in publicly held corporations may be either nominal, tainted by a conflict of interest, coerced, or impoverished."[21] In Eisenberg's view, share-holder consent is "nominal" when (as permitted under proxy rules) the shareholder does not vote at all and management votes on his behalf, or shares held by the broker or broker's depository are voted with no direction from the beneficial owner. Shareholder consent is "tainted" by a conflict of interest when an institutional investor votes in favor of a management proposal it would otherwise oppose, due to commercial ties to the company management.

Shareholder consent is "coerced" when, for example, management ties an action that is attractive to shareholders, like a special dividend, to passage of a provision that may be contrary to their interests. For instance, in 1989, shareholders of Ramada Inc. were asked to approve a package of antitakeover measures, bundled with a generous cash payment.[22] And shareholder consent is "impoverished" when "for example, shareholders may vote for a rule proposed by management even though they would prefer a different rule, because the proposed rule is better than the rule it replaces and management's control over the agenda effectively limits the shareholders' choice to the existing rule or the proposed rule."[23] This is a reflection of management's vastly superior access to the proxy, both procedurally (in terms of resources) and substantively (in terms of appropriate subject matter). Eisenberg has described shareholders as "disenfranchised."

The disenfranchisement of the modern shareholder has been developing for over a century, but it took the events of the last decade to bring it to public attention. In the 1980s, the takeover era itself was a symptom of the problems created by the failure to link ownership and control. As we describe below in more detail, the abuses of shareholders by both managers and raiders made it clear that there was not enough accountability to shareholders, and that this lack of accountability was detrimental to the competitiveness and vitality of American companies. But, as noted above, the fact that the disconnect was inadvertent was irrelevant to one important fact – it was convenient, even ideal, for those whom it most benefited. When efforts to reconnect ownership and control began in the mid-1980s, shareholders found that the very problem of their inability to act made it all but impossible to regain their ability to hold corporate management accountable, especially when corporate management had no interest in changing a system which was working very well from their perspective.

As a result, Harvard Professor Michael Jensen predicted in *The End of the Public Corporation* that the "ownerless" modern venture without the discipline of accountability would inevitably be unable to compete. He saw that the leveraged buyouts that had reconnected management and ownership at the end of the 1980s as the model for the future.

## FRACTIONATED OWNERSHIP

In addition to the separation of ownership and control, there are several other respects in which share ownership in the modern corporation differs from traditional notions of ownership.

- *Numerical:* There are so many owners of the largest American corporations that it makes little sense to consider any one of them an "owner" in the sense of an individual with an economic interest in being informed about and involved in corporate affairs.
- *Legal:* The splitting of ownership between a legal title holder (the trustee) and beneficial owners (trust beneficiaries of all kinds, including pensioners and mutual fund participants) has created a welter of separate interests. The relationships between fiduciary and beneficiary are usually stipulated by a specific governing

law. Trustees can be individuals or special purpose corporations; beneficiaries can be individuals or classes of individuals, whose identities may not be known for many years.

- *Functional:* "It has often been said that the owner of a horse is responsible. If the horse lives he must feed it. If the horse dies he must bury it. No such responsibility attaches to a share of stock."[24]

A corporate shareholder owns a share certificate, but this piece of paper does not accord him the rights and responsibilities traditionally associated with ownership. Berle and Means observe that, "Most important of all, the position of ownership has changed from that of an active to that of a passive agent. In place of actual physical properties over which the owner could exercise direction and for which he was responsible, the owner now holds a piece of paper representing a set of rights and expectation with respect to an enterprise. But over the enterprise and over the physical property – the instruments of production – in which he has an interest, the owner has little control. At the same time he bears no responsibility with respect to the enterprise or its physical property.[25]

- *Personal:* "The spiritual values that formerly went with ownership have been separated from it. Physical property capable of being shaped by its owner could bring to him direct satisfaction apart from the income it yielded in more concrete form. It represented an extension of his own personality."[26]

## Case in Point: Junior Invests in Boothbay Harbor

The traditional relationship between entitlement to receive the benefits from a venture and responsibility for its impact on society was charmingly put at the beginning of the century, as a father advises his son in *Main Street and Wall Street,* written in 1926:

Now, Junior, before you go to college I want to give you my investment in the Boothbay Harbor Electric Light Co. This concern serves our old neighbors and friends, and I want you to feel a continuing interest in, and a responsibility for, our share in this local enterprise. If properly managed it should be a benefit to this community; and it will yield you an income to be applied to your education through the next few years. But you must never forget that you are partly responsible for this undertaking. Our family had a hand in starting it. That responsibility is an inseparable part of your ownership. I read something the other day, in an opinion by Justice Brandeis of the US Supreme Court, which bears this out: "There is no such thing to my mind . . . as an innocent stockholder. He may be innocent in fact, but socially he cannot be held innocent. He accepts the benefits of the system. It is his business and his obligation to see that those who represent him carry out a policy which is consistent with the public welfare." He is right in that. This accountability for wealth underlies and justifies the whole institution of private property upon which the government of our great country is founded.[27]

Contrast Junior and his father with today's shareholder, who will be represented by Junior's son Trip, now an employee of Widget Co., a midsized manufacturing company with a "defined benefit" pension plan. That means that no matter what he puts in before he retires, once he does, he is guaranteed a set retirement check every month. Let's say that Trip has been with the company for 20 years, with about another 15 to go before retirement, keeping in mind that his office mates, one who just started work and one who is five years from retirement, might have very different sets of priorities. Trip and his colleagues are a far cry from Junior, who had a "sense of responsibility" for the companies he invests in; indeed, Trip could not tell you what stocks he holds, bought by several investment managers who are hired by the named fiduciary designated by the corporate chairman. Trip "owns" a minuscule fraction of perhaps thousands of publicly traded companies. He has not only no say about which securities are purchased on his behalf; he doesn't even find out until after the fact, sometimes not even then. Between Junior and Boothbay there was a reliable system of communication. Between Trip and Boothbay there is an investment manager, a custodian, a trustee, a named fiduciary, and the CEO of Trip's employer, Widget Co.

Meanwhile, Trip and the other employees whose pension money is invested really have no legally enforceable interest with respect to a particular holding of the plan. Their only right is to be paid the promised benefits. Whether that comes from stocks, bonds, or gold bullion is irrelevant to him. Trip's only right is to require that the trustee act loyally and competently in his interest.

That could be complicated. The trustee, usually a bank, may have business relationships that create uncomfortable conflicts, putting him in a situation quite different from Junior's. For example, the trustee will be voting stock in the same companies it makes loans to or handles payrolls for. There have been a number of reports of cases where a trustee attempting to vote against corporate management was stopped by his own management.[28] Why fight it?

After all, the shareholder has no economic interest whatsoever in the quality of his voting decision, beyond avoiding liability. No enforcement action has ever been brought and no damages have ever been awarded for breach of duty in voting proxies. Trustees earn no incentive compensation, no matter how much energy and skill they devote to ownership responsibilities.[29] And, crucially, the corporation knows how he votes, while Trip has no idea. The trustee has nothing to lose, and everything to gain, from routine votes with management. Even if the trustee wanted to view his ownership responsibility more energetically, it would be all but impossible as a practical matter due to further inhibitions to shareholder activism arising out of the problems of "collective action" and "free riding," the pervasive problem of conflict of interest by institutional trustees, the legal obstacles imposed by the federal "proxy rules" and state law and state court acquiescence to management entrenchment – all described later in substantial detail.

Meanwhile, at the top of the chain, the CEO's interest in the investment in Boothbay is also quite different from Trip's or Junior's. His interest is, first and foremost, being able to pay Trip his "defined benefit" when he retires, with a minimum of contribution by Widget Co. and, probably, a minimum involvement of his own time – after all, pension benefits don't have much to do with the products or sales of the company. So the CEO will push the investment managers to provide results (while he decries the "short-term perspective" of investors with other CEOs). If he is involved, he is faced with what has been called "ERISA's Fundamental Contradiction."[30] On one hand, as a corporate manager, he would tend to favor provisions that, on the other hand, as a shareholder or director, he might find unduly protective of management.

In the 1920s, Trip's father, Junior, and his grandfather, who spoke of Boothbay Harbor with such proprietary interest, felt a real connection to the company they invested in. In the 1990s, the trustee, the custodian, the investment managers, and the CEO stand between Boothbay and Trip.

There is a fair measure of agreement that ownership is necessary, but it has been little consensus on how to make it meaningful or indeed how to pinpoint it.

## THE SEPARATION OF OWNERSHIP AND CONTROL, PART 2: THE TAKEOVER ERA

As explained above, one of the essential rights of ownership is the right to transfer ownership to someone else. Indeed, in making transferability a priority, owners of common stock were willing, for most of this century, to relinquish some of the other rights of ownership. In order for the stock to be freely transferable, shareholders had to have limited liability and shares had to trade at a fairly low rate. Both conditions loosened the connection between ownership and control. In order to have limited liability, shareholders had to give up control over any but the most basic corporate decisions. In order to keep trading prices low enough to ensure liquidity, shareholders had to allow their companies to issue millions of shares of stock, making it almost impossible for any one investor to hold a meaningful stake. The result was the "Wall Street Rule." Recognizing that transferability was the only real right the shareholder had, this rule provided that investors should "vote with management or sell the shares." The theory was that shareholders could send a powerful message to a company's management by selling out, ideally in enough of a block to depress the share value. Ultimately, the theory continues, the stock price would fall enough to make the company an attractive takeover target. This risk would then keep management acting in the interest of shareholders.[31] As Edward Jay Epstein points out,

> [T]his economic theory requires more than a shareholder being free to sell his holdings to another investor. Merely selling shares is analogous to political refugees leaving a dictatorship by "voting with their feet." While it may solve their personal problem, it does not end, or necessarily even weaken, the dictatorship – though it might weaken the economy. Similarly, just the exchange of one powerless shareholder for another in a corporation, while it may lessen the market price of shares, will not dislodge management – or even threaten it. On the contrary, if dissident shareholders leave, it may even bring about further entrenchment of management – especially if management can pass new bylaws in the interim.
> This theory works if, and only if, shareholders can sell their shares eventually to an investor who has the power to take over the company – and fire the ruling board of directors.[32]

In the 1980s, the seismic impact of takeovers, junk bonds, and the growth of institutional investors jolted every aspect of the corporate structure, down to its tectonic plates. Perhaps the most unexpected shift was the way the musty, academic question of "corporate governance" became the focus of intense debate. Once exclusively the province of scholars and theorists, the arcane vocabulary of governance was reforged as each of the corporation's component groups blew cobwebs off the antique terminology and employed it to redefine its role and that of the corporation.

But one reason the debate had become so tangential to the reality of politics and business was that most of the theories about corporate governance bore little relation to the reality. Indeed, the theories assumed the status, and the role, of myth. And myth has both advantages and disadvantages as the basis for debate. The theory was that corporations were managed by officers, under a system of checks and balances provided by the board of directors and the shareholders. All three groups, acting in their self-interest, would maximize profit within the confines of the legal system, and all three groups would benefit, as would society as a whole, including the groups now termed "stakeholders" – employees, customers, suppliers, and the community. The reality was that there was no system of checks. Corporate governance had become completely out of balance.

That lack of balance was revealed by the collision of two developments of the 1980s, both the collateral and unanticipated results of another set of priorities. The first was the rise of the institutional investor. Even those who worked hardest for the passage of the Employee Retirement Income Security Act (ERISA) of 1974 never anticipated that in less than 20 years the funds subject to its standards would hold a third of the stock of American companies. Institutional holdings mushroomed in the 1970s and 1980s, creating a category of investor that was big, smart, and obligated as a fiduciary to exercise shareholder ownership rights if it was "prudent" and "for the exclusive purpose" of protecting the interests of pension plan participants to do so.

Meanwhile, the takeover era was giving shareholders plenty to react to. Both raiders and management took advantage of shareholder disenfranchisement and there were extraordinary abuses, which we will discuss below. All of a sudden proxy cards asked for more than approval of the auditors and the management slate of directors. The value of ownership rights became clear just as for the first time there emerged a group of owners sophisticated enough to understand them, obligated enough as fiduciaries to exercise them, and big enough so that when they did exercise them, they made a real difference. But it took them a while to do so, and during that time corporate boards and managers were able to diminish further the value of share ownership. We will come back to this issue when we discuss the role of the board as fiduciary in the next chapter, but will discuss its impact on ownership here.

As mentioned above, most of the technology and systems developed for the stock market were designed with liquidity and transferability as the primary goal. Transferability has been so important, in fact, that the market has willingly, if inadvertently, relinquished many of the other rights of ownership, in order to preserve it. In early days, stock certificates were like checks or like other kinds of property; you transferred stock by giving someone the actual certificate. As recently as the early 1950s, at least five documents were necessary for each transfer of stock, all pinned together with great ceremony by a man who worked behind a cage in the front of the office. This system worked, briefly. In the summer of 1950, for example, the market never traded over 750,000 shares in a day.

The system, however, was inadequate for the volume that would come. It was cumbersome, and too invasive of shareholder privacy. In the late 1980s, as policy makers debated "circuit breakers" to slow down or even stop trading (as a way of preventing a stock market crash like the 500-point drop in October of 1987), the New York Stock Exchange was trading upwards of 290 million shares a day.

Universal transferability also critically changed the nature of the shareholders' relationship to the corporate structure. As an investor, the stockholder had to look to corporate performance for protection and enhancement of his investment; he had to consider the efficacy of capital investments, and he was directly influenced by how the corporation conducted itself and how society perceived that conduct. In the absence of readily available "exit," or sale, the traditional shareholder used "voice," or ownership rights.[33] "[T]he corporation with transferable shares converted the underlying long-term risk of a very large amount of capital into a short-term risk of small amounts of capital. Because marketable corporate shares were readily salable at prices quoted daily (or more often), their owners were not tied to the enterprise for the life of its capital equipment, but could pocket their gains or cut their losses whenever they judged it advisable. *Marketable shares converted the proprietor's long-term risk to the investor's short-term risk . . .*"[34] The increased number of shares and ease of transferability acted as a vicious circle because the inability to use "voice" to influence corporate activity made "exit" the only option.

It is virtually impossible to argue that effective monitoring is cost-effective for investors whose profit is principally derived from buying and selling in the short term. The prospect of buying low and selling high is so beguiling that a lucrative industry of "active money management" has flourished, notwithstanding the reality that institutional investors are the market and, therefore, cannot hope to beat its performance. As Charles D. Ellis, onetime President of the Institute of Chartered Financial Analysts, noted: "Investment management, as traditionally practiced, is based on a single basic belief: Professional investment managers *can* beat the market. That premise appears to be false, particularly for the very large institutions that manage most of the assets of most trusts, pension funds, and endowments, because their institutions have effectively become the market."[35]

William Fouse, chairman of Mellon Capital Management, says that pension fund management is "like monkeys trading bananas in trees." As he observed in an interview with *Forbes* writer Dyan Machan, "The money managers end up with a lot of the bananas."[36] The efforts by pension fund fiduciaries to find active money managers who can beat the market over time have been unsuccessful. Most pension funds give their money to whichever manager did well the previous year, and given the statistical "regression to the mean," the odds are that manager will not do as well in the future.

An alternative strategy is "indexing," in which a fund buys every stock in a given index, such as the S&P 500. The holdings are held, not traded, so the fund neither beats the market nor underperforms it – but replicates it. A *Forbes* headline summed up the simplicity of such a strategy: "Don't Just Do Something, Sit There."[37]

Decisions are often based on recommendations by consultants. But consultants rarely recommend indexing. "[I]t would put them out of business if everyone did it. Pension funds pay consultants for objective advice on which funds to hire, but the same consultants charge managers fees for measuring the managers' performance. . . . There are plenty of stories about managers who are recommended by the consultants on the grounds that the managers pay the consultants the biggest fees."[38]

A rare contrarian exception is the General Mills pension fund, which has dared to "break entirely out of the cycle. . . . Instead of firing the stock picker who happens to be performing below the mean in a given year, General Mills gives him more money, taking from highest-ranked performer." As a result, General Mills has produced one of the best long-term records with 17 percent annualized equity return over the 15 years ending in 1992.[39] It is therefore not surprising that a study of 135 funds with $700 billion in assets concluded that "There was no positive correlation between performance and money spent on staff, managers, and other high-priced advice to get it."[40]

Of course every investor, whether individual or institutional, hopes that it can be the exception and can beat the averages. This is reminiscent of the line about the poker game, "If we all play well, we can all make money." This hope, rather than any statistical evidence, accounts in part for the change in the way shareholders see themselves today: no longer as an owner but as a speculator.

Of course another of the incentives for a minimal sense of ownership by money managers is short-term self-interest. Active trading produces immediate transaction costs. Monitoring involves the commitment of resources for gains that are not immediately quantifiable, with the possible exception of shareholders who are large enough and aggressive enough to underwrite contests for control. In the longer term, this has involved a high price for the business system as whole.

Transferability has had consequences for corporations as well. It means that the interests of shareholder and managers are based on incompatible premises. The investor will want to sell at the first sign that the stock may have reached its trading peak, whereas the manager wants stable, long-term investors. The American corporate system was initially based on the permanence of investor capital. But while the capital may have remained in place, the owners kept changing. Unintentionally, the growth of the institutional investors may have served to reintroduce stability in stock ownership. But that could not happen until the institutional investors were shocked into activism by the abuses of the takeover era.

An essential part of the theoretical underpinning for the market was the notion that shareholders should sell to each other, and as often as possible to keep the markets "efficient." During the takeover era, it became clear that, though the system was designed to promote transferability above all, there was one kind of transfer that the system would not tolerate: the transfer of power from one group to another. Despite a strong theoretical commitment to "the market for corporate control," as soon as the means to create a genuine market were developed, corporations, lawyers, and legislators, even judges, worked quickly to obliterate it.

One unjustifiable practice was called a "two-tier tender offer." A two-tier offer was used to accomplish what was then the largest non-oil takeover in history, R.J. Reynolds' $4.5 billion acquisition of Nabisco in 1985. In such a deal, a buyer would offer, for example, $10 per share over the market price to everyone who tendered – until 51 percent had been received. The last 49 percent to line up would be left, like Oliver Twist, asking for more. What they would get would be thinner than Oliver's gruel – such as notes for the tender not payable for 15 years. For reasons that will become clear later in this chapter, institutional investors were invariably at the front of the line in such offers – as fiduciaries, they couldn't refuse an offer of $10 now rather than $10 in 15 years.

## A FRAMEWORK FOR PARTICIPATION

The regulatory framework governing the issuance and trading of public securities and the functioning of exchanges was almost entirely set up by two landmark statutes of the New Deal era. Congress passed the 1933 Securities Act and 1934 Securities and Exchange Act after exhaustive debate and in response to over-whelming evidence of mismanagement, deception and outright fraud during the stock market boom of the late 1920s. In the Public Utility Holding Company Act of 1935 and the Investment Company Act of 1940, multiple classes of common stock with differing voting characteristics were flatly prohibited for the affected companies. Rather than attempt with industrial compa-nies to remedy specific mistakes or abuses, lawmakers attempted a far more difficult task; they tried to set up a process of corporate accountability – an impartial set of rules preserving the widest possible latitude for shareholders to protect their financial inter-ests. In searching for a reliable and familiar model, they turned to America's own traditions of political accountability.

Shareholders were seen as voters, boards of directors as elected representatives, proxy solicitations as election campaigns, corpo-rate charters and by-laws as constitutions and amendments. Just as political democracy acted to guarantee the legitimacy of govern-mental or public power, the theory went, so corporate democracy would control – and therefore legitimate – the otherwise uncontrol-lable growth of power in the hands of private individuals. Under-pinning that corporate democracy, as universal franchise underpinned its political counterpart, was the principle of one share, one vote.

## OWNERSHIP AND RESPONSIBILITY:
## NO INNOCENT SHAREHOLDER

What is the accountability of the shareholders themselves? Supreme Court Justice Louis D. Brandeis, who had a distinguished legal career defending both individual and public rights in large corporations, wrote passionately about the moral aspects of ownership of shares. His comments on page 89 quoted in part in the Boothbay Harbor case, are a poignant reminder of how far modern stock ownership has strayed from its origins. They are as true today as when written almost a century ago.

To my mind there is no such thing as an innocent purchaser of stocks. It is entirely contrary, not only to our laws but to what ought to be our whole attitude toward investments, that the person who has a chance of profit by going into an enterprise, or the chance of getting a larger return than he could get on a perfectly safe mortgage or bond – that he should have the chance of gain without any responsibility. The idea of such persons being innocent in the sense of not letting them take the consequences of their acts is, to my mind, highly immoral and is bound to work out, if pursued, in very evil results to the community. When a person buys stock in any of those organizations of doubtful validity and of doubtful practices, he is not innocent; he is guilty constructively by law and should be deemed so by the community and held up to a responsibility; precisely to the same responsibility that the English owners of Irish estates have been held up, although it was their bailiffs who were guilty of nearly every oppression that attended the absentee landlordism of Ireland.

He may be innocent in fact, but socially he cannot be held innocent. He accepts the benefits of a system. It is his business and his obligation to see that those who represent him carry out a policy which is consistent with the public welfare. If he fails in that, so far as a stockholder fails in producing a result, that stockholder must be held absolutely responsible, except so far as it shall affirmatively appear that the stockholder endeavored to produce different results and was overridden by a majority. Stockholders cannot be innocent merely by reason of the fact that they have not personally had anything to do with the decision of questions arising in the conduct of the business. That they have personally selected gentlemen or given their proxies to select gentlemen of high standing in the community, is not sufficient to relieve them from responsibility.

From the standpoint of the community, the welfare of the community, and the welfare of the workers in the company, what is called a democratization in the ownership through the distribution of the stock dissipates altogether the responsibility of stockholders, particularly of those with five shares, ten shares, or fifty shares. They recognize that they have no influence in a corporation of hundreds of millions of dollars' capital. Consequently they consider it immaterial whatever they do, or omit to do. The net result is that the men who are in control it becomes almost impossible to dislodge, unless there should be such a scandal in the corporation as to make it clearly necessary for the people on the outside to combine for self-protection. Probably even that necessity would not be sufficient to ensure a new management. That comes rarely except when those in control withdraw because they have been found guilty of reprehensible practices resulting in financial failure.

The wide distribution of stock, instead of being a blessing, constitutes, to my mind, one of the gravest dangers to the community. It is absentee landlordism of the worst kind. It is more dangerous, far more dangerous than the landlordism from which Ireland suffered. There, at all events, control was centered in a few individuals. By the distribution of nominal control among ten thousand or a hundred thousand stockholders, there is developed a sense of absolute irresponsibility on the part of the person who holds the stock. The few men that are in position continue absolute control without any responsibility except that to their stockholders of continuing and possibly increasing the dividends.

That responsibility, while proper enough in a way, may lead to action directly contrary to the public interest.

Everyone should know that the denial of minority representation on boards of directors has resulted in the domination of most corporations by one or two men; and in practically banishing all criticism of the dominant power. And even where the board is not so dominated, there is too often that "harmonious co-operation" among directors which secures for each, in his own line, a due share of the corporation's favors.

Minority stockholders rarely have the knowledge of the facts which is essential to an effective appeal, whether it be made to the directors, to the whole body of stockholders, or to the courts. Besides, the financial burden and the risks incident to any attempt of individual stockholders to interfere with an existing management is ordinarily prohibitive. Proceedings to avoid contracts with directors are, therefore, seldom brought, except after a radical change in the membership of the board. And radical changes in a board's membership are rare.

Protection to minority stockholders demands that corporations be prohibited absolutely from making contracts in which a director has a private interest, and that all such contracts be declared not voidable merely, but absolutely void.[41]

And what of the institutional shareholders? The extra overlay of fiduciary obligation requires them to act if it appears reasonably cost-effective to do so. While an individual is free to ignore both Justice Brandeis's concern and his own wallet by ignoring his rights and responsibilities as corporation owner, institutions, as trustees, enjoy no such liberty. They are legally obligated to manage all trust assets, including those relating to ownership, prudently. And institutional investors, individually and collectively, are so large that it will be increasingly clear that oversight is not only cost-effective but a more reliable investment than many of the alternatives, including active trading.[42]

Yet it is indisputable that shareholders have largely been unable to exercise the responsibilities of ownership of American corporations. In some respects, this "ownership failure" is due to the difference between tangible and intangible property.

As discussed above, the liquidity of shareownership has diluted the notions of ownership and responsibility and created obstacles to their exercise.

## TO SELL OR NOT TO SELL: THE PRISONER'S DILEMMA

The incentives driving shareholder actions can be compared to the famous logical problem called "the prisoner's dilemma." Two co-conspirators are captured and placed in separate cells by the police. They are each told that if neither confesses, they will both go to jail for five years. If one confesses, he will go free but the other will be sentenced to ten years. If both confess, both go to jail for eight years. Each must sit, unable to communicate with the other, and decide what to do. The dilemma is that an action that may benefit the individual making the choice (whether silence or confession) may have adverse consequences for the group (prison), whereas an action that benefits the group (silence) may have adverse consequences for the individual (prison, if the other confesses). This is also referred to as the problem of "collective choice" and the "free rider" problem. Any shareholder who wants to exercise ownership rights to influence a company must undertake all of the expenses, for only a pro rata share of the gains, if there are any. This problem has also produced one of this field's better oxymorons, by giving rise to the term for shareholders who deem it uneconomic to become involved in governance: "rational ignorance." This leads to votes against the investor's own interest in dual class exchange offers, and sales against the investor's own interest in two-tier offers.

## WHO THE INSTITUTIONAL INVESTORS ARE

The largest groups of institutional shareholders had the following holdings in 1992:[43]

|                              | $ trillion |
|------------------------------|------------|
| Private pension funds[44]    | 3.16       |
| State/local pension funds    | 0.95       |
| Investment companies         | 1.34       |
| Insurance companies          | 1.62       |
| Bank trusts                  | 1.02       |
| Foundations/endowments       | 0.18       |

The increase in institutional funds has been extraordinarily rapid. In 1970, institutional assets stood at $672 billion. Over the next decade, that figure grew to $1.9 trillion. From 1980 to 1990, the value of institutional assets tripled, to $6.3 trillion. Even in the last two years, the figure has increased a further 30 percent, to over $8 trillion. With as much as 31 percent of these assets in equities,[45] institutions represent a powerful stockholding force. Indeed, by 1990, institutions owned more than 50 percent of all US equity, though that figure dipped in 1992 to 47 percent.[46] Clearly, concerns of institutional investors should be of the utmost importance to corporate management.

These institutions have one very significant thing in common. All are subject to the highest standard of care and prudence our legal system has developed, the fiduciary standard. In Justice Benjamin Cardozo's classic terms, they must be "above the morals of the marketplace." Beyond this guiding standard, however, the groups of institutions have little in common with each other. As one observer noted, "institutional investors are by no means a monolithic group."[47]

One consistent theme is the problem of collective choice, as described in the "prisoner's dilemma" above. Another is the problem of agency costs. All institutional investors, by definition, are acting on behalf of others, whether pension plan participants, insurance policy holders, trust beneficiaries, or the less well-defined beneficiaries of charities and endowments. As you read the descriptions below, look carefully at this issue in particular. One way to begin is to ask which party has which information. For example, in almost every case, the beneficial owner of stock managed by an institutional investor has no idea how the proxies for that stock are voted. On the other hand, despite the growing popularity of "confidential voting," the corporation issuing the stock does know how the proxies are voted, and by whom. The Boothbay Harbor case in point illustrates this point.

*Bank trusts* Banks make up one large category of institutional investor, as trustees for everyone from pension plans to private estates. Trust administration is dominated by the complexities of federal income, gift, and estate taxes. Like other institutions, trusts have different classes of beneficiaries who have different kinds of interests.

In most instances, trusts are irrevocable, and, unless there is fraud, which is almost impossible to discover or prove, the bank can expect to continue to serve and collect fees as trustee, regardless of its investment performance. The security of the trust business may well be the reason for the traditional poor investment performance by banks. After all, in quite literal terms, they – unlike the beneficiaries – have nothing to lose. The trust contains "other people's money."

Banks generally get the most profitable, and certainly the most interesting, portion of their business from prominent local corporations. The smaller the community in which the bank is located, the more completely its tone is apt to be dominated by the locally based businesses. Banks, especially trust departments, do not encourage innovation, especially positions that are contrary to corporate management's recommendations on proxies.

## Cases in Point

R.P. Scherer A rare lawsuit exposed the conflicts of interest that can occur in these situations. In the late 1980s, Karla Scherer watched her husband, as CEO, ruin the R.P. Scherer Corporation, the company her father founded. As a major shareholder and board member, Ms. Scherer soon realized that the inefficiently run company was more valuable to shareholders if it was sold. However, the board repeatedly refused to consider this option, forcing her to take the matter to shareholders in the form of a proxy fight for board seats. She filed a lawsuit, challenging the way her trust shares were being voted. Scherer recalls the most devastating blow to the ultimately successful campaign to force a sale was when she had to deal with her own trustees. "Manufacturers National Bank, the trustee of two trusts created by my father for my brother and me, indicated it would vote all 470,400 shares for management, in direct opposition to our wishes. Remember the bank's chairman sat on our board and collected director's fees as well as more than half a million dollars in interest on loans to Scherer. During the trial, the then head of the bank's trust department admitted under oath that he did not know what the 'prudent man' rule was. He also stated that he had arrived at his decision to vote the stock for management in less than 10 minutes, without conferring with us and after affording management an opportunity to plead its case over lunch in a private dining room at the Detroit Club." The court initially ordered the appointment of an independent voting trustee, but the ruling was reversed.

**Citicorp** The officer of Citicorp responsible for voting proxies determined that a proxy proposal made by Boeing management in 1987 was contrary to the interests of the shareholders, so she voted against it. She was summoned to the office of the chief executive officer to be reminded that Boeing was an important customer of the bank.

*Mutual funds* Mutual funds are trusts, according to the terms of the Investment Company Act of 1940, which governs them. Otherwise, they bear little resemblance to the other institutional investors because of one important difference: they are designed for total liquidity. The "one-night stands" of institutional investment, they are designed for investors who come in and out on a daily basis, or at least those who want the flexibility to do so.

The investors are entitled to take their money out at any time, at whatever the price is that day. The investment manager has no control over what he will have to pay out or when he will be forced to liquidate a holding. So he views his investments as collateral; they are simply there to make good on the promise to shareholders to redeem their shares at any time. This is not the kind of relationship to encourage a long-term attitude toward any particular company the fund happens to invest in, and if there is a tender offer at any premium over the trading price, mutual fund investment managers have to grab it.

In the face of the real need to attract new money and to retain the investors he has in a world of perpetual and precise competition, the mutual fund manager cannot concern himself with the long term, because his investors may all show up today, and he must be prepared to stand and deliver.

## Case in Point: T. Rowe Price and Texaco

Investment firm T. Rowe Price held substantial Texaco stock in various accounts during Carl Icahn's proxy contest for that company in 1988. Its investment managers voted the stock in one account for Icahn and the stock in another account for incumbent Texaco management. Their justification was that one fund was explicitly short-term in orientation, while the other was long-term, and that this was no different from having one fund buy the stock while the other was selling it.

*Insurance companies* Insurance is the only major industry that has successfully avoided any significant federal regulation, although "special accounts" and subsidiary manager investments are subject to ERISA and other federal rules. Life and casualty insurance companies prefer to deal with state legislatures, with whom they have historically had a close relationship.

State law has until most recent times severely circumscribed the extent to which insurers are allowed to invest their own funds in equities. Even today, only 14 percent of insurance fund assets are invested in common stocks. The current limit on stock is 20 percent of a life insurer's assets, or one-half of its surplus. But insurers still may not take influential blocks: life insurers may not put more than 2 percent of the insurance company's assets into the stock of any single insurer, and property and casualty insurers may not control a non-insurance company.[48]

Insurance companies, perhaps more than any other class of institutional investor, have a symbiosis with the companies in which they invest. First, they are usually holders of debt securities of any company in which they have an equity investment; debt instruments are very compatible with their needs because they have a reliable, set payout. Second, they typically have – or would like to have – a commercial relationship with the company by providing insurance or a product to meet the company's pension obligations. Third, like most other institutional shareholders, they are under no obligation to report to their customers on their proxy voting (but the companies whose proxies they vote – and with whom they do business – do know). Finally, like all other shareholders, the collective choice problem makes any form of activism uneconomic. Therefore, it is not surprising that the insurance industry consistently votes with management, regardless of the impact on share value. For example, one Midwestern insurance company wrote that its policy "is to support management positions on normal corporate policy and matters falling within the conduct of a company's ordinary business operations."[49]

*Universities and foundations* Universities and foundations are institutional shareholders because they are funded through endowments. People contribute to a fund, and the interest that fund generates is used for whatever charitable or educational purpose the endowment permits. In 1991, the J. Paul Getty Trust had $3.98 billion. The Ford Foundation had $5.83 billion, and the MacArthur Foundation had $3.13 billion. This money is put into widely diversified investments, including common stock. Although these organizations have "not for profit" status under US tax laws, they seek returns as rigorously as any other investor. But they have not been rigorous in the exercise of their stock ownership rights (or responsibilities).

Foundations and universities are no less subject to commercial pressures than banks and insurance companies. After all, their money comes from alumni, who are often business executives, and from businesses themselves. One study reported that in 1985 corporate contributions to American universities and colleges "surpassed donations from alumni for the first time."[50] Indeed, nonprofits are "selling" a much less tangible product, so they must be especially diplomatic. Foundation and university trustees are usually drawn from the business community. The trustees of the Ford Foundation, of Harvard, of the New York Public Library, or of any public museum or symphony are drawn from the same list as the directors of the largest corporations. Many corporate boards include members of the academic community, whose programs and schools receive large contributions from the grateful companies.

## Case in Point: Interlocking Directors

The dean of a university served as head of the compensation committee of the company headed by the chairman of his university's board. The CEO and his company were both large contributors and the company funded a good deal of the university's research. They played crucial roles in approving each other's pay plans, a clear conflict of interests.

*Pension plans* "We own the economy now," said Carol O'Cleireacain, then New York City finance commissioner and trustee of four city employee pension funds with nearly $50 billion of assets.[51] David Ball, director of the Pension and Welfare Benefits Administration that oversees billions of dollars in pension assets, said that institutions could accurately borrow a phrase from the comic strip, Pogo: "We have met the marketplace and they is us."[52] The

California Public Employees' Retirement System grows about $1 billion every two months – "in a year more than four times the median market value of a *Fortune 500* industrial company; in a year, enough to buy all the common stock of General Motors, with enough left to buy five tankfuls of gasoline for each vehicle it makes."[53] Because of their size and importance, we will devote the next section to pension funds.

## THE BIGGEST POOL OF MONEY IN THE WORLD

The largest institutional investors, the group that includes the largest collection of investment capital in the world, are the pension funds. One of the most important elements to understanding the current state of corporate governance, as well as its future direction and potential, is an understanding of this group. Although they are very diverse in many ways, they share several important characteristics. As we examine their impact not just on corporate governance, but also on competitiveness and productivity, we need to understand the impact of the most important characteristic they have in common: they are all trustees. A money manager who does not perform may lose clients. A trustee who does not perform may pay a fine, be permanently prohibited from managing pension money, even go to jail. This is certainly a good way to protect the pension funds, but it is almost as certainly not a good way to move markets. The problem is that no one ever realized, when they established the pension system, that it would quickly take over the market, for rather Gresham-like reasons.[54]

After World War II, the US government provided generous tax incentives to encourage individuals and employers to make provision for retirement income. The program was subsidized three ways:

- the employer's payments to the plan were deductible for federal income tax purposes;
- all transactions by the plan – buying, selling, collecting income – were exempt from tax; and
- the recipient is allowed to stagger the receipt of payments to fall into the most advantageous year from a tax point of view.

This huge federal subsidy transferred national savings from savings banks to pension systems as individuals responded to the tax incentives. They preferred to save 100-cent dollars in retirement plans rather than 50-cent dollars in the savings bank. Thus, over

30 percent of all the equity investments in the country are held in public and private pension plans. This means that the largest accumulation of investment capital in the world was the responsibility of trustees, who have a perspective (and set of incentives) very different from the strictly economic "invisible hand" of the capital markets.

While in theory the trustees are vitally committed to earning the highest possible rate of return, in reality there is little incentive for most of them to perform better than the actuarially defined return necessary to meet an actuarially defined payout (for a defined-benefit plan) or a market rate of return (for a defined-contribution plan).

A defined-benefit pension plan specifies the level of benefits it will pay, or the method of determining those benefits, but not the amount of company contributions. Contributions are determined actuarially on the basis of the benefits expected to become payable. A defined-contribution plan specifies the amount of contributions, but not the level of benefits. The size of the pension is determined by how much (or how little) is in the account at the time the plan participant retires.

The assets in a public plan are assumed by the actuaries to earn a particular rate of return – typically 8 percent in 1993, higher in earlier years. Clearly, if the plan can earn a consistently higher rate of return than the one assumed, the amount of money required to be paid in by the state from taxes can be reduced. In the case of private pension systems, this translates in higher earnings for the corporation and, presumably, bonuses for the pension manager. With public plans and civil service salaries, however, there are no bonuses (though in some cases there may be political benefits). In general, though, the individual responsible for the investment of public plan funds has no incentive to achieve beyond the mandated averages. As Edward V. Regan, former Comptroller of the State of New York, said: "Nobody ever got elected to anything by beating the S&P 500. On the other hand, for one bad investment, they'll throw you out." It is not surprising that Regan responded by investing in an "index." This meant that the state pension fund performed exactly as well as the Standard & Poors 500; in essence it *was* the S&P 500.[55]

The "invisible hand" is now the hand of these trustees of public (state, municipal, federal) and private (corporate and union) pension plans. Peter Drucker called this "The Unseen Revolution" in 1976, noting that "If 'socialism' is defined as 'ownership of the

means of production by the workers' – and this is both the ortho-
dox and the only rigorous definition – then the United States is
the first truly 'Socialist' country."[56]

> Shortly before the year 2000, there will be more workers in compa-
> nies that are more than 15 percent employee held than in the entire
> US trade union movement. *The property rights of workers will
> dwarf labor laws as an option for influence in corporations.* For
> the first time since the 1930s, America will see a new wave of
> employee activism – one more likely to be low key and business
> oriented than the early trade union movement. But this time unions
> will be joined by company-wide employee associations – *ad hoc*
> and coordinated – asking for a say because they are either the
> dominant shareholder or the second major shareholder in the firm.[57]

The defined-benefit plan is declining in popularity among private
American companies. Few new ones are being started, and many
existing plans are being terminated. Defined-benefit plans with
cost-of-living adjustments (COLAs) are an effort to insulate a
particular class of citizens from the economic vagaries of the world
by guaranteeing them a set level of buying power, no matter what
the rate of inflation. This is a very expensive commitment, and
companies and states are increasingly reluctant to assume it.

The alternative is defined-contribution plans. Because the
amount that the employer and the employee pay in is fixed, the
employee has a certain control over the investment of the funds.
The funds are entirely his (subject to restricted use for statutorily
permitted purposes like the purchase of a residence or for education
costs), and so is the risk of gain and loss. The employer ceases to
play a buffering role either with respect to the performance of
plan investments or with respect to inflation in the outside world.

It may appear that employees have lost financial ground in the
trend toward defined-contribution plans, because of the loss of
security. It is only in defined-benefit plans that the employer acts
as guarantor of a set level of purchasing power after retirement.
But defined-contribution plans have advantages for the plan participant as well, including the ability to change jobs and to take the
benefits along. The ultimate problem lies in investment policy. As
we have pointed out above, the trustee of the entire defined-benefit
pool has the luxury of making the optimum long-term investment
in stocks. On the other hand, the individual acting as his own
"trustee" for a defined-contribution plan, worried on a day-to-
day basis about preserving his retirement fund, is apt to invest in

bonds. He will be satisfied with losing only a little bit as long as he avoids running the risk of losing a lot. Thus, the assets committed to an individual under a defined-contribution scheme are apt to be invested less profitably, and the aggregate will have a massive long-term impact on what funds are actually available in retirement.

As public funds gradually evolve from defined benefit to defined contribution, plan participants will have increasing involvement. Although the trustee will manage plan assets and retain ownership responsibilities with respect to plan stocks, plan participants will exercise more choice selecting investment categories (stocks or bonds), as in the FERSA example below.

## Case in Point: Maine State Retirement System

The Maine State Retirement System (MSRS), has a typical defined-benefit plan. Like most public pension plans in the United States, it offers participants "defined benefits" on retirement. The employee is paid an amount based on the cost of living as well as other factors. The formula takes into account expected raises, inflation, and differing retirement ages. The formula is the number of years of service times 1/50 times the average of the final three years' pay.

This produces an ideal result for a "typical" career state employee; after 35 years of service, an individual can retire at age 62 with a pension calculated as 70 percent of "final pay." Public plans generally provide for a level of "inflation protection" for payments. In Maine, there is a cap of up to 4 percent per year. The State is required to pay into the plan every year an amount calculated by actuaries to be sufficient, if invested according to the assumed returns, to produce an adequate amount of capital to pay the system's commitments as they mature.

Maine's promise to make "defined-benefit" payments to participants is enforceable whether or not there are assets in the pension plan. If the plan does not have enough, it will have to come out of tax revenues. The purpose of the plan (and the basis of the actuaries' calculations of the amount of annual payments) is to match pension payments with the benefits from the service of the participant. Like social security, it is something of a Ponzi scheme. Today's workers pay in money that is immediately sent out to today's retirees.

To make the system work, then, today's taxpayers must pay in as well. The portion of their taxes allotted to the pension system must be enough, when invested, to provide today's public employees with a suitable pension when they actually do retire. The amounts in the pension plan serve two purposes. They serve intergenerational fairness by assuring that those who receive the benefits pay the full costs. They also act as a buffer (if not a complete guarantee) against the changing politics and priorities of the state budgetary process. While a state can (and does) break some promises, the legislature makes it a little more difficult by segregating pension assets in an independent trust (difficult, but not impossible – see the discussion of ETIs, later in this chapter).

The dynamics of a defined-benefit system are skewed heavily in favor of an individual who works until the end of the anticipated term of service. In the State of Maine system a hypothetical defined-benefit participant only begins to get a portion of the state's contribution during the last third of his term. After that, his interest soars.

The liability assumptions have been subject to great change over the past half dozen years:

- in 1987 there was an increase of about $0.5 billion to reflect a change in assumptions as to the retirement age;

- in 1992, assumptions were changed $0.45 billion to reflect the level of pay increases at career end (and to reflect vacation and sick pay).

The Maine State Constitution requires a vote of the electorate before debt can be incurred. But pension liabilities cannot be controlled by the political process. In Maine, the level of actuarially unfunded liabilities in the MSRS approaches $5 billion, almost ten times the amount authorized by popular vote. The aggregate level of state debt today is about $0.6 billion. To put it bluntly, the MSRS actuaries have created more state debt over the last six years than the voters of the State of Maine have authorized in 200 years.

State employee compensation is bargained, but pension obligations are legislated. This means that lobbying is the mode of employee involvement. In 1992, in an effort to reduce state expenditures, the legislature modified benefits for all employees with fewer than seven years creditable service. They excluded from the definition of "earnable compensation" payment received for unused sick leave or vacation; raised the minimum age for retirement with full benefits by two years to 62; and increased the penalty for retirement before the minimum age. The state employees went to court, arguing that as soon as they accepted employment they had in effect accepted a contract providing that the state would provide them with the benefits at that time, and that they could not be reduced. Other states, like California, have ruled in favor of the employees in these challenges. The lower court in Maine did so, too, but it was reversed by the state Supreme Court, which ruled that only benefits actually due could not be changed; those merely anticipated could be.

The "conventional wisdom" is that defined-benefit plans are "cheaper" than defined contribution in the sense that less benefit is actually received under the former system. The reason is that so few defined-benefit plan participants actually serve the optimal period of time; the others are losers. Thus someone who leaves before ten years is not vested; 35 years of employment is essential for optimization.

The defined-benefit system creates winners and losers. Every employee hopes that he or she will win. Importantly, for the political process, the losers are usually not available to testify, litigate, or lobby. Thus, the impression prevails that all is well, when less than 30 percent of those entering the system ultimately receive their full rewards. A defined-contribution system is transparent; you can see what is yours and what you see is what you get (and complain about).

A public pension system enjoys special status within governmental institutions:

- it has substantial money;

- the state can decline to make requisite payments for a sustained period of time and there is no immediate adverse impact; and

- the impact is sufficiently complex, long range, and diffused that no one seems to be hurt by deficiencies.

Governments are increasingly being driven to extremes in efforts to balance their budgets. Roughly speaking there are three alternatives:

- raise taxes, which can be political suicide;

- cut back programs, which can also be politically disastrous;

- postpone, reduce, eliminate, but – above all else – decline to pay timely the actuarially determined amounts into the pension system.

Clearly, the pension system is the easiest target. The extent of political profligacy has been obscured over the last decade only by the raging "bull" market. In recent years, the percentage of equity holdings has gradually increased, so that now about 70 percent of Maine's investments are in stocks. A rising market covers all manner of sins, or has so far. Note that the Maine legislature recently increased the employee contribution from 6.5 percent to 7.65 percent. According to a newsletter published by the National Association of Public Pension Attorneys, "No sound actuarial reason was given for this increase. It is reported that the State Legislature did it simply to reduce the employer contribution so as to solve state budget problems unrelated to the retirement fund."[58]

The efficacy of the defined-benefit system, where no one really has a sense of owning something specific, depends ultimately on the level of discipline in the political system. Indeed, there have been challenges to the cost-of-living increases granted to defined-benefit plan participants, on the grounds that these increases should be considered "gifts." In one such suit, the challengers argued that the money belongs to the government, and not the retirees, because the government administers the plans and the government determines when or if cost-of-living increases are payable.

If one has no confidence in the capacity of government to be held to its commitments, a defined-benefit system is less desirable than a defined-contribution system where an individual has a continual sense of ownership with respect to the specific assets in their retirement account, bolstered by regular reports of its status. It seems likely that tens of thousands of participants in a defined-contribution system would be better motivated, informed, and able than defined-benefit plan participants to compel government to make the promised payments into the plan and to prevent it from wasting the assets already in the plan.

A fascinating study of the public and private pension fund cultures was described in the 1992 book *Fortune and Folly*[59] by anthropologist William M. O'Barr and law professor John M. Conley. They approached the pension fund world just as they might an unusual tribal culture. "[T]o fit better into the native environment, we exchanged our academic tweeds for field clothes – in this case, blue suits from Brooks Brothers rather than khakis from an army surplus store – and set out to live with the natives and observe their ways of life."[60]

Perhaps the most interesting part of the book is its description of the cultural differences between the private and public pension funds. For example: "Private fund officials often talk about their accountability to the sponsoring corporation's bottom line, or at least to the sponsor's corporate notion of successful management. Their public counterparts talk instead about the press and the ballot box as the instruments of day-to-day accountability."[61] The result, according to the authors, is that public funds' primary goal is to avoid poor performance, while private funds try to achieve superior performance – a fine, but very important distinction that is both the cause and the result of the diff. ng incentives (pay and otherwise) of the two systems.

This distinction stems in part from what the authors call, in true anthropological terms, "creation myths." These "oral histories" about the origins of the pension system reveal, in their differing emphasis on particular aspects, what each systems' assumptions and goals are. "The creation myths we heard at private funds tended to be centered around important individuals and to convey the teller's sense of the corporation's culture and personality."[62] In these stories, "cultural influences predominate over economic ones."[63] Private fund "creation myths" tend to emphasize a visionary leader who created the pension fund to provide for loyal employees and their dependents. Interestingly, these myths focus on the origins of the pension fund at the particular company and not on the establishment of the overall structure of private pension funds under ERISA, which was enacted in 1974.

O'Barr and Conley found that public fund "creation myths," too, focus on "history and politics, but the history was scandalous and the politics was external. (Ironically, much of the impetus for ERISA came from widespread corruption in the *public* pension system, which ERISA left untouched.) Once again, financial analysis was not a primary determinant of structures and strategies."[64] In contrast to the private fund managers, who see themselves as living up to the "creator's" vision of economic security for fellow workers, the public fund managers see themselves as protecting their fellow workers from those who would try to benefit themselves, politically or financially, to the detriment of the workers. While both are fiduciaries, operating under the strictest standard for integrity and loyalty imposed by our legal system, the "creation myths" reveal an important difference in the way each sees their obligations and goals.

But the authors found that there was one point on which public and private pension funds were alike – their efforts to avoid accountability for the consequences of their investment decisions. This is understandable in a field where even the most capable professionals have so little ability to control or even predict what the market will do. The 20-year effort of the federal government to gain control over the Teamsters' union and the "looting" of the New York City plans created a generation of risk-averse fiduciaries.

Perhaps *Fortune and Folly*'s most important conclusion is:

In every interview we conducted, fund executives talked at length about assuming, assigning, or avoiding responsibility. As we listened to them, it often seemed as if the funds had been designed for the purpose of shifting responsibility away from identifiable individuals. They described four specific mechanisms for displacing responsibility and avoiding blame; burying decisions in the bureaucracy, blaming someone else, blaming the market, or claiming their hands were tied by the law.[65]

## PENSION PLANS AS INVESTORS

Before we consider the question of pension funds as owners (as participants in the corporate governance system), we must take a brief look at the bigger question of pension funds as buyers and sellers. The fiduciary standard for prudent investment works fine in the situation for which it was designed, protecting the assets of a trust beneficiary, like a minor inheriting property. It does not work when it is applied to a pot of money that constitutes the largest single collection of investment capital. There are simply not enough "prudent" investments around to sustain all of that money. So what you get is what we have now, too much investment in large-capital blue chip stocks and not enough in everything else.

This is what happens when a horde of "prudent experts" go to the marketplace to look for diversified and seasoned investments. It is inevitable when they are faced with a choice between rational (in economic terms) or prudent (in legal terms) investments. The problem is that we need a system that invests to encourage risk, and we have a system that invests to discourage it.

The data show that pension money has not, by and large, provided needed new capital or new employment. During the decade of the eighties, the S&P 500 corporations typically *reduced* their capital by buying back stock. And this (over)investment in the largest companies failed to create new jobs. Artificial inflation of investment in large-capitalization companies thus had no meaningful benefits either to those companies or to the pension beneficiary investors themselves. And of course it has provided no special benefits to participants in the pension plan, the employees and retirees. With all of the pension managers grouped together in the S&P 500, it is not surprising that none of them, over time, beats the market and that so many of them have taken the savings available by eliminating the transaction costs in active trading and investing in "index funds" that replicate the market. The challenge is finding a way to ensure that this essentially permanent holding gives the market the feedback that it needs.

## PENSION PLANS AS OWNERS

The only result of passive investing is active owning. Says James Dowling, chairman of Burson-Marsteller, the public relations firm that recently established a corporate governance practice to advise CEOs and boards on how to operate in the changed environment: "The public funds have so much money that they find it's harder to find new companies to invest in than to try to turn around poorly performing ones." Says Jennifer Morales, executive director of the Houston Firemen's Relief Retirement Fund: "We don't want to sell. If a company can be improved, why should we be the ones to leave?"[66]

Public and private pension funds are the largest single component of equity ownership – 28 percent of the total equity in the country and growing. And, with an average of 30 years from the time money comes in to the time it has to be paid out, they are the ultimate long-term holder. For that reason, we need to understand their impact on the capital markets and on corporate performance. They bring significant advantages and disadvantages over the old system of highly fractionated individual investment.

**Advantages:**

- Their size and expertise minimizes the collective choice problem discussed above. They are sophisticated enough to understand when activism is necessary and large enough to make it effective (and cost-effective) to do so. The holdings of pension funds are large enough to alleviate the free-rider problem that makes shareholder information and action economically nonrational (and therefore imprudent for fiduciaries).
- They are widely held – almost 100 million Americans have interests in employee benefit plans – so their pension trustees are good proxies for the public interest. It is virtually inconceivable that something would be in the interest of pensioners that is not in the interest of society at large.
- Pension plans are less restricted by commercial conflicts of interest than are other institutional investors, like banks, insurance companies, mutual funds, and other classes of institutional investors. (Note, however, that there are still significant commercial conflicts of interest, as shown by the Citicorp example.)
- For political and investment reasons, pension plans are becoming increasingly "indexed" in their equity holdings. This makes them

both universal and permanent shareholders. Their holdings are so diversified that they have the incentive to represent the ownership sector (and the economy) generally rather than any specific industries or companies. This endows them with a breadth of concern that naturally aligns with the public interest. For example, pension funds can be concerned with vocational education, pollution, and retraining, whereas an owner with a perspective limited to a particular company or industry would consider these to be unacceptable expenses because of competitiveness problems. Robert Reich, the Secretary of Labor, urged institutional investors against the short-term view that cutting payrolls boosted the immediate bottom line. Instead, he told institutions to adopt a long-term perspective, arguing that retraining programs and heightened employee security can enhance productivity. Reich said: "You should be aware of the full consequences of the signals you send and the positions you take, not just in the current round of play, but in the next, and the next. Stewardship of the future, after all, is the essence of your profession."[67]

- The private pension system is administered under ERISA, an existing Federal law that preempts state involvement. The administration of this law in its definition of the scope of fiduciary responsibilities by the Pension & Welfare Benefits Administration (PWBA) of the US Department of Labor has succeeded in creating a standard that has been widely followed by the states in the operation of public pension systems. The essential legal structure needed to govern these investors is already in place.

**Disadvantages:**

The disadvantages are in general a function of what we do not know, and they can best be stated as questions.

- Who watches the watchers? Who should watch them? Who can?
- What are the qualifications of the trustees? What should they be?
- Are the trustees genuinely accountable to their own beneficiaries or are we simply substituting one unaccountable bureaucracy for another?

One way to address these questions is to make the qualifications of the trustees (like the qualifications for members of boards of directors) explicit and public. But there is another disadvantage that is more subtle and complex:

- What is the impact on the capital markets of having such a high percentage of the available capital invested by fiduciaries?

More than $2 trillion is now under the control of laws that effectively relegate pension assets to permanent yet docile holdings in large, established companies. The result is "excess diversification and insufficient innovation."[68] This means overinvestment in large companies and underinvestment in emerging opportunities. By nature and by law the objectives of fiduciaries are low risk. This can hamper market efficiency, because for the first time a significant portion of the investment is managed for some goal other than maximum returns. Both public and private pension funds have thus been criticized for being underinclusive in their investment strategy, for failing to recognize the opportunities that may be higher risk but may also be higher return. They have been encouraged to behave more like venture capitalists.

But they have also been criticized for being overinclusive, for making investments for reasons other than returns. Social investing (or economically targeted investing) falls into this category, as well as some of the attempts to fund corporate pension funds with the corporation's own stock. Both are described in more detail in the following section. It is useful to apply the same overlay of questions in connection with the management of pension funds that we do with corporations: *Who has the best information and the fewest conflicts of interest? Who is in the best position to make the decisions, and does that person have authority to do so?*

## PUBLIC PENSION FUNDS

The public pension funds have been the most visible of the institutional investors with regard to governance issues. They include pension funds for state and municipal employees, ranging from teachers and civic workers, to firefighters and police, and they oversee nearly a trillion dollars. It is important to note that of this very large group, only a handful have been actively involved in governance initiatives. One of these activists noted,

> There might be lots of noise and action, and there might be talk about all the new, awakened shareholders and institutional investors, but there's really not much more than a dozen public pension funds involved. And they call the tune. In fact if you took the CalPERS and the New York City pension fund and TIAA–CREF out of the equation along with our fund [New York State] and Wisconsin, Pennsylvania and to some extent Florida, you might have very little activism at all.[69]

In terms of their own governance, the public plans are all organized differently. Some are directed by bureaucrats, some by politically appointed officials, and some by elected officials. The $70 billion California Public Employees' Retirement System (CalPERS), for example, is overseen by trustees appointed through a variety of mechanisms, who are intimately involved, whereas the New York State employee's fund is overseen by a single trustee, one of only four statewide elected officials.

The people who oversee the public pension funds come from a wider variety of backgrounds than the money managers who are responsible for other kinds of institutional investments. The CalP-ERS board, for example, includes union officials and political appointees who oversee the staff (both inside and outside the civil service) and both professional money managers and staff with other kinds of expertise. They cannot compete salary-wise with other institutional investors for the top investment professionals (though, ironically, they may end up employing those same professionals by retaining their companies to manage their assets). This is because, with rare exceptions like the 1993 decision by CalPERS to give its CEO a performance-based bonus, the public plan pay schemes are designed for political, not economic reasons. As one public pension CEO said, "If I do a good job, I get $100,000. If I do a great job, I get $100,000." Several senior officials lost their jobs in the Washington state pension fund, when their very lucrative investments with LBO fund KKR became perceived as a political liability.

Actuaries can tell any defined-benefit plan exactly what its liquidity needs will be and how much cash it will need over the next ten years to meet retirees' entitlements. The balance of the fund really is "permanent." All of the long-term analyses of rates of return to be derived from different classes of investment prove that returns from common stocks beat the returns from bonds or money market funds – or any other investment medium for that matter. This means that it is all but impossible to justify any investment for the public plans (except for a small percentage of Treasury Bills to meet their liquidity needs), other than common equity.

So the conservative approach described by Regan prevails. The "prudent man" degenerated into a "lowest common denominator" approach. There is no incentive to do better than others, and every incentive to be safely in the middle of the pack.

In this context, let's examine the role of the public funds in corporate governance. We have already established that they are not strictly motivated by economic returns. And it is all but tautological to say that they are motivated by political concerns. To the extent that the public plans do become involved with corporate governance, they raise the very real specter of "back door" socialism. What is the role of the state when it becomes a major shareholder, even **the** major shareholder of American business? To what extent do we really want elected officials overseeing the managers of American business?

The incentives, expertise, and goals of business and government are so different, at such fundamental levels, that this is a complicated – and crucial – question. The trustees of public plans act on behalf of a very diverse group, including current employees (at all stages of their employment) and retirees. The trustees themselves are a diverse group, including employees, retirees, and others, including political appointees, elected officials, and a wide range of experts – investors, bankers, actuaries, insurance professionals. Usually they are paid just a nominal per diem fee for their work. While this attracts people with a high level of public spiritedness, there is a certain impracticality in trying to manage the operations of a truly mammoth investment and retirement system under the direction of people whose expertise is often in other areas, and who are not paid enough to be able to devote a substantial amount of time to this task. There is also a substantial political impediment to hiring people outside the government – especially at the prices that the market demands for people who manage money. This is a significant disadvantage.

The public fund board of trustees must reach a perilous equilibrium between plan participant representatives and political appointees. There are frequent disagreements on questions of funding and investment. The plan participants' top priority is safety of the fund and the politicians are interested in politics – on the budget side and on the investment side.

The result is a tendency toward compromise. CalPERS' success is firmly based on a realistic assessment of the limits of its practical ability to force issues. "We have a strong predisposition to accommodation," CalPERS' former CEO Dale Hanson explained in a lecture to the Harvard Business School.[70] The political realities (both internally, in Hanson's relationship with his own board and his fiduciary obligation to plan participants, and externally, as a government agency reporting to the governor) placed a premium on compromise. The economic realities ("rational ignorance") may place an even larger premium on compromise. Perhaps the public pension funds' most significant contribution has been to make the world an uncomfortable place for a director of an underperforming company. "Hanson is adamant that he does not seek to oust CEOs . . . Also CalPERS insists it does not seek to name its own people to boards, although it does push hard for independent directors."[71]

Many public funds, as well as many union funds, belong to the Council of Institutional Investors (CII). The Washington-based group acts as a resource for its members, holding conferences, providing information and acting as a clearinghouse, occasionally issuing policy papers. Recently, several corporate funds joined the Council as well, perhaps in a sort of "If you can't beat them, join them" move. It will be interesting to see which group has more of an impact on the other.

The public pension plans differ in their perspectives, their policies, and their politics. But they are all fiduciaries, obligated by law to protect the interests of their plan beneficiaries, the public employees. And they all have a high degree of independence because they are not dependent on commercial relationships with those in whom they invest. This makes it easier for them to become involved in governance issues. The Maine State Retirement System has successfully brought suit against Travelers' Insurance company to recover a portion of an investment negligently managed.

But public institutions have relationships too, and like their private counterparts, those relationships can affect investment strategies, proxy votes, and other governance activity. They are subject to political considerations, as the cases below demonstrate.

## Cases in Point: Public Fund Activism

- When the Wisconsin state pension fund wanted to object to General Motors' $742.8 million forced greenmail payment to Ross Perot, it was stopped by the governor, who was trying to get General Motors to build some plants in his state.
- When Shearson Lehman Hutton (as it was then called) assisted in the takeover of a Pennsylvania company called Koppers, many local residents (and politicians) were concerned about possible job losses. Shearson was not only acting as investment banker for the acquiring firm, but also as a participant. Shearson had loaned $500 million of its own funds to the acquirer and had agreed to purchase 46 percent of Koppers for itself if the takeover was successful. The state held some Koppers stock in its pension fund. It was not enough to stop the takeover, but it was enough to slow the effort down. The state treasurer suspended all state business, including bond business, with Shearson and its subsidi-

aries. Three Shearson subsidiaries were eliminated from consideration for management of state pension fund assets. The takeover was ultimately completed in a manner that satisfied the state's concerns about jobs, and the suspension was removed.

- The New York State United Teachers Fund sold its investment in the Tribune Company when employees of the Tribune's *New York Daily News* went on strike in 1991. The fund stated that, "our policy is not to invest in any project, corporation, or stock that is anti-union."

- Several police pension funds used the pension fund's proxies in Time Warner, parent company of Ice-T's record label, to protest the Ice-T "Cop Killer" record.

- Dr. David Bronner, manager of the Alabama State Pension Fund, invested $120 million to build the "Robert Trent Jones Golf Trail," seven huge golf complexes across the state. He has built so many office towers and parking garages in downtown Montgomery that he is the most active developer in that city. "Officially just the bureaucrat who manages money for teachers and state employees, Dr. Bronner has come to view himself as the personal guardian of Alabama's future."[72] He emphasizes the economic benefits to the state of his investments, arguing that the golf courses will increase tourism.

- The New Jersey state pension fund required by state law to disinvest all holdings in companies doing business with South Africa, ended up selling out of two New Jersey pharmaceutical companies whose only dealing with South Africa was the sale of medicine used exclusively by black South Africans. The *Wall Street Journal* estimated that the disinvestment policy has cost the plan between $330–$515 million in two years.[73] Is there any reason not to treat this as an expenditure, subject to the same procedural protections and deliberations as other expenditures of public funds? New York City's pension fund was able to adopt a more flexible policy on South Africa. It began by writing letters to express its concerns, then sponsored and supported a number of shareholder resolutions, calling for companies to adopt the Sullivan Principles making a commitment to providing equal opportunity in their South African facilities. They sold out of a limited number of companies that they determined had business dealings that promoted apartheid, like those who do business with the police and military there. Regan, of the New York State pension fund, took a different approach. Facing annual legislative proposals along the inflexible lines enacted in New Jersey, Regan used the fund's shares to commence a massive program of shareholder resolutions calling for disinvestment from South Africa, instead of divesting. Regan's view was that mandated sale of stocks (for any reason) would impose unreasonable financial costs on the portfolio and force higher contributions from the taxpayers. By use of the shareholder franchise, he negotiated results with the companies, arguing that he met the objectives of divestment legislation without incurring the significant financial losses.

- In 1991, California governor Pete Wilson initiated what some observers called a "hostile takeover" of the state's pension funds to reduce the budget deficit and gain more control over the trustees.

- New York State Comptroller Regan voted the state pension fund's proxies in favor of management in the Texaco proxy contest. In a series of newspaper articles he was accused of basing this vote on the campaign contributions of the dissident candidate, Carl Icahn. Icahn was a contributor to Regan's political opponent. Regan was subjected to a grand jury investigation.

- The inspector general of the state of Massachusetts issued a report finding that state pension fund officials had hired outside financial advisers based on friendships and political relationships rather than by competitive bidding, then created phony, backdated documents to conceal the fact that they had not adequately researched the firms' performance in advance.

Recently, there has been an increasing number of investigations of state and city pension funds and the way they make their investment decisions.[74] Federal investigators examined the pension fund of the Commonwealth of Virginia, following the governor's (unsuccessful) attempt to use some of the pension fund's real estate for a new football stadium for the Washington Redskins. The state legislature also hired an investment firm to examine the state fund's operations, including its investment policies and procedures. In Minnesota, former state pension fund employees pled guilty to charges of embezzlement.

## ECONOMICALLY TARGETED INVESTMENTS

A number of states are experimenting with "social investing" (recently renamed "economically targeted investments" or ETI), the investment of state pension funds in local companies, programs, or securities which may not meet traditional standards for risk and return. A Commission convened by New York Governor Mario Cuomo released a report in 1989 called "Our Money's Worth," recommending that the state pension fund consider the impact of its investments on the state economy as one aspect of its investment strategy. It also recommended the creation of a state agency to act as a clearinghouse to find these investments, and this agency was in fact created the following year.

Professor D. Jeanne Patterson of Indiana University published a thoughtful analysis of the ETI programs of the public pension funds in the Great Lakes States (Michigan, Illinois, Ohio, Wisconsin, Indiana) in 1992. She found that the "targeted investments" averaged about four percentage points below the S&P 500 stock index over a five-year period, and about two percentage points below the Wilshire 5,000 index during the same period. Citing Harvard Professor E. Merrick Dodd's well-known argument that "It is not for the trustee to be public-spirited with his beneficiary's property," she concludes that "there will be continuing pressure for federal controls because of the excesses of a few systems."[75] She adds that "we must remember that the use of [pension employee retirement system funds] to *subsidize* economic development efforts is inappropriate," citing Regan's view that "the greatest good a [state pension fund] can do for its state is to maximize return on investments and reduce the contributions necessary from taxpayers.[76] In hearings held in June of 1995, congressional leaders criticized the Department of Labor for encouraging ETIs, despite the Department's unequivocal commitment to returns as the determining criteria for investment. Look at the discussion of private pension funds' version of ETIs later in this chapter. Compare this to claims made in a recent lawsuit by a group of ministers and lay employees charging that their pension funds' environmental and political investment restrictions resulted in inferior financial performance. Predictably, their complaint provoked references to the necessity of choosing between God and mammon, but it also showed the difficulty in pinpointing which is which.

## FEDERAL EMPLOYEE RETIREMENT SYSTEM

In 1986, the US government established what will in time be the largest institutional investor in the world, the Federal Employee Retirement System (FERS). Up to that point, the federal employees had operated outside of the Social Security system. Like Social Security, the federal retirement system had no "fund" – money paid in by today's workers was immediately sent out to retirees. FERS was created in large part to help bail out Social Security by adding the federal employees to the pot, and by making their part of the pot a growing one. The Federal Employee Retirement System

Act of 1986 (FERSA) made it possible for the first time for federal employees to create "defined-contribution plans" that employees could invest in a variety of securities of their choice, including equities.

Congress wanted to allow federal employees the benefits of being allowed to invest their retirement funds in equity securities (which, as noted elsewhere in this book, according to all of the long-term analyses, have the best rate of return of all classes of available investment). The creation of FERS was not a simple matter of politics or policy, however. It raised a number of troubling issues, many of which were discussed in congressional hearings. As we have noted, widespread private ownership is viewed as an essential ingredient of democratic government and free enterprise. But the federal government already exerts enormous power over the private sector. What would the impact be if we made Uncle Sam the country's largest shareholder as well? Congress was reluctant to give an agency of government – the trustees of the pension fund – power over the private economy. When President John F. Kennedy became angry with the steel companies, he mobilized the government's purchasing power to force them to retract a price increase. What could he have done if the United States was also the steel industry's largest shareholder? (For a suggested scenario, see the Koppers case in point.)

No one wanted to create a system in which federal officials could through purchase or sale of the securities of a particular industry – or, even in an extreme case, a particular company – compel corporate America to comply with or even support the policies of a particular government. No one wanted federal employees with regulatory and enforcement authority over industries and companies to be able to buy and sell and vote proxies in these companies through their pension funds. Would an employee of the Environmental Protection Agency go short on a company he knew was soon to be the target of an enforcement effort? Would an employee of the Food and Drug Administration buy stock in the company whose experimental medication he was testing? Would an employee of the Occupational Safety and Health Administration over- or under-regulate a particular industry depending on what was in his portfolio? The possibilities for abuse were almost endless.

FERSA solved that problem by limiting the options for investment. The law required that equity investments be in an "index" that reflected the economy as a whole. The trustees selected the

S&P 500 and appointed Wells Fargo to administer the equity fund.

That solved the issue of buying and selling, but it left the issue of voting and other corporate governance opportunities. At the legislative hearings on FERSA, the issue was raised explicitly. Republican Senator Ted Stevens from Alaska and former Social Security Commissioner Stan Ross engaged in an illuminating dialogue. It shows that everyone wished to avoid "back door socialism." As a result, FERSA provides simply that: "The Board, other government agencies, the Executive Director, an employee, a member, a former employee, and a former member may not exercise voting rights associated with the ownership of securities by the Thrift Savings Fund."[77]

The trustees were made responsible for management of FERSA's assets and yet were prohibited from being involved in the "ownership" portion of the security. They delegated voting power to Wells Fargo.

The story of the federal retirement system's ownership of equity securities illustrates the fractionalization of ownership. The layers of ownership exemplify the evolution from the individual shareholder to the institutional shareholder.

- Trustees appointed by the President with the consent of the Senate are the legal owner of the interest in Wells Fargo's S&P 500 Index Fund.
- The trustees of the index fund are the legal owners of the portfolio equity securities.
- The federal employee – the beneficial owner – has no right to make a decision about whether to buy or sell stock in a particular company. Indeed, he hasn't even chosen a particular equity index (the FERSA trustees did that); he has only elected to invest a portion of his retirement plan in the equity mode.
- Neither the federal plan trustees nor the federal employee are legally permitted to exercise their ownership rights respecting shares of common stock.
- Ownership responsibilities are dumped onto Wells Fargo. An index fund is committed to market returns. It cannot compete with other index funds on returns. Although there is some competition between various indexes, the major basis for competition is on fees. Index funds save money because they do not have to hire analysts to follow companies and make investment decisions. Whatever resources Wells commits to getting information in order to be able to monitor its portfolio companies effectively make it less competitive both with other index funds and other

modes of equity investment. In addition, it faces the "collective choice" and "free rider" problems mentioned in the discussion of the prisoner's dilemma.

It is hard to consider an individual federal employee as the owner of portfolio companies. His interest is fractionalized among 500 companies and he is forbidden by law to make any decision with respect to the shares of a particular company. Those who are entrusted with "ownership" responsibility have a pervasive economic disincentive to discharge them in a substantively meaningful way.

Furthermore, the federal government has not confronted its own massive underfunding problems. "If the government were forced to adhere to the same accounting standards (as private funds), retirement programs for civilian and military employees would be underfunded by more than $1 trillion. What's more, if Uncle Sam were required to reserve for pensions as they are accrued by workers – the way corporations are – the federal budget deficit would be roughly one-third higher.... Thanks to aging baby boomers within the civil service, the funds needed to cover annual benefit payments by 2010 are expected to nearly triple, to $160 billion."[78]

## TIAA–CREF

The Teachers Insurance and Annuity Association–College Retirement Equities Fund (TIAA–CREF) is in a category of its own, a pension fund that is neither quite public nor quite private. The $125 billion fund manages pension money for 1.5 million teachers and other employees of tax-exempt organizations. It has $52 billion in equity securities. Its size and its unique position have given it unusual freedom from commercial or political restrictions on involvement with corporate governance. It is therefore not surprising that it has often been first, if not most visible, with shareholder initiatives. Its proposal to put International Paper's poison pill to a shareholder vote was the first such proposal by an institutional investor to be voted on. And it pioneered the "preferred placement" initiatives, asking companies not to offer preferred equities to "white squires" without shareholder approval.

In 1993, the fund announced a broader program, and released a detailed list of their corporate governance policies, saying that "TIAA–CREF acknowledges a responsibility to be an advocate for improved corporate governance and performance discipline."[79]

The policies provided the basis on which TIAA–CREF said it intended to pursue all of their portfolio companies. "The significance is not the three or four laggards you catch – it's that you get the herd to run," said Chairman John Biggs. "We need to scare all the animals."[80] One "animal" scared by TIAA–CREF in 1995 was the board of W.R. Grace, which adopted reforms including the ouster of its CEO and Chairman, following complaints by TIAA–CREF.

TIAA–CREF's policy statement focused on the board of directors. The policy statement encouraged boards with a majority of outside, independent directors, and said that key board committees should be made up exclusively of independents. Moreover, TIAA–CREF did not believe that directors who have other business dealings with the corporation (as a legal representative for instance) should be considered independent.[81] Biggs said that the fund would be willing to withhold votes for directors "where companies don't have an effective, independent board challenging the CEO."[82]

The policy statement also gave considerable space to a discussion of executive compensation issues – specifically, determining what constitutes "excessive" compensation, evaluating the soundness of policies and criteria for setting compensation, and deciding what constitutes adequate disclosure. There is some irony in the fact that CREF's own 1993 proxy statement, issued to its plan participant/shareholders, included a shareholder resolution concerning the executive compensation at CREF itself, complaining about the CEO's salary of over $1 million a year.

## PRIVATE PENSION FUNDS

The largest category of institutional investors is pension funds managed for the benefit of employees of private companies. ERISA, the law that governs private pension funds, was intended to encourage private companies to create pension plans, and to protect the money in those plans once they were created. The statute was designed to resolve questions of conflicts of interest and liability that had left the private pension system uncertain, even chaotic. The two public interest problems it was designed to solve were underfunded pensions and unvested pensions. "These are the institutions then that create the distinctive ERISA problems: funding, with managerial direction of the funds, and underfunding, with government guarantees of performance."[83]

ERISA funds are most often handled by outside money managers who range from one extreme to the other in their focus on proxy voting. A recent trend, endorsed by the Business Roundtable, is for plan sponsors to leave other aspects of the fund management outside, but to take the proxy voting in-house. Given the natural pro-management outlook of people who are, after all, part of management, this can be expected to result in more consistently pro-management votes. But in all cases, whether the money is managed in-house or outside, "The brute fact that managers control their own firms' pensions is central. Few managers want their pension more active in the corporate governance of the firm . . . Although arising from other intentions, (ERISA's) doctrines fit well with managerial goals of shareholder passivity."[84]

Despite their size, ERISA funds face the same problem of "collective choice" and "free riders" that all shareholders do: Can it be prudent for them to expend resources, knowing that, without the ability to communicate with other shareholders, any positive results are unlikely? Even if the results are positive, any returns to the active shareholder will only be proportionate to its holdings, all of the other shareholders getting a free ride.

For private pension funds, perhaps, this problem is presented most sharply. To the extent that a company's pension department adopts an activist posture with respect to portfolio companies, it risks retribution: retaliation in the marketplace and invitation to other pension professionals to take an equally aggressive view of their own functioning. All the more reason, then, to do nothing, to try to maximize value by trading, despite the fact that all evidence indicates that the majority of those who do so fail to outperform the market.

ERISA fiduciaries must meet all of the obligations of prudence and diligence that any trustee must meet under the common law. The ERISA statute starts with that standard and then imposes obligations beyond those of traditional trust law. One reason for the additional obligation is that ERISA permits a "non-neutral fiduciary,"[85] which would not be allowed under the common law of trusts. Under traditional trust law, the first requirement for a trustee is that he or she must be "neutral," and must have no conflicts of interest that would interfere with the ability to administer the trust assets in the sole interest of the trust beneficiary. But it is a fact of ERISA that in pension plans, unlike traditional trusts, there is an inevitable and inherent conflict of interest. Employers and employees are both settlors (the party that provides the pension) and beneficiaries (the party that receives the pension). And the plan sponsor is the party at risk of having to make up the difference if the plan is poorly run, even if there is no negligence, a level of risk that a "neutral" trustee does not have to face.

ERISA requires that a "named fiduciary"[86] with responsibility for the plan be designated by the company, called a "plan sponsor."[87] Typically, a major corporation designates a committee of the board of directors as the "named fiduciary." ERISA recognizes that these people are too busy and important to watch over the pension fund money, so it permits them to delegate authority (and responsibility and potential liability) to an investment manager. So long as the selection of the investment manager is prudent, and the plan sponsor monitors its performance, the plan sponsor company will not be liable for the investment manager's mistakes. The standard is utterly process oriented. As long as there is a reasonable process, and it is followed, the Department of Labor (DOL) will not second-guess the results. This applies to all investment decisions, whether buy-sell decisions or decisions on the exercise of proxy voting and other governance rights.

The passage of ERISA in 1974 put the fear of God into trustees of private systems. There was almost as much of an impact on the public systems, which usually *de facto* hold themselves to the ERISA standard, at least in terms of process. With liability avoidance as the primary goal, the trustees developed the practice of hiring consultants of all kinds and shapes to advise the trustees. By and large these consultants have succeeded in placing a floor beneath which the trustees feel they cannot go. The stress is on "process." The "process" is simple: "Walk slowly and cover your tracks." (This is reflected in the conclusions of O'Barr and Conley cited above.) And this is the basic message of consultants' elegant presentations, often in exotic locales, to which pension fiduciaries are invited, all designed to shield the trustees from liability no matter what actually happens with their investments.[88]

ERISA funds have not been noticeably active in exercising ownership rights. The issues of pension fund management (and the small subset of issues that come up for a vote on proxies) are remote from whatever goods or services the plan sponsor company produces, so it is easier to file the pension fund away under "human resources."[89] And, as we have seen in the case of the public pension funds, meaningful exercise of the ownership rights of private pension assets is thankless. No investment manager, in-house or outside, ever got paid extra for voting proxies well, because that would mean a number of votes against management recommendations. For that reason, the ERISA funds have been among the least visible of institutional shareholders.

There is some evidence of change, however. In 1991, departing from their usual pro-management line, the ERISA funds sharply distinguished themselves from at least some traditional management positions in the letter to the SEC from the Committee on Investment of Employee Benefit Assets (CIEBA).[90] CIEBA's 40 members are corporate benefit plan sponsors, representing $600 billion in collective assets managed on behalf of eight million plan participants. The letter gave guarded backing for proxy rule changes that were often opposed by top company managements. For instance, CIEBA said that any changes to the proxy process should include giving shareholders a vote when companies want to adopt a "poison pill" or other antitakeover defenses.

### Cases in Point: Campbell Soup, General Motors

> **Campbell Soup** In July of 1993, Campbell Soup Company's $1 billion pension fund became the first major ERISA plan to make a commitment to "investing" in shareholder activism. Until that point, institutional shareholder activism had been largely the province of public pension funds. Proud of its own corporate governance structure and record, Campbell's pension fund announced that it would direct the firms managing their pension fund's equity investments to vote their proxies against companies that elect more than three inside directors or reprice stock options after falling stock prices leave them with little value. Campbell's also said it would direct its money managers to vote their proxies to emphasize linking executive pay to performance.

One set of conflicts concerns the contribution of company stock to the pension fund. PPG Industries announced that it would contribute 1.5 million of its shares to its pension fund and Tenneco, Inc. announced that, having already contributed 225,000 of its own shares, it would next contribute the 3.2 million shares it owns in Cummins Engine, Inc., a joint venture partner. A Tenneco spokeswoman said, "It was a way to achieve two things, to bring pension funding closer to where it needs to be, and to do so without using cash."[91] IBM planned to put up to 15 million shares into its pension fund. Chrysler contributed 30 million shares to its pension plans in 1991, when the stock was trading at around $10 a share, about one-fifth of what it was three years later. A

Chrysler executive supports this approach: "The beauty of contributing stock to your pension fund is that the act of contributing increases the equity base of the company, and if, in fact, the stock appreciates in value, the benefit goes to the pension fund."[92] An executive at another company noted that his company saved time and investment banking fees by contributing stock to the pension fund instead of presenting it to the public equity market. But none of them mentioned any benefits to plan participants.

Westinghouse contributed 22 million shares trading at $16.50 in 1991, about three dollars a share more than the stock price in 1994, when the company contributed a further 16 million shares. On the other hand, Xerox guidelines prohibit such donations. "We feel there is enough exposure on the part of the employees to the fortunes of Xerox, and there ought not to be additional exposure through the pension fund," said Myra Drucker, assistant treasurer.[93] This is a good example of the problems of the "non-neutral fiduciary," because what is best from the perspective of the corporation's financial structure (forced sale of company stock to the friendliest and longest-term possible hands), may not be best from the perspective of the plan beneficiaries, whose pension money is tied up in stock that may not be the best possible investment.

## Case in Point: "Universal Widget"

Universal Widget's pension plan holds the largest block of the company's stock. Universal's performance has been very poor over the past ten years, following a series of disastrous acquisitions and declining market share. The plan trustee is a major bank that also handles Universal's commercial accounts. It routinely votes the proxies in the pension fund for management. Under what circumstances do "prudence" and "diligence" require action on the part of the trustee, either shareholder proposals, withholding votes for the board, or more aggressive initiatives? In other words, how bad does it have to get?

Many observers are concerned that the pension system may require a bail-out that will make the savings and loan crisis look small. In 1993, the Pension Benefit Guaranty Corporation, a federal government agency that insures private pension systems, announced that the unfunded liabilities of just the worst 50 pension plans alone grew 31 percent over the previous year, to $38 billion, of which $31.7 billion is guaranteed by the PBGC (and the tax-payers).

If fiduciaries are genuinely "required" to vote independently, it will be all but impossible for commercial conflicts to interfere. Mark Roe says that "ERISA's key fiduciary restraint is *not* to force passivity but to *reinforce* whatever the prevailing practice is. ERISA mandates imitation." He recommends consideration of four possible changes to ERISA doctrine to enable more effective shareholder monitoring: a safe harbor specifying that an ERISA fiduciary could meet its diversification goals with "say, 20 or 50 stocks in different industries," "netting" for big block investments (absent wrongdoing), limiting the liability of pension funds to the business judgment rule for boardroom actions, and scrutinizing pension managers more carefully when they have conflicts of interest stemming from their position as corporate managers.

## THE SLEEPING GIANT AWAKENS: SHAREHOLDER PROXY PROPOSALS ON GOVERNANCE ISSUES

As noted above, some institutional shareholders became more active in exercising the rights of share ownership in the late 1980s. Initially a reaction to the abuses of the takeover era, this activism gained a life of its own as it focused on performance – and on boards of directors as the place to go when performance was unsatisfactory.

The reach and power of this trend can be seen in the number of shareholder proposals and the number of votes in favor of them. For many years these proposals were the exclusive province of legendary corporate "gadflies" like the Gilbert brothers, Evelyn Y. Davis, and Wilma Soss. Soss inspired the delightful play (later a movie) "The Solid Gold Cadillac," still remarkably relevant to current corporate governance issues.

This small group, cheered on by a few, ridiculed by more, and dreaded by corporate management, really created the field of shareholder activism. In 1932, the late Lewis Gilbert attended the annual meeting of New York City's Consolidated Gas Co. Gilbert was unhappy with the chairman's refusal to recognize shareholder questions from the floor. He and his brother John Gilbert began buying stock (their investment policy was "never sell") and attending meetings. Their actions led to the SEC's adopting rule 14a-8 in 1942, giving shareholders the right to have their proposals included in the company's proxy statements. The early gadflies began submitting shareholder resolutions on corporate governance topics like executive compensation, cumulative voting, and the location of the annual meeting.

Their approach was noted with approval by public interest advocates in the 1960s, and the range of topics for shareholder proposals expanded beyond the governance realm into social activism. Public pension funds, union pension funds, and church groups sponsored shareholder resolutions on "social policy" issues like investment in South Africa or the sale of infant formula. The vote of less than 3 percent for Ralph Nader's 1970 "Campaign GM" shareholder proposals was hailed as a victory of unprecedented levels for a shareholder initiative. These groups have continued to submit social policy proposals, which have received votes of up to 20 percent. Some of these proposals have become something of a hybrid, combining elements of social policy and corporate governance. These include proposals regarding tobacco, defense manufacturing, environmental issues, South Africa, and Northern Ireland. Many of the resolutions sponsored on these subjects are sponsored by members of the Interfaith Center on Corporate Responsibility, an organization that promotes corporate social accountability. Typically, social proposals achieve a 7–10 percent vote from shareholders.

Other proposals in this category concern the employment practices of the corporation. In 1993, US District Court judge Kimba Wood overturned the SEC's determination that Wal-Mart did not have to include a shareholder resolution asking the company to issue a report in its affirmative action and equal employment opportunity programs. The resolution was sponsored by the Amalgamated Clothing and Textile Workers Union and several church groups.[94] The SEC found that the proposal concerned "ordinary business," which, as the exclusive province of corporate managers, was not appropriate for shareholder initiatives. This was a reversal of the SEC's policy before 1991, when they viewed employment issues as raising important policy questions. Judge Wood agreed with the earlier view. Similarly, in 1993, the New York City Employees Retirement System (NYCERS) sued the SEC after the agency allowed Cracker Barrel Old Country Store Inc. to exclude NYCERS' resolution asking the company to rescind its policy prohibiting gay employees. The SEC agreed with Cracker Barrel that the issue came under the heading of "ordinary business" and was thus not suitable for shareholder comment. NYCERS argued that the issue had broader economic implications: "Limiting the available talent pool from which a company can choose employees and managers puts that company at a disadvantage in the labor marketplace" said NYCERS chairwoman, Carol O'Cleireacain.[95]

The United Shareholders Association (USA), founded in 1986 by T. Boone Pickens, had thousands of members in all 50 states and became a powerful force for activism by individual investors, providing information about companies, issues, and the mechanics of filing. USA members filed a large proportion of the shareholder resolutions each year, and USA was instrumental in persuading the SEC to amend the proxy rules and was a prominent commentator on executive pay issues. It announced that it would close down in 1993, but many of its members promised to continue its fight. One group, the Investors Rights Association of America, submitted 60 proposals in 1995, and received votes from 35–63 percent.

By the late 1980s, many major companies, particularly poorly performing companies, routinely had at least one shareholder resolution, sometimes as many as five or six, submitted by individuals, union pension funds, church groups, and public pension funds. Even though virtually all shareholder resolutions are precatory only, companies have increasingly responded to them, often negotiating with proponents so that the proposals are not voted on at the annual meeting. USA found, in its last year, that 29 of 50 resolutions were withdrawn after successful negotiation. CalPERS found that eleven of the twelve companies they targeted were prepared to make concessions.

As institutional investors began to use governance resolutions to fight disenfranchising antitakeover devices corporate management installed to protect themselves from changes in control, the levels of support grew. A little more than 20 years after Campaign GM, shareholder resolutions routinely get votes ranging from 20 to 40 percent, and occasionally even get majority support. In 1987, the first corporate governance resolutions from institutional investors (mostly relating to poison pills) were submitted at 34 companies, with votes in favor ranging from about 20 to 30 percent. A year later, two of these resolutions got majority votes, one concerning a poison pill, one prohibiting payment of greenmail. Both were at companies where proxy contests for control provided a good deal of visibility (and engendered a good deal of shareholder support). The more significant development that year, though, was the "Avon letter," issued by the DOL on February 23. As described in greater detail below, it was the first formal ruling by the agency with jurisdiction over the ERISA funds that the right to vote proxies was a "plan asset." Money managers across the country began to establish procedures and policies for voting proxies.

But the following year, in 1989, there was the first proxy contest that was not over director candidates, but over corporate governance.

## Case in Point: Honeywell

A large individual shareholder of Honeywell joined with two public pension funds and Institutional Shareholder Services, Inc.,[96] to prevent management from adopting two of management's proposed changes. The company wanted to stagger the election of directors and to eliminate the right of the shareholders to act by written consent, instead of waiting for the annual meeting. The *ad hoc* coalition circulated its own proxy card and was successful at preventing management from getting the necessary level of support. Over the three-month period of the initiative, Honeywell common stock rose 22 percent, with each state of the contest sparking a favorable market reaction. While takeover rumors played a role, the market clearly recognized the value of active shareholder involvement in an underperforming company. The individual investor who paid the costs of the solicitation got a substantial return on his investment in activism – as did the other Honeywell shareholders.

In 1990, shareholder resolutions on governance, mostly from public pension funds, continued to receive growing support. Two resolutions got majority votes, the first majority votes without a formal proxy solicitation. But the most important corporate governance issue of the year was the battle over Pennsylvania's controversial new antitakeover law. Like most states, Pennsylvania adopted new laws to protect companies incorporated there from takeovers. But it went further, with a second set of amendments, when local company Armstrong World became a takeover target. The 1990 amendment was objected to so strongly by shareholders that nearly one-third of the state's companies (including over 60 percent of the Fortune 500 companies located in the state) opted out of at least one of its provisions.

In 1991, there was an unprecedented level of cooperation and negotiation between shareholders and managements. Many of the shareholder resolutions submitted by institutional investors were withdrawn, following discussions with management and agreed-upon changes. Representatives of the shareholder and corporate community negotiated a "Compact Between Owners and Directors" that was published in *Harvard Business Review*.

Significant as the Compact was, however, the 1991 proxy season demonstrated that managements and investors had not become instant bedfellows. One of the top governance stories of the year was Robert Monks's proxy contest for one board seat at Sears, Roebuck.

And in the same year, for the first time, a corporate governance issue exploded, leaving the business pages to land on the front pages, the editorial pages, even the comic pages. The issue was, of course, executive compensation (see discussions in chapter 4). Even the business press used terms like "obscene" and "out of control" in describing the level of pay received by some top executives. Politicians and the mass media made it a central issue. And shareholders came full circle, with shareholder proposals reminiscent of the proposals by the Gilbert brothers, half a century ago. In 1991, ITT CEO Rand Araskog's pay increased by 103 percent to more than $11 million, in a year when ITT's shareholders watched the value of their stock decline 18 percent. Pressure from shareholder groups led the company to overhaul its compensation scheme for the top 500 employees, with very positive effects on the company's stock price. Also in 1991, the SEC reversed its long-term policy and allowed shareholder resolutions about pay. It gave the go-ahead to ten resolutions, all submitted by individual shareholders.

These resolutions were presented at annual meetings in the spring of 1992. While none got a majority vote, they all received substantial support, and one got 44 percent. Overall, though, the volume of shareholder proposals was down in 1992, largely because both shareholders and management were more interested in trying to find common ground through less confrontational methods. Many individual and institutional investors withdrew their proposals after successful negotiations.

CalPERS, long at the vanguard of institutional shareholder activism, announced itself "kinder and gentler," and did not submit any shareholder resolutions that year. Instead it targeted a dozen underperforming companies, many with compensation schemes that had several of their widely distributed list of "danger signals" developed for them by compensation guru Graef Crystal. Although some companies stonewalled CalPERS (until their failure to respond was reported in the press), many of the companies were willling to meet and negotiate.

Boards of directors did respond to the increased levels of shareholder activism, and not just in making concessions to avoid shareholder resolutions. In just over twelve months – between October 1992 and December 1993 – the CEOs of no less than six major companies were pressured to resign in light of the long-term under-performance of the companies they managed. The six companies were:

- General Motors
- American Express
- Westinghouse
- IBM
- Eastman Kodak
- Borden Inc.

They were followed by the departures of the CEOs of K-Mart, Morrison-Knudson, and W.R. Grace. These oustings represented nothing less than a sea-change in American governance. Boards of directors were finally holding managements accountable for poor performance. The "Pharonic" CEO had given way to the fired CEO.

## FOCUS ON THE BOARD

It was clear in 1992 and 1993 that large institutional shareholders, legislators, and even the corporate community had begun to look to boards to provide a more independent review of corporate performance, direction, and strategy. CalPERS CEO Dale Hanson told a group of corporate managers, "We are no longer into CEO bashing. We are now into director-bashing."

From the shareholder perspective, the "just vote no" strategy became an increasingly important mechanism for sending a vote of no confidence. The 1 percent "withhold" vote at ITT in 1991 was overtaken in 1992 by 2 percent withhold votes at Dial and GM, 3 percent withhold votes at American Express, 4 percent at Westinghouse, Unisys, Occidental Petroleum, 6 percent at Sears and Travelers, and a stunning 9 percent at Champion International.

Further concerns about the board have been reflected in share-holder resolutions calling for separate individuals to serve as chairman and CEO, compensation and nominating committees to be entirely made up of independent outside directors, and an overall majority of independent outside directors on the board as a whole.

Then New York State Comptroller Edward V. Regan circulated a proposal to permit large shareholders access to the company's proxy statement for brief evaluations of the performance of the board. In 1992, Robert Monks submitted a shareholder proposal at Exxon which would permit the creation of a Shareholder Advisory Committee, a group of shareholders, elected by shareholders, to meet (at company expense).[97] This group would be permitted to include its comments on the company in the corporate proxy statement. The California Public Employees' Retirement System negotiated the creation of such a committee with Ryder, and is currently discussing similar committees with other companies.

## SEC'S PROXY REFORM

But the most significant development since the original adoption of the rules governing shareholder proposals was probably the October 1992 adoption of the SEC's proxy reform rule amendments. The initial proposal, in 1991, elicited an avalanche of comments. Nearly every representative of management objected; nearly every representative of shareholders supported them. The new rules make it easier for shareholders who are not seeking control of a company to communicate with each other. Previous rules required any shareholder who wants to communicate with more than ten other shareholders to have his comments approved by the SEC before they could be circulated. The new rules eliminated the SEC's role as editor/censor of this material, and required only that a copy be filed. Other aspects of the proposal made it easier for shareholders to get their material to each other.

The new rules will make possible more effective shareholder oversight. But managers, directors, and shareholders must keep in mind that just as shareholders' liability is limited, so is their agenda. The rules governing the appropriate topics for shareholder resolutions have not changed, and the SEC shows no indications of changing them in the future. Shareholders do not have the expertise, the resources, or the right to get involved in matters of day-to-day management, and should not become involved in second-guessing "ordinary business." Indeed, such involvement is currently prohibited by sections of the proxy rules that are not under consideration for change.

But as Benjamin Graham and David L. Dodd argued over a half century ago, shareholders do have the right and responsibility to focus their attention on matters where "the interest of the officers and the stockholders may be in conflict," including executive compensation.[98] Developments since the time of Graham and

Dodd have shown that shareholders must also be vigilant about preserving the full integrity – and value – of their stock ownership rights. For example, their right to vote may be diluted by a classified board or by dual class capitalization, and their right to transfer stock to a willing buyer at a mutually agreeable price may be abrogated by the adoption of a "poison pill." (For a discussion of "poison pills" and other devices adopted during the takeover era that encroached on the rights of shareholders, see chapter 3.) These kinds of issues present conflicts of interest not contemplated at the time of Graham and Dodd's first edition, as shareholders are interested in accountability and officers and directors are interested in protecting themselves. Even if poison pills are good, there is a potential conflict of interests between shareholders and management in the design and timing of a pill. For that reason, shareholders argued that they should be submitted to a shareholder vote.

Of course, the shareholders' most important function as monitors concerns their election of the directors. As noted above, the "just vote no" strategy is an increasingly important way for shareholders to send a message of concern about the performance of a company or its board of directors. Company proxy statements reveal information about whether individual directors attend 75 percent of the meetings, how much stock they own, which committees they serve on, whether they have other financial connections to the company. Shareholders can withhold votes for directors who do not attend meetings, who hold no stock, who serve on committees that approve bad compensation schemes, or who have conflicts of interest. While even a majority of "withhold" votes cannot keep an unopposed director candidate off the board, it can send an effective message to the board, to management, and maybe even to members of the financial community who may be considering running a dissident slate.

As we have shown, institutional investors are transforming the world of corporate governance. The issues they must consider in voting proxies are more complicated and diverse, with economic and fiduciary consequences to consider and evaluate. The priorities of the institutional investor community are evolving quickly, past the secondary (and reactive) issues of poison pills and staggered boards and toward the central (and active) concerns of board composition, independence, and effectiveness. The "New Compact Between Owners and Directors," drafted by a committee of shareholder and management representatives, shows the commitment by both parties to better board oversight.

It is not only the shareholder community that has changed in the last decade. The corporate community has also changed, in response to the increased ownership focus of shareholders, even in cases where shareholders have not taken any overt action. John Wilcox of Georgeson, one of the leading proxy solicitation firms, reports that many of his clients decided not to make certain changes that would require shareholder approval, after Georgeson advised them that they would have trouble getting a majority vote.

Many companies are restructuring their boards of directors in response to governance concerns raised by the shareholder, financial, and legal communities. SpencerStuart's annual Board Index (analyzing board trends and practices at 100 major companies) shows some dramatic shifts. Over the past five years, as a result of direct shareholder activism and of indirect pressures, there has been a net loss of 91 inside directorships and a net gain of two outside directorships. The median ratio of outsiders to insiders is now 3:1, and more than a quarter of the boards in the study had a ratio of 5:1 or greater. Only seven of the boards in the survey had a majority of inside directors. A survey of 653 CEOs conducted by the National Association of Corporate Directors revealed virtually unanimous support for "small, pro-active, informed and truly independent boards."[99] In many cases, companies have responded to shareholder resolutions asking for a majority of independent directors on the board, by agreeing without putting the proposal to a vote.

## INVESTING IN ACTIVISM

The changes in the SEC rules and in the size and kind of shareholder have changed the cost-benefit calculus of shareholder activism. The Gordon Group's *Active Investing in the US Equity Market: Past Performance and Future Prospects* (December 2, 1992) provides the most persuasive analysis to date of the value to be realized from effective shareholder activism. The report, which combines its own ground-breaking research with an exhaustive study of the massive traditional literature on the subject and considers several new approaches, concludes that, "a partnership catalyzing such activity [proxy initiatives, board candidacy] can expect to provide a return substantially above the baseline expected return on a passive equity investment." The report goes on to quantify this potential return as up to 30 percent in excess of the S&P 500.

Several sources cited earlier lend strong support to the proposition that activism is good for corporate health and shareholder value. Columbia Law School professor Bernard Black has written a thoroughly reasoned and documented argument for the efficacy of ownership involvement.[100] Former US Treasury Department Corporate Finance Director Michael Jacobs forcefully argued in *Short-term America* that poor governance results in a higher cost of capital that in turn inhibits competitiveness.[101] This theme is echoed in Harvard Business School Professor Michael Porter's portion of the Council on Competitiveness report released in June 1992.[102] A similar conclusion, based on global analysis, was reached by the two international governance studies mentioned earlier in this section, Oxford Analytica's Board Directors and Corporate Governance and the Pacific Institute's *Redressing Imbalances in Japanese Corporate Governance*. The Oxford Analytica report, discussed in greater length in chapter 5 of this book, found that in order to compete for capital, corporations will have to give investors more of a role in governance. The willingness of Daimler-Benz to make governance changes to accommodate the requirements of the New York Stock Exchange and Rupert Murdoch's rejection from the Australian Exchange are real-life examples.

In early 1992, and again in 1995, Wilshire Associates' Steve Nesbitt analyzed several years of CalPERS shareholder initiatives and concluded that the effort was highly profitable to the system; the program companies showed a five-year return of 54.4 percent above the S&P 500 index. Significantly, the initiatives did not have to be "successful" (gain majority support) in order to produce those returns.[103] And the market saw other examples of the "returns" on activism. The stock of Sears, Roebuck went up almost 10 percent on the day that the management acceded to shareholder pressure to stick to its core business and divest the financial services divisions. Honeywell stock went up 22 percent during the shareholder opposition to two management-sponsored proposals to decrease accountability to shareholders. Michael Jacobs's second book, published in 1993, argues that shareholders, even individual shareholders, can outperform the market by "breaking the Wall Street rule" and exercising ownership rights instead of buying and selling.[104]

To the extent that it becomes part of the "conventional wisdom" that a corporation with informed and effectively involved owners is worth more in the marketplace than one without them, a burden is placed on pension fund trustees – who are, after all, the majority owners of American corporations – to develop the ability to act as owners. Informed and effective participation by shareholders in today's equity markets requires new structures and procedures. Few exist already, and those are still in the very earliest stages of development.

This gap between governance forms and the reality they confront is not new. In 1960, Harvard law professor Abram Chayes wrote that "Ownership fragmented into shares was ownership diluted. It no longer corresponded to effective control over company operations." He found that there were no "institutional arrangements" that could "make it possible for many scattered individuals to concert their suffrages on issues sufficiently defined to warrant meaningful conclusions about an expression of their will."[105]

## NEW MODELS AND NEW PARADIGMS

In the absence of effective mechanisms for channeling shareholder power, some individuals and institutions have sought a way to hold management accountable – often by joining it.

### Cases in Point: from DuPont to Relationship Investing

Du Pont at General Motors In an article in *Harvard Business Review*, William Taylor held out Pierre S. du Pont (the first in the distinguished industrial lineage) as a large shareholder and chairman of a troubled General Motors corporation. Du Pont was both the substantial owner and the chief executive of the DuPont Company, which in turn owned a substantial stake in General Motors. Acting as an owner, much along the lines Brandeis contemplated for "Junior's" father at Boothbay Harbor, du Pont was able to provide the focus and energy to ensure that General Motors emerged as the dominant force in the world automotive industry for a half century. But du Pont's very effectiveness raised questions. In 1957, in the context of the trust-busting concerns of that era, the United States Supreme Court ordered the DuPont Company to divest itself of its holdings of General Motors on the grounds that the relationship violated the nation's laws against restraint on competition.
Robert Galvin at Motorola Compare du Pont's involvement at General Motors to Robert Galvin's current role at Motorola. Structurally, Motorola has few of the corporate governance provisions that are designed to promote accountability. But Motorola may not need structural accountability as long as it has Galvin, a brilliant man who knows the industry, serves on the board, *and* holds almost $500 million worth of Motorola stock, equal to nearly 2 percent of the company. This model has its own drawbacks, however. When

Motorola's outstanding CEO, George M.C. Fisher left Motorola in late 1993 to head Eastman Kodak, many observers concluded that the Galvin family involvement in the company limited Fisher's prospects for advancement, as Galvin's son Chris seemed likely to become Chairman.

**Rosen at Compaq** A model of ownership similar to du Pont's may be found in the venture capital industry. Venture capitalists provide start-up money to entrepreneurs with ideas for high-technology developments that may not come to the market for years.

Such companies as Apple Computer and Federal Express owed their success to venture capital. But venture capitalists provide more than money. They are involved and informed investors who closely monitor the company, generally hold a seat or two on the board, provide technical assistance, and help attract further capital, directors, managers and suppliers. As one entrepreneur said of his relationship with his venture capitalist: "Think of it as you would marriage."

Sevin Rosen Management, one of the most successful venture capital funds during the 1980s, invested $2.5 million in Compaq when the computer company was still little more than an idea. A few years later, that investment was worth over $40 million.

Sevin Rosen was closely involved with the running of Compaq. Indeed, the company's co-founder, Benjamin M. Rosen, served as the non-executive chairman of the board. Thus Compaq, like General Motors in the 1920s, was headed by a chairman with a significant ownership stake in the company. Rosen's presence proved to be vitally important when Compaq hit some hard times. In Rosen's words:

From [Compaq's] start-up of operations in 1983, we enjoyed an unbroken eight-year run of rising sales, earnings, and stock price. We went from start-up to $3 billion sales in record time, achieved Fortune 500 status in three years, an all-time record, and were flying high. We were recognized for producing PCs with the highest performance and quality, but also with the highest prices. No matter though, for the market clearly was willing to pay up for the best.

And then in the second quarter of 1991, a funny thing happened on the way to prosperity. Our sales flattened, our earnings dropped, and our stock price plummeted. In the third quarter, we faced our first-ever quarterly loss. What had happened was that competition was intensifying and product price was becoming much more important to customers. Yet we were locked in to a product line characterized by high costs and high prices.

Over a period of several months, it became clear that management and the board disagreed sharply over whether the problems we were facing were a short-term peturbation (management's view) or a long-term structural mismatch between the company's product line and the marketplace (the board's view). After intensive study and discussion, the board concluded that only a management change and a corporate strategy revamping would restore the company's growth and profitability.

We effected the changes in October 1991. We installed a new CEO and president, who in turn redirected the company's product strategy, marketing strategy, and, of critical importance, focused on a drastic cost-reduction strategy.

The results of these changes have been electric. As we reported to shareholders just this morning, sales and earnings for the March [1993] quarter were more than double those of a year ago and unit growth more than tripled. Our market share is up substantially, and our stock price has risen from the 20s into the 50s.

**Warren Buffett** Some people think that a modern version of the ideal owner is Warren Buffett, the only person to reach the *Forbes* list of the country's wealthiest people through investments alone. Buffett is chief investment officer and principal owner (with a holding of 44 percent) of Berkshire Hathaway. Shareholders applauded Buffett's willingness to assume the position of chief executive officer in the disgraced banking firm Salomon Brothers (now Salomon, Inc.). He served with equity position, Buffett's involvement has given a "free ride" – or at least a discounted ride – to the rest of the shareholders.

But the ride is not always free, even with Buffett. It shouldn't be. In many corporate investments, Berkshire Hathaway insists on the purchase of a special class of convertible preferred stock, which guarantees a better return than ordinary common stock. In effect, Buffett is reducing the free rider problem by charging a fee for his perceived – and, in the case of Salomon, proven – ability to add value to the company. This may be the ultimate example of the modern-day owner – big enough to make a difference, smart enough to make a valuable difference, and valuable enough to be paid for at least some portion of the difference that his contribution makes.

Buffet is one of the rare examples of a shareholder who is willing and able to intervene on behalf of the whole class of owners in return for some approximation of the value he confers on other shareholders. In his incarnation as holder of convertible preferred stock, Buffett is one model of an ideal modern owner. In July 1989, Buffett rescued Gillette Co. from a hostile takeover bid by Coniston Partners. Buffett paid $600 million for preferred shares paying a guaranteed dividend of 8.75 percent. In 1991, Buffett performed similar rescue missions at possible takeover candidates, USAir and Champion International.

On the other hand, this kind of convertible preferred investment can be viewed as (or used as) an opportunistic entrenchment of existing management, as some of the "white knight" or "white squire" investors were in the 1980s.

**Relationship investing** As discussed in greater detail in chapter 5, in other countries, "relationship investors" provide monitoring that many observers credit for making a substantial contribution to industrial competitiveness. The German Hausbank, with capacity to provide all manner of financing, places its own executives on the supervisory boards of corporations. The bank benefits from this relationship through the payment of fees and otherwise. The Japanese members of a *kereitsu* are financiers, customers, suppliers, and owners of each other. The ownership interest is an entrée to a more profound commercial relationship. Monitoring is not so much a function of ownership, but rather one of preserving a valuable commercial relationship.

In order for this kind of involvement by owners to work, the owner's stake in the enterprise must align his interest with the interest of the shareholder more than his other organizational interests create conflicts.

Even the legendary Buffett is only human and cannot be expected to guide more than a dozen corporations at a time.

The role of activist investor is unlikely to be assumed by any of the categories of institutional investor outlined in this chapter, because each of them faces commercial or political restrictions. Financial institutions are all subject to constraints against owning sufficiently large percentages of the outstanding stock of particular companies. With commercial banks, there is the prohibition of Glass-Steagall; mutual fund holdings are limited by the Investment Company Act of 1940; insurance companies are limited by state law; private pension plans are required by ERISA to diversify as widely as possible; the federal system under FERSA is limited to equity investment through index funds. These provisions, enacted independently, have a cumulative impact of preventing the financial sector executives from being able to exercise control over commercial sector executives – to keep Main Street independent of Wall Street.

Like many barriers, the wall between Main Street and Wall Street was constructed out of mistrust and misunderstanding. It is probably based on what Columbia Professor Mark Roe has recently chronicled as the pervasive American distrust against centralized "money trust" power.[106] But this attitude may be based more in myth than reality. The reality is that Main Street needs Wall Street, and not just its money, more than ever. Unless finance executives can monitor portfolio companies, it is unlikely that a meaningful system of accountability based on institutional investors will be established.

Look at the chief executive of the largest institutional investor, CalPERS. No one, inside CalPERS or inside corporate management, has ever suggested that it would be useful or even appropriate for the CEO of CalPERS to take a role in a portfolio company comparable to that taken by Buffett in Salomon Brothers. It is a question not of expertise but of culture; with public plan officials, one can only ask: Is it possible to make an owner out of a bureaucrat? An employee of a public pension system appears to have none of the characteristics of an owner. The CEO's incentive compensation aside, he bears none of the risk of loss if the value of the investment declines; his own career progress is only tangentially related to the performance of a particular company. Indeed, according to a memorandum prepared by the CalPERS fiduciary counsel, the public pension fund employee is prohibited from becoming a director in the affairs of the company, due to conflicts of interest like restrictions on trading.

Despite this non-owner mindset, public plan officials, even those who preside over index funds, can be credible candidates for some kinds of investor activism. For one thing, they can be counted on to do their duty, in this case their fiduciary duty. To what extent is that duty compatible with the kind of focus and expertise required for meaningful monitoring of corporate performance? As we consider different models of shareholder involvement, we must keep in mind the strengths and the limits of the different categories of investor. Public plan officials face a set of conflicts and a set of impediments to obtaining information different from other institutional investors. This is, in a way, their greatest strength. Their inherent limitations may be what is needed to assure an elementary level of monitoring while protecting against undue interference. A public official, acting as trustee, can insist that a portfolio company perform at or above the level of its peer group. He can insist on a governance structure that will enable the board to do the closer monitoring that is beyond the capability of the shareholders. Indeed, that is what CalPERS and some of the other public pension funds have done over the past few years and – with the additional opportunities made available to them through the revised SEC shareholder communication rules and the increased oversight of pay/performance linkages – what they can be expected to do in the future.

It is interesting to note that although CalPERS had an early and visible role in raising issues of concern with James Robinson of American Express, they did not play a significant role in resolving the issues. The institutional shareholders who pushed Robinson to leave the company were not the public pension plans but the white-shoe Wall Street funds like Alliance Capital and J.P. Morgan. Two very different kinds of shareholders played two very different kinds of roles, each one the other could not play.

CalPERS could play a public role in identifying the problems, but could not follow through with something as specific and even radical as insisting that the CEO step down. This is because CalPERS' equity portfolio is almost entirely indexed, even with limited experimental forays into "relationship investing." In essence, indexed funds replicate the market. Their investment is not based on any particularized knowledge about the individual companies. If they select a target, based on poor performance, they must then invest the time and resources in trying to understand the company and its problems. When CalPERS representatives speak with any CEO about their holdings in the company he heads (and this is rare, no more than a dozen or so each year of the more than 6,000 companies whose securities they hold), they recognize that they own all of that company's competitors, suppliers, corporate customers, potential takeover targets, or acquirers. Given these broad holdings, public pension funds cannot be sufficiently informed about their holdings to make recommendations about strategic issues (assuming they could do so without violating insider trading restrictions, triggering concerns about "pension fund socialism" or exceeding the limits of the legitimate shareholder agenda).

For these reasons, public pension plans can be visible, but they cannot be very specific. For this reason, they focus on issues of process – confidential voting, annual election of directors, the independence of the directors on key committees, and similar issues.

The Wall Street investment firms are on the other end of the spectrum. They are stock-pickers. They buy into the company because of what they know about it, not because it happens to be on the index. Their "investment" in learning about the company is made already; it's a sunk cost. These institutional investors were not willing to take the commercial risks of making public statements or filing shareholder resolutions, but they were willing and able to meet with the new CEO of American Express to insist that James Robinson had to leave. They were rumored to be involved in the departures of CEOs at Borden and some other companies and in the search for a new CEO at IBM even in determining the price of divestitures at W.R. Grace in 1996. This will increasingly be the pattern. After all, these same firms are very used to negotiating what are in essence governance issues on the bond side of the business. As governance is more unignorably translated into value, negotiations will become a part of the equity side as well.

On both sides of the institutional investor spectrum, then, there are potential plausible candidates for at least some forms of active monitoring. But the "carrot" of increased shareholder value is not enough to make it happen, in a world where the collective choice problem and political and economic reprisals present overwhelming obstacles. Neither the public pension funds nor the money managers will be willing or able to act as quickly, as publicly, or as meaningfully as is necessary for optimal monitoring. If ownership must provide more than the primary level of assuring honesty and minimal competency, both will have to follow. Others will have to lead.

## THE "IDEAL OWNER"

In the search for the ideal owner, it is useful to start with Harvard Business School Professor Michael Porter's recent statement about the current American situation.

> Perhaps the most basic weaknesses in the American system is transient ownership, in which institutional agents are drawn to current earnings, unwilling to invest in understanding the fundamental prospects of companies, and unable and unwilling to work with companies to build long-term earning power. . . . The natural instinct of many managers is to seek fragmented ownership to preserve their independence from owners in decision-making. . . . *The long-term interests of companies would be better served by having a smaller number of long-term or near-permanent owners, whose goals are better aligned with those of the corporation.* . . . Ideally, the controlling stake would be in the hands of a relatively few long-term owners. . . . These long-term owners would commit to maintaining ownership for an extended period, and to becoming fully-informed about the company. In return for a long-term ownership commitment, however, must come a restructuring of the role of owners in governance. Long-term owners must have insider status, full access to information, influence with management and seats on the board . . . Under the new structure, management will be judged on the

basis of its ability to build long-term competitive position and earning power, not current earnings of stock price.[107]

Where are the "smaller number of long-term or near-permanent owners, whose goals are better aligned with those of the corporation?" Locating the ideal owner (or its closest approximation in our system) does not permit us to lose sight of the limits of ownership involvement. No one is suggesting that shareholders should second-guess corporate managers on "ordinary business" decisions. The contract between shareholders and the companies they invest in provides, in essence, that in exchange for limited liability shareholders will have a limited scope of authority and a limited agenda. Shareholders are not there to tell corporations how to run their business; they should be there, and they are beginning to be there, to tell corporations that they need to do a better job.

The ideal owner must be someone who has the information, the ability, and the alignment of interests with other corporate constituencies to provide the optimal level of monitoring. It is important to keep in mind, though, that the optimal level of monitoring is in part a function of the narrow range of appropriate issues for shareholder involvement.

The shareholder agenda should focus only on assuring that the interests of directors and management are aligned with those of the shareholder and that when a conflict of interest is presented, the shareholders make the decisions. As Ira Millstein, noted governance authority and advisor to outside directors, has said,

> Where there is a 'problem' company, an institution can ask for meetings with the board, pose the problem, and determine whether the board is dealing with it or ignoring it. . . . In our system, if the shareholder satisfies itself that the board is knowledgeable, diligent, aware of the problems and attempting to deal with them, generally this should suffice.[108]

In order to make this possible, shareholders must be able to act when necessary to preserve the full integrity – and value – of ownership rights themselves. Any ideal shareholder must be vigilant about preventing dilution of the right to vote (by a classified board or by dual-class capitalization, for example) and preserving the right to transfer the stock to a willing buyer at a mutually agreeable price (which could be abrogated by the adoption of a poison pill).

If any institutional investor is to be the ideal owner, the trustees must exercise their ownership rights with the "care, skill, prudence, and diligence" and "for the exclusive benefit" of the retirement plan participants (the employees), the people who are, after all, the real owners. That is the standard for ERISA fiduciaries (very similar to the common law and statutory standards applicable to other fiduciaries as well). This means that the "real owners" have their own obligation to monitor; they must not only delegate to their elected representatives (directors or trustees) the responsibility of safeguarding share value; they must assume part of it themselves. The trustees responsible for monitoring the accountability of corporate managers must themselves be genuinely accountable to their beneficiaries, whether they are elected officials, civil servants, or hired fund managers.

The system of accountability for those who manage institutional funds is not perfect. There are often efforts to dilute the accountability further, as with economically targeted investments. In general, however, it has worked well. New York State's Comptroller is sole fiduciary for the state fund. He is not only accountable as a fiduciary, he is accountable through the electoral process. The State Comptroller is one of four statewide elected officials. While he does not have trustees, he has advisory councils made up of the representatives of beneficiaries and other groups. The CalPERS' CEO meets with his trustees (some of whom are elected by the beneficiaries directly, some appointed by state elected officials) for one week out of each month.

Former New York State Comptroller Edward V. Regan is not so sure that the present state is satisfactory. "This leaves us then exactly where we started. Shareholders, directors, and the public react only after the economic damage has been done, to the detriment of the company and the nation. It leaves us with the activist pension systems presumably without the ability (and maybe the will) to stand up and oppose a company whose performance is deteriorating (not deteriorated), to force that company to turn around by attempting to fire, in a public manner, a prestigious board of directors."[109]

What the public pension funds can do is put the pressure of publicity on the board. The board may very well react (as did the boards of IBM, GM, Westinghouse, and American Express). As Mr. Regan said, "The point is to alert board members that a significant number of shareholders do not believe they are doing their job." Perhaps the shareholder movement's most significant contribution is to make the world an uncomfortable place for a director of an underperforming company.

## PENSION FUNDS AS "IDEAL OWNERS"

*The Economist* sees the ideal owner in activist institutions, ranging from pension funds to brokerage firms:

> So everything now depends on financial institutions pressing even harder for reforms to make boards of directors behave more like overseers, and less like the chief executives' collection of puppets. . . . Financial institutions must also fight to restore their rights as shareholders, lobbying for the dismantling of state takeover restrictions which have provided no protection to workers, only to top managers. Institutions should also demand that shareholder democracy be allowed to operate. . . . But there is more to be done. In the age of the computer, access to shareholder lists should be cheap and simple, not jealously guarded by the boss; that would make it easier to solicit support from other shareholders. Institutions would then be able to use their clout in big firms to elect directors, who would be obliged to represent only their collective interest as owners. Chief executives would still run their firms; but, like any other employee, they would also have a boss. And when they failed at their jobs, they would face the sack.[110]

Public and private pension funds have many of the qualities necessary to play this kind of role. Their ownership, by virtue of their size and their time horizons, is as close to permanent as possible. And because of this near-permanent stake, their interest is far-sighted enough to incorporate the long-term interests of the corporation and (as an essential element of those interests) the interests of the employees, customers, suppliers, and the community.

Leadership cannot come only from the public plans. It must also come from the private (ERISA) plans. In addition to the benefits of size and long-term time horizons they share with public pension plans, they have the additional advantage of greater familiarity with business needs and the financial expertise of professionals whose qualifications price them out of the public plan market. In order for them to serve this role, the "non-neutral fiduciary" who administers the pension fund must recognize that involved ownership is essential to the healthy continuance of the capitalist system – and that it will make them money. And they must be willing to create and support a system with the resources and the insulation from reprisals to do the job.

Exercising ownership rights with regard to a limited agenda, and meeting the requirements of a strict fiduciary standard, means that a trustee voting proxies does not have to know how to make widgets, or even how to improve an underperforming company's widget manufacturing operation or marketing strategy. The trustee must only be able to identify an underperforming company and determine, within the limited options available to the shareholder, which one is appropriate. A meeting with management? A nonbinding shareholder resolution? A vote against a compensation plan that does not provide the right incentives? A "withhold" vote for a board that is not doing its job? Limiting shareholders to a narrow range of substantive concerns and to a narrow range of procedural options is an important protection against abuse.

There is another important protection to limit any possible damage from a trustee who is wrong (whether through inaccuracy or political motivation) in identifying an underperforming company or in selecting a particular mechanism for making changes. Unless the trustee can persuade enough of the other shareholders to support the initiative, nothing will happen, and management will continue to move in the same direction, enhanced by the demonstration of support by a majority of the shareholders.

## IS THE "IDEAL OWNER" ENOUGH?

If we assume something more is needed, some entity that can initiate more than symbolic involvement, what model is appropriate?

One answer may be found in groups like the *ad hoc* "roots group," a collection of pension fund and corporate attorneys that designed the "Compact for Owners and Directors," or "New Foundations," a collection of many of the most thoughtful academics, institutional investors, and corporate executives working in this area that convened by Harvard Law School in 1993. As described by the *New York Times*: "In an attempt to smooth the often contentious relationships between corporations and their shareholders, a group has been formed based at Harvard University, to create a road map for communication without confrontation."[111] This reflects the perspective of convener John Pound, of Harvard's John F. Kennedy School.

Groups like these can improve communications and even develop new standards. But they cannot initiate action to make changes at particular companies. Given the limits on even the most

likely candidates for active monitoring, additional structures may
be necessary. For example, new classes of special purpose securities
can encourage more effective involvement by pension funds. The
kind of preferred shares issued for Warren Buffett in many of the
companies in which he invests can also give institutional shareholders the incentives (and compensation) necessary to reduce the free
rider problem and make active monitoring worthwhile. Pension
funds can take advantage of their size and their limited need for
liquidity by insisting that the market present them with specialized
instruments to meet their situation.

Another possibility is adding the "stick" of enforcement to the
"carrot" of increased value. The Department of Labor could issue
new regulations requiring ERISA trustees to demonstrate that they
have acted "for the exclusive benefit of plan participants" in their
voting and governance actions, including consideration of (and
participation in) more active involvement in corporate governance.
This would reduce the collective choice problem because many of
any company's largest shareholders would be required to consider
shareholder initiatives as an alternative to selling out. Furthermore
it would spread to other institutional investors as well. Once a
fiduciary standard is created and rigorously enforced for ERISA
fiduciaries, other institutional investors tend to follow.[112]

In addition to voluntary action from groups like New Foundations and forced action from regulatory impetus, there are some
options available to shareholders who want to strengthen their
ability to respond to underperforming management and boards.
Two options developed by the authors of this book were designed
to bridge the gap created by the collective choice and free rider
problems – the gap between the level of activism that is optimal
for individual shareholders (even large ones) and that which is
optimal for maximum corporate performance.

The first of these options involves amending the corporation's
by-laws to enable long-term shareholders to monitor the overall
direction of the enterprise. It would require either the board or
(in some states) the shareholders to enact this amendment. The
by-law is designed to permit "rational involvement" instead of
"rational ignorance." The by-law amendment would create a
shareholder committee, made up of a class of "long-term shareholders" (defined in terms of the length and size of their ownership,
perhaps $5 million worth of common shares for three years, per-
mitting groups to form in order to meet the minimum level).
These long-term shareholders would be permitted to nominate

candidates for a special committee. Those candidates would be submitted to a shareholder vote, on the same proxy as the board of directors.

The shareholder committee's primary task would be to exercise control over the board's priorities and composition. This will ensure that they spend their time on issues that are suitable, from the perspective of their abilities, their resources, and their interests.[113]

> Rational apathy, the typical shareholder's attitude toward corporate governance, will not undermine shareholder committees. First, the committees need not participate in directing the company, they will only nominate directors to do the job. *The mere fact that the directors will know that they have been chosen by investors should make them more responsive to shareholder concerns.* Second, the committee should have access to corporate resources to obtain and generate information it needs; individual members need not spend much of their own money. Third, where individual expenses are incurred, they will be justified by investors' large holdings in the company and the utility of the expenses in performing the usual portfolio management functions. There are signs that institutions are willing to perform these tasks.[114]

The committee members would be compensated and have a budget to permit them to retain a lawyer, compensation consultant, accountant, or banker to aid in their task of monitoring the board of directors. Most important, the committee would have access to the company proxy statement for a brief statement of its findings and recommendations, not annually, but possibly once every three years. The objective is to find a balance between allowing ownership to be effectively exercised when it is necessary and allowing it to interfere with "ordinary business." This would not mean that shareholders will start acting as another board of directors or as officers. It would be a mistake to create another self-perpetuating body: a new bureaucracy to monitor an old bureaucracy.

The second option is a new kind of institutional investor, one designed to be the "ideal owner," in partnership with the existing institutions. This would be a partnership organized for the purpose of capturing the profits available due to inefficiencies in the marketplace relating to governance. The partnership would buy shares in undervalued companies, push for governance reforms, and benefit from the value of those reforms. It is what Michael Porter described when he recommended that institutional investors increase the size of their stakes and create special funds to test these new (governance-based) investment approaches. The authors have such a partnership structure, named LENS.

Other investment firms have also focused on turning around underperforming companies, though their strategy has been a little different from that of LENS. They have selected mid-size to small companies, where an investment of $10 million or more buys a significant stake. And in general they have acted more like venture capitalists than mere shareholders, getting seats on the board and becoming involved in the company's operations, with little or no publicity, rather than using governance initiatives and working publicly with institutional shareholders.

Much of the focus of this chapter has been on the incentives, disincentives, and impediments shareholders have in fulfilling their "legendary monitoring role." In order to understand that issue more fully, however, we need to examine it from another perspective, the perspective of those who are "elected" by shareholders and owe the duties of care and loyalty to shareholders. So, in chapter 3, we turn to the board of directors.

## NOTES

1. Quoted in Milton Friedman, *Capitalism and Freedom* (University of Chicago Press, Chicago, 1962), p. 26.
2. "The holder of shares owns no part of the corporate property as such . . . He has, however, an equitable interest in the property, the extent of which interest is determined by the number of shares held." Arthur L. Helliwell, *Stock and Stockholders* (Keefe-Davidson, St. Paul, Minn., 1903), p. 3 (citations omitted). "It is incorporeal and intangible. The interest, thus being abstract, cannot, during the life of the corporation, be reduced to possession" (id., pp. 6–7, citations omitted).
3. Adam Smith, *Wealth of Nations* (Modern Library ed., New York, 1937), p. 423.
4. For a discussion of Chile's privatization policies, see Rita Koselka, "A Better Way To Do It," *Forbes,* Oct. 28, 1991. For a discussion of privatization in Britain see chapter 5, p. 303.
5. John J. Clancy, *The Invisible Powers: The Language of Business* (Lexington Books, Lexington, MA), 1989, p. 10.
6. Alfred F. Conard, *Corporations in Perspective* (Foundation Press, New York, 1976), p. 7.
7. Arthur M. Schlesinger, Jr., *The Age of Jackson* (Little, Brown, Boston, 1945), p. 75.

8. Harvey H. Segal, *Corporate Makeover: The Reshaping of the American Economy* (Viking, New York, 1989), pp. 5–6.
9. Id., p. 6.
10. Id., p. 7.
11. All information for this case study was taken from Alfred D. Chandler, *The Visible Hand: The Managerial Revolution in American Business* (Harvard University Press, Cambridge MA, 1977).
12. David Halberstam, *The Reckoning* (William Morrow, New York, 1986), pp. 227–8 (emphasis in the original).
13. Id., p. 232.
14. Id., pp. 232–3.
15. Id., p. 234.
16. See Edward J. Epstein, "Who Owns the Corporation?" a Twentieth Century Fund Paper (Priority Press Publications, New York, 1986).
17. Adolf A. Berle and Gardiner C. Means, *The Modern Corporation and Private Property* (Transaction Publishers, 1991 ed.), p. 8.
18. The effects of increasing the number of shares, and thus holders, has become increasingly limited due to the rise of institutional investors.
19. Ease of transferability is not a priority for Warren Buffet, whose Berkshire Hathaway trades in four figures per share. But he is a rare exception – most companies split their stock before it reaches $100 a share.
20. Melvin Aron Eisenberg, "The Structure of Corporation Law," *Columbia Law Review*, 89, 7, Nov. 1989, p. 1461.
21. Id., p. 1474.
22. Marlene Givant Star, "Paying for Approval," *Pension and Investment Age*, July 24, 1989, p. 1.
23. Eisenberg, supra, p. 1477.
24. Berle and Means, supra, p. 64.
25. Id.
26. Id.
27. William Z. Ripley, *Main Street and Wall Street* (Scholars Book Company, Kansas, 1972) (reissue of original edition of 1926), pp. 78–9. The quotation from Brandeis is not from his opinions on the Supreme Court, but rather from testimony before the Commission on Industrial Relations, Jan. 23, 1913, p. 7660.
28. See the R.P. Scherer case in point, p. 121.
29. The Department of Labor in 1985 issued a release permitting incentive compensation in limited cases.
30. Daniel Fischel and John H. Langbein, "ERISA's Fundamental Contradiction: The Exclusive Benefit Rule," *University of Chicago Law Review*, Sept. 1988 (55:4), pp. 1105–60.
31. See Henry G. Manne, "Some Theoretical Aspects of Share Voting," *Columbia Law Review*, 64, 8, 1964 pp. 1430–45. Also, Andrei

Shleifer and Robert W. Vishny, "Large Shareholders and Corporate Control," *Journal of Political Economy,* 1986, 94, 31, pp. 461–88.

32. Epstein, supra, pp. 24–5.

33. Albert O. Hirschman noted that deterioration in performance of an institution produces two options for its members and consumers: exit, "some customers stop buying the firm's products or some members leave the organization," and voice, "the firm's customers or the organization's members express their dissatisfaction directly to management or to some other authority to which management is subordinate or through general protest addressed to anyone who cares to listen." See, *Exit, Voice, and Loyalty: Responses to Decline in Firms, Organizations, and States* (Harvard University Press, Cambridge, MA, 1970), p. 4.

34. Nathan Rosenberg and L.E. Birdsall, Jr., *How the West Grew Rich, The Economic Transformation of the Industrial World* (Basic Books, New York, 1986), at p. 229. Emphasis added.

35. Charles D. Ellis, *Investment Policy* (Dow Jones-Irwin, Homewood, IL, 1989), p. 5.

36. Dyan Machan, "Monkey Business," *Forbes,* Oct. 25, 1993, p. 184.

37. Jonathon Clements, "Don't Just Do Something, Sit There," *Forbes,* Dec. 26, 1988, p. 142.

38. Machan, supra, p. 190.

39. Id., p. 188.

40. Id., p. 190.

41. *Guide To A Microfilm Edition of The Public Papers of Justice Louis Dembitz Brandeis.* In the Jacob and Bertha Goldfarb Library of Brandeis University. Document 128. Testimony before the Senate Committee On Interstate Commerce, 62nd Congress, 2nd Session, Hearings On Control of Corporations, Persons, and Firms Engaged in Interstate Commerce, 1(Pt. XVI), pp. 1146–91 (Dec. 14–16, 1911).

42. See Stephen L. Nesbitt, "Study Links Shareholder Proposals And Improved Stock Performance," Wilshire Associates, Feb. 13, 1992; Stephen L. Nesbitt, "Long Term Rewards From Corporate Governance," Wilshire Associates, Jan. 5, 1994; Lilli A. Gordon, John Pound, "Active Investing in the US Equity Market: Past Performance and Future Prospects," Gordon Group Inc., Dec. 2, 1992; Michael T. Jacobs, *Break the Wall Street Rule* (Addison-Wesley, Reading, MA, 1993).

43. Figures from "The Brancato Report on Institutional Investment," 1, 1, Dec. 1993.

44. Includes both Private Trusteed funds and Private Insured funds.

45. "The Brancato Report on Institutional Investment," 1, 1, Dec. 1993. Brancato reports that in 1992, institutional investors held

31.3 percent of their assets in equities, representing a value of $2.6 trillion.

46. Id.

47. Carolyn Kay Brancato, "Breakdown of Total Assets by Type of Institutional Investor, 1989," Riverside Economic Research, Feb. 21, 1991.

48. Mark J. Roe, "Legal Restraints on Ownership and Control of Public Companies," Paper presented at the Conference on the Structure and Governance of Enterprise, Harvard Business School, March 29–31, p. 8.

49. James E. Heard and Howard D. Sherman, "Conflicts of Interest in the Proxy Voting System," Investor Responsibility Research Center, 1987, p. 22

50. Larry Rohter, "Corporations Pass Alumni in Donations to Colleges," New York Times, April 29, 1986, p. A 16.

51. Thomas A. Stewart, "The King Is Dead," Fortune, Jan. 14, 1993, p. 35.

52. Speech of David Ball to the Financial Executives Institute, January 23, 1990.

53. Id., p. 36.

54. Named for Sir Thomas Gresham, the Gresham Law states that bad money will always drive out good.

55. For a discussion of an index strategy, see note 57.

56. Peter Drucker, The Unseen Revolution: How Pension Fund Socialism Came to America (Harper & Row, New York, 1976), p. 1.

57. Joseph Raphael Blasi and Douglas Lynn Kruse, The New Owners: The Mass Emergence of Employee Ownership in Public Companies and What it Means to American Business (HarperBusiness, New York, 1991), p. 3 (emphasis added).

58. The NAPPA Report, 7, 4, Nov. 1993, p. 3.

59. William M. O'Barr and John M. Conley, Fortune and Folly: The Wealth and Power of Institutional Investing, with economic analysis by Carolyn Kay Brancato (Business One Irwin, Homewood, IL, 1992).

60. Id., p. 6.

61. Id., p. 140.

62. Id., p. 78.

63. Id., p. 80.

64. Id., p. 82. One of the public fund mangers interviewed for this book said, describing the reason for the laws establishing the current system, "There was no formal accountability mechanism (before these laws). At that time, there were more than a dozen funds and several hundred million dollars. And at one of the funds in particular, one of the treasurers did a lot of business with a particular broker. And it was a very easy thing to do. I'm not

suggesting that this was a venal form of a scandal so much as it was just falling into what are normal political practices." (Id., p. 83.)

65. Id., p. 85 (emphasis added). See also Pound's piece on Balance in Governance.

66. Thomas A. Stewart, "The King Is Dead," *Fortune,* Jan. 11, 1993, p. 36.

67. Robert Reich, "Of Butchers and Bakers," Address to the Council of Institutional Investors, Oct. 8, 1993.

68. Mark J. Roe, "The Modern Corporation and Private Pensions," *UCLA Law Review,* 41, 1, Oct. 1993, p. 96.

69. Regan, supra, pp. 2, 3.

70. Dale Hanson's speech to the Harvard Business School, Dec. 3, 1992.

71. Paul Sweeney, "How CalPERS Can Ruin a CEO's Day," *Global Finance,* Feb. 1993.

72. E.S. Browning, "Alabama Pension Chief Achieves a Rare Feat: He Stirs Controversy," *Wall Street Journal,* Feb. 4, 1994, p. 1.

73. James A. White, "Divestment Proves Costly and Hard," *Wall Street Journal,* Feb. 22, 1989, p. C1.

74. For example, David Vise, "Va. Pension Fund Hires Too Many Advisers, Report Says," *Washington Post,* Dec. 14, 1993, p. D1; also, David Vise, "DC Pension Plan Mishandled," Washington Post, Aug. 17, 1993; also, David Vise, "City Office Probes Pension Trustee," *Washington Post,* Aug. 16 1993, p. A1.

75. Dr. D. Jeanne Patterson, *The Use of Public Employee Retirement System Resources for Economic Development in the Great Lakes States* (Institute for Development Strategies, Indiana University, 1992), p. 114.

76. Id., p. 118, emphasis in the original.

77. Federal Employees' Retirement System Act of 1986, Section 8438 (g).

78. Editorial, "The Biggest Pension Scofflaw? Uncle Sam," *Business Week,* Dec. 6, 1993, p. 186.

79. TIAA–CREF Policy Statement on Corporate Governance, Sept. 17, 1993.

80. Leslie Scism, "Teacher's Pension Plan to Give Firms Tough Exams," *Wall Street Journal,* Oct. 6, 1993, p. C1.

81. TIAA–CREF Policy Statement on Corporate Governance, Sept. 17, 1993.

82. Scism, supra, p. C1.

83. Roe, supra, p. 83.

84. Id., p. 77.

85. See Daniel Fischel and John H. Langbein, "ERISA's Fundamental Contradiction: The Exclusive Benefit Rule," *University of Chicago Law Review,* 55(4), Sept. 1988, pp. 1105–60.

86. Employees' Retirement Income Security Act (ERISA), 1974, Section 402(a)(2).

87. ERISA, Section 3 (16)(B).

88. Money managers have an incentive to trade shares thanks to the "soft dollar" industry. Soft dollars or soft commissions are those arrangements whereby a fund manager agrees, whether formally or informally, to provide a broker with a certain commission flow each year in return for various financial services, such as analysts' research, portfolio valuation or information systems. Some argue that soft dollar arrangements encourage money managers to trade shares regardless of the value to the ultimate beneficiary.

89. The government seemed to agree – administration of ERISA was given to the Labor Department, not to the Treasury Department.

90. Letter from J. Grills, chairman of CIEBA, to Linda Cane, director of the Division of Corporate Finance, SEC, Feb. 25, 1991. CIEBA is a committee of the Financial Executives Institute, a professional association of 13,500 senior financial executives.

91. Leslie Scism and Albert R. Karr, "Retirees Share in Company Fortunes as Corporations Put Stock in Pensions," *Wall Street Journal,* Nov. 17, 1993, p. C1.

92. Id., p. C22.

93. Id.

94. See Judge Kimba Wood's ruling in *Amalgamated Clothing and Textile Workers Union v. Wal-Mart Stores Inc.*

95. Marlene Givant Star, "SEC Sued in Proxy Dispute," *Pensions and Investments,* March 8, 1993, p. 2. In the fall of 1993, Judge Kimba Wood of the U.S. District Court for the Southern District of New York declared the SEC's decision improper. While its appeal is pending, the SEC must refrain from issuing any more no action letters under the proxy rule (14a-8 (c)7).

96. The authors were, at that time, President and General Counsel of Institutional Shareholder Services, Inc.

97. In 1993, the California Public Employees' Retirement Fund sponsored a similar shareholder advisory committee resolution at Pennzoil Co. The SEC, however, ruled that Pennzoil could exclude the proposal from its proxy because a provision calling for reimbursement of the committee's members contravened Delaware law, Pennzoil's state of incorporation. CalPERS offered to redraft the resolution, but the SEC still refused to demand that Pennzoil include the resolution in its proxy.

98. Benjamin Graham and David L. Dodd, *Securities Analysis* (McGraw-Hill, New York, 1934), pp. 51–511.

99. NACD 1992 Corporate Governance Survey, National Association of Corporate Directors, Washington, DC, 1992, p. i.

100. Bernard S. Black, "Institutional Investors and Corporate Governance: the Case for Institutional Voice," *Journal of Applied Corporate Finance,* Fall 1992.

101. Michael T. Jacobs, *Short-term America: The Causes and Cures of Our Business Myopia* (Harvard Business School Press, Cambridge, MA, 1991).
102. Michael E. Porter, *Capital Choices: Changing the Way America Invests in Industry,* Research Report to the Council on Competitiveness and co-sponsored by the Harvard Business School, June 1992.
103. In Jan. 1994, Nesbitt completed a second study on CalPERS' activism, finding that 24 companies targeted by CalPERS had each lagged the S&P 500 Index by an average 86 percentage points in total for the five prior years. But for the four years subsequent to CalPERS' involvement, those same companies each exceeded the index by an average 109 percentage points. See Stephen L. Nesbitt, "Long Term Rewards From Corporate Governance," Wilshire Associates, Jan. 5, 1994.
104. Michael T. Jacobs, *Break the Wall Street Rule: Outperform the Stock Market by Investing as an Owner* (Addison-Wesley, Reading, MA, 1993).
105. Abram Chayes, in his Dec. 1960 introduction to John P. Davis, *Corporations* (originally published 1897, republished Capricorn Press, New York, 1961), pp. xvii–xviii.
106. Roe, supra, p. 77.
107. Porter, supra, p. 91 (emphasis added).
108. Ira Millstein, "The Evolving Role of Institutional Investors in Corporate Governance," prepared for American Bar Association Panel, Institutional Investors: Monolithic or Diverse?, Aug. 10, 1992, pp. 42–3.
109. Edward Regan, "U.S. Competitiveness: Financial Markets and Corporate Governance," Synopsis of Remarks Delivered at the Conference on Global Views on Performance Measurement, Financial Executives Research Fund, Dallas, Dec. 16, 1992, pp. 4–5.
110. "Getting Rid of the Boss," *The Economist,* Feb. 6, 1993.
111. Leslie Wayne, "Assuaging Investor Discontent," *New York Times,* Feb. 3, 1993.
112. In late 1993, the Supreme Court ruled that group annuities held by insurance companies were subject to ERISA. Peviously, only state regulations applied to such investments. *John Hancock Mutual Life Insurance Co. v. Harris Trust & Savings Bank, as trustee of the Sperry Master Retirement Trust No. 2,* US Supreme Court, Dec. 13, 1993. See also, Albert B. Crenshaw, "Court Backs Curbs on Pension Risks," *Washington Post,* Dec. 14, 1993, p. D1.
113. George W. Dent, Jr., "Toward Unifying Ownership and Control in the Public Corporation," *Wisconsin Law Review,* 1989, No. 5, p. 881.
114. Id., p. 908, emphasis added.

# 3
# Directors: Monitoring

Boards of directors are a crucial part of the corporate structure. They are the link between the people who provide capital (the shareholders) and the people who use that capital to create value (the managers). This means that boards are the overlap between the small, powerful group that runs the company and a huge, diffuse, and relatively powerless group that simply wishes to see the company run well.

The board's primary role is to monitor management on behalf of the shareholders. In this chapter, we will discuss the mechanisms and structures used to keep managers accountable to the board as well as the mechanisms and structures used to keep the directors accountable to the shareholders.

The strength – and indeed survival – of any corporation depends on a balance of two distinct powers: the power of those who own the corporation and the power of those who run it. A corporation depends on shareholders for capital, but reserves the day-to-day running of the enterprise for management. This creates opportunities for efficiencies far beyond what any one owner/manager, or even a group of owner/managers, could accomplish. It also creates opportunities for abuse.

This was the conundrum that almost stopped corporations before they began. Karl Marx and Adam Smith did not agree on much, but they both thought that the corporate form of organization was unworkable, and for remarkably similar reasons. They questioned whether it is possible to create a structure that will operate efficiently and fairly, despite the fact that there is a separation between ownership and control. Adam Smith criticized both those who invested in joint-stock companies, and those who managed them. Of the investors he wrote that they "seldom pretend to understand anything of the business of the company"; and of the directors, he said: "Being the managers of other people's money rather than of their own, it cannot well be expected that they should watch over it with the same anxious vigilance with which the partners in a private co-partnery frequently watch over their own."[1] Put another way, is there any system to make a manager care as much about the company's performance as a shareholder does?

Corporations cannot be run by consensus. Managers must be given the power to make decisions quickly and to take reasonable risks. If every managerial decision had to be communicated to the company's owners, much less ratified by them, industrial progress would be paralyzed, and everyone would lose.

Yet while shareholders delegate substantial powers to management, they need assurance that power won't be abused.

The single major challenge addressed by corporate governance is how to grant managers enormous discretionary power over the conduct of the business while holding them accountable for the use of that power.

Shareholders cannot possibly oversee the managers they hire. A company's owners may number in the tens of thousands, diffused worldwide. So shareholders are granted the right to elect representatives to oversee the management of the company on their behalf – the board of directors. Directors are representatives of owners (or, in closely held companies, the owners themselves), whose purpose under law is to safeguard the assets of the corporation.

The board acts as a fulcrum between the owners and controllers of a corporation. They are the middlemen (and a very few middlewomen!) who provide balance between a small group of key managers based in corporate headquarters and a vast group of shareholders spread all over the world. In theory, at least, the law imposes on the board a strict and absolute fiduciary duty to ensure that a company is run in the long-term interests of the owners, the shareholders. The reality, as we will see later in this chapter, is a little less certain.

## A BRIEF HISTORY OF ANGLO-AMERICAN BOARDS

US boards carried on a tradition that began with the earliest form of corporate organization, the joint stock companies. In the British colonies, as in Great Britain itself, the group of people who oversaw the company would meet regularly. Fine furniture was expensive in those days, and few people in trade had chairs or tables to contain the group. So the men sat on stools, around a long board laid across two sawhorses. The group was named "the board," after the makeshift table they worked at. And the leader of the group, who did not have to sit on a stool, by reason of his prestigious perch, was named the "chair-man."

The first commerce in America was conducted by two British enterprises, operating under royal charter: the Virginia Company of London and the Virginia Company of Plymouth. These companies were governed by two bodies. The first was a local council – a management board of colonists responsible for day-to-day operations in the new land. This council was accountable to a second, more powerful, body in London. This "supervisory board" was answerable to the sovereign, and responsible for more general matters of policy and strategy.

Following the American Revolution, the new republic had to devise its own forms of governance. An early leader was one of the joint authors of the *Federalist Papers,* and the nation's first Secretary of the Treasury, Alexander Hamilton. In November 1791, the New Jersey Legislature passed a bill authorizing Hamilton's "Society for Establishing Useful Manufactures" (or SUM, as it was known). The society was allowed to produce goods ranging from sailcloth to women's shoes.

The governance of Hamilton's corporation was remarkably similar to that of today's largest companies. The Society's prospectus declared: "The affairs of the company [are] to be under the management of thirteen directors." Hamilton also created an early audit committee. He devised a Committee of Inspectors, separate from the board of directors, made up of five shareholders. They were generally chosen from among defeated directorship candidates, though shareholders could elect any five of their fellow stockholders. These inspectors were granted access to the company's books, and given power of review over all the company's affairs.[2]

## TODAY'S TYPICAL BOARD

Hamilton would have no trouble recognizing the corporate board of today. The structure and composition of boardrooms have changed surprisingly little in 200 years. Average board size has remained at about 15, give or take a director or two. Audit committees remain an important force in board life. And most of today's directors come from the same segment of the population as the directors of SUM, the commercial elite.

Nonetheless, organizations that have tracked shifts in board size, composition, and structure see significant changes.

*Size* In 1993 the annual survey of the largest 100 boards conducted by executive search firm SpencerStuart found that boards were shrinking slightly, with half of the boards surveyed having 13 or fewer, compared to the average of 15 in 1988.

*Inside/Outside Mix* SpencerStuart found more outside independent directors, with a net loss of 128 insiders on the boards surveyed over the five-year period. The average was three insiders, but 14 of the boards had only one insider, the CEO.

*Diversity* In 1991, exactly 200 years after the chartering of SUM, consulting firm Korn/Ferry noted "a dramatic rise in the representation of women and minorities." This trend has continued. In its 1993 report, Korn/Ferry noted that the number of boards seating women had risen to 60 percent in 1993, up from 11 percent in 1973. Over the same period, the number of boards with minority representation had increased to 38 percent from 9 percent.[3]

*Meetings* While boards' meeting frequency has declined slightly – the average board met seven times a year in 1992, down from eight meetings a year in 1988[4] – this may be the result of the increased reliance on board committees. The number of committees, number of outsiders on committees, and number of committee meetings have all been increasing.

Most companies have some or all of the following committees:

- Nominating: selects candidates for the board
- Compensation: sets executive pay
- Audit: reviews reports of outside audit firm and oversees internal audit and accounting procedures
- Finance: oversees the investing of the company's funds and reviews the capital needs and allocations of the company
- Executive: approves important decisions between full board meetings

Many companies have other committees whose role is to ensure that the company is a good "corporate citizen." These include: public policy, corporate responsibility, and environment.

*Ownership* From 1990 to 1993, the number of companies providing stock plans for their directors more than doubled. According to SpencerStuart, 20 percent pay some part of the directors' annual retainer in stock, or offer that option.

Board meetings usually follow an agenda compiled by management, though directors can ask for items to be included. The agenda, plus relevant information, is typically sent to directors a couple of days before the meeting.

A meeting may feature a special presentation by a non-board insider, such as a divisional head. Alternatively, the company may schedule special board trips to foreign or regional headquarters.

Some companies schedule special meetings for the outside directors to meet alone, in order to evaluate the CEO and senior managers when they are not present.

## BOARD DUTIES: THE LEGAL FRAMEWORK

The responsibility of today's boards of directors is little different from what it was in Hamilton's day. Compare Hamilton's statement of the role of the board with today's General Corporation Law of the State of Delaware, which reads: "The business and affairs of every corporation organized under this chapter shall be managed by or under the direction of a board of directors."[5] Of course, since Hamilton's day, the legal implications of such statements have been examined and developed in enormous depth. Today, an enormously complex, ever-changing body of law governs the role of the corporate board of directors.

Legally, most jurisdictions describe the director as having two duties, the duty of care and the duty of loyalty. And directors' conduct will be judged according to the "business judgment rule."

*Duty of loyalty* means that a director must demonstrate unyielding loyalty to the company's shareholders. Thus, if a director sat on the boards of two companies with conflicting interests (both trying to buy a third business, for example), he would be forced to resign from one board because clearly he could not demonstrate loyalty to the shareholders of both companies at the same time.

*Duty of care* means that a director must exercise due diligence in making decisions. He must discover as much information as possible on the question at issue and be able to show that, in reaching a decision, he has considered all reasonable alternatives.

When a director can demonstrate that he has acted with all due loyalty and exercised all possible care, the courts will not second-guess his decision. In other words, the court will defer to his *business judgment*. Unless a decision made by directors and managers is clearly self-dealing or negligent, the court will not challenge it, whether or not it was a "good" decision in light of subsequent developments.

Of course, these laws offer only a general definition of the director's role. The law, after all, must be sufficiently flexible to cope with ever-changing business developments that are forever challenging directors with new issues and questions to resolve. As we shall see later, the takeover era of the 1980s caused a fundamental re-evaluation of these concepts.

Many people have tried to step beyond the legal definitions of a board's duties and develop more specific descriptions of the responsibilities of the directors. The Business Roundtable, representing the largest US corporations, describes the duties of the board as follows:

The board of directors has five primary functions:

1. Select, regularly evaluate, and, if necessary, replace the chief executive officer. Determine management compensation. Review succession planning.
2. Review and, where appropriate, approve the financial objectives, major strategies, and plans of the corporation.
3. Provide advice and counsel to top management.
4. Select and recommend to shareholders for election an appropriate slate of candidates for the board of directors; evaluate board processes and performance.
5. Review the adequacy of the systems to comply with all applicable laws/regulations.[6]

Other groups have developed similar lists. The following, for instance, is the guide developed by the American Law Institute:

1. Elect, evaluate, and, where appropriate, dismiss the principal senior executives.
2. Oversee the conduct of the corporation's business, with a view to evaluation on an ongoing basis, whether the corporation's resources are being managed in a manner consistent with [enhancing shareholder gain, within the law, within ethical considerations, and while directing a reasonable amount of resources to public welfare and humanitarian purposes].
3. Review and approve corporate plans and actions that the board and principal senior executives consider major and changes in accounting principles that the board consider material.
4. Perform such other functions as are prescribed by law, or assigned to the board under a standard of the corporation.[7]

These lists, though they differ in emphasis, sum up the generally accepted duties of the board. Beneath such umbrella definitions stand the myriad details that the board might attend to: quarterly results and management's projections for the next quarter; the company's long-term strategic goals; its capital structure; debt financing; resource allocation; the need to buy or sell assets; dividend policy; research and development projects; the status of the corporation's competitors; or the company's global prospects.

Most commentators agree, however, that umbrella definitions do not adequately describe a job that has lofty – and nebulous – responsibilities. The difficulty lies in the fact that although boards of directors are burdened with the responsibility of ensuring that management runs the enterprise efficiently, they are not permitted (as a practical or legal matter) to become intimately involved in the running of the company. The board is there to evaluate performance, and to respond promptly if it is not satisfactory.

The board is not sufficiently involved in the day-to-day decisions of the company to determine how the company should be managed – that is the job of the executives. As one academic comments: "Outside directors likely have the most difficult job of all – not running the store – but making sure that the individuals running the store run the store as well as possible."[8] As a result, many believe that the primary responsibility of directors is to see that they have the best management talent available – the best people to run the store – and to replace them promptly if performance slips.[9]

Other descriptions of a board's responsibility are more general in their approach. Sir John Harvey-Jones, the highly successful chief executive of Imperial Chemical Industries in the United Kingdom during the 1970s and 1980s, sums up the difficulty of defining the director's role:

> Management consultants are there for every conceivable part of the manager's job. But you try getting advice, guidance, a course, or a specialist book on the skills of being a good director of a company, and you will find almost nothing except a great deal of mystique.
>
> The job of the board is all to do with creating momentum, movement, improvement and direction. If the board is not taking the company purposely in the future, who is? It is because of boards' failure to create tomorrow's company out of today's that so many famous names in industry continue to disappear.[10]

From this description, one commentator who has served on many boards describes his role as "creating tomorrow's corporation out of today's."[11]

## THE BOARD–MANAGEMENT RELATIONSHIP

The existence of boards, according to both the legal definitions of the board's role and Sir John's description, is based on the premise that they oversee management, select executives who will do the best job, and fire them when they don't. In other words, management serves at the pleasure of the board. The reality is the exact opposite. Directors are beholden to management for nomination, compensation, and information. Moreover, many directors are unable or unwilling to devote the time or energy necessary to oversee the operation of the company, or to make a financial commitment to its success.

As management guru Peter Drucker puts it, "Whenever an institution malfunctions as consistently as boards of directors have in nearly every major fiasco of the last 40 or 50 years, it is futile to blame men. It is the institution that malfunctions."[12] Allowing so many CEOs to receive gargantuan compensation for mediocre returns is just one symptom of the ineffectuality of boards over the past decade.

In this section we will draw on actual cases to show how various aspects of board organization serve to work against the representation of shareholders.

## INFORMATION FLOW

Directors can never know as much about the operation of the company as management, so they are dependent on being supplied with necessary, accurate, and timely information. Sarah A.B. Teslik, Executive Director of the Council of Institutional Investors, an association representing $650 billion in investment capital, described the problems a director might face in a newsletter to CII clients.

> What if some very clever record keeping is occurring to mask problems that may or may not be detectable by auditors? Or what if a few big customers are angry about problems that could be fixed but haven't yet dropped their accounts (and the leader either doesn't know or doesn't want to reveal this)? Since the outside world can, by and large, detect many of the bigger, or later-stage problems without your help, it is presumably these kinds of nascent or potential problems that you [the director] are mostly there to detect, prevent, or remedy.
>
> But how do you do this if the source of virtually all your information is the leader? The fact is, in too many cases, you don't. Because you can't. Because, under the circumstances, no one can.
>
> There isn't much point in fussing over the definition of an independent director, or the existence or makeup of board committees, or the procedures for electing directors if the information they get is inadequate. What can even the most brilliant and properly moti-

vated director do if he or she lacks needed, accurate, or timely information?[13]

Unfortunately, the corporate history books are full of boards who knew too little too late.

## Cases in Point: RJR Nabisco, Lone Star Industries, Tambrands

**RJR Nabisco** CEO Tylee Wilson spent $68 million developing an ultimately disastrous "smokeless" cigarette without telling the board. As chronicled in *Barbarians at the Gate,* an epic of corporate excess, Wilson's directors were livid that he had far exceeded his spending limits without board approval.

> "Why didn't you tell us about this sooner?" Juanita Kreps demanded. "You trust hundreds of company people working on this project; you trust dozens of people at an ad agency you're working with; you trust outside suppliers and scientists, but you don't trust us," she said. "I, for one, absolutely resent that."[14]

Wilson's successor, F. Ross Johnson, behaved similarly. He handled his board with a combination of lavish perquisites and meager information. He arranged for his directors to rub shoulders with celebrities, use corporate planes and apartments, and even endowed chairs at their alma maters. All this made it hard for directors to push him on tough questions.

Two *Wall Street Journal* reporters described the life of an RJR Nabisco board member: "A seat on RJR Nabisco's board was almost like Easy Street: lucrative directors' fees, fat consulting contracts, and the constant loving care of the company's president and chief executive officer, F. Ross Johnson. "I sometimes feel like the director of transportation," he once remarked, after ordering up a corporate jet for a board member. "But if I'm there for them, they'll be there for me."[15] While he was dazzling his hand-picked directors, who could expect them to complain about his jets and country clubs?

**Lone Star Industries** The Lone Star board ordered a special inquiry into the expenses of CEO James Stewart, following a *Business Week* article that criticized his lifestyle at a time of company cutbacks. The inquiry alleged that Stewart billed the company $1.1 million for "purely personal expenses," including taking his personal music teacher on Lone Star trips to three continents. The nine-man board, including such luminaries as Robert L. Strauss, later Ambassador to Russia, never scrutinized Stewart's expenses. "You make an assumption that the CEO is honest and prudent," said David Wallace, an outsider who succeeded Mr. Stewart. "We didn't know what he was doing." In 1990, Lone Star filed for bankruptcy protection.[16]

**Tambrands, Inc.** On June 1, 1993, Martin F.C. Emmett was fired as the CEO of Tambrands Inc., the manufacturer of feminine hygiene products. Seemingly, his ouster was a routine affair, given the increasingly troubled operations of the company. Market share for Tampax, the company's leading product, had dropped 8 percent since mid-1992, and share value had declined by a third in less than six months. The board apparently fired Emmett after he failed to outline a satisfactory recovery strategy.

Ten weeks after the firing, the *Wall Street Journal* reported that Emmett's departure had opened a walk-in closet full of skeletons. The story demonstrates the extent to which an executive can keep his board in the dark. The *Wall Street Journal* commented that the story raises "murky ethical issues hinged on friendships, business relationships and, ultimately, a board's role in policing corporate operations."[17]

The scandal was based on Emmett's unusually close relationship with two principals in a consulting firm called Personnel Corp. of North America (PCA) – the firm that had originally landed Emmett his job at Tambrands. Immediately after Emmett's departure, Tambrands ended most of its contacts with PCA.

PCA's two principals were long-time friends of Emmett's. During his tenure, he steered contracts worth $2 million to PCA, including compensation, pension administration, and outplacement. Not only did he retain the firm, but the two principals were placed on individual retainers that exceeded the salaries of most of Tambrands' officers.

Emmett's relationship with the PCA executives dated back to the mid-1970s, when PCA principals David R. Meredith and Jack L. Lederer conducted a compensation study for Standard Brands Inc., where Emmett was then an executive. When Standard Brands merged with Nabisco in 1981, Emmett referred PCA to Nabisco, and PCA was awarded a contract. When Emmett left Nabisco to chair the investment banking subsidiary of Security Pacific in New York, PCA followed also.

Even in those days, Emmett enjoyed the trappings of executive privilege. Emmett's boss in the Standard Brands' days was the same Ross Johnson described above, who went on from Standard Brands to be CEO of both Nabisco and, following the merger with R.J. Reynolds, RJR Nabisco. *Barbarians at the Gate* describes Emmett's career at Standard Brands: "Johnson lavished gifts on Emmett, including a luxurious corporate apartment and an unlimited expense account." When Emmett was being hunted to head Tambrands, at least one executive search firm report commented on Emmett's apparent taste for the high life.

Lynn Salvage, a director who left the board in 1991, told the *Wall Street Journal* that once PCA had been retained, the two partners "did everything in their power to get [Emmett] the most lucrative compensation scheme they could."[18] Pearl Meyer, a compensation consultant with her own firm, described the PCA consultants as "very capable and energetic advocates on [Emmett's] behalf."[19] Mr. Emmett's stock options and benefits were more appropriate for a company twice Tambrands size. He received options to buy nearly 600,000 Tambrands shares over the years; in December of 1992 he exercised options for 150,000 shares, which he sold at a profit of over $5 million.[20]

PCA also argued that the board was underpaid. Following this advice, the board voted to increase its annual retainer from $13,000 to $20,000, and to award themselves options on 1,100 shares annually.

Following his ouster, Emmett still had ten years to exercise his remaining 450,000 stock options – a severance package negotiated by PCA in 1992. He currently works from an office provided by PCA in their Connecticut headquarters.

Of course, not many executives try to push the limits as far as the CEOs of RJR Nabisco, Lone Star, or Tambrands. There are few examples of managers actively trying to mislead the board. And not many boards allow themselves to be kept in the dark for so long. However, it is inevitable that executives will be more fully informed than the board, so there is inevitably an obvious problem deciding what information should be shared. At Polaroid, the board was unaware that employee groups opposed swapping various compensation benefits for an enlarged ESOP. Though a court ultimately determined that this information was immaterial, the example shows the kinds of conflicts of interest present in management–board relationships and the effect they can have on access to information and decision-making.

Who has the ultimate responsibility for the corporation? Who is genuinely responsible for a company? And who should have control – management or the board? Legally, the answer is clear; in the final analysis the board has the responsibility for the company and, is, therefore, the ultimate fountain of power. It is in practice, not in law, that the problems arise. Management has the expertise, infrastructure, and time to run and control the company. Given this degree of management domination, how can a board still exercise its responsibility? Can an entrepreneurial, energetic management run the company and at the same time reserve the ultimate control for the board? How do the board and management determine who should wear the "crown"? We believe the board carries more than *de jure* responsibility for the corporation. The paradox is how to allow both bodies to retain effective control without diminishing the initiative and motivation of either. The paradox creates tensions that are vexing for many corporations, causing friction at the top and considerable loss of energy. . . . The complexity of the responsibility for corporate governance requires that management and the board find a comfortable, dynamic, balance of power between them. There will always be tension, but the tension that exists is not altogether bad. Like stress, a certain amount enhances creativity and productivity.[21]

Director Information Checklist: What information should the board have? One veteran board member produced the following list.[22]

- Operating statements, balance sheets, and statements of cash flow that compare current period and year to date results to plan and last year.
- Management comments about the foregoing that explain the reasons for variations from plan and provide a revised forecast of results for the remainder of the year.
- Share of market information.
- Minutes of management committee meetings.
- Key media articles on the company and competition.
- Financial analysts' reports for the company and major competitors.
- Consumer preference surveys.
- Employee attitude surveys.

Robert K. Mueller, former outside chairman of A.D. Little and a veteran director, recently summed it up in his ninth book on boards of directors: "Ignorance is no excuse."[23]

There are ways to ensure that directors are well informed. Home Depot, Inc., for instance, requires its directors to spend at least one full day a month at one of its stores, and to visit eight to ten stores a quarter, both in and out of the areas in which they live. Bernard Marcus, CEO of Home Depot, described the process:

They go in as a customer first, then they announce themselves and make themselves available to the employees of the company. . . . It's a very, very good way for the board members to get a different feel for what's happening in the company. Typically, on a board, everything is filtered through the Chairman; everything you want the directors to know comes from him. Here we tell our board members to get out in the field. When they do this, they come back with recommendations. It's been very valuable for both sides – from our side as operators and for the board members for their knowledge of the company."[24]

## THE CEO/CHAIRMAN

In 76 percent of the largest US companies, the chief executive is also the chairman of the board.[25] In England, by contrast, the figure is roughly reversed, with only one-third of the largest companies having a joint CEO/Chairman.[26] Note, however, that UK boards have a higher percentage of inside directors as well.

We discussed earlier how the very existence of the board is based on the need for accountability. The board exists to keep management accountable for the vast discretionary power it wields. Thus, when the chairman of the board is also the CEO, it makes management accountable to a body led by management. It can mean that the CEO is put in the position of evaluating his own performance. For the same reason that we do not allow students to grade their own exams, that presents risks in the corporate context as well.

According to Harold Geneen, former CEO and Chairman of ITT Corp.,

> If the board of directors is really there to represent the interests of the stockholders, what is the chief executive doing on the board? Doesn't he have a conflict of interest? He's the professional manager. He cannot represent the shareholders and impartially sit in judgment of himself.[27]

In its 1992 survey of company directors, Korn/Ferry found that just under 20 percent believed that separating the CEO and chairman positions would have a "very negative impact" on boardroom performance. A little more than 20 percent thought it would have a "very positive impact" and not quite 60 percent thought the impact of separating the roles would be neutral.[28] Those who thought separating the roles would have a negative impact thought it important that a company be led by one person. "You've got to have one boss," said one respondent to the Korn/Ferry survey "Don't second guess him." Another said, "The CEO and the chairman need to be intimately involved in the business, so I believe they should be the same person. If they are not, the chairman would be a figurehead or would usurp the role of the CEO."

Those who were in favor of separating the roles believed it would lead to more objective evaluation of the CEO, and create an environment of greater accountability. One outside director commented that when the CEO is also the chairman there is "too great a temptation to 'tilt' things toward protecting CEO career interests."

The majority who believed that splitting the jobs was an unimportant issue typically commented that the chairman was simply the one who chaired the meetings, and that this was merely an argument about titles. While there has not been much empirical work done on this issue, at least one study found that companies with separate CEOs and chairmen consistently outperform those companies that combine the roles.[29]

That may be, but resistance is predictably high. Combining the two positions does not mean that a CEO who is also chairman will inevitably manipulate his board, but it does give him that opportunity. Board chairmanship can mean much more than parliamentary procedure. In the hands of a skilled power broker, the CEO/chairman can shift the locus of power to management and away from the board. Hugh Parker comments:

> In the final analysis a board of directors can only be as effective as its chairman wants it to be. It is the chairman who, over time, is the main architect of the board – i.e., of its composition, agendas, priorities, and procedures. The chairman chooses the directors he wants and uses them (or not) as he wishes. A chairman who wants a strong, independent, and effective board will in time have such a board. But the reverse is equally true: a chairman who wants a passive and uninvolved board to rubber-stamp his own decisions can in time also achieve such a board.

## CATCH 22: THE EX-CEO AS DIRECTOR

In 1991, Institutional Shareholder Services (ISS), a consulting firm that advises institutional investors on corporate governance issues, found that 27 percent of S&P 500 companies had a former CEO of their company as a board member.[30] Six companies even had two former CEOs on the board. There are a number of possible problems.

> They could dominate the board agenda and decisions . . . many, if not all, inside directors may owe their jobs to the retiring CEO, and would be reluctant to contradict his views out of a sense of

loyalty and/or fear: CEOs often continue to exercise enormous power even after their retirement. The same combination of fear and loyalty can appear to the non-executive directors recruited by the retiring CEO.[31]

But one current Fortune 500 CEO and chairman told ISS that most retired CEOs recognize the problem posed by their continuing presence and, to give the new CEO a chance to assert his own leadership, they stay silent on major policy questions.

The author of the ISS report, Howard D. Sherman, concluded, "In short, it is a Catch 22 for a retired CEO. Retired CEOs who care about their successor may not be effective directors. Retired CEOs who want to dominate the board should not be in the board at all."

But the ex-CEO has vast experience, and probably has more knowledge of the company than anyone else. How can shareholders make the best use of that knowledge? ISS recommended that the company should keep the CEO off the board, but keep him on as a consultant. Look at the news reports surrounding CEO departures to determine how many are kept on as "consultants" to see if you can tell how often this is a bribe to get them to leave. Recent examples that appear to fit this category include Paul Lego at Westinghouse. Lego was forced by the board to resign as CEO and Chairman of Westinghouse in January 1993. Despite the fact that Lego was, to all intents and purposes, fired, he received a two-year consulting contract at $600,000 a year (marginally less than the $700,000 salary he received as CEO). This was in addition to a severance payment of $800,000 and a lifetime annual pension of $910,000. If Lego's services were still useful to the company, why was he removed from his CEO post, and if he was fired for poor performance, why were the shareholders paying for his consulting services?

Interestingly, some CEOs told ISS that too much emphasis was put on keeping the ex-CEO around. Sir Adrian Cadbury, the esteemed former chairman of Cadbury Schweppes Plc, said, "I personally favor CEOs making a clean break with their companies on retirement. I would like to see this become the accepted practice with the possibility of a consultancy as an exception. . . . I am skeptical of the real value to a company of past experience, however vast."

Walter Wriston, ex-CEO of Citicorp and member of numerous boards as an outside director, made much the same point as Cadbury:

One reason for mandatory retirement is to assure the corporation of fresh leadership to meet changing conditions. If the new leadership wants to consult the old, no corporate structure is necessary; if consultation is not desired, no corporate arrangement will assure it. On the other hand, if the new CEO wants to get moving with his or her agenda, a board seat occupied by the retired CEO may be seen as an impediment to getting on with the job, particularly if new management feels that radical measures are called for.

One CEO who asked that he and his company remain anonymous said his company gave its outgoing chiefs an informal role:

> We strongly feel that "one should not look over the shoulder of a successor," for it could inhibit and restrict his freedom of action. We have always been fortunate that the retiring and incoming CEOs have had close and supportive relationships and that they could hold informal conversations on significant issues. Thus the new CEO could have the benefit of the counsel of the departed CEO if he sought it. The important consideration here is that the initiative in seeking such counsel must come from the new CEO. The retired CEO does not call or visit the incumbent CEO to offer advice unless it is requested.

## DIRECTOR NOMINATION

In 95 percent of large US companies, candidates are recommended to the board by a nominating committee.[32] The full board approves the recommendations. Director candidates are interviewed by the full board (including the CEO), and then "elected" (actually ratified) by a shareholder vote. In theory, this structure permits the board to evaluate director nominees independently, and to protect against management packing the board with its own allies. But Korn/Ferry found in 1991 that 82 percent of board vacancies were filled via recommendations from the chairman. Given that at nearly 80 percent of companies the chairman is also the CEO, it is clear that in reality the CEO plays an important, even dominant role in the selection of director candidates.

"Nominating committees all too often are a sham, pure and simple," said Dale Hanson, then CEO of the California Public Employees' Retirement System, before a House of Representatives Subcommittee.[33] In England, a 1992 PRO-Ned survey found that 86 percent of directors were "dissatisfied with the amateur approach adopted by companies of appointing non-executive directors." The fact that we speak of directors as "representing" or being "elected" by shareholders when the shareholders play no role in their nomination is evidence of the challenge we face in trying to understand corporate governance.

## Case in Point: A Director's Departure

A food service company made an ill-advised acquisition attempt for a restaurant group. The acquisition ended up costing the company over $680,000 – a large sum for a small-capitalization firm. One of the directors worried that the aborted acquisition might leave the company's directors liable for damages in a shareholder lawsuit charging that the directors had not acted with sufficient care or loyalty. He was particularly concerned because the CEO had canceled all board meetings for several months while he negotiated the ultimately unsuccessful deal.

After the CEO refused to schedule a board meeting, the director suggested to some of his fellow outside directors that they meet, separately from the insiders, to discuss their potential liability. For instance, he thought they should consider whether it might be wise for them to hire independent counsel.

None of the other outsiders accepted his invitation. Rather, they informed the CEO (who also served as chairman) of his suggestion. The director received a letter from the company's outside counsel accusing him of attempting to set up "clandestine" meetings. At the next full meeting of the board, the first held in over five months, the director was informed that he would not be renominated as a director at the company's next annual meeting. In other words, he was fired.

The director sent a letter to the CEO/chairman, requesting that his "resignation" be fully explained in the company proxy statement. He wrote:

I believe that the number of board of directors' meetings has not been sufficient to keep the board members as informed as I feel they should be about the activities of the company . . .

I am opposed to your having increased the compensation of officers of the Company without having come to the board, first. Not only was it contrary to the By Laws, but reflects our differences in philosophy as regards your view of the Board's functions . . .

I thought the fact that my name was not set forth to be nominated as a director and to be voted upon at the next annual meeting because of "philosophical differences" with you was not in the company's or its shareholders' best interest. Although I may have views that are contrary to yours, even you have, in the past, indicated that it was good for the Company. This action (albeit with the concurrence of the rest of the Board) once again reflects your desire to have control over the Board . . .

I feel that an independent compensation committee should be appointed and that it set up performance standards, evaluate achievements, and judge corporate results.

I would recommend that the positions of Board Chairman and Chief Executive Officer be separated, as you presently have too much control.

## Case in Point: A Director Demands More from the Board

A director at another company wrote this letter to a CEO who had been in place for about two years:

I have been thinking about the issues facing [our company], and I have become convinced that we have to come to grips with the mission and performance of the board. Everyone will agree that the board is responsible for strategic direction and management succession. But in my view, there is no single model of optimal board/management interrelationship. What this means, then, is that the board must constantly re-evaluate itself to make sure that it has the best possible structure for the company's present needs. The best results will obtain from recognition that change is always needed, that directors and management need to be committed to an ongoing process of self-examination and criticism, and that the balance will constantly be in flux. Until we have adopted an explicit "mission" for the board, we cannot adequately monitor our performance fairly, and if we cannot monitor ourselves, we cannot monitor the performance of the company or of you as CEO.

You inherited a board that was used to reacting to what was presented to us, and not used to asking for more. As a matter of personality and style, John [the former CEO] had little use for a board. For a long time the board acquiesced, as John produced superior results. During this period, the board was essentially limited to a consultative and oversight role (I refer to this later as a "watch-dog" board). I believe that during at least part of this period, you served for him the role that a board often serves, providing feedback, support, and analysis.

The board has changed little, but the company you inherited is a very different one from the [company] of John's heyday. And you do not have a number two officer playing the same role for you as you played for John. In other words, the players are different, the challenges are different, and it is time for the board to be different, too. To go back to the two primary responsibilities of the board:

*Strategic direction* We have already established a goal: $5 of earnings per share within five (now three and a half) years; and $10/share within ten years. With our core business in worldwide recession, simply maintaining our position – approximately $100 million per year in cash flow – is a substantial accomplishment.

It should not, however, permit us to lose sight of our longer term objectives. Do we have an industrial strategy as to how we are going to achieve these earnings targets? Is it going to be from internal growth? Or by acquisition? In what industrial sectors?

Do we have a financial strategy? If we are going to achieve our growth targets we will need substantial additional capital. My own sense is that the "cost" of equity capital is low. Our year-end closing price of 51 5/8 indicates a price/earnings multiple of 31. Have we decided to wait for a time when we can demonstrate an actual need for new capital or will we be opportunistic and go to the marketplace when capital is available on an historically attractive basis? These are the questions that the board should be considering right now. If we do not, I fear that we may be allowing a uniquely attractive time for raising additional capital to pass without adequate consideration.

*CEO selection, evaluation, succession* You have urged the board to evaluate your performance annually, and it is encouraging that we actually started this process in 1993. I find this to be a very constructive process.

But I am concerned about the issue of succession. When John was CEO, we knew we could turn to you. But I do not think any of the directors have a clear idea as to whom we would turn in the event that you were no longer able to serve. We need to make sure that you have a back-up. Any company is only as strong as its officer cadre. At present we are very "thin on the ground." The board must turn to this issue promptly.

These are the two most important responsibilities of a board of directors. It seems clear to me that our board needs to do more with regard to both. The fact that we have not done well enough in either of these areas demonstrates the importance of devoting time to examining ourselves to determine how we can improve our structure and composition to ensure that we function more effectively in the future.

It is very difficult – but absolutely essential – for our board to redefine itself to address our changing needs. This company needs a strong board.

Somebody needs to get this process started. I think it makes the most sense for you to take the initiative, to make sure that we develop a structure that accords with your sense of the company's needs today.

I found it useful to think of the possible roles of a board by keeping two matrices in mind. The first is a vertical matrix that illustrates a range of involvement – from a primarily re-active "watchdog" role on one end to a role as a fully participating partner with management to active participation, as boards often play in crisis situations like the board of General Motors a year ago or the board of Paramount right now. Second is a horizontal matrix that is a spectrum of modes of activity – ranging from exclusive focus on the strategic and succession issues that are always the core of the board's responsibility to setting policy, substantively analyzing tactical options, implementation, monitoring, and evaluation.

As far as I am concerned, a board could perfectly properly decide to locate itself anywhere on the graph emanating from these matrices. At the risk of redundancy, there is no "right" answer, but there is a "wrong" one. What is wrong is to have no defined role, no mission, no explicit benchmarks against which performance of the board can be evaluated. That is what I worry about here. In particular, I worry about the time we spend reviewing operating results instead of looking at the larger picture. None of us on the board has the time, the expertise, or the wish to become deeply enough involved in the day-to-day affairs of the company to evaluate these results in any meaningful way; even if that was an appropriate role for the board to play, this is not the group of people to play it.

In order to make sure that the board addresses the right issues, based on the right information, I think it might make sense for us to appoint an outside director as part-time chairman of the board. If that does not seem right to you, perhaps we could follow the advice of Marty Lipton and Jay Lorsch and appoint a "lead director" to help focus the outside directors on the agenda and other governance concerns. We should also have regular meetings of the outside directors in executive session at least twice a year. This is in no way a reflection on you and in no way intended to go behind your back. It is just the best way to make sure that the directors can talk to each other about what kinds of questions they want to ask. This is often mentioned by critics of boards as a key element in improving their performance.

Our board has really not "jelled." I think that is because we have not agreed on an explicit set of goals. Certainly, it is not lack of personal financial investment or personal commitment. What I am looking for is a shared sense of commitment, a sense that $5 per share within five years is more than just a slogan; that it represents a commitment by all of us to an extremely challenging and rewarding task; that we are each deeply personally committed to its achievement; that we discuss alternatives; that we see ourselves as successful or failures in terms of achieving the objective. I think having regular meetings of the outside directors would help a great deal.

In the absence of having a strong back-up within the company, it seems to me that you can make very good use of increased board involvement. I would like the board to be more of a resource for you than the rubber stamp with a micro perspective I feel that we have been. I am asking you to allow us to give you all that we can.

Empowered shareholders should focus on the board of directors – its composition and its agenda. The job of effectively involved shareholders can be simply described as ensuring that the board of directors does its job. This means making sure that the right people are on the board, that they are focusing on the right issues, and that they operate under a structure that enables them to ask the right questions and reach the right answers. This is the answer to the agency costs issues, the most effective way for the ownership to exercise the appropriate level of control.

## DIRECTOR COMPENSATION

A director serving on the board of a major corporation will normally have a retainer of about $20,000 to $30,000, with another $6,000 or so for attending full board and committee meetings. Adding the retainers and meeting fees makes the median annual board payment of $36,000. The largest combined fee in 1991 was $81,364 paid by ITT. The lowest was Loew's Corp. which paid $15,000.[34] Out of the 100 companies surveyed by SpencerStuart in 1991, 79 had retirement plans for their directors (more than twice as many as in 1986). The numbers do not seem big – unless you consider them on an hourly basis, in which case they are almost at the same scale as the CEOs whose pay hit the headlines. And there is more. At least 24 of the companies made stock grants in addition to the retainers. Finally, there are the legendary perquisites, from life insurance policies, to use of the corporate plane or other facilities, to endowed chairs at the director's alma mater. Most companies also give directors huge discounts on whatever they produce – not much value if they make ball-bearings, but invaluable if it is an airline. Retail company directors get free merchandise or discounts. At General Motors, directors received a new car every ninety days.

For a job that seldom demands more than two weeks a year, the compensation is generous, especially for those who serve on several boards in addition to full-time jobs. President Clinton's transition team chief, Vernon Jordon, earned $504,000 in fees from nine of the boards on which he served in 1992, and, if he'd retired from all his board positions in 1993, he would receive $160,000 annually in retirement fees. Directors often get business from the companies for their law, consulting, or investment banking firms as well.

These pay schemes bear no relation to the performance of the company – or, of course, to the performance of the director. A director will receive his retainer and fees, no matter what. His compensation will not rise in good years, nor fall in bad. Such a scheme provides no incentive. The stock component in some director's compensation packages is rarely significant enough to make the company's performance an issue. Thus, not only do most directors not hold a significant portion of their worth in the company's stock, but their pay is not designed to align their interests with shareholders. A 1995 report by the National Association of Corporate Directors Commission on Director Compensation recommended that a substantial component of the director's compensation be in stock, and that all consulting fees, life and health insurance, and charitable contributions be eliminated.

## INTERLOCKS

As mentioned earlier, the most popular type of director is a top executive of another company. Eighty-six percent of billion-dollar company boards included at least one CEO/COO of another company.[35] This means that managers of one company serve to oversee the managers of another. Though this may create something of the appearance of a generalized conflict of interests, that potential conflict is probably outweighed by the knowledge of trends and transactions that high-level corporate officers can bring to a board. What is troublesome, however, is the more specific set of conflicts arising from the number of managers who sit on each other's boards.[36] Sixty-five percent of outside directors serve on two or more boards, and 89 percent of inside directors are outside directors on other companies' boards. A fifth of all directors serve on four boards or more.[37] The *New York Times* even found five pairs of companies where executives sat on each other's compensation committees.[38] In the words of Justice Louis Brandeis, "The practice of interlocking directorships is the root of many evils."[39] American Express CEO James Robinson relied particularly on the support of Drew Lewis, CEO of Union Pacific. Robinson sits not just on the board of that company, but also on the compensation committee. The case study describes a host of other relationships that helped to undermine the independence of Amex's outside directors. Carter Hawley Hale CEO Philip Hawley relied on the Bank of America for support in arranging a voting scheme for employee stock in the face of a takeover. Hawley sat on the executive committee of the Bank of America's board, and chaired its compensation committee.

## TIME AND MONEY

Directors' ability to oversee management is further undermined by the fact that many directors are unable to devote sufficient time or resources to the job. The following comment was made by two of America's most astute observers of corporate boardrooms, Martin Lipton of Wachtell, Lipton, Rosen & Katz in New York and Jay Lorsch, Senior Associate dean of the Harvard Business School:

> Based on our experience, the most widely shared problem directors have is a lack of time to carry out their duties. The typical board meets less than eight times annually. Even with committee meetings and informal gatherings before or after the formal board meeting, directors rarely spend as much as a working day together in and around each meeting. Further, in many boardrooms too much of this limited time is occupied with reports from management and various formalities. In essence, the limited time outside directors have together is not used in a meaningful exchange of ideas among themselves or with management/inside directors.[40]

Lipton and Lorsch go on to say that for a director to do his or her job properly, he or she needs to devote at least 100 hours annually on the job. But because so many directors serve on more than one board, in addition to a full-time job, they are quite unable to contribute that much time.

As mentioned earlier, according to Korn/Ferry's 1992 survey of Fortune 1000 directors, more than 20 percent of respondents served four or more boards as an outside director. Consider a busy executive who has an important and demanding full-time job and who also sits on four boards. It is inconceivable that he will be able to devote 400 hours (or nearly seven 60-hour weeks) to his outside boards. In reality, that executive would devote far less than 100 hours to each of his outside boards, which is simply not enough time to do the job that, in theory, he is expected to do.

Though rare, there are "super-directors" who claim to be able to serve on numerous boards. One respondent to the Korn/Ferry 1992 survey served on 11 boards.[41] Former Secretary of Defense, Frank Carlucci, serves on no less than 20 for-profit company boards, and on a dozen non-profits. This is in addition to a full-time job as chairman of the Carlyle Group. According to the *Washington Post,* Carlucci had a board meeting for one of his outside interests every single working day in 1992, including one that he attended by phone from his doctor's waiting room.[42] It is our opinion that no one, however talented, can hope to sit on the boards of that many companies and effectively monitor the management of each.

As well as being unable to commit in terms of time, many directors are unable or unwilling to commit money. If directors are to be the representatives of shareholders, then it is not too much to demand that they be shareholders. Yet all too often, outside directors hold, at best, only small proportions of their net worth, and merely token holdings at worst. For example, at the 1993 Westinghouse annual meeting, Robert A.G. Monks (one of the authors of this book) was able to announce that his firm's $3 million holding represented more stock held by the entire board of directors put together, and nearly three times more than all the outside directors (including Frank Carlucci) put together. Carlucci had invested a total of $8,000 for each year he had served on the board. A 1996 study listed him as the country's worst director.

Nor is Westinghouse an isolated example. In 1993 there were 140 companies in the S&P 500 (or about 28 percent) with a director who owned no stock at all in the company.[43] Many boards include directors with a token holding of 100 shares. In cases like these, despite concerns about reputation and personal pride, directors may not have enough incentive to be aggressive in evaluating and overseeing management. One survey suggested that directors do not see a problem with an absence of stock holding. A 1989 polling of Fortune 1000 directors found that 69 percent of respondents agreed that "directors are likely to have the same commitment to representing shareholders' interests regardless of their equity holdings."[44] A 1996 survey by Directorship concluded – based on a survey of directors themselves – that the money was immaterial. On the other hand, empirical studies consistently show a strong correlation between director stock ownership and superior performance.

## THE DIRECTOR'S ROLE IN CRISIS

Boards of directors receive attention only when faced with a crisis, like disastrous performance or a hostile bid. Too often, it has seemed that they only pay attention when there is a crisis. There seems to be little concern with what a director is supposed to do, if anything, to *prevent* a corporate crisis. This seems to be one problem that directors' concern with their own reputation does not address; a survey of directors in 1989 showed that they themselves regarded the boards of IBM and General Motors as the most prestigious on which to serve.[45] It is no coincidence that both companies suffered precipitous decline with no apparent reaction by the board.

More recently, there has been some change as the General Motors' board's decision to replace the CEO was seen as something of a challenge and a grant of authority to other boards. As we describe in chapter 2, the period from September 1992 through December 1993 appeared to be an open season on chief executives. The CEOs of General Motors, Westinghouse, American Express, IBM, Eastman Kodak, Scott Paper, and Borden were all pressured to resign in the face of their companies' long-term underperformance. These moves were heralded in the media as a breakthrough in boardroom activism.[46] Yet in all these instances the board took the necessary drastic action years too late. At IBM, Akers resigned only after the company's market value had halved in six months, following a $5 billion loss in 1992. At American Express, Robinson was allowed to pursue a course of reckless financial expansion for seventeen years. Why does it take boards so long to respond to deep-seated competitive problems? And, if one of the leading responsibilities of directors is to evaluate the performance of the CEO, why do boards wait too long for proof of managerial incompetence before making a move?

Judge William E. Allen, chancellor of the Delaware court, and leading expert on the judicial implications of corporate governance, described the "fire alarm" problem in a 1991 speech: "The view of the responsibilities of membership of the board of directors of public companies is, in my opinion badly deficient. It ignores a most basic responsibility: the duty to monitor the performance of senior management in an informed way. Outside directors should function as active monitors of corporate management, not just in crisis, but continually."

One of the most important reasons that boards have failed to fulfill their role as monitors is also the most intangible – the culture of the boardroom. By "culture" we refer to the psychology of belonging to a board – the collegiate atmosphere that prevents any one member speaking out against the prevailing view. It is the existence of this culture that leads to boards being accused of being "old boys' clubs."

The problem is that it is difficult to speak out against management when the CEO controls the board's agenda, information, compensation, and composition.

A 1989 survey in the United Kingdom found that one-third of directors agreed that "don't rock the boat" was the unspoken credo of most boardrooms. The same survey reported that virtually all boardroom votes are unanimous, and a spirit of "we must agree to disagree"is strongly discouraged in today's boardrooms. As one CEO said, "I often say my directors can come in and vote one of two ways – either 'yes' or 'I resign.' "[47] The problem has been well summarized by New York lawyer Ira Millstein and former lawyer Winthrop Knowlton:

(Directors) appear, in theory, to have immense power and flexibility. They can help shape their corporations' missions in a great variety of ways, provided only that they create plausible evidence that they have taken their primary obligation to shareholders adequately into account. They can (and do) stimulate CEOs to formulate long-range plans. They can dismiss the CEO if they do not like these plans or the way he carries them out. They can urge management on to higher standards of performance through an arsenal of sophisticated incentives: salary increases, bonuses, options, and a variety of grants. And yet, the gut feeling in their stomach is that their role is an exceedingly limited one. They feel they do not have time enough to know the company's products well and to know, especially, how truly competitive these products are. They do not have time enough to tour company plants, talk to middle managers, hear alternative points of view. While they can, in theory, criticize CEOs, punish them, and even remove them, there is immense reluctance to do so. This is an individual they themselves have selected. This is an individual who has far more information at his fingertips than they do, who is (surprising as it may seem to many corporate critics) usually devoting every waking hour to the firm's affairs, and who is in need of every bit of support the board can give. A number of outside directors who have managed or may still be managing companies of their own are particularly sensitive to this.[48]

Millstein and Knowlton comment further:

> Whether [the board's] activities here take on an active or a passive coloration, whether boards respond only to crisis or to specific kinds of issues and the rest of the time restrict their activities to formal, even ritualistic review, depends in large measure on the kinds of people the directors are, the personality and operating style of the CEO, past board practice, and the challenges that the particular corporation faces.[49]

## "INDEPENDENT" OUTSIDE DIRECTORS

One trend that has characterized boards of directors over the last 20 years has been the rise of the "independent" outside director. While definitions of "independence" vary, most agree that in order to be "independent," a director must have no connection to the company other than the seat on the board. This excludes not just full-time employees of the company, but also family members of employees and the company's lawyer, banker, and consultant. Some include people with connections to the company's suppliers, customers, debtors or creditors, or interlocking directors. Some definitions include direct or indirect recipients of corporate charitable donations, like the heads of universities or foundations. In its report on the relationship between independent directors and corporate performance, Faulk & Co. considered any director was not independent if he held five percent or more of the stock – a most unusual restriction, and one that, according to most lights, utterly skewed the results. Some definitions are so restrictive that they all but require that the CEO has never met the candidate. The theory is that if the director is a friend of the CEO, it is just as difficult for him to be objective as it would be if he was an employee.

A number of high-profile corporate crimes in the 1970s prompted a fresh look at the role of directors. The Watergate affair caused several illegal campaign contributions to come to light. On the international front, sleazy tales emerged of corporations bribing foreign officials to keep out competition. Observers wondered why boards of directors, whose job it was to prevent such transgressions, had failed in their duty.

Academics, investors, and others began to put more emphasis on the importance of independent directors – directors not primarily employed by the company. Outsiders are not dependent on the chief executive for promotion, or for legal or consulting business.

Thus, they are relatively free from conflicts of interest, and better able to protect the owners' interests. This philosophy prompted companies to raise the number of outside directors in America's boardrooms, and, more importantly, the ratio of outsiders to insiders on the typical board. Corporate apologists and critics alike agreed, at least in theory, that if outsiders command a powerful majority in the boardroom, they will be better able to check any tendency of those in top management to abuse their positions of power.[50]

True or not, the notion of raising the ratio of outsiders to insiders on corporate boards proved extremely popular. Over the last two decades, America's boardrooms have witnessed a remarkable growth in the power of independent outside directors – in 1973, insiders occupied 38 percent of the seats in the average boardroom; today that ratio has dropped to 25 percent.[51] As we discuss later, however, these directors have not always been willing to use this power. "Independence" can also mean "indifference." More recent efforts have been directed not just at making sure that boards have independent directors but also at giving them a structure that makes it possible for them to monitor more effectively.

One early reform that had an enormous impact on the importance of the independent directors was a requirement by the New York Stock Exchange in 1978 that every listed company had to have an audit committee made up of a majority of outside directors. This forced companies to have at least two outsiders on their board. According to a SpencerStuart boardroom survey in 1990: "The ratio of outside to inside directorships, which climbed steadily during the 1980s, reached a new high in 1990."

> 1980: 20 boards had an outside/inside ratio of 3:1 or greater.
> 1990: 51 boards did.
>
> 1980: 20 boards had an outside/inside ratio of 4:1 or greater.
> 1990: 40 boards reported such a ratio.

There are other indications that outside directors have become an increasingly dominant force on corporate boards:

> 1980: 7 boards had just one or two insiders, and 51 companies had six insiders or more.
> 1990: 27 companies had one or two insiders, and 24 had six or more.

SpencerStuart concluded: "Since 1980 . . . the combined total number of inside directors for all the SSBI companies has fallen from 584 to 410. That's a decline of nearly 30 percent."[52] The number of affiliated outsiders has also declined.

> 1980: 32 percent of boards reported seating one of their own outside lawyers.
> 1990: The incidence had dropped to 21 percent.[53]

The insider-outsider ratios continue to rise in the 1990s:

> Today, some boards (14 out of SpencerStuart's sample of 100 in 1993) report only one inside director, the CEO.[54]

What does all this really mean? Although there is much theory and some data to recommend outside directors, their impact is still difficult to quantify, and research on this subject remains limited.[55]

## Case in Point: Sears

> The "independence" of independent directors selected by management was put into focus when Robert A.G. Monks, co-author of this book, ran a campaign to be an independent director of Sears in 1991. At Sears, where the CEO also served as chairman of the board, CEO of the largest operating division, and head of the board's nominating committee, outside directors not selected by management are so threatening that Sears budgeted $5.5 million (22 times Monks's budget) to defeat his candidacy.

In 1971, a Harvard Business School Professor named Myles Mace conducted a landmark study of boards, and concluded that directors were "ornaments on a corporate Christmas tree." His description echoed one company chairman who once described directors as "the parsley on the fish."[56] Since Mace's day, things have improved markedly, but directors still have a long way to go before they exercise their power on behalf of shareholders' interests.

Boards of directors, despite the much-ballyhooed rise of the independent outside director, have seldom succeeded in effectively overseeing management. Rather, the CEO/chairman wields the power in the boardroom, and directors mostly serve at his pleasure. This is not to say that directors do nothing, or that they cannot check managerial abuse. But it is true that boards are mostly reactive, not proactive.

Millstein and Knowlton put it this way:

> Directors are forced to spend a great deal of their time – in our view, most of it – going by "the numbers" and by "the book," endlessly reviewing financial results, making sure their tracks are covered, and helping their companies mostly, we feel, by the exercise of negative virtues: reducing risks, preventing egregious mistakes, making sure things are "in order."[57]

Not all boards fail in their duty to oversee management. It's worth looking at a contrary example, where a board has responded promptly to resolve a company's problems.

## Case in Point: Compaq Computers

Ben Rosen, a venture capitalist with a significant stake in Compaq, served as the non-executive chairman of the company's board. After the stock price of the company plummeted, matched by Compaq's first ever quarterly loss, a major disagreement developed between management and the board as to how the company should address the crisis. The board believed the company needed a fundamental shift in strategy, and the company's founder and CEO, Rod Canion, was forced to resign. The result was vastly increased earnings over the next year and a doubling of the stock price. In testimony to the House of Representatives, Rosen described the criteria for a strong board:

> (1) An outside, independent chairman; all directors, with the exception of the CEO, should be outsiders. (2) Board members who all have meaningful ownership in the company, making them natural allies of the shareholder owners. (3) Key committees that exclude the CEO. (4) Boards that are relatively small, to increase their effectiveness. In addition, reciprocal directorships should be discouraged, if not eliminated.

Compaq had such a board, which was vital as the company faced a difficult period:

> Compaq Computer, after a period of meteoric and profitable growth, ran into serious difficulties engendered by fundamental shifts in the marketplace. Our historical recipe for success was out of tune with the new needs of customers. For the first time,

the board and management differed on the fundamental direction of the company. Because the board was composed of all-outside directors (except the CEO), had a non-CEO chairman, and was small (seven members), it was able to act dispassionately and entirely in the interests of the corporation. The board moved promptly, and the rest, as they say, is history.[58]

We have seen in the previous section how the boardroom system conspires against genuine representation of owners' interests.

The corporate structure has two provisions designed to ensure that directors are genuinely acting in the interests of the shareholders: the electoral process and the fiduciary standard.

## DIRECTOR ELECTION

In theory, directors, like politicians, are elected by their constituents. This system, like representative democracy, is predicated on the assumption that if shareholders don't approve of their representatives, they will "throw the bums out."

As noted above, however, most observers will agree that the electoral process has not been an effective mechanism for assuring that directors represent the interests of the shareholders. Edward J. Epstein says that shareholder elections "are procedurally much more akin to the elections held by the Communist party of North Korea than those held in Western democracies."[59] The reality backs him up. Management picks the slate of candidates, no one runs against them, and management counts the votes. Managers even know how shareholders vote. As soon as the votes come in, they can call and try to persuade (or pressure) those who vote against them. And, of course, management has access to the corporate treasury to finance its search for candidates and solicit support for their election, while anyone running against them must put up their own money. (Successful dissident slates often get reimbursed, however, once they are in office.) Management has access to the shareholder list; a dissident shareholder faces significant obstacles, though fewer following the 1992 SEC rule changes.

In this section, we will look at how the electoral system can be manipulated to reduce the efficacy of shareholder voting rights. As mentioned above, in reality, it is more of a ratification than an election, because in more than 99 percent of the votes, the management candidates run without opposition. So the "election" is really just a formality. Except for the rare case of a proxy contest, where those trying for control of the company nominate (and finance) a competing slate of directors, there is no chance of the nominees not being elected. Shareholders cannot vote "no" to unopposed directors. They can only abstain by withholding their support. And their abstentions carry little weight; it only takes one yes vote from a single shareholder to get a slate of unopposed candidates elected, no matter how many shareholders refuse to support them.

Moreover, corporate managers often seek to limit shareholders' voting rights. They argue, correctly, that corporations cannot be run by referenda. However, there is a difference between governing a company as a "town hall" and allowing shareholders a voice in the governance of the corporation they own.

## STAGGERED BOARDS

Until the mid-to-late 1980s, it was the all but universal practice for all directors to be elected at each annual meeting of shareholders. Thus, a director would serve a succession of yearly terms until either retirement or a decision was made by the nominating committee not to renominate him.

The takeover era, however, raised the possibility of raiders being able to take over a company by nominating a separate slate of directors and seeking votes from shareholders to vote for the dissident's slate over management's.

As a protective device, companies began to nominate directors for three staggered sets of three-year terms. Thus, the board would be divided into three sets, or classes, of directors who would each be nominated for re-election every three years. This way, an acquirer would have to run a dissident slate three years running to gain control of the board – an impossibly long time to maintain a hostile bid.

This practice became especially popular in the late 1980s. By 1991, 51 percent of sample companies elected directors to three-year terms, up from 33 percent in 1986.[60] And the Commonwealth of Massachusetts enacted a law *requiring* all companies incorporated there to adopt a staggered board structure, just to protect one local company from a prospective hostile acquirer.

In adopting a staggered (or classified) board structure, management argued that the moves assured the "continuity" of board service. This ignored the fact that it should be up to the shareholders whether they wish their directors to continue representing them or not.

Studies performed by Securities and Exchange Commission economists support the view that classified boards are contrary to shareholder interests. These studies demonstrate that adoption of a classified board can result in loss of share value.[61] There is the greater issue of accountability, however. Shareholder advocates believe that holders have the right to vote on all of their directors every year.[62] They believe that staggered boards, in protecting directors from raiders, also serve to "protect" the board from the company's shareholders. In making it more difficult for an outsider to present shareholders with an alternative, the staggered board structure makes it even more difficult for shareholders to play a meaningful role in the election of directors.

## CONFIDENTIAL VOTING

Conflicts of interest, both political and commercial, make confidential voting an important issue to many shareholders. These conflicts are inherent in any situation where management (or its agents) is counting the non-confidential votes. This is the practice that prevails in the vast (though shrinking) majority of corporations. Thus, corporate managers know as soon as the votes come in who has voted and how they voted. Since new proxies can be submitted at any time up to the moment votes are counted, intense pressure can be placed on shareholders who also happen to have a close business relationship with the company in question. It is common practice for companies to call dissident shareholders and persuade them to change their votes to support management[63] (see the discussion of conflicts of interest among institutional investors in chapter 2). But the beneficial holders, for example, the individuals who are pension plan participants or investors in mutual funds, have no way of finding out how votes are cast on their behalf. For that reason, it is easy for institutional investors to succumb to pressure to vote with management.

Though few companies have adopted some form of confidential voting policy, the number is increasing quickly,[64] in part because the corporate community has decided that it costs them little and means a lot to shareholder activists. But some of these policies are written very narrowly. Many of them do not apply in case of a proxy contest, exactly the situation where confidential voting proponents argue they are most needed.

The Department of Labor has directed ERISA fiduciaries to monitor the way that proxies are voted by the money managers they retain,[65] which means that money managers must disclose their votes to the fiduciaries. There are two important aspects of full disclosure missing (or at least not explicit) in this requirement, however. First, the disclosure may apparently be in general or aggregate form. Unless the ERISA fiduciary insists on more detail, the information may be disclosed as "number of votes cast in favor of management-sponsored proxy issues relating to stock option plans" rather than "vote on the stock option plan proposed by Widget Co." Second, the disclosure is made to the ERISA plan fiduciaries, and not to the beneficial holders, the plan participants, or to the public. Still, this requirement does provide information to at least some of those who make the decision about which money managers to use. And the state of California now requires institutional investors subject to state law to make public the record of their proxy votes in order to limit their liability for any failure to cast the votes appropriately.

Despite these mandates, the electoral system still falls short of providing shareholders with any meaningful ability to make a change in the board. This raises the expectations for the fiduciary standard as the foundation for the corporate structure's legitimacy even higher. As discussed earlier, this standard means that a director is legally bound to an unwavering loyalty to the shareholders, and must pursue their interests with the greatest of care and diligence. To understand the operation of this standard in practice better, we will examine its greatest modern-day challenge, the takeover era.

## IMPACT OF THE TAKEOVER ERA ON THE ROLE OF THE BOARD

In the 1950s, corporate lawyers felt that their job had been done – they had no questions left to answer! As academic Bayless Manning put it in 1962: "Corporation law, as a field of intellectual effort, is dead in the United States."[66]

Twenty-five years later, however, the takeover era turned Manning's statement on its head. The creation of financial instruments to finance takeovers of any company, of virtually any size, presented directors with the most demanding challenges in corporate history.

Justifying decisions in terms of benefits to shareholders is one thing when the issues relate to marketing or research and development, and quite another when they relate to whether the entity will continue in its current state or be swallowed up by another company. And making a decision that affects the job security of the CEO who brought you on the board (to say nothing of your own job security as a director) is of necessity less dispassionate than making a decision about ordinary business.

The early takeovers (and efforts to block takeovers) challenged in court produced judicial decisions reflecting concerns about the difficulty directors would have in acting on behalf of the shareholders when the interests of management, and perhaps the directors' own interests, could be different.

The early challenges to takeover defenses produced case law that reflected traditional notions of the director's duty, and traditional concerns that corporate managers and directors would have a natural tendency to protect their own interests to the detriment of the shareholders'. In the most important of the early cases, *Trans Union* (discussed below), the court ruled against directors for agreeing to a sale of the company in a manner that seemed almost impetuous. Since the board had not taken enough steps to ensure that they were getting the best price, ruled the court, they had not met their duty as fiduciaries. In *Trans Union,* the board gave in too easily.

In the next wave of cases, the courts objected when the boards did not give in easily enough. Those cases, including Revlon and *Unocal,* concerned efforts by boards to block takeovers. When shareholders sued, the courts had to decide whether there was any limit to the defensive maneuvers a board could undertake in the face of an offer to buy the company.

## THE DELAWARE FACTOR

Most of the cases relating to takeovers have been decided by the Delaware courts, because most big companies are incorporated there. Some other courts have addressed the business judgment rule. The New York court ruled, for example, that issuing a block of stock to an ESOP and a wholly controlled subsidiary, just to avoid a takeover, violated the duty of loyalty.[67] But, in general, Delaware has a lock on the Fortune 500, and when it seemed that decisions limiting the protection of the business judgment rule might lead companies to incorporate elsewhere, the Delaware courts began to back off (see "Delaware puts out," chapter 1).

### Case in Point: Trans Union

In the landmark case of *Smith v. Van Gorkom,*[68] directors were found to have violated their fiduciary duty over the sale of Trans

Union. The CEO of Trans Union, Jerome William Van Gorkom, suggested to potential buyer Jay Pritzker that $55 per share would be a good offer for his company, without consulting anyone on his board. When the board did meet to discuss the deal, Van Gorkom did not tell them that it was he who had suggested that figure to Pritzker, and he did not tell them how he had arrived at it. He did not ask the board whether it was the best price, just whether it was a fair price.

After about two hours, the board approved the deal, subject to two conditions: first, that the company could accept (though not solicit) another offer during a "market test" period, and second, to facilitate other offers, that the company could share proprietary information with other potential bidders.

The market test was a brief one. With the permission of his board, Van Gorkom signed the merger agreement that evening, although, the court found, at the time the agreement was executed neither Van Gorkom nor any director had read it.[69] Trans Union issued a press release announcing a "definitive" merger agreement, "subject to approval by stockholders."

The shareholders did approve the deal, but one shareholder sued. The lower court upheld the actions of the directors, but the Delaware Supreme Court reversed that finding, ruling that the Trans Union directors were "grossly negligent" in failing to make an independent determination of whether Van Gorkom did a complete job of evaluating the price and negotiating the terms of the merger agreement, and in failing to understand the transaction themselves.

The issue was not the substance of the decision; the court never said whether $55 per share was too low or too high. Instead, the issue was one of process. The court ruled that the directors had not taken adequate steps to be able to evaluate the offer. The substantial premium over the market price, the "market test" period for entertaining other offers, the advice of counsel that they might be violating their duty as fiduciaries if they failed to approve the merger, and the shareholder vote were not sufficient to make up for the board's failure to evaluate the deal independently. It should be noted that this was a close case – two justices dissented, finding the directors' actions reasonable. Controversy notwithstanding, however, *Van Gorkom* became the litmus test for director's duty.

The primary impact of the *Van Gorkom* case has been on the process for arriving at decisions, not on the substance of the decisions themselves. Courts have been very careful not to substitute their business judgment for that of boards. As long as a process is followed, the courts will defer to it. But the processes themselves have little substantive meaning. Law firms present boards with routine check-lists of options which are then "considered" just to make a strong record in case of a challenge in court, rather than for any substantive purpose. And sometimes, the record does not even need to be very strong, as in the Time-Warner case, where all the steps taken to establish due care and deliberation were taken in consideration of a deal that was different in every major respect (except management compensation) than the deal that went through.

## Case in Point: Revlon and Unocal

In *Unocal*,[70] the court expressed its concern with the "omnipresent specter" that a board would act to protect its own interests when faced with a takeover offer. For that reason, any action to protect the company from a contest for control would be reviewed with special care by a court reviewing a challenge, based on the assumption that the board and the top managers had a conflict of interests between what was best for them and what was best for the shareholders.

While the courts normally give directors' "business judgment" great deference, in takeover cases (as in other cases of possible conflicts of interest), directors would have what the law calls a "burden of proof" and therefore have to show "good faith and reasonable investigation" before the courts would defer to their decision. They also have to show that, unlike the actions of the Trans Union directors, their decisions were "informed." Directors' decisions must also meet another test: they must be "reasonably relationed to the threats posed."[71] Directors are not supposed to use an atom bomb to fight a squirt gun; if they do, it must be assumed that their primary interest is their own job security.

When Revlon adopted a poison pill[72] in reaction to Pantry Pride's offer of $45 a share, that was "reasonable in relation to the threat posed."[73] But when Pantry Pride increased its offer to $53, the defensive measures were no longer reasonable. At that point, according to the court, "it became apparent to all that the break-up of the company was inevitable"[74] and "the directors' role changed from defenders of the corporate bastion to auctioneers charged with getting the best price for the stockholders at a sale of the company."[75]

The court lambasted the directors' decision to grant favorable treatment to a white knight[76] whose offer was only $1 per share more than Pantry Pride's, even though its offer provided more protection to note-holders. "[T]he directors cannot fulfill their enhanced *Unocal* duties by playing favorites with the contending factions. Market forces must be allowed to operate freely to bring the target's shareholders the best price available for their equity."[77]

The court decided that once a company was "for sale," the only factor to be considered was the best price for shareholders; any other interest was a breach of the directors' fiduciary duty of loyalty.

The court specifically addressed the issue of "stakeholders." As discussed in chapter 2, these non-shareholder constituencies also have an interest in the company and have sought to advance these interests at the board level. The court said that although boards may consider other interests, "there are fundamental limitations on that prerogative. A board may have regard for various constituencies in discharging its responsibilities, provided that there are rationally related benefits accruing to the stockholders. . . . However, such concern for non-stockholder interests is inappropriate when an auction among active bidders is in progress, and the object is no longer to protect or maintain the corporate enterprise but to sell it to the highest bidder."[78]

## HOW DID BOARDS RESPOND?

A noticeable by-product of the takeover era was the abuse of shareholders, as management demonstrated that the market for corporate control was a chimera. Boards of directors and management joined to protect their companies from the threat of a hostile raid, but ironically, they only distanced themselves from their own shareholders. By the end of the 1980s, most large companies bristled with a host of "antitakeover" devices – collectively known as "shark repellents" – that only served to render management and the board still *less* accountable than they had been before. As we saw in chapter 2, these protective devices were one of the main reasons for the emergence of shareholder activists, and the dismantling of such devices was one of their main early aims.

*Greenmail* Possibly the most unconscionable way of avoiding takeover, greenmail forced shareholders to bear the cost of management's incumbency. There is a reason "greenmail" sounds a lot like "blackmail," though it is really more like extortion. Someone buys a large stake in the company and begins to make his presence known, perhaps by making noises about trying to take over the company. Management does not want him, so they offer to buy him out, at a substantial bonus over the market price of the stock. Raiders achieve huge profits without even having to make a bid for the company; managers are able to keep their jobs. But all other shareholders are left with the market trading price – which often went down as a result of a large cash payment being made to silence a potential dissenting voice.

One of the earliest payments of greenmail was in 1984. The Bass brothers had acquired 9.9 percent of Texaco, and were known to be interested in purchasing the other 90.1 percent. Instead, Texaco's management paid the Bass brothers $1.3 billion for the stock, a $137 million premium over the market price. In other terms, the Bass brothers were able to sell their stock for $55 per share, while the vast majority of shareholders could only get $35. The payment so infuriated the then Treasurer of California, Jesse Unruh, that he formed the highly influential Council of Institutional Investors to lobby for improved shareholder rights.

Greenmail provides a perfect example of board neglect. Directors should not permit managers to pay huge sums of shareholders' money merely to avoid possible loss of control. In all likelihood it was not in Texaco's interest to be taken over by the Bass brothers, but that is something for the market to decide. Moreover, the majority of shareholders should have been allowed to decide if selling their shares to the Basses was in their best interests. The Texaco board should have let the company's shareholders make that choice.

*"Poison Pills"* In November 1985, in *Moran v. Household International, Inc.,* the Delaware Supreme Court upheld a company's right to adopt "shareholder rights plans," as they are called by corporate managers, or "poison pills" as they are called by everyone else. Moreover, the Delaware court allowed a pill to be created without shareholder approval. The plans usually take the form of rights or warrants issued to shareholders that are worthless unless triggered by a hostile acquisition attempt. If triggered, pills give shareholders the ability to purchase shares from, or sell shares back to, the target company (the "flip-in" pill) and/or the potential acquirer (the "flip-over" pill). While a pill has the effect of entrenching a company from an unsolicited takeover, it also protects shareholders from such coercive practices as two-tier offers.

The widely used flip-over plan gives target shareholders the right to purchase shares of the potential acquirer's common stock at a steep discount, usually 50 percent, should the acquirer attempt a second-stage merger not approved by the target's board. Since the built-in discount would encourage all of the target shareholders to exercise their rights and purchase shares from the acquirer, and since the potential acquirer's shareholders would be prevented from participating, the result would be that the acquirer's pre-existing shareholders would find their own equity interests substantially diluted once the pill is triggered and the rights exercised. Here lieth the "poison" in the pill.

The flip-in plan is often combined with a flip-over plan. Upon the triggering event, rights in a flip-in plan allow target shareholders to purchase shares of their own company at a steep discount, again usually 50 percent. The right is discriminatory in that the potential acquirer is excluded from participating if the pill is triggered by an action not approved by the target's board.

The pill is a "doomsday device" with such potent wealth-destroying characteristics that no bidder has ever dared proceed to the point of causing a pill actually to become operative.

A poison pill gives the board veto power over any bid for the company, no matter how beneficial to the shareholders. If the board opposes the bid, it can sit back and wait for the pill to be triggered – usually when an acquirer has purchased 15 or 20 percent. If the board is in favor of an acquisition, it can simply redeem the pill. The board can both create and redeem the pill without shareholder approval. Thus, while we have stated that shareholders have a basic right to sell their stock to whoever they please, "poison pills" showed that shareholders could only sell to people pre-approved by the board.

By the end of the 1980s, over 1,000 companies had implemented a poison pill. Meanwhile, academics studied the effects on share-holder value. The evidence has been inconclusive. One type of study has examined the price movement of company stock follow-ing the adoption of a pill. Some have suggested that adoption of a pill increases share value; some say the opposite. Another set of studies has focused on how pills are used in practice. Some of these suggest that companies with pills generally receive higher takeover premiums than companies without pills; others disagree.[79]

As the takeover market has declined in recent years, so the need for protective devices such as pills lessened.[80] As described in chapter 2, shareholders have consistently sponsored resolutions calling for the redemption of pills, with considerable success.[81] There is some evidence that firms that abandon their pill experience short-term positive gains, as the market recognizes that the com-pany has become more susceptible to the discipline of the takeover market.[82]

Some companies, rather than canceling the pill outright, have modified the plan to create a "chewable" pill. This pill is not a "doomsday device" triggered by hostile interest, but a pill that sets certain conditions on an unsolicited bid. Thus, if a bid is fully financed, and is made for all shares, then a "chewable pill" generally won't be triggered. In many ways, such a device is beneficial to shareholders since it ensures that any bid made for the company is a fair one.

There are other takeover defenses that also seek to prevent shareholders being coerced by such bids as two-tier offers. For instance, a "fair price provision" requires an acquirer to pay the same price for all shares bought, rather than only paying a premium for a sufficient number of shares to gain control.

Another popular strategy was the "white knight" defense. A "white knight" is a friendly third party who agrees to buy a significant portion of stock to keep it out of the acquirer's hands. This strategy was used successfully at both Polaroid and Carter Hawley Hale. A similar strategy involves creating a new class of shareholder with unequal voting rights. Shares may be issued to friendly shareholders (usually management) with greater voting power than that which applies to common stock. Thus, friendly interests may control few of the shares but many of the votes.

Other takeover defenses are less shareholder friendly, and give the impression that the target management would rather destroy the company than let it be taken over. For instance, a "crown jewel" strategy could result in a target company divesting itself of its most valuable assets. In this defense, the target company would sell or otherwise "lock up" the company's most valuable assets – its core business, for instance. Thus, the acquirer would be faced with undertaking an expensive takeover bid for a far less valuable company. Of course, this strategy only averts takeover at the cost of the dismemberment of the target company.

Still more risky was the "PacMan" defense, in which the target company made a bid for the acquirer. This "I'll-eat-you-before-you-eat-me" strategy was used most famously in the takeover battle between Bendix and Martin Marietta. In 1982, Bendix announced its intention to purchase Marietta; Marietta responded by making a tender offer for Bendix shares. Months later, United Technologies joined the battle by proposing to buy Bendix at a higher price than Marietta was offering. Ultimately, both companies were bought by Allied Corporation.

Perhaps the most bizarre strategy ever adopted was the so-called "Jewish Dentist" defense, pioneered by leading takeover lawyer Joe Flom, in 1975. Sterndent, a manufacturer of dental equipment, was under attack from Magus Corp., a foreign-based conglomerate. Flom found that 10 percent of Magus was owned by the Kuwait Investment Company. Since Sterndent sold most of its products to dentists, many of whom were Jewish, Flom argued that an Arab-financed takeover would negatively effect Sterndent's operations as its customers would shop elsewhere. Flom was also able to find a white knight for Sterndent, and Magus backed off.[83]

The causes and effects of takeovers, and whether management is justified in opposing a takeover without recourse to a shareholder vote, is still a matter of raging debate. Takeover lawyer Martin Lipton believes that the takeover era was disastrous for corporate America, and that such devices as poison pills are necessary to allow managers to run their companies without continually looking over their shoulders for a possible hostile bid. By contrast, raiders such as T. Boone Pickens believe the takeover era restored market accountability, by exposing poorly performing companies to the threat of correction. In many ways the debate has been rendered irrelevant by history – with the collapse of junk-bond financing in 1989, large-scale takeovers are now few and far between, a notable exception being the contest for Paramount Communications.[84] However, the years of increased takeover activity did raise a host of new questions regarding the role and responsibilities of the board. These questions remain as pertinent today as they did during the go-go takeover years.

**Recommendations for the Future**

Academics, judges, legislators, shareholders, managers, board advisers, and even directors themselves have made a number of recommendations for improving the operation of boards. The directors of General Motors, KMart, and American Express overcame the obstacles of the current structure to respond to crises. In this section we will discuss some of these proposals to improve the performance of boards of directors that might allow – or even encourage – boards to pre-empt crises.

The post-takeover era has resulted in a new focus on independent directors as a group separate from the other directors. Increasingly, shareholders are looking to outsiders – who are willing to own a significant block of stock – to take the lead on board issues. They are also asking for more of a role in setting the criteria for board service, if not involvement in the selection of the candidates themselves.

**THE FUTURE OF DIRECTOR COMPENSATION**

Director compensation is an issue of increasing concern. Pay for performance is just as important with directors as it is with executives. As with executive pay, the important question in director pay is not "how much" but "how." Of course, the assumption of risk should be rewarded. It is often said that directors are paid far too much for what they do, but not nearly enough for what they ought to do. If directors are prepared to link their own wealth to the performance of the company, then they should be paid more. No shareholder objects to directors who make a lot of money as long as the shareholders make a lot of money, too.

An article in *Directors and Boards* magazine by Marcia Lewis correctly recommends that director compensation should be more closely tied to corporate performance. And she rightly suggests that more share ownership makes better directors. But she comes up with the wrong mechanism for assuring that directors hold more stock. The problem is clear from the title of her piece: "Give Directors Restricted Stock."[85] Directors' stock should not be a gift. Nor should it be a replacement for a pension, as she recommends. Otherwise, stock awards would merely be a way of exchanging one marginal compensation supplement for another. Programs "to facilitate share acquisition" are not meaningful unless the value of the incentives is directly and explicitly set off against current compensation levels. As Crystal writes:

> Giving the directors more stock is not a bad idea *per se*. But I strongly suspect that the critics who were pushing for more stock had in mind some form of capital contribution by the directors, perhaps cutting the cash compensation of the outside directors and then substituting shares of stock with an equivalent economic value. I even more strongly suspect that the critics didn't have in mind letting the outside directors continue to receive their usual cash compensation and then giving them free shares of stock and stock options on top of that.[86]

Unless carefully designed, stock-related compensation (in the form of stock options and/or outright grants) for directors could encourage measures that attempt to engineer a short-term increase in the stock price at the sacrifice of long-term viability for the company (for example, drastically reducing R&D). This can be addressed by the use of awards of restricted stock vesting 12 to 36 months after the director retires from the board. A growing trend is deferral or conversion of retainer and fees for up to a 50 percent discount of the current stock price; however, these programs should be designed so that they do not interfere with the board's ability to limit the terms of directors they do not want to keep on the board.

But the most important goal here is for directors to have enough of their own financial future at risk to think like shareholders. Lawrence Tucker of Brown Brothers Harriman was a director on one board in which the other outside directors' average investment in the company was nearly $1 million apiece. He said: "Believe me, that is a board that pays attention . . . I've never seen the pocket calculators come out so quickly in my life."[87]

Director compensation is one of the most sensitive and complex tasks facing the board and the company, because, by definition, no member of the board can view the issue without conflicts. For that reason, many observers, including the National Association of Corporate Directors, recommend that boards should impose procedural safeguards to ensure credibility, including enhanced disclosure, review, eliminating consulting fees, life and health insurance, and charitable contributions, with exclusive reliance on stock-based pay. Safeguards include full disclosure of director compensation in the proxy statement, with supporting data justifying the approach, and submitting the director compensation plan to a review by an independent expert (not the company's or the board's compensation consultants) from time to time, publishing a summary of that review in the proxy statement. But even that will not be enough unless shareholders review director pay disclosures carefully, and respond by withholding votes for directors who approve poor pay plans, and submitting resolutions to make sure that director pay plans are designed to align the interests of directors with shareholders.

## INCREASING INDEPENDENT DIRECTORS' AUTHORITY

It intuitively seems a good rule of thumb to have a majority of the directors be independent. Shareholders have submitted proposals asking that companies have a majority of outside directors, or that crucial committees like nominating, audit, and compensation be made up exclusively of outside directors. Some companies, including General Motors in 1991 (which already had a majority of outside directors, and just adopted a by-law making it formal) agreed to the terms of the proposals, so they never went to a vote.[88]

Proposals to split the positions of chairman and CEO fall into this category as well. In 1992, a shareholder resolution advising that Sears, Roebuck separate the two positions won 27 percent of the vote. The following year, the proposal was resubmitted and won 32 percent. The sponsor of the resolution at Sears explained the reasons for recommending a split:

> I believe a person in the position of Chairman/CEO is subject to an inherent conflict of interest that the shareholders of Sears can no longer afford. This conflict, in my opinion, results from the obvious concentration of power and lack of accountability that results from combining the two positions. The CEO is the company's most senior manager, responsible for executing corporate strategy. When the same individual is chairman of the board of directors, which is charged with the duty of monitoring management on behalf of shareholders, it can create an untenable situation.[89]

Sears has so far resisted the pressure, but other companies, also targeted by shareholders, have not. At General Motors, Westinghouse, and American Express – companies where the chief executive was forced to resign – the board took the opportunity to separate the roles of CEO and chairman, at least for a transitional period.

Many governance activists have backed the moves to separate the roles. Jamie Heard, president of Institutional Shareholder Services, said: "The goal here is really not to emasculate CEOs, the goal is to empower the board."[90] Jay W. Lorsch, of the Harvard Business School called such a separation "the single most significant thing to do" by a company's board.[91] John Nash of the National Association of Corporate Directors said that CEOs' attitude is that: " 'It's my company and it's my board.' They don't get it that it's not."[92]

### Martin Lipton's "Quinquennium" Proposal

Interestingly, the management side has also focused on independent directors as an important protection from abuse and entrenchment. In addition to the "modest proposal" mentioned above and described more fully below, Martin Lipton, the leading takeover lawyer on the management side, has produced a "quinquennial election" proposal. This would be a process to elect the entire slate of directors only once every five years. At that election, however, shareholders meeting some threshold would have access to the proxy to nominate their own candidates and comment on management's performance. And if the company had not met its own (publicly stated) goals, the board would be liable to lose any proxy fight.

Lipton's model "looks to the outside director as the primary monitor of the business performance of corporate managers." He argues that the proposal strengthens the role of the independent director by sharpening his incentive to perform (due to greater risk of losing the seat on the board), and by helping to remove current barriers to obtaining business information. The proposal would also limit the number of boards on which an outside director could serve to three, and it would increase their compensation.

### "A Market for Independent Directors"

A widely circulated proposal by Stanford's Ronald J. Gilson and Harvard's Reinier Kraakman suggests that institutional investors create "a market for independent directors" by "recruiting a class of outside directors who actively monitor public corporations, much as LBO sponsors or universal banks in Japan and Germany actively monitor their own companies."[93] They suggest that the institutions, perhaps through some coordinating entity like the CII or ISS, develop a cadre of full-time directors whose entire professional obligation would be to serve as director of five or six companies. Gilson and Kraakman point out that the institutions have the votes to make this possible. They suggest that compliance with SEC rules should not be too burdensome, as control is not at issue (though they recognize that reform of the proxy rules would be a significant help). And they suggest that a director of five companies is unlikely to become co-opted by any one of them.

The National Association of Corporate Directors (NACD) is a trade association based in Washington, led by President John Nash and Chairman Jean Head Sisco. NACD provides courses, studies, surveys, and materials, hosts conferences, convenes working groups on topics like executive compensation and CEO and director evaluation, and tracks and comments on legislation. Its publications include *Director's Monthly*. NACD also evaluates boards and maintains a database of director candidates.

Many observers have recommended adoption of the British "PRO NED" model, a clearinghouse/head-hunting firm to provide boards with qualified independent ("non-executive" in the UK) directors. PRO NED stands for the Promotion of Non-Executive Directors. PRO NED was established in 1982 under the sponsorship of a group of financial and industrial institutions, including The Bank of England, the Institutional Shareholders Committee, and the Confederation of British Industry. Sir Adrian Cadbury, chairman of PRO NED, described the group as having three main tasks:

1. To promote the wider use of non-executive directors through publicity and other means; to provide general guidance for non-executive directors on the discharge of their duties; and to contribute to current thinking on the structure of company boards, the role of non-executive directors, and legislative and other developments (including prospective developments in the EEC) concerning these matters. PRO NED holds seminars and discussions on aspects of the non-executive director's role and work.
2. To maintain an extensive register of names of actual and/or potential non-executive directors, of high quality and of a wide range of business experience and qualifications.
3. To provide companies on request with the names of suitable candidates for their boards, of the right quality and background, from which a choice may be made; and to give help on the assessment of the overall capabilities of individual candidates and of their suitability for particular appointments.

### "Designated Director"

An interesting legislative initiative enacted in Michigan permits companies incorporated there to designate an independent director, meeting certain criteria, for special compensation, rights (including communication with shareholders at company expense), and responsibilities (including determinations on indemnification, transactions that raise conflicts questions, and derivative litigation). This designation is limited to a three-year term. Significantly, companies who exercise this option have more limited liability. An organization called the Independent Director Foundation encourages companies to take advantage of the new Michigan law. It also gathers information on the way that independent directors are used, and hopes to encourage other states, the exchanges, or federal regulators to adopt similar laws. They will maintain a roster of qualified candidates.

### "Just Vote No"

In November of 1990, former SEC Commissioner Joseph Grundfest urged members of the CII to "just vote no" – to withhold votes for directors as a way of sending a strong message of concern to managements and boards of underperforming companies. The members of the Council were receptive. According to a scholarly and painstakingly documented follow-up by Grundfest himself, institutional investors representing more than $269 billion in equities have used this mechanism.

His article gets right to the point: "The takeover wars are over. Management won."[94] To the extent that the market for corporate control was effective in disciplining and removing inefficient managers in the 1980s, it is no longer available.

Grundfest recommends "just vote no" as an alternative. He argues that the withhold vote's symbolic nature (it cannot prevent the election of unopposed candidates) is its strength. It will not leave a vacuum at the company's top or upset the company's governance structure. But it will send an embarrassingly public "vote of no confidence" to the board, thus providing an incentive for improved performance. That could mean making the hard decision to get rid of the CEO; a decision that recently increased value by more than $2.7 billion at just four companies examined in the article. Grundfest also does a cost-benefit analysis of a "just vote no" strategy and concludes that the costs (mechanics, information, coordination, publicity – good and bad) and the conflicts (with money manager's clients or other commercial relationships) are more than outweighed by the benefits: "Symbols . . . have consequences. A successful 'just vote no' campaign can reduce internal reforms as a result of social pressures that lead board members to engage in more effective monitoring. Alternatively, a substantial 'just vote no' turnout can increase the probability of a hostile proxy contest or tender offer that will be treated more kindly by the courts precisely because it follows a significant 'just vote no' turnout."

Grundfest's approach has been supported by some CEOs. H. Brewster (Bruce) Atwater, CEO of General Mills and then Chairman of the Business Roundtable's Special Task Force on Corporate Governance, has encouraged disgruntled institutions to "just vote no." In a 1991 Senate hearing on shareholder rights, Atwater testified: "I know of no board that would not be moved dramatically by as little as 20 percent of the shareholder votes being withheld for the election of directors. The board would perceive itself as being vulnerable and would do everything in its power to attempt to correct the situation which led to this shareholder vote of no confidence."[95]

Shareholders can send a strong message of concern, not only to the company's directors and management, but also to anyone considering running a dissident slate. This response by shareholders strikes a good balance between the need for oversight by shareholders and the need for stability and continuity in the management of corporations.

## "Compact for Owners and Directors"

The "Compact for Owners and Directors" developed by representatives of shareholders and management, assigns to outside directors the responsibility for evaluating the CEO and screening and recommending new directors. It also recommends that outside directors meet alone, at least once a year.

## Board Evaluation

The National Association of Corporate Directors published a report on the performance evaluation of CEOs, boards, and directors in 1994. Prepared by a Blue Ribbon Commission of directors, shareholders, academics, and corporate officers, the report urged boards to develop a system for setting goals and evaluating the performance of individual directors, board committees, and the board as a whole. One key recommendation was a separate evaluation of the CEO in his capacity as chairman, if the CEO serves in both positions.

## Lipton/Lorsch's "Modest Proposal"

Academic Jay Lorsch and corporate lawyer Marty Lipton co-wrote an article entitled "A Modest Proposal for Improved Corporate Governance." They described their ideas as modest, not because they were modest in scope, but because (unlike Lipton's Quinquennium idea) their implementation would not require the involvement of Congress, the SEC, or the stock exchanges. Rather, the authors argued, their proposals could be implemented simply via the willingness of boards of directors and management.

Lipton and Lorsch offer some basic structural changes – such as shrinking the size of the board, increasing the time spent by directors on board service, and limiting the number of boards that a director serves – and some reforms that they believe would encourage director independence. For example, they suggest that boards chaired by the CEO should identify a "lead director," taken from one of the independent outsiders.

> What this person is called is not important, but his or her duties are important. We believe that the CEO/Chairman should consult with this lead director on the following matters: the selection of board committee members and chairpersons; the board's meeting

agendas; the adequacy of information directors receive; and the effectiveness of the board meeting process.

Furthermore, Lipton and Lorsch argue that a board with a designated lead director would be able to establish a better system of CEO evaluation, and thus deal more effectively with the possibility that the only person to judge the CEO's performance would be the CEO himself. While arguing that specific rules can't suit every company, the authors produce detailed guidelines for evaluating the CEO.

1. The assessment should be based on company performance, and the progress the CEO has made toward his or her personal long- and short-range goals. Such personal goals would constitute the major extraordinary initiatives the CEO wanted to achieve, e.g., developing and selecting a successor; expanding into markets internationally; making a major acquisition; creating a significant joint venture. We contemplate that short-term goals will be agreed upon annually among the CEO and the independent directors. The longer-term goals might have a three- to five-year horizon, but would be reviewed annually and changed as necessary.
2. Each director would make an individual assessment of the CEO's performance. These assessments then would be synthesized to reveal the tendency, as well as any range of views. This synthesis could be done by the lead director, or by a small group or committee of independent directors.
3. The CEO would receive this synthesized feedback in a confidential manner in which both he or she and the independent directors were comfortable.
4. After the CEO had time to reflect on it and to develop a response, he or she would then discuss his or her reactions to the assessment with all the independent directors. This discussion also should focus on any changes in goals for the company or the CEO which seem appropriate.

## MAKING DIRECTORS GENUINELY "INDEPENDENT"

The primary conclusion of this chapter is that America's boards of directors have, more often than not, failed to protect shareholders' interests. In one respect, this was inevitable. We demand too much of corporate boards. We expect directors to accept usually less than $50,000 a year, devote less than two weeks' work a year, and still be able to monitor a company that may generate billions in sales with hundreds of thousands of employees in dozens of countries. There is the theory of the fiduciary standard holding them accountable, and the reality of actually being able to.

Independent directors were meant to be a means to an end. It was thought that informed, intelligent, and wise directors, of proven integrity, bound by a fiduciary standard, would effectively oversee management. Being outsiders, they wouldn't face the conflicts that might face, say, the chief operating officer, reluctant to criticize his boss and in no position to call for his ouster. The idea proved to be a mirage. Independence is an intangible concept. Outsiders cannot be guaranteed to be independent, any more than insiders can be assumed to be deferent. Personality plays a strong role, so that the CEO's strong-minded brother may be able to evaluate the boss's performance while a more compliant outsider may not.

Directors do not become independent just because they have no economic ties to the company beyond their job as a director. Disinterested outsiders can mean uninterested outsiders. The key is not "independence," arbitrarily defined, but whether a director's interests are aligned with those of the shareholders. If a director is to represent the interests of the shareholders, he must share those interests. More, he must be intimately familiar with those interests. Put simply, he must be a shareholder.

The key to a good board is ownership. Each director's personal worth should be closely tied to the fortunes of the company. No director is going to remain passive if a quarter, or even a tenth, of his net worth is at stake.

The CEO of Wall Street securities house Salomon Inc. described that company's criteria for board membership. The first such criterion was: "Be owner oriented – usually best demonstrated by an investment in Salomon's stock that is significant in relation to the individual's net worth."[96]

## INVOLVEMENT BY SHAREHOLDERS

Whether it is the Exxon Committee or a LENS-like special purpose monitoring organization, there are a number of proposals for shareholders to assert and exercise control over the selection and ordering of priorities of the board through some kind of collective action vehicle.[97] One such vehicle is the shareholder committee described in chapter 2. *"The mere fact that the directors will know that they have been chosen by investors should make them more responsive to shareholder concerns."*[98]

## NOTES

1. Adam Smith, *The Wealth of Nations* (New York: Random House edition, 1937), pp. 699–700.
2. For more on the governance of SUM, see Stanley C. Vance, *Corporate Leadership: Boards, Directors, and Strategy* (McGraw-Hill, New York, 1983), pp. 3–6.
3. Korn/Ferry International, "Board of Directors, Twentieth Annual Study," 1993.
4. Id.
5. Delaware General Corporation Law Annotated Franchise Tax Law Uniform Limited Partnership Act. As of Feb. 2, 1988.
6. The Business Roundtable, *Corporate Governance and American Competitiveness,* March 1990, p. 7.
7. American Law Institute, *Principles of Corporate Governance: Analysis and Recommendation,* Draft 2, 1984, pp. 66–7.
8. Wayne Marr, "Do Independent Outside Directors Improve Corporate Performance?" Research Paper, Clemson University, College of Commerce and Industry, July 1991, p. 1.
9. Attorney Ira M. Millstein of Weil, Gotschal & Manges in New York, says that in addition to hiring, monitoring, and firing CEOs, directors are there to "certify" them. This means that when corporate performance suffers, directors need to judge whether this is because of or despite CEO performance. If it is the former, they must replace the CEO. If it is the latter, they can provide support in the form of "certification." See Ira M. Millstein, "The Evolution of the Certifying Board," *The Business Lawyer,* 48, 4 (Aug. 1993), pp. 1485–97. Also see "Corporate Governance Headed in the Right Direction," *Director's Monthly,* 18, 1 (Jan. 1994), p. 1. Note, however, that the ability to make this distinction requires a level of independence and commitment from directors that has been difficult to find in the past, as the examples in this chapter show.
10. John Harvey-Jones, *Making It Happen* (London: Collins, 1988), p. 147. For more on ICI, see the case in point in chapter 1.
11. Hugh Parker, "The Company Chairman – His Role and Responsibilities," *Long Range Planning,* 23, 4 (1990), pp. 35–43.
12. Peter Drucker, "The Bored Board," in *Toward the Next Economics and Other Essays* (Harper & Row, New York, 1981), p. 110.
13. "The Governance of Oozcskblnya," CII Central, Newsletter for Members of the Council of Institutional Investors, 6, 8 (Aug. 1993).
14. Bryan Burrough and John Helyar, *Barbarians at the Gate* (Harper & Row, New York, 1990), p. 75.
15. Bryan Burrough and John Helyar, "RJR Nabisco Board Asserts Independence in Buy-Out Decisions," *Wall Street Journal,* Nov. 10, 88, p. A1.

16. Joann S. Lublin, "More Chief Executives Are Being Forced Out by Tougher Boards," *Wall Street Journal,* June 6, 1991, p. A1.
17. Suein L. Hwang, "Fired Tambrands CEO Was Unusually Close to a Consulting Firm," *Wall Street Journal,* Aug. 23, 1993, p. A1.
18. Id.
19. Id.
20. Id.
21. Ada Demb and F. Friedrich Neubauer, *The Corporate Board – Confronting the Paradoxes* (Oxford University Press, Oxford, 1992), pp. 70, 97.
22. Walter Salmon, "Crisis Prevention: How to Gear Up Your Board," *Harvard Business Review,* Jan.–Feb. 1993, p. 69.
23. Robert K. Mueller, *Building a Power Partnership: CEOs and Their Boards of Directors* (Amacom, New York, 1993). Of Mueller's 16 books, nine have concerned boards. A tenth book on boards should appear in 1996.
24. Bernard Marcus, "How Directors Mind the Store at Home Depot," *Directorship Magazine,* XVII, 10 (Oct. 1992), p. 1.
25. Korn/Ferry International, "Board of Directors, Twentieth Annual Study," 1993.
26. Oxford Analytica, *Board Directors and Corporate Governance: Trends in the G7 Countries Over the Next Ten Years,* a study prepared for Russell Reynolds Associates, Price Waterhouse, Goldman Sachs International, Gibson, Dun & Crutcher, by Oxford Analytica Ltd, Oxford, England, Sept. 1992, p. 65.
27. Egon Zehnder International, *Corporate Issues Monitor,* USA, IV, 1 (1989).
28. See also the 1992 NACD survey, supra, for a similar result.
29. P.L. Rechner and D.R. Dalton, "CEO Duality and Organizational Performance: A Longitudinal Analysis," *Strategic Management Journal,* 12, 1991, pp. 155–60.
30. The figure is bigger for larger companies. In 1994, Boardroom Consultants of New York found that 38.6 percent of the 300 largest public companies retained the former CEO as a board member. However, that figure was down from previous years. See Marlene Givant Star, "Few CEOs Stay with the Board," *Pensions and Investments,* Jan. 24, 1994, p. 11.
31. Howard D. Sherman, "Catch 22: The Retired CEO as Company Director," Institutional Shareholder Services, July 15, 1991.
32. Korn/Ferry Organizational Consulting, "Reinventing Corporate Governance: Directors Prepare for the 21st Century. Results of *Fortune* Company Directors," Jan. 1993.
33. Dale Hanson, Hearing before the Subcommittee on Telecommunications and Finance of the Committee on Energy and Commerce, House of Representatives, Aug. 2, 1989.

34. SpencerStuart Board Index, 1991 Proxy Report.
35. Korn/Ferry International, 1989 annual study of boards. The study found the following makeup at billion dollar companies: 86 percent included at least one CEO/COO of another company, and 74 percent included at least one retired executive from another company.
36. The interlocking compensation committee practice may not be widespread, but it is common enough to have prompted a new SEC disclosure requirement in 1992. The amendments to executive compensation disclosure mentioned earlier include a requirement that companies disclose compensation committee interlocks.
37. Korn/Ferry Organizational Consulting, supra.
38. Alison Leigh Cowan, "Board Room Back Scratching?" *New York Times,* June 2, 1993, p. D1.
39. Louis Brandeis, Pujo Committee: House Committee on Banking and Currency, "Investigation of Concentration of Control of Money and Credit," House Report, No. 1593, Feb. 28, 1913.
40. Martin Lipton and Jay W. Lorsch, "A Modest Proposal for Improved Corporate Governance," *The Business Lawyer,* 48, 1, Nov. 1992, p. 64.
41. Korn/Ferry Organizational Consulting, supra.
42. Kathleen Day, "Frank Carlucci and the Corporate Whirl," *The Washington Post,* Feb. 7, 1993, p. H1.
43. Institutional Shareholder Services, Proxy Voting Manual, third ed., Jan. 1993, p. 3.13.
44. Egon Zehnder International, supra IV, 1 (1989).
45. Id.
46. Dana Wechlser and Nancy Rotenier, "Goodbye to Berle & Means," *Forbes,* Jan. 3, 1993, p. 100.
47. Barbara Lyne, "The Executive Life," *New York Times,* Jan. 2, 1992.
48. Ira M. Millstein and Winthrop Knowlton, "Can the Board of Directors Help the American Corporation Earn the Immortality it Holds So Dear? An Examination of Our System of Corporate Governance With Recommendations for Change," Research Paper, Center for Business and Government, John F. Kennedy School of Government, Harvard University, Jan. 1988.
49. Id.
50. Stanley C. Vance, *Corporate Leadership: Boards, Directors and Strategy* (McGraw-Hill, New York, 1983), p. 50.
51. Korn/Ferry International, Board of Directors Twentieth Annual Study, 1993. According to Vance (Id.), a sampling of over 1000 directors in 1963 found that 59.3 percent were insiders.
52. SpencerStuart Board Index, 1991.
53. Id.
54. SpencerStuart Board Index, 1993.
55. See, for example, Elmer W. Johnson, "An Insider's Call for Outside Direction," *Harvard Business Review,* March-April 1990, pp.

46–55; and Sir Adrian Cadbury, The Company Chairman (Fitzwilliam, London, 1990).

56. Arthur Fleischer, Geoffrey C. Hazard, and Miriam Z. Kipper, *Board Games* (Little, Brown, Boston, 1988), p. 3.

57. Ira M. Millstein and Winthrop Knowlton, supra.

58. Testimony of Benjamin M. Rosen, before the Subcommittee on Telecommunications and Finance, Committee on Energy and Commerce, United States House of Representatives, April 21, 1993.

59. Edward J. Epstein, "Who Owns the Corporation?," A Twentieth Century Fund Paper (Priority Press, New York, 1986), p. 13.

60. SpencerStuart Board Index, 1991.

61. Securities and Exchange Commission, "Shark Repellents and Stock Prices: The Effects of Antitakeover Amendments Since 1980," Office of the Chief Economist, Washington, DC, July 1985, p. 5.

62. See the resolution sponsored by John J. Gilbert at the Sears, Roebuck & Co. annual meeting, 1993.

63. See Dale Hanson's testimony to the Subcommittee on Telecommunications and Finance of the Committee on Energy and Commerce, House of Representatives, Aug. 2, 1989. Hanson testified that following a CalPERS-sponsored shareholder resolution at USAir, "The representative from USAir said, 'Gee, you guys had us worried. We had to call many shareholders back 3 or 4 times to get them to change the vote because it looked like you were going to win.' "

64. According to the United Shareholders Association "1992 Shareholder 1,000" review of America's 1,000 largest companies, only 74 had some form of confidential policy.

65. See the "Avon Letter," US Department of Labor, Feb. 23, 1988: "Finally the Department notes that section 404(a)(1)(B) requires the named fiduciary appointing the investment manager to periodically monitor the activities of the investment manager with respect to the management of plan assets. In general, this duty would encompass the monitoring of decisions made and actions taken by investment managers with regard to proxy voting." See also appendix 9.

66. Bayless Manning, "The Shareholder Appraisal Remedy: An Essay for Frank Coker," 72 *Yale Law Journal*, 223, 245 (1962).

67. *Norlin Corp. v. Rooney, Pace Inc.*, 744 F.2d 255 (2d Cir. 1984), applying New York law. See also discussion of the use of ESOPs to defend against takeovers at the end of this chapter.

68. *Smith v. Van Gorkom*, 488 A.2d 858 (Del. 1985). For a summary of Van Gorkom and other landmark legal case summaries, see Stanley Foster Reed and Alexandra Reed Lajoux, *The Art of M&A: A Merger/Acquisition/Buyout Guide* (Business One Irwin, 1995), pp. 805–23.

69. Id., p. 869.

70. *Unocal Corp. v. Mesa Petroleum Co.*, 493 A.2d 946 (Del. 1985).

71. Id., p. 956.
72. For a discussion of "poison pills" see page 213.
73. *Revlon, Inc. v. MacAndrews & Forbes Holdings, Inc.,* 506 A.2d 173, 181 (Del. 1986).
74. Id., p. 182.
75. Id., p. 182.
76. For a definition of "white knights" see page 213.
77. Id., p. 184.
78. 506 A.2d 173, 182 (Del. 1986).
79. See, for example, Analysis Group, Inc., "The Effects of Poison Pills on Shareholders: A Synthesis of Recent Evidence," Belmont, MA, Nov. 4, 1988; Office of the Chief Economist, Securities and Exchange Commission, "The Economics of Poison Pills," March 5, 1986; Office of the Chief Economist, Securities and Exchange Commission, "The Effects of Poison Pills on the Wealth of Target Shareholders," Oct. 26, 1986; Michael Ryngaert, "The Effect of Poison Pill Securities on Shareholder Wealth," *Journal of Financial Economics,* 20 (1988), pp. 377–417; Nancy Sheridan, "Impact of Stockholder Rights Plan on Stock Price," Kidder, Peabody & Co., New York, June 15, 1986; Richard Wines, "Poison Pill Impact Study," Georgeson & Co., New York, March 31, 1988; and Richard Wines "Poison Pill Impact Study II," Georgeson & Co., New York, Oct. 31, 1988.
80. Note, however, that in Jan. 1994, Time Warner reinstated the poison pill that it had eliminated three years previously. The company brought back the pill after Seagram, the Canadian spirits company, purchased over 11 percent of Time Warner on the open market. Time Warner defended the reinstatement of the pill, saying it wished to prevent Seagram from exercising "creeping control" over the company. See Laura Landro and Eben Shapiro, "Time Warner Protects Itself Against Seagram," *Wall Street Journal,* Jan. 21, 1994, p. A3.
81. At Hartmarx, a majority of shareholders voted to redeem a poison pill two years in a row, but the company still refused to do so.
82. Michael Ryngaert, "The Effect of Poison Pill Securities on Shareholder Wealth," *Journal of Financial Economics,* 20 (1988).
83. Robert Slater, *The Titans of Takeover* (Prentice Hall, Englewood Cliffs, NJ, 1987), p. 155.
84. See Robert Comment and G. William Schwert, "Poison or Placebo? Evidence on the Deterrent and Wealth Effects of Modern Antitakeover Measures," Bradley Policy Research Center, William E. Simon Graduate School of Business Administration, University of Rochester, March 11, 1993. Their figures show that takeover activity tripled between 1975 and 1988, but that by 1990, takeover rates were back to 1975 levels. However, in 1993, a very 1980s-style takeover

battle developed as Paramount Communications Inc., was forced to auction itself following a friendly offer from Viacom Inc., and a competing, hostile offer from QVC Inc.

85. Marcia Lewis, "Give Directors Restricted Stock," *Directors and Boards,* 16, 4 (Summer 1992).

86. Graef Crystal, *In Search of Excess* (W.W. Norton, New York, 1991), p. 229.

87. Lawrence Tucker, *Investor's Business Daily,* July 7, 1993, Finance; p. 4.

88. Support for independent directors as a legitimating force comes from other sources as well. The controversial one share, one vote proposal submitted for SEC approval by the AMEX in 1976 provides that dual class recapitalizations through exchange offers (which can be coercive) will only be permitted if one-third of the directors are independent, or if holders of low-voting stock have the exclusive right to elect 25 percent of the directors.

89. Sears, Roebuck & Co. 1992 proxy statement, pp. 16–17.

90. Editorial Roundtable, "Chair and CEO: Should the Jobs Be Split?" *The Corporate Governance Advisor,* April–May 1993.

91. Judith H. Dobrzynski, "Chairman and CEO: One Hat Too Many," *Business Week,* Nov. 18, 1991, p. 124.

92. Id.

93. Ronald J. Gilson and Reinier Kraakman, "Reinventing the Outside Director: An Agenda for Institutional Investors," Presented at the Salomon Brothers Center and Rutgers Centers Conference on The Fiduciary Responsibilities of Institutional Investors, June 14–15, 1990.

94. Joseph A. Grundfest, "Just Vote No: A Minimalist Strategy for Dealing with Barbarians Inside the Gates," 45 *Stanford Law Review,* 4, April 1993.

95. H. Brewster Atwater, Senate Testimony, Subcommittee on Securities, Oct. 17, 1991.

96. Robert E. Denham, "Envisioning New Relationships Between Corporations and Intelligent Investors," Speech to the Institutional Investor Project of the Columbia University School of Law conference on "Relational Investing," May 7, 1993.

97. George W. Dent, Jr., "Toward Unifying Ownership and Control in the Public Corporation," *Wisconsin Law Review,* 1989, 5, p. 881.

98. Id., p. 908, emphasis added.

# 4

# Management: Performance

Management of the modern corporation involves a series of herculean tasks. Many of the corporate governance issues concerning corporate management have been raised earlier, in the discussions of the corporation, the role of shareholders, and the CEO's relationship with directors. In this section, we will begin by examining some of these issues from the perspective of management.

## INTRODUCTION

In January 1993, a *Fortune* magazine cover story had a provocative headline echoing the Declaration of Independence: "The King Is Dead." It went on: "Booted bosses, ornery owners, and beefed-up boards reflect a historic shift in corporate power. The imperial CEO has had his day – long live the shareholders." The article ran down a list of deposed CEOs, 13 from the Fortune 500 in just 18 months. How did this happen? Veteran journalist Thomas Stewart saw the events in Shakespearean terms:

> And in the encircling tents, their armor glittering, their coffers brimming with gold, the Bolingbrokes of the piece: institutional investors, activist shareholders, and even the boards of directors themselves, the king's own court, to whom he gave preferment, now demanding his obeisance – if not his head. . . . What's manifest here is large, basic, and historic.[1]

Stewart explained where the idea of the "CEO-King" began:

> The passing of generations had attenuated the power of founding families (noted Adolf Berle and Gardiner Means), while the rise of the public corporation had spread ownership among tens of thousands of individual shareholders, none of whom could cast a meaningful vote in the governance of their companies. The result, Berle and Means showed, was a new class of professional managers who owned little of the corporation they nevertheless controlled. The merest whim of the imperial executive echoed like thunder down a valley. The CEO has to be careful, ran an old joke at General

Electric; if he asks for a cup of coffee, somebody might run out and buy Brazil.[2]

But Stewart went on to say that, "paradoxically, executive leadership is becoming more indispensable than ever. Only the executive can mediate among the multitude of constituencies vying to influence every corporation: investors and lenders, communities, employees (who may be big investors), customers. The CEO may be on a shorter leash, but he's a more valuable dog."[3] Like Harvard's John Pound, who said that in the future CEOs will be more like a politician than a monarch, negotiating agreement with all of the different parts of the corporate constituency, long-time counsel to CEOs and directors Ira Millstein advises CEOs to adjust to a more consensus-based corporate governance structure. He wrote, in an article addressed to CEOs: "I ask you . . . to determine to what extent the board procedures at your companies encourage independence and hence suggest credibility. After all, if you don't, shareholders, plaintiffs, and the government may."[4]

In any relationship, especially one as intertwined as the CEO/board/shareholder relationship, changes in one party have an impact on the others. As shareholders and directors have become more active, the imperial CEO in the GE joke has begun to seem like a quaint cartoon figure.

But it was only a very short time ago that CEOs (and their lawyers) were quite comfortable with the idea that the CEO was, if not a king, then a benevolent dictator. Just three years before the "King Is Dead" cover story, *Fortune* magazine ran a cover story about the "Pharonic CEO," noting: "Pharaoh in all his glory would have envied today's CEOs their perquisites and ever-sweetening pay. Too busy living the cosseted life, America's managerial élite have lost touch with the humble employee. Workers' faith in top management is collapsing. CEOs who don't come down from the heights are in for trouble."[5] The article predicted that CEOs could not expect the support of employees who consider them out of touch. "Hourly workers and supervisors indeed agree that 'we're all in this together,' but what 'we're in' turns out to be a frame of mind that mistrusts senior management's intentions, doubts its competence, and resents its self-congratulatory pay."

Interestingly, the insistence on change came not from employees, but from elements never mentioned in the article: the shareholders and the board.

## WHAT DO WE WANT FROM THE CEO?

The one certainty in business, as in life, is change. If it were possible, we all – investors, lenders, communities, employees, customers – would want a CEO who could predict the future and guide the company accordingly. Since that is impossible, what we want is a CEO who is able, by virtue of ability, expertise, resources, and authority, to keep the company not just ready for change but ready to benefit from changes, even to lead them. The CEO must be powerful enough to do the job, but accountable enough to make sure it is done correctly. The challenge for all of the participants in corporate governance is to make sure that there is enough of a balance between the two so that, overall, the decisions made by the CEO are in the long-term interests of the shareholders (and thus by definition all other constituencies) rather than in his own interests.

One of the key areas for achieving and evaluating this balance is executive compensation, discussed later in this chapter. The essential conflict between the goals of shareholders and management is not over the amount of pay but over its variability and risk. Shareholders want a compensation plan with maximum variability based on corporate performance, and management's natural tendency is to want a compensation plan with maximum security. Before we can understand how to best link management compensation to corporate performance, however, we must take a look at how we measure corporate performance.

### QUALITY: THE VALUE OF TQM

"Total Quality Management" (TQM) has been hailed as a success ever since its emergence as a movement in the years following World War II. Quantification of its value was developed by the international accounting firm of Ernst & Young, which joined with the American Quality Foundation in 1992 to study 900 specific management practices deemed to deliver "quality management" in four countries and four industries over a five-year period. They identified specific practices that had improved profitability (defined as return on assets), productivity (defined as value-added per employee), and quality (using a specified rating system) during that period. According to the report, these practices bring low performing employees up to acceptable (or better) performance, moderate performers up to high performance, and encourage high performers to stay at that level or improve even further.

The presence of these practices can be another indicator of a company's likely future performance. They are as follows.

- Three-dimensional strategy, including exploration of new horizons, selectivity (the ability to focus on the key imperatives), and drive (a passion for being the best).
- Making wisdom contagious, including empowering independence, interaction, and communication among employees, focusing on group performance rather than individual performance.
- External processes, including benchmarking (particularly of marketing systems, delivery and distribution systems, and service after delivery systems – all relating to the link between the company and its customers), systems for feedback from suppliers and customers.
- Continuous innovation, based on the internal and external evaluations outlined above.[6]

All methods of evaluating a company's value and performance are useful for evaluating the CEO. But perhaps one of the clearest indications of CEO quality is the structure of the organization itself. In general, the more diversified and conglomerated the company, the more likely it is to reflect the CEO's empire building and the less likely that it demonstrates focus and commitment to shareholder value. As one management consultant put it, "The design trick is to be small where small is beautiful and then be big where big is beautiful."[7]

## Case in Point: AT&T and NCR

In the years after the end of the go-go years of the takeover era, there was only one genuinely hostile takeover, and it was not by a raider like Carl Icahn or Donald Trump; it was AT&T's purchase of NCR. When NCR, a very entrepreneurial enterprise, made the classic argument of the target, that its special culture and constituencies required its independence (indeed, it was a pioneer of the constituency concept), it fell on deaf ears, ironically the ears of a board of directors that included several CEO veterans who had fought off their would-be hostile acquirers, characterizing them as all but in league with the devil. Under their direction, AT&T, the giant bureaucracy, was willing to go forward at (literally) almost any cost. And the shareholders were hard pressed to refuse. "As a stockholder, I have to say, 'Take the money and run. . . .' It's a major premium on the market by a qualified buyer. I don't see how they can say 'no.' "[8] (Note that by all accounts, AT&T then proceeded to destroy NCR.)

If, as one thoughtful consultant argues, in order to master change, the primary requirement for organizational health over the long term is a continual sense of renewal, then what investors and other corporate constituents most want from the CEO is someone who will create a "culture of questions."

> If you look at the history of companies, there's an irony in that, the more successful they become, the more convinced they become of their knowledge and the rightness of their view of the world, and the more arrogant and insular they become. Whatever helped them become successful in the past becomes institutionalized. The more successful, the more institutionalized, and the more this is a danger. It's not surprising that the problems at GM or IBM or Sears developed while the companies were clearly their industry leaders.[9]

## "DINOSAURS"

In the spring of 1993, *Fortune* writer Carol Loomis wrote a cover story entitled "The Dinosaurs" about companies whose annual value had declined both in absolute and in comparative terms over the previous two decades. The dinosaurs of the title were IBM, long thought of as the most profitable and the "best" company in the world; General Motors – the defining enterprise in a quintessentially American industry; and Sears, Roebuck – the greatest merchant of them all. All three of these companies were valued by the marketplace in 1993 much less generously than in earlier times.

The market became persuaded that these companies' ability to manage their assets to produce a flow of cash for owners in the future had deteriorated. One way to answer this question is by looking at those companies that *didn't* lose their top billing. Three companies maintained their positions as the most highly valued companies in the world: Exxon, AT&T, and General Electric.

### Cases in Point: Exxon, AT&T, and General Electric

- The world market for oil has been such that Exxon has not been required to alter radically its strategy to stay ahead. Exxon, unlike Sears, IBM, or General Motors, has not been the victim of a dramatically shifting marketplace.
- Ironically, AT&T has survived because, unlike IBM, it lost an antitrust case and was required to break itself up into seven "Baby Bell" companies. The breakup forced a rigorous redefinition of the company's mission. IBM, by contrast, emerged from the anti-

trust suit victorious but floundered as a result of its failure to undertake just such a review.[10]

- In 1980, General Electric was a huge and sprawling conglomerate, though in rock-solid financial condition – AAA bond rating, and a handsome 19.5 percent return on equity.[11] The company was the eleventh largest corporation in *Fortune*'s list of the most highly valued companies in the United States. In December 1980, the company announced the appointment of a new CEO and chairman, John F. Welch. Jack Welch did not believe that GE's respectable results reflected the true value that the company could generate. Over the succeeding decade Welch shook up the conglomerate from top to bottom. It is arguable whether, without Welch, GE would still feature in *Fortune*'s list of the world's largest companies.

  Welch insisted that each of GE's divisions be the number one or number two business of its kind in the world. Any business that failed to meet this test would be sold. Over the next decade, GE sold or closed almost $10 billion worth of businesses and product lines, and over $18 billion was spent on acquiring further businesses to boost those that remained. Notable acquisitions included Kidder Peabody in 1986 to join GE Financial Services, and NBC to join GE's broadcasting operations.

  But Welch was not satisfied with merely buying and selling businesses. His aim was to drive change through every part of GE's massive operation. He wanted the company to be as lean and responsive as the smallest startup. Partly, he did this by downsizing the company, and stretching middle management to the limit. Welch's notion was that if employees were overworked, they would spend less time in committee meetings or on other bureaucratic procedures that inhibited the company's ability to respond.[12] The effects of these changes were far-reaching – GE shed over 100,000 employees through the 1980s. While Welch was criticized for these cuts, and while many managers complained that the changes undermined security and loyalty, evidence of their worth was made plain in ever-improving financial results.

  Welch wished to reinvigorate every employee, from the bottom up. Welch wanted full-scale cultural change at GE, and that meant shaking up the entire workforce. Welch introduced a concept called "workout," a practice similar to German methods of employee relations. Workout introduced sessions in which 50 to 100 employees, generally chosen to represent a cross-section in terms of rank and tenure, would meet for two days to discuss their work. The lowliest employees were encouraged to make suggestions as to how their job could be made easier or more efficient, and how ingrained bad habits could be eliminated. In its first two years, more than 2,000 workout sessions were held, some including suppliers and customers.

Though some have criticized Welch's "empowerment" approach as futile,[13] there can be no doubting the impact that Welch's changes have had on the bottom line. Between 1980 and 1990, GE's net earnings improved from $1.5 billion to $4.3 billion. And between 1980 and 1989, GE's market value rose from $12 billion (number 11 on *Fortune*'s list) to $58 billion (number two). In 1993, GE finally topped the list, with a market value of $89 billion.[14] Clearly, GE would not be joining the "dinosaurs."

As far as the "dinosaurs" are concerned, however, there can be no doubt that the failure of IBM, GM, and Sears was at least partly a failure of governance. It is not surprising, for instance, that the problems at Sears developed when the same person held the jobs of CEO, chairman of the board, CEO of the largest (and worst-performing) operating division, chairman of the nominating committee of the board, and trustee of the 25 percent of the company's stock that was held on behalf of the employees. The company had circumvented all of the systems set up to ensure that the right questions would be asked by putting the same person in all of the positions that were supposed to monitor each other. It is impossible to identify what Hirschman calls "repairable lapses"[15] when the same person is both making the decisions and evaluating them.

The best way to make sure that the right questions are asked of the right people is to create a structure that aligns the interests of the CEO with the long-term interests of the shareholders as much as possible. Indeed, it is just this alignment that gives managers the expertise and the credibility to do their job effectively.

Although managers are self-interested, this interest can be aligned with that of investors through automatic devices, devices that are useless when those in control are "disinterested;" hence the apparent contradiction that self-interested managers have more freedom than disinterested regulators.[16]

## EXECUTIVE COMPENSATION

It took the abuses of the takeover era to wake up the institutional investors, and almost before they got started, the takeover era ended. But by that time, a new issue took over: excessive CEO

compensation. In some ways, this was an ideal corporate governance issue for the new activists. Complaints about compensation
could be made in a sound bite, with political, economic, and even
gossip appeal. This was the first corporate governance issue to go
from the financial pages to the front pages to the editorial pages
to the comic pages – even "Doonesbury" got in a few digs. And
this was not just some Capraesque populist movement. No one
complained about the money Bill Gates made at Microsoft, and
few complained about Michael Eisner's pay at Disney. But when
pay was not related to performance, the business press was just
as outraged as the shareholders. Even *Forbes*'s cover story on
executive pay bore a banner headline: "It doesn't make sense."[17]

It was also an issue uniquely suitable for being addressed by
shareholders. Compensation for performance is the perfect issue;
no shareholder initiative could have a more direct impact on shareholder value. If compensation is connected to performance, all
other shareholder initiatives become secondary. If compensation
is unrelated to performance, however, all the shareholder resolutions in the world won't make a difference.

The role of the shareholders with regard to compensation starts
with one simple point: compensation presents an investment
opportunity. The compensation plan is a clear indicator of the
company's value as an investment. It reveals what the CEO's
incentives are. If homeowners are deciding between two realtors
who want to sell their house – one who charges a flat fee and one
who charges a percentage of the sale price – they know they are
likely to do better with the one whose compensation is tied to
the money they themselves will eventually receive. Similarly, a
shareholder should want to invest in a CEO whose compensation
depends on the money the shareholder will receive. Compensation
plans also reveal what the company's goals are and how confident
the CEO and board are of the company's future.

Graef Crystal, in his book on executive compensation, *In Search
of Excess,*[18] discusses the impact that compensation plans should
have on stock-picking by sophisticated investors. His conclusion
that restricted stock grants are made by boards who do not think
the stock will go up is supported by his data on companies that
have made these awards. If his analysis is correct, selling short on
companies that make restricted stock grants should be a highly
profitable investment strategy.

Furthermore, compensation issues present shareholders with
some of their most cost-effective (highly leveraged) opportunities

for "investing" in shareholder initiatives. A shareholder can submit a shareholder proposal about executive compensation for little more than the cost of a stamp. Shareholders can distribute information about their views to other shareholders under the enormously simplified revised proxy rules for little more than the cost of a couple of dozen letters or phone calls. With a high likelihood of improving returns through this visible focus, and negligible, if any, downside risk, this is an "investment" that shareholders, especially fiduciary shareholders, will find increasingly appealing.

Shareholder initiatives on compensation have special appeal. CEOs get paid a lot for one reason – because they take risks. Their compensation should provide the appropriate incentives for those risks. To the extent that a shareholder initiative can better align these incentives, it is an investment with substantial returns.

The question, then, is not whether there will be increased activism by shareholders on the subject of compensation; the question is what form it will take. With the exception of a few extremists, shareholders have not objected to chief executives earning a lot of money. Roberto Goizueta's $81 million stock grant got four standing ovations from the Coca-Cola shareholders, who were delighted with the 38.2 percent annual returns during his tenure. What shareholders have objected to is chief executives being paid a lot of money without earning it; their focus has been on strengthening the link between pay and performance.

It's a very small group at the top of the compensation scale: rock stars, movie stars, athletes, investment bankers, and CEOs. All but CEOs are compensated for performance. And it is not coincidental that, of that group, CEOs are the only ones who pick the people who set their compensation. In all of the other categories, pay and performance are closely linked. Madonna made $38 million in 1991, almost all of it relating to her record sales. But she was paid union scale for her appearance in the movie *Dick Tracy,* that year, due to the low box office returns for her most recent films. Investment bankers who earned bonuses in the millions in the 1980s were living on unemployment checks in the 1990s. But statistics showed that CEOs do well regardless of performance, and the publicity for those numbers provided much of the momentum for the reforms on compensation disclosure.[19]

Of course, some of the fuss missed the point. United Airlines' Steve Wolf didn't really make $18.3 million in one year as cited in *Business Week;* most of his gains were from long-term stock options. And despite the headlines, in many, perhaps even most cases, compensation is not outrageous. The problem is that the extreme cases point out the failure of the system as a whole. If shareholders, as the consumers of executive compensation, cannot act when it is out of control, the system simply isn't working. Executive compensation unrelated to performance is just one symptom of a corporate governance system that fails to ensure management accountability.

The issue is not only matching compensation to performance. There is almost always some standard that can be used to support a bonus, and compensation consultants are good at providing a mix of "performance plans" that ensure that at least one of them will pay off. Crystal's book devotes an entire chapter to document in devastating detail the compensation package of Time Warner's late chairman, Steve Ross, dubbed by Crystal "The Prince of Pay." Ross's seven different long-term incentive plans included $21.1 million in stock options, $69.6 million in bonus units (plus $3.8 million in dividend equivalent payments), and another set of units that would pay out based on the stock's highest average price over an eight-week period over the previous two years.[20] There was also another set of units tied to the Warner stock price that paid him $58.7 million because the stock was valued at the time of the acquisition by Time. According to Crystal, "[h]is total take from all seven plans was $236 million over a period of effectively 17 years or about $14 million a year."[21] And it is worth noting that Ross's employment contracts were voted on by a board that included five officers of his company, without whom the contract would not have been approved.

Ross's performance at Warner may have been terrific. The problem was that the high compensation was almost coincidental; the compensation plan did not link compensation to performance. The issue shareholders should focus on is not just tying compensation to performance, but really improving performance.

It is all very well to talk about incentive plans, but all the incentives in the world cannot work if there are other impediments to getting the job done. Some so-called "incentive plans" can be manipulated. Targets can be hit by divesting a subsidiary instead of increasing product sales. More important, there is no incentive plan that can make a weekend athlete into an Olympic gold medalist. And no incentive plan will make a CEO who is in over his head suddenly able to turn the company around.

As mentioned at the beginning of this section, there is an inherent conflict of interest between shareholders and management with regard to compensation. It is important to note, however, that the conflict is not over the amount of compensation, but over the variability of the compensation. Shareholders want compensation to vary with performance as much as possible, while managers understandably want as much certainty as possible; even those who want a lot of variability on the upside are less willing to allow it on the downside.

This inherent conflict did not become obvious until the early 1990s, when executive compensation became the subject of magazine cover stories, *Nightline* and *Crossfire* debates on television, and hearings before the US Congress. In 1991, CalPERS called for shareholders to withhold their votes from the board of directors of ITT, where CEO Rand Aroskog's compensation more than doubled as the stock sank. The 1 percent of "withhold" votes cast led to a massive overhaul of the company's compensation plan. At Fairchild, an overpaying company that merited an entire chapter in Crystal's book, the board approved substantial revisions to the company's compensation plan, including a $250,000 cut in CEO Jeffrey Steiner's cash compensation, cancellation of 50,000 options, and agreement to no new options until 1993 and no raises until 1996. This was in settlement of a shareholder lawsuit, worth noting because courts are very reluctant to permit challenges to executive compensation.

General Dynamics reacted to the sobriquet "Generous Dynamics," accorded it by *Business Week* for a compensation package that gave its executives double their salary for a ten-day rise in stock prices. The company called a special meeting to get shareholder approval for substantial changes after pressure from shareholders – and a visit from *60 Minutes*. United Airlines executives agreed to increased disclosure of their compensation in the proxy statement, after negotiations with the United Shareholders Association. Many companies announced cuts; at USAir, the directors took a 20 percent compensation cut, to mirror the cuts they were asking of employees.

In 1992, the focus on compensation continued, as the SEC reversed its long-time policy and allowed advisory (non-binding) shareholder resolutions on compensation. These included the following proposals.

- Amend the company's severance package to prohibit payouts to any executive if, in the three preceding years, return on share-

holder equity was less than 8 percent (Equimark) – 16.5 percent in favor
- Abolish the short-term incentive plan for senior managers (Bell Atlantic) – 16.4 percent in favor
- Cap compensation at a multiple of the average-paid worker (Baltimore Gas & Electric) – 12.7 percent in favor
- Eliminate management bonus plan until stock regains its 1986 price level of $27 per share (Grumman) – dropped by proponent
- Fine outside directors $1,000 for failing to attend board meetings (Aetna Life) – 8.5 percent in favor
- Prohibit repricing of underwater stock options (Chrysler) – 7 percent in favor
- Disclose executives' severance packages (Kodak) – dropped by proponent
- Eliminate directors' retirement plan (Black Hills Corp.) – 44 percent in favor

In 1993, individuals submitted several hundred proposals seeking to limit executive compensation.[22] Support for these proposals was unexpectedly high, given that shareholders were only allowed to sponsor pay-related resolutions in 1992. The proposals received an average support of 18.8 percent.

The media and the politicians emphasized the size of certain executive compensation packages. Shareholders focused, as Michael Jensen and Kevin Murphy put it, not on "how much," but on "how."[23] Two crucial elements of the "how" are stock options and restricted stock grants, and shareholders began to make some important distinctions.

Compensation consultants Towers Perrin found that the average face value of stock options to CEOs has doubled in the last decade, to more than twice the value of annual compensation.

> "The salary of the chief executive of the large corporation is not a market award for achievement. It is frequently in the nature of a warm personal gesture by the individual to himself." *John Kenneth Galbraith*

## STOCK OPTIONS

Stock options, of course, are supposed to be the ultimate example of compensation for performance. The company gives the option recipient the right to purchase a block of the company's stock at some specified point in the future at a "strike price" set at the time of award, often the current trading price. So if the stock rises between the time of award and the time the option is exercised, the executive will get the benefit of the gain, without having had to make the capital expenditure to buy the stock. (For information about the controversy on valuing and expensing stock options, see the discussion in chapter 1.)

Theoretically, at least, the person granted the options will not make any money unless the stock goes up. A typical description of a stock option plan notes, "The company's stock option program is designed to focus attention on stock values, and to develop Company ownership, promote employee loyalty, reward long-term business success and develop a parallel interest between key employees and shareholders." But as one compensation consultant argues, market and industry factors (over which company management have no control) account for about two-thirds of the a stock price's movement.[24] Warren Buffett noted in one of his annual reports that stock options do not tie individual performance to individual compensation:

> Of course, stock options often go to talented, value-adding managers and sometimes deliver them rewards that are perfectly appropriate. (Indeed, managers who are really exceptional almost always get far less than they should.) But when the result is equitable, it is accidental. Once granted, the option is blind to individual performance. Because it is irrevocable and unconditional (so long as a manager stays in the company), the sluggard receives rewards from his options precisely as does the star. A managerial Rip Van Winkle, ready to doze for ten years, could not wish for a better "incentive" system . . .
>
> Ironically, the rhetoric about options frequently describes them as desirable because they put owners and managers in the same financial boat. In reality, the boats are far different. No owner has ever escaped the burden of capital costs, whereas a holder of a fixed-price option bears no capital costs at all. An owner must weigh upside potential against downside risk; an option holder has no downside. In fact, the business project in which you would wish to have an option frequently is a project in which you would reject ownership. (I'll be happy to accept a lottery ticket as a gift – but I'll never buy one.)[25]

Fans of options say that they are effective in motivating long-term performance. But Philip Morris gave CEO Hamish Maxwell options on 500,000 shares on his retirement, when motivation and performance were scarcely relevant.

But the most troubling aspect of stock option awards is "repricing," reissuing stock options when the stock price is below the option price. Companies that have repriced executive options included Apple Computers, Salomon Brothers, and Occidental Petroleum.[26] This removes all of the risks to management (and all of the benefits to shareholders) of a stock option grant. For the purpose of incentives, it is just like giving the managers cash. One of the most beneficial aspects of shareholder involvement is that repricing of stock options has all but disappeared.

But at the same time another kind of option award with almost no relation to performance is gaining in popularity. That is the awarding of huge option grants, so that even an increase of one dollar a share will lead to a million-dollar payoff, even if the gain is at or even less than the rest of the market. Like repricing, enormous option grants remove any downside from the compensation plan. Leon Hirsch, CEO of US Surgical, was awarded so many options that his compensation risk was all but removed. Four years' worth of grants gave him nearly six million shares on option. If the stock climbed by as little as one dollar he would make $5.9 million. As then-SEC chairman Richard Breeden noted, "Mega-grants of options are an increasing and quite disturbing trend. Some mega options make mini sense for shareholders . . . shareholders are entitled to expect the directors who make those awards to have an affirmative reason for every award and its pricing."[27]

## Case in Point: Borden

At Borden, weeks after the proxy statement explained that the CEO did not get a bonus because the company had not met its performance goals, the board awarded the CEO options to purchase 100,000 shares of the company's common stock at a price to be set in the future, subject to shareholder approval at the next annual meeting. Furthermore, according to the employment contract, "In the event that the Stock Option Plan is not approved by shareholders at the Corporation's next annual meeting of shareholders, the Corporation shall provide the executive with compensation of equivalent value as determined by the Compensation Committee." In other words, if the shareholders decided that the CEO should not get the new stock options, the CEO would get the equivalent in the form of cash. Note: this plan also provided that the company would pay for two residences for the CEO, along with all applicable taxes. Note further that despite the contract's provision that the CEO could not be removed for any reason other than commission of a felony, he was removed within six months of signing this contract. While he no longer had the job, this did not affect his salary, which will be paid for the full five years of the contract.

What shareholders look for in options is some way to make sure that they tie returns to the particular company's performance rather than to the performance of the market as a whole. One way to do this is to index the options, so that the "strike price" rises with the stock market. That way, the compensation reflects the performance of the particular company's stock. Another option is to grant the options at a price greater than the current stock price. Compensation consultant Ira Kay, of Hay Group management consultants, says that committees should build downside risk into their plans by *selling* jumbo stock option grants, paying bonuses for executives who retain option shares, and granting premium options. Shareholders are becoming more sophisticated about compensation. According to the Investor Responsibility Research Center, the percentage of shareholders voting against option plans was 3.5 percent in 1988, and 12 percent in 1991. The enhanced disclosure required by the amendments to Section 402 will permit shareholders to be more discriminating about option proposals in the future.

## RESTRICTED STOCK

Instead of stock options, some companies make "restricted stock grants," awarding stock with limits on its transferability for a set time, usually two or three years, but sometimes for the executive's tenure with the company. Crystal is leery of restricted stock grants, arguing that they should be a signal to the market that even management does not think that the stock price will go up. They are low in risk. An executive granted restricted stock will always make money, unless the stock goes down to zero. Compare Lee Iacocca's compen-sation plans at the beginning of his time at Chrysler with the plan at the end. He once ran Chrysler for a dollar a year, but with some "monster (very large) options" that paid out $43 million in six years. On the other hand, between 1983 and 1987, Iacocca received 455,000 shares of restricted stock. By the end of the 1980s, Chrysler stock had halved. In 1991, Chrysler's bonus-eligible executives received grants of restricted stock, with restrictions that lapsed within months. Since they paid nothing for these grants, this was additional compensation that was all upside and little downside.

## SHAREHOLDER CONCERNS: SEVERAL WAYS TO PAY DAY

Some other issues of recent shareholder concern include the following abusive compensation practices:

*The "guaranteed bonus" – the ultimate oxymoron* Time Warner executives were told that their bonus would not be less than 125 percent of salary. Although Champion's Andrew Sigler had a bonus that could theoretically swing from 0 percent of salary to 110 percent, the target he had to reach in order to qualify was set very low. If his performance merely matched the plan set down at the beginning of the year, he was rewarded with a 66 percent of salary bonus. To receive no bonus, Sigler would have had to underperform drastically the goals he has a good deal of say in setting. In 1991, a year in which earnings per share was 0.84 percent, Sigler received a bonus of $294,000.

*Bundled proposals* Companies often tie proposals unpopular with shareholders to special dividends or other inducements. New rules issued by the SEC in the fall of 1992 prohibit this "bundling." Interpretation of this rule will probably be required in the context of omnibus stock option or other compensation-related proposals, but as of this writing it has not yet been tested.

*Deliberate obfuscation* New executive compensation disclosure rules promulgated by the SEC in 1992 (discussed in greater detail below) were designed to prevent companies disguising compensation awards in pages of numbing legal narrative. As soon as the new rules were issued, however, lawyers and compensation consultants began designing ways to make compensation less clear to shareholders.

In part, increased attempts to evade disclosure have been thwarted by the revisions to the shareholder communication rules. The SEC's express exemption of proxy analysis services from the pre-clearance provisions of the proxy rules gives more latitude to the firms that are in the business of dissecting and revealing compensation plans. Smart corporate management, concerned about good investor relations, will not seek to evade the new requirements, but rather will see them as an opportunity for effective communication of corporate objectives and their relationship to performance.

In 1993, a new compensation rule was proposed that many predict will give management new motivation to disguise the true amounts of their compensation. The 1993 Budget eliminated the deductibility of most compensation over $1 million, except for performance-based compensation meeting specified criteria. At least some compensation consultants thought that this rule would merely provide a new test of their ingenuity. The *Wall Street Journal* reported: "Few, if any, companies intend to respond to the law by cutting big compensation packages."[28] Favorite gimmicks include: deferring more pay until after retirement, creating a two-tier bonus arrangement, and altering stock option plans by setting a maximum number of possible options that may be awarded. One compensation consultant told the *Journal:* "The professional fees generated by this piece of legislation will far outweigh the tax revenue it generates."[29]

*The Christmas tree* Many compensation plans contain elements that are in themselves admirable, but in combination with a host of other plans add up to a package that has no sensitivity to performance. For example, stock options and performance unit plans are all too often usually an addition to compensation packages, not a substitute for something else.

*Compensation plans that are all upside and no downside* These plans include any grants of stock or stock options that fail to discount for overall market gains, or that are cushioned against loss of value through compensatory bonuses or repricing. Management will face increased opposition to these kinds of plans.

*Phony cuts* All of a sudden, no one wants to be in the top quartile any more. In 1991, while corporate profits declined by 15 percent, nearly double 1990, CEO compensation gained 3.9 percent. Some companies made highly publicized "cuts," but again, all too often, these "cuts" were more than made up for by mega stock options or other awards. Today, smart shareholders, particularly institutional shareholders, will not be fooled by such management sleight of hand. The "withhold" vote at Westinghouse in 1992 reflected shareholder concern over just such an award.

## FUTURE DIRECTIONS

In October 1992, the SEC promulgated two sets of rule changes that will likely have far-reaching consequences on shareholders' ability to ensure that executive pay is performance related.

First, the SEC demanded that companies reveal and display compensation information in the proxy statement in a clear and comprehensible manner. From the 1993 proxy season forward, companies were required to publish a summary compensation table for the five highest paid executives, giving separate disclosure of salary, bonuses, and other annual compensation. Stock options, stock appreciation rights, and other long-term incentive payouts also had to be disclosed. Two tables were also required under the new rules. The first table lists all stock option grants, and their estimated value given a range of possible stock price increases. A second table required companies to include a chart comparing a corporation's total five-year return to shareholders to a broad market index (such as the S&P 500) and an industry peer group. Thus, shareholders can, at a glance, gauge the performance of their company and decide if the compensation they are paying executives is justified.[30]

A second rule change freed shareholders from burdensome disclosure requirements. Henceforth, shareholders who are concerned about excessive shareholder pay can discuss the issue with other like-minded shareholders.

All indications are that shareholders will continue to use the improved disclosure about compensation required by the new rules to make decisions about "just voting no" for directors, and the increased flexibility of the SEC's new Section 14 communication rules to share information about their analyses, their compensation-related proposals, and their voting decisions.

The fact sheet accompanying these two SEC rule-making changes notes that the SEC's intention is not to create new causes of action for shareholder litigation, but to give shareholders a better basis on which to evaluate the directors. The requirement that the names of the compensation committee members appear below the committee's statements on the compensation plan[31] will help shareholders connect the plans to the individuals responsible for adopting them. The requirement that interlocks be disclosed will enable shareholders to withhold votes for those directors who appear to have conflicts of interest.

Improved disclosure is also important to investors because it will enable them to make an informed investment decision, whether it is voting proxies or deciding to buy or sell a company's stock. Nothing is of greater interest to an investor considering whether to buy or sell than whether the company has an incentive scheme that aligns the interests of management and shareholders. Nothing is of more interest to a shareholder who is considering candidates for election to the board (including members of the compensation committee) than the priorities reflected in the compensation plan they approve and the independence of the members of the committee. Shareholders will use the increased clarity and consistency of the information available to them to make decisions about when to buy and sell, and about when to submit or support a shareholder initiative. Directors and management will no longer have the luxury of the SEC pre-clearance rules to track shareholder communication on these issues. Smart managers will want to seize the initiative to reach out to the shareholders and address their concerns.

Compensation should be seen as one item – and an important one – on the board's report card. How does a board balance the sometimes conflicting interests of managers and shareholders? The way the board reconciles these interests is a very significant indicator of their focus, independence, and ability. Bad compensation schemes are not the disease; they are the symptom. The disease is bad boards, and shareholders are now persuaded that bad boards must be fixed.

The new rules do not mean that CEOs will be paid less; it means that they will be paid better. Shareholders have learned that if they do not make sure they get what they pay for, they will certainly pay too much for what they get. In the words of then SEC chairman Richard Breeden, echoing his predecessor of the Carter administration in the late 1970s, Harold Williams, "The best protection against abuses in executive compensation is a simple weapon – the cleansing power of sunlight and the power of an informed shareholder base."[32]

## EMPLOYEES: COMPENSATION AND OWNERSHIP

The employer puts his money into . . . business and the workman his life. The one has as much right as the other to regulate that business. *Clarence Darrow*

Scholars from law and economics, and, more recently, from management theory, have shown that giving employees more authority over their work and more of an ownership interest makes companies stronger and more productive. Some even suggest that employment itself creates a form of ownership, echoing the sentiments of Clarence Darrow quoted above.[33] The role of the employees in corporate governance is another area where it is particularly useful to examine models from different countries. As the examples in this section show, a number of different approaches have worked very well.

Many times each day, every employee is faced with a choice between performing the job to maximize benefit for the company or performing it to benefit himself. What is the best way to make sure that the employee will be likely to make the right decision? Let's look at one such choice: business travel. Once the employee leaves the office, he has a number of opportunities to affect the returns to the firm from the trip. He can fly first class, with very little, if any, benefit to the company. He can schedule the trip to make the time or the place more congenial for him. He can pad his expense vouchers and keep the difference. Most companies address this "agency cost" issue by imposing rules. Employees below a certain level, for example, must fly coach. They must get extra approval for travel that includes a Friday or Monday, to make sure the trips are not designed to give the employee a free weekend away from home. A few rare companies, like Semco (see case study below) take the opposite approach. Their view is that if they trust the employee to conduct their business in their interests, they trust him to arrange travel in their interests as well.

Trust alone is not enough, however. What makes this approach possible is that it is just one part of a system of involvement, ownership, information, and authority that minimizes agency costs. The CEO of Semco says that development of prescriptive rules diverts the company's attention from its objectives, provides a false sense of security for executives, creates work for bean counters, and "teach(es) men to stone dinosaurs and start fires with sticks."[34] Rules of this kind are more likely to be used to shield someone from accountability ("I was following the rule!") than to create accountability.

If we accept that the advantage of the corporate structure is that it enables different groups to combine capital and labor for the benefit of all of them, we must recognize that one of the core issues is how those benefits are divided.

Indeed, the debate over this issue goes back to Plato, who wrote extensively on the subject of property in virtually all of his works. Karl Marx argued that "ownership" ultimately belonged to those whose labor created a "product." The capitalist employer enjoys what Marx called "surplus value." He meant that all value is the result of work. The capitalist employer pays the worker less than the value he produces and keeps the surplus for himself as profit. Marx predicted that in future socialist economies workers may receive "from the social supply of [the] means of consumption a share corresponding to their labor time."[35]

Shann Turnbull, an Australian scholar and businessman, considers the question of "surplus value" from a modern perspective. His perspective is that of an investor in a resource-rich but capital-poor country trying to induce foreign investment to create jobs and wealth. In that context, "[i]t does not make good business or macro economic sense to pay foreign investors more than they require to attract their investment. It is simply not a good deal to export surplus profits. It should be considered economically subversive to use corporate concepts which provide external interests with unknown, uncontrolled and unlimited financial claims on a host community."[36]

Turnbull analyzes the factors involved in making a decision to invest: "it is the time horizon rather than the rate of return which becomes the overriding factor for investment decisions" by large institutions.[37] Each sets a rate of return that must be yielded if the investment is to be accepted; this can be translated into the number of years necessary to pay back the original investment. And this in turn relates to risk – the shorter the time period for payback, the less the risk. In balancing risk and return, investors traded off maximization of potential profit to secure protection against risk. Turnbull hazards as a rule of thumb: "We may conclude from the above analysis, that as a rule, all cash received from an investment after ten years represents surplus profits or incentives."[38] This leads to his most important conclusion: "[I]t is evident that investors do not require perpetual property rights to provide them with the incentive to invest."[39] After the investor has recovered sufficient cash to compensate him (or, to look at it another way, to incentivize him) for risking the initial investment, ownership entitlement may be directed to other corporate constituencies – pre-eminently, the employees.

Go back to our original questions: What decisions must be made? Who is in the best position to make each decision? Does that person have the authority to make it? Over the long term, the employees may be the ones who are in the best position to decide many aspects of corporate direction, based on their superior access to information and their minimal conflicts of interest. After all, no one has a longer term commitment to the company or a more closely aligned interest in the company's long-term vitality.

The employees do not just represent members of the community; they *are* the members of the community. When it comes to questions of factoring in the long-term and allocating externalities, they may have the fewest agency costs or conflicts of interest.

## Four Reasons for Employee Ownership

- Owners are the only party affected by corporations who are able to monitor its activities at the micro and macro levels. Put another way, they have minimal agency costs.
- Ownership is a responsibility as well as a right. As the party with the ultimate interest in enterprise, owners not only can, they should be responsible for its impact on society. Because of their ability to represent the interests of the suppliers of work and capital and the interests of the community, employees are well suited to this role.
- Ownership requires a level of vigilance that is hard to obtain from a holder of securities, a rather indirect form of "ownership" at best.
- In order for the ownership function to be discharged within the corporate structure, there must be "owners" who are:
  1. rationally informed and involved;
  2. unrestricted by laws and regulations in the exercise of their ownership; and
  3. free from the "morbidity" arising out of remove from active involvement in the venture.

This concept is also very relevant to the macro perspective, going back to the discussion of the basis for establishing the corporate structure. From the earliest times, the law has created barriers to limiting the use of property or removing it from commerce for an indefinite period of time.

This characterization of share capital in perpetual ventures acting as a permanent drain on productivity recalls the view of capital in the middle ages.[40] It is not difficult to make an analogous argument about the provider of capital. While the "ownership" changes continuously, as shares are bought and sold, the uses of capital are still limited by the "dead hands" that established the structure.

Many observers argue that giving the passive shareholder perpetual rights to the ultimate fruits of enterprise promotes economic inequality and perpetuates a dead hand element at the heart of the national economy. Their position is that whatever value the provider of capital contributed has long since been rewarded, and the continued siphoning of the fruit of enterprise must diminish the opportunity, and therefore the incentive and the morale of others who must make a living from the enterprise. They conclude that thus, even if a venture has perpetual existence, the entitlement of "owners" can be appropriately limited to a set term. The theory is that the corporation evolves from a structure that best benefits from widely dispersed public ownership (with the inducements of limited liability and easy transferability to attract capital) to a structure that is ultimately hampered by it. As the company matures, the best guarantee of continuous renewal is ownership by a group more vitally connected to the enterprise.

There is a lot of appeal in the notion that those who provide the labor have an "ownership" right to the economic value of a corporation. One of the great business leaders of the years between the two world wars was Owen D. Young, for many years the CEO of the General Electric Company and a genuine "industrial statesman." In a 1927 speech at the dedication of the George P. Baker building at the Harvard Business School, he shared a vision of ownership of corporations by their employees seldom before or since articulated by business leaders.

Perhaps some day we may be able to organize the human beings engaged in a particular undertaking so that they truly will be the employer buying capital as a commodity in the market at the lowest price. It will be necessary for them to provide an adequate guarantee fund in order to buy their capital at all. If that is realized, the human beings will then be entitled to all the profits over the cost of capital. I hope the day may come when these great business organizations will truly belong to the men who are giving their lives and their efforts to them, I care not in what capacity. Then they will use capital truly as a tool and they will be all interested in working it to the highest economic advantage. Then an idle machine will mean to every man in the plant who sees it an unproductive charge against himself. Then every piece of material not in motion will mean to the man who sees it an unproductive charge against himself. Then we shall have zest in labor, provided the leadership is competent and the division fair. Then we shall dispose, once and for all, of the charge that in industry organizations are autocratic and not democratic. Then we shall have all the opportunities for a cultural wage which the business can provide. Then, in a word, men will be as free in cooperative undertakings and subject only to the same limitations and chances as men in individual businesses. Then we shall have no hired men.[41]

This same theme – the ultimate ownership of an enterprise by its employees – is prevalent in modern day Japan. "For instance, when asked about who owns the company, in theory most Japanese, reply the shareholders, but when asked who in fact owns the company, they reply the employees."[42] The author of those words, Ben Makihara, is the American-educated CEO of a Japanese company, Mitsubishi. A second-generation career Mitsubishi employee, he is married to the daughter of the company's founder, whose family was divested of substantially all of its ownership in the Mitsubishi group following World War II. Makihara, thus, is connected to his company in a way few employees are.

In the half century since Hiroshima, Japan has been single-minded about creating an exporting industrial colossus. Executives work without holiday and for pay levels very much less than their counterparts in the West; employees hold themselves to standards of diligence that are viewed with awe all over the world, and the government has supported and encouraged this effort. The results have been extraordinary; in one generation Japan has gone from total destruction to ascendancy over the world's economy.[43]

Robert Ozaki in *Human Capitalism*[44] describes this essentially Japanese creation first by contrasting it with the conventional Western prototype and then by carefully evoking a structure based on mutual concern that is capable of moral judgments:

> Contemporary capitalists typically are not insiders involved in the affairs of the firm they "own." They are interested in the company only to the extent that it serves their own interest. At a sign of unprofitability, they have the option of selling their shares and investing their money in another firm. Understandably, they are interested in short-run maximization of the firm's profit; the executives who opt for long-term growth at the expense of short-term profits run the risk of losing their positions . . .
>
> An individual will predictably be motivated when he assumes rights and responsibilities for his conduct. The contemporary firm is a grouping of many individuals. For it to behave like a highly motivated individual, it must, freely and independently of outside interference, be able to make its own decisions toward maximization of its own gains, and at the same time it must take responsibility for the consequences of its failure.
>
> There are different ways to construct a firm so that it can control its own destiny and in effect become a well-motivated quasi-person. A worker-owned and -managed producer–cooperative type firm is one alternative . . .

The humanistic firm has enabled itself to behave like a motivated individual by separating ownership from control through mutual stockholding, an extensive reliance on debt financing, and (more recently) the use of accumulated earnings.

Management and workers form one group, exercising joint sovereignty and sharing a common interest. The firm's gain is their gain. Given the internalized nature of the human-resources market, they must pay a high price if their firm fails.

The ethos of the humanistic firm requires new thinking about the very concept of ownership and control. Ownership of the humanistic firm is clearly not public in the socialist sense, nor is it purely private in the capitalist sense. It is not somewhere in between, either, and cannot be well articulated under the dichotomy of public versus private ownership. The members of the humanistic firm do not perceive their firm to be owned by stockholders. They may not legally own it, yet it belongs to them, as they occupy the firm and operate its facilities. One may argue that this is an instance of usufruct and that they are usufructuaries. These terms are not satisfactory, however, since usufruct implies that the property one is authorized to use is privately owned by someone else, whereas the members of the humanistic firm do not consider themselves to be leasing their firm from capitalists. In the absence of the appropriate expression, we might say that they are the quasi-private owners of the firm.

Shann Turnbull proposes a specific mechanism for transferring ownership from shareholders to others. "A dynamic tenure system transfers property rights from investors to operational stakeholders after the investors' time horizon. This would encourage those people who are operationally involved in the creation of surplus profits to promote further profits. In this way, the inefficiency and inequity of surplus profits being returned to investors is replaced with improved efficiency and equity arising from stakeholder control and ownership."[45]

## EMPLOYEE STOCK OWNERSHIP PLANS

In the United States, we have another approach that, at least partially, transfers ownership from outside shareholders to employees, the employee stock ownership plan (ESOP). ESOPs were created in 1974 by two forces: the legislative efforts of legendary Louisiana Democrat and long-time Senate Finance Committee chairman Russell Long and the philosophical evangelicalism of Louis Kelso, who dedicated his career to advancing employee ownership. Kelso wrote:

The problem with conventional financing techniques is that they address only the productive power of enterprise and the enhancement of the earning power of the rich minority. Sustaining or increasing the earning power of the majority of consumers who are dependent entirely upon the earnings of their labor, or upon welfare, is left to government or governmentally assisted redistribution of income and to chance.[46]

In Kelso's view, there are no developed mechanisms through which an individual – no matter how talented or hard working – can secure "capital" in exchange for his work. Kelso has promoted "self-financeability" by which employees "earn" a capital position as a result of their labor. This requires tax incentives and credit arrangements. "Thus, the logic of a market economy itself, that legitimate income must be earned by participation in production, requires a form of capital credit for the acquisition of capital ownership by individuals who will use its income to support their consumption of goods and services."[47]

The ESOP is the modern American effort to enable employees to acquire meaningful ownership interests in the firms in which they work. Conceptually, ESOPs work rather as Turnbull has urged. The government provides a substantial tax incentive for companies to borrow in order to be able to acquire their own stock in the ESOP trust, which is then distributed to employees over a long period of years corresponding with their continued employment – or in Turnbull's terms, when the ownership entitlement of the original investor expires. ESOPs, like the one at Polaroid, which are "stockholder neutral," are funded by the deferral of raises and bonuses by employees.[48] Over a relatively short period of time, employees can acquire a significant block of their company's stock. Indeed, it is not uncommon that the employee benefit plan is substantially the largest owner of large modern corporations – for example, Sears, Roebuck and Westinghouse. Lockheed corporation carried this a logical step further: the company intended its ESOP to become the majority holder of its equity securities.

Note, however, that in some cases corporate management has used the ESOP form to protect itself from prospective hostile acquirers. In these cases, employee ownership is arguably only the extension of management's desire to maintain its incumbency.

Some substantial questions remain as to whether ESOPs will carry out their authors' intention of making owners out of employees. Their status as "trusts" under ERISA and their use as financing devices for the fundamental benefit of management or outside entrepreneurs have severely restricted their utility as ownership vehicles for employees.

In 1985 concern about the role of workers in worker ownership surfaced from an unexpected quarter. In proposals that stunned traditional supporters of ESOPs, the Reagan administration, acting through the Treasury Department, called for fundamental changes in the ESOP as part of the giant tax reform package. The administration said that employees must have all the rights of direct ownership, including voting rights and in some circumstances dividend rights, if employee ownership were to merit the tax expenditures it demanded. It questioned whether ESOPs that restrict the "traditional incidents of ownership" could really improve profitability or employee motivation. The administration proposed to remove ESOPs from retirement law and continue to encourage them with tax incentives as a socially desirable goal. It called the bluff of ESOP apologists by saying plainly that, if ESOPs were not retirement plans, they should be vehicles of real ownership.[49]

In 1986, after 12 years of active ESOP advocacy, Senator Long made a last effort before his retirement to make sure that ESOP legislation would be seen primarily as intending to enable employee ownership:

The Congress has made clear its interest in encouraging employee ownership plans as a bold and innovative technique of corporate finance for strengthening the free enterprise system. The Congress intends that such plans be used in a wide variety of corporate financing transactions as a means of encouraging employers to include their employees as beneficiaries of such transactions. The Congress is deeply concerned that the objectives sought by this series of laws will be made unattainable by regulations and rulings which treat employee stock ownership plans as conventional retirement plans, which reduce the freedom of employee stock ownership trusts and employers to take the necessary steps to utilize ESOPs in a wide variety of corporate transactions, and which otherwise impede the establishment and success of these plans.[50]

## Case in Point: United Airlines and Employee Ownership

In late 1992, the employees of United Airlines agreed to buy 53 percent of the company (63 percent, if the stock price hits certain levels in the plan's first year), in exchange for about $5 billion in wage and work-rule concessions over the next six years. This is the biggest and most dramatic example of a growing trend toward employee ownership. The objective of the employees in designing this deal was to save their jobs. To stay employed, they were willing to take pay cuts of 10 to 17 percent. In addition, there were other concessions, like unpaid lunch breaks and reduced pension plan contributions. It is unlikely that they would have been willing to make these concessions without majority ownership to guarantee the management of their choice. Interestingly, however, the 13-member board of directors has seats for only four employee representatives, one from each of the three unions and one to represent non-union employees.

Compare the employee ownership plans at other companies. At Wierton Steel, the company did extremely well at first, ahead of its peers. But the board replaced the CEO, a favorite of employees, with an outsider, a mutual-fund executive. A worker group filed a shareholder suit accusing the officers and directors of mismanagement. The board's efforts to raise capital (and dilute the workers' share) by issuing new stock led to a major battle.

## Case in Point: Semco

Semco is a Brazilian manufacturer of industrial equipment that achieved a 600 percent growth rate and moved from 56th to 4th in its industry over a ten-year period when the country's economy was depressed. Productivity increased by nearly 700 percent. And there is tremendous employee loyalty; they have had periods of up to 14 months without a single departure, and one recent help wanted ad attracted 1,400 applications.

CEO Ricardo Semler, who took over from his father when he was in his early 20s, abolished the hierarchy in favor of a system that allowed the workers to set their own production quotas, hours, and salaries. Twelve layers of management in a traditional pyramid structure was reduced to three layers in a structure based on concentric circles.

All financial information is available and openly discussed; everyone down to the cleaning staff gets trained to read balance sheets and cash flow statements. Employees evaluate their bosses. Prospective managers are interviewed by those they will be supervising. Everyone participates in major decisions, such as the location of a new factory or the acquisition of a new division. There are no receptionists, secretaries, or assistants, no executive dining rooms, or reserved parking spaces. People wear what they like and design their working space as they like. "At Semco, we have stripped away the unnecessary perks and privileges that feed the ego but hurt the balance sheet and distract everyone from the crucial corporate tasks of making, selling, billing, and collecting."[51] Although the union originally resisted broadening job classifications, which were seen as protection against pressure for (unfairly) higher productivity, they became enthusiastic when they found that they would determine the goals and how to reach them.

Semco's profit sharing plan is largely determined by the workers themselves. "Profit sharing has worked so well that once, during negotiations over a new labor contract, a union leader argued that too big a raise would over-extend the company."[52]

"I think we're proving that worker involvement doesn't mean that bosses lose power," writes Semler. "What we do strip away is the blind, irrational authoritarianism that diminishes productivity. . . . In restructuring Semco, we've picked the best from many systems. From capitalism we take the ideals of personal freedom, individualism, and competition. From the theory, not the practice, of socialism we have learned to control greed and share information and power. The Japanese have taught us the value of flexibility, although we shrink from their family-like ties to the company and their automatic veneration of elders. We want people to advance because of competence, not longevity or conformity."[53]

## Case in Point: The "Temping" of the Workplace

In contrast to the notion of employees as partners, or even owners, is the increased reliance on temporary employees. As companies save storage and other carrying costs with "just in time" inventory, they are increasingly taking advantage of the benefits of "just in time" employees. In 1993, the largest single private employer in the United States was a temp agency, Manpower, Inc., with roughly 600,000 people on its payroll. By some calculations, one in four employees in the United States are now members of the "contingency workforce." Once thought of as a place to call if the receptionist was out sick or on vacation, these agencies are now relied on for "outsourcing" facilities for photocopying, word processing, accounting, and other technical operations. Some companies even go to temp firms for higher level employees. Many hospitals outsource their emergency rooms to independent groups of physicians. Matthew Harrison works for Imcor, a firm that supplies high-level temporary employees. Reflecting on his experience as a high-level employee at four companies in seven years, he said, "There can be a real value in having a throwaway executive, who can come in and do unpleasant, nasty things like kill off a few sacred cows."[54] British consultant Charles Handy says, "Instead of being a castle, a home for life for its defenders, an organization will be more like an apartment block, an association of temporary residents gathered together for mutual convenience. . . . (Corporations will still conduct business) but to do so they will no longer need to employ."[55]

Manpower CEO Mitchell Fromstein says that outsourcing is a good choice when there is high turnover (with high training costs) and when work is highly cyclical. Unquestionably, temping has made some companies more productive, and it has provided flexibility for workers like parents of young children and others who do not want the demands of a full-time career. But it has also been used as a tax dodge, at least in the view of the US Internal Revenue Service, which has insisted on recategorizing some 439,000 workers as employees (and therefore subject to withholding requirements). And it has been used as a way to avoid the cost of benefits; temp agencies do not give the employees they send out to other companies comprehensive health and pension benefits.

## MONDRAGÓN AND SYMMETRY: INTEGRATION OF EMPLOYEES, OWNERS, AND DIRECTORS

Governance is ultimately concerned with the alignment of information, incentive, and capacity to act. The challenge is aligning the responsibilities and authorities of all of the various constituencies to achieve the optimal conditions for growth and renewal. One of the most dramatic examples is the employee-owned enterprise, essentially taking the ESOP to its final conclusion. In this model, the two constituencies with the largest interest in the success of the venture are identical. It is not perfect; there are problems with the dual nature of the workers' interest, for example. In the short run, they want to maximize their compensation for work performed, but as owners they have a long-term interest in maximizing the value of the enterprise. Overall, however, this model probably does the best job of minimizing agency costs.

### Case in Point: Mondragón and "Cooperative Entrepreneurship" or "Cooperation Instead of Competition"

The Mondragón cooperatives were founded as a training facility for apprentices by a priest and some students in a small Basque city in the north of Spain. It has grown from 23 employees in one cooperative in 1956 to 19,500 employees in more than 100 enterprises in 1986. In 1987 the sales were $1.6 billion, including $310 million in exports. Mondragón includes a large bank, a chain of department stores, schools, clinics, high-tech firms, appliance manufacturers, and machine shops. The individual cooperatives range in size from six employees to 2,000, from one location to 180. Mondragón is almost like a living organism, with each enterprise like a cell that divides when it grows too large. (In this way, it is similar to Semco, which compares itself to an amoeba.) There is no set limit, but practice has shown that 400–500 members is the maximum, since "beyond that size bureaucracy almost unavoidably intrudes and attenuates cooperative intimacy and solidarity."[56] Its achievement is not just in its growth, but in the success rate of the enterprises; there have been only three failures. Perhaps its greatest strengths are the commitment of its members (based in part on their role in its governance) and the cooperatives' ability to respond to change (based in part on the system for communication and the flexibility of the structure).

Its organization is designed to match entitlement and responsibility.

Ultimate power resides in the general assembly in which all members not only have the right, but the obligation, to vote. The General Assembly meets at least annually. The Governing Council is the top policy-making body of the firm, which is elected on the basis of one vote per worker. The governing council includes only worker-members. Key executives may attend council meetings, but they are not members of the council.

Members of the Governing Council are elected every two years for four-year terms. Members are not specially compensated for their council responsibilities but continue to be paid their regular salaries. The Council has overall responsibility for management policies and programs. It selects the manager, who serves for a four-year term unless he is deposed by the Council. There is an audit committee consisting of three persons elected by the members.

There is also a Management Council, which consists of the manager and chief department heads. Finally, there is a Social Council, which has the right to advise the governing council on matters such as safety and health on the job, social security, systems of compensation, and social work activities or projects.

Mondragón is thus a structure of interested parties. No one is permitted access to the governance structure who has not made a material contribution of personal resources to the enterprise. No one is permitted the speculative profits that arise out of public ownership. Thus, a level of alignment is possible, because only interested parties are involved in setting values. The vagaries of the outside world are not permitted to upset the careful economic equilibrium of a Mondragón cooperative. In a sense, Mondragón is saying that jobs and the continuity of the enterprise are too important to permit the involvement of the speculative money interests.

## CONCLUSION

We return to our original questions: Who is in the best position to make a given decision about the direction of a corporation, and does that person or group have the necessary authority? The material we have covered has given us a context for developing the answers. The person or group in the best position to make any decision about the corporation's direction is determined by two factors: conflicts of interest and information. Decisions should be made by those with the fewest conflicts and the most information.

This applies from the smallest decision to the largest. Who should decide what color the walls should be painted in the workroom? The people who work in that room have the best information about which color suits them best. Furthermore, looking at them as a group, there is no possible conflict of interests because there are no agency costs; they are deciding something that affects them. The question of how often the walls should be painted is another question, however. Workers are not in the best position to determine how often the money should be spent to repaint. They would be acting as agents for management if they made this decision, and the agency costs would be considerable. There is a way to minimize these agency costs, if so desired by any of the parties, of course. If the workers are meaningfully responsible for budget allocation (which is a system with some benefits), they will "feel" the impact of the decision enough to align their interests with those of management.

The corporate structure has been so robust that it has outgrown most of the structures, including the political structures, designed to control it. Accountability must come from within; and that requires an effective governance system that is itself accountable. All three major players in corporate governance, the board, the shareholders, and the management must be able to act and must be motivated and informed enough to act correctly. There is no one perfect corporate governance model, just as there is no one perfect financial structure. The ultimate aim of a corporate governance structure must be that it is continually re-evaluated so that the governance structure itself can adapt to changing times and needs.

## NOTES

1. Thomas A. Stewart, "The King Is Dead," *Fortune,* Jan. 14, 1993, p. 34.
2. Id., p. 35.
3. Id., p. 40.
4. Ira M. Millstein, "Advising a CEO on Boardroom Relations," *American Lawyer,* Nov. 1993, p. 87.
5. "The Pharaonic CEO," *Fortune,* Dec. 4, 1989.
6. "Quality: How the Best Get Better," Excerpts from the International Quality Study$^{SM}$ Best Practices Report, *Directors Monthly,* Nov. 1992, pp. 6–8.
7. "It Could Happen to Us," Interview with David A. Nadler, in *Across the Board,* Oct. 1993, p. 28.
8. Randall Smith, John J. Kelle, and John R. Wilke, "AT&T Launches $6.12 Billion Cash Offer for NCR After Rejection of Its Stock Bid," *Wall Street Journal,* Dec. 6, 1990, p. A3.
9. Interview with David A. Nadler, supra, Oct. p. 28.
10. See James B. Stewart, "Whales and Sharks," *New Yorker,* Feb. 15, 1993.
11. "General Electric, Strategic Position – 1981," Harvard Business School Case Study 9–381–174, March 24, 1993, p. 1.
12. See "General Electric: Jack Welch's Second Wave (A)," Harvard Business School Case Study 9–391–248, April 2, 1993.
13. Id.
14. See Chris Roush, "GE Brings Good Things to Shareholders," *Business Week,* Jan. 17, 1994, p. 6.
15. Albert O. Hirschman, *Exit, Voice, and Loyalty: Responses to Decline in Firms, Organizations, and States* (Harvard University Press, Cambridge, MA, 1970).
16. Frank H. Easterbrook and Daniel R. Fischel, "The Corporate Contract," 89 *Columbia Law Review,* 7, Nov. 1989, p. 1418.
17. *Forbes,* May 27, 1991.
18. Graef Crystal, *In Search of Excess* (W.W. Norton, New York, 1991).
19. See Graef Crystal's study for the United Shareholders Association, "Executive Compensation in Corporate America 1991," and Graef Crystal, "The Compensation 500: What America's Top CEOs Should Be Paid This Year," *Financial World,* Oct. 29, 1991. For press coverage, see Michelle Osborne, "Author's Recipe for CEO Pay," *USA Today,* Oct. 9, 1991; Robert J. McCartney, "Quoth the Maven, Cut Some More," Washington Post, Jan. 29, 1992; Alison Leigh Cowan, "The Gadfly CEOs Want to Swat," *New York Times,* Feb. 2, 1992.
20. Graef Crystal, supra, pp. 51–85.
21. Id., p. 75.

22. Jill Lyons, "Individuals Lead the Way on 1993 Pay Proposals," *ISSue Alert,* June 1993, VIII, 6.

23. Michael C. Jensen and Kevin J. Murphy, "CEO Incentives: It's Not How Much You Pay, It's How," *Harvard Business Review,* May-June 1990, p. 138.

24. See Towers Perrin, "XYZ Company: Weaknesses of Conventional Stock Option Plans and a Proposed Solution: An Indexed Stock Option Plan," New York, 1991.

25. Berkshire Hathaway, Inc., Annual Report to Shareholders, 1985, p. 12.

26. Crystal, supra, p. 134.

27. Statement of Richard Breeden, Chairman of SEC, at open meeting of the Commission, Oct. 15, 1992.

28. Joann Lublin, "Companies Seek Loopholes for Executive Pay Deduction," *Wall Street Journal,* Nov. 19, 1993, p. B1.

29. Id.

30. See Jamie E. Heard, "How New SEC Rules Impact '93 Proxy Season," *ISSue Alert,* Nov. 1992, VII, 11.

31. See *The Federal Register,* 57, 204, Oct. 21, 1992, p. 48138.

32. "Shareholder Communication and Executive Compensation," Opening statement of Richard C. Breeden, Chairman of the Securities and Exchange Commission at the open meeting of the Commission, Oct. 15, 1992.

33. See, for example, Joseph W. Singer, "Reliance Interest in Property," 40 *Stanford Law Review* 611 (1988) and "Jobs and Justice: Rethinking the Stakeholder Debate," 43 *University of Toronto Law Journal* 475 (1993) and materials cited therein.

34. Ricardo Semler, *Maverick: The Success Story Behind the World's Most Unusual Workplace* (Warner Books, New York, 1993), p. 97.

35. Ivan Alexander, *Foundations of Business* (Basil Blackwell, Oxford, 1990), p. 93.

36. Shann Turnbull, *Reinventing Corporations,* IOS, 1991, p. 176.

37. Id., p. 177.

38. Id.

39. Id., p. 179.

40. Morbid capital is a graphic name for a phenomenon that is explicitly articulated in the British common law of property, which became part of the American common law of property with the adoption of the US Constitution in 1789. It relates to two limitations on the rights that a person possesses with respect to a thing he or she owns. Specifically, a private property owner may not (1) use that property to cause injury to the property or person of another, or (2) use that property in ways that injure the public interest or the public welfare. "Morbid capital . . . beggars others by depriving them of the economic opportunity to increase their earnings as capital workers."

Louis O. Kelso and Patricia Hetter Kelso, *Democracy and Economic Power – Extending the ESOP Revolution* (Ballinger, Cambridge, MA, 1986), p. 36.

41. Owen D. Young, Dedication Address, June 4, 1927, published in *Harvard Business Review*, 4, pp. 385, 392.

42. Private letter from Ben Makihara letter to Robert A.G. Monks.

43. A complete discussion of the political, cultural, strategic, and financial reasons for Japan's economic growth is beyond the scope of this book. We will therefore consider only one aspect, the role of the employee as owner.

44. Robert S. Ozaki, *Human Capitalism* (Penguin Books, London, 1991), p. 18.

45. Shann Turnbull, "Democratic Capitalism; Self-Financing Local Ownership and Control," prepared for the *Symposium on the Interplay of Economics and Politics in Economic Transformations in Russia and Central Europe*, March 27, 1993, p. 7.

46. Louis O. Kelso and Patricia Hetter Kelso, supra (Ballinger, Cambridge, MA, 1986), p. 47.

47. Id., p. 45.

48. They are "stockholder neutral" because the formation of the ESOP does not require the creation of any new shares that would dilute existing shareholders' equity.

49. Joseph R. Blasi, *Employee Ownership, Revolution or Ripoff?* (Ballinger, Cambridge, MA, 1988), p. 154.

50. *The Congressional Record*, Sept. 18, 1986, H7744–46.

51. Semler, supra, p. 4.

52. Id.

53. Id., pp. 4–5.

54. Jaclyn Fierman, "The Contingency Work Force," *Fortune*, Jan. 24, 1994, p. 31.

55. Id.

56. Roy Morrison, *We Build the Road as We Travel* (New Society Publishers, 1991), p. 13.

# 5

# Re-Empowering the Shareholders:
# A Proposed Agenda for Action

## INTRODUCTION

Balancing the conflict between individual freedom and institutional power has challenged human society since people first began to live together in communities. Complexity and specialization required a system of rules and a level of obedience to leaders. Too few rules led to anarchy. Too many restrictions led to rebellion.

In early history, institutional power was most often represented by the church or the government (of course the most powerful kings knew enough to represent both). In the century to come, as multi-national corporations create the "borderless world" of global markets and global employers, the focus will be on ensuring that corporate power is compatible with the rights of individuals in a democracy. The corporation can give the ultimate scope and expression to individual genius; this creative force has improved the living standard of billions of human beings. The challenge is to encourage the liberating energy without imposing unacceptable costs on individuals and society.

The only way to do that is to make sure that there is a meaningful level of accountability. As the outreach of worldwide communications, financial markets, and industrial enterprises exponentially expands in ways we can only begin to imagine, we must rethink the traditional concepts by which corporate power was to be held accountable to the marketplace and to the community. The very aspects of corporate design which have made it so robust are those that have made it a powerful "externalizing machine," doing everything it can to impose the costs of its activities on everyone else. The problem is that a corporation is designed for perpetual life, but the people who make its decisions tend to think in terms of their own tenure. The result is the failure of corporations to meet their most important challenge – the continuous propulsion toward renewal that is necessary to evaluate risk and master change. The challenge of corporate governance is to create something as close to a perpetual-motion machine as possible, a structure that continuously evaluates and corrects its course to stay competitive.

## The Goal of Governance

The goal of corporate governance is to find a way to maximize wealth creation over time, in a manner that does not impose inappropriate costs on third parties or on society as a whole. Wealth creation can be looked at from a macro perspective (including the wealth created for employees and the community as well as investors), although doing so requires rigorous and quantitative calculations to prevent vague "stakeholder" claims. Inappropriate costs can include agency costs imposed on investors as reflected, for example, in excessive CEO pay. They also include externalized costs imposed on society at large, like pollution, price fixing, and other criminal behavior.

An effective corporate governance system requires a system of checks and balances, assuring that the right questions get asked ("Do we need to revise our corporate strategy? Our asset mix? Our organizational structure? Our allocation of resources? How is the CEO doing? How is the board doing?") of the right people (those with the best access to information, the fewest conflicts of interest, and the authority to make the decisions and see they get implemented). Since the one certainty in life, whether corporate or not, is change, the one goal we have for corporate governance is that it optimally enables corporations to respond to, affect, and even lead change. All governance systems should be evaluated on this basis.

In order to respond to change, you have to both be aware of it and be able to determine and implement the right response to it. Both require constant questioning, evaluation, and re-evaluation. A corporate governance system that is not effective is one in which questions are raised too late, or not at all, or are decided by people who are unable to evaluate them properly. The result of an ineffective system of corporate governance is the use of power without a level of accountability sufficient to ensure that it is exercised to maximize wealth creation. As we examine the corporate failures of the past decades, we see failures of individual corporate behemoths as symbols of the failure of the corporate structure as a mechanism for tying together the use of power and the accountability for the consequences of its exercise.

In order to understand what needs to be done, we must first ask what we are trying to achieve, not just in the context of the corporate structure, but in the societal systems that create and surround it. Other systems place equality or stability or the good of the group as a whole as their most important priority, but the capitalist system prizes individual liberty above everything else. The basis of our system is the belief that the greatest benefit to the greatest number will come from a system in which each person profits according to his or her contribution.

It is not entirely Darwinian or libertarian, of course. We have social programs and legislatively imposed standards to ensure that those who are unable to achieve a certain level of contribution will nevertheless have food, shelter, education, and health care. But our system is designed to make Horatio Alger stories possible, and our heroes are those, from Andrew Carnegie to Walt Disney to Sam Walton to Bill Gates, who have exceeded even Alger's dreams of success. For that reason, we leave to the individual and to the structures they create a broad range of decisions and judgments, believing that the individual should have as much freedom as possible to pursue success as he defines it. When we do impose limits, they are designed to resolve problems of externalities and conflicts of interests. For example, we reduce occupational injuries by establishing health and safety standards, reasoning that the costs they impose on corporations and their investors are exceeded by the benefits to the individual employees and to society as a whole.

As we look at corporate governance, then, we evaluate the options by measuring them against the goals of protecting individual liberty, maximizing wealth, and managing change. This requires most of all, a balance of power between the distinct elements of the corporation. Even the smallest company, owned and operated by the same people, cannot operate by consensus. Some authority must be delegated. If too little is delegated, the enterprise will not be able to benefit from expertise and specialization. Decision making will take so long that opportunities will be missed. If too much authority is delegated, the result will be a lack of coordination and consistency that can be very expensive. The benefit of sharing expertise and experience will also be missed. The challenge is to find the right level of delegation, at all levels in the corporation. Which decisions should be made on the spot, and which should be reviewed before implementation? Which divisions (counsel's office, marketing, finance) within the company should be brought in, and at which stages? Which decisions must be left to the board? Which must be decided by shareholders?

Perhaps the most difficult task in designing and operating the corporation is achieving the optimal balance between power and accountability. We want all people in the corporation to have power to perform their tasks, so long as there is enough accountability to ensure that those tasks are performed for the benefit of the owners over the long term. While this applies to every individual who has any decision-making authority, we will discuss the issues in terms of categories of people, primarily owners (shareholders), managers (top executives), directors, and employees. Each of these categories has important connections to each of the others. There is in place, at least in theory, a system of checks and balances designed to permit the appropriate scope of authority (power) and limit the abuse of that authority (accountability).

Corporate power itself is not the issue. To the extent that corporate managers determine many of the most important aspects of people's lives, including what they will buy and the conditions of their employment, they may be in a better position to make those determinations than the alternatives, like, for example, the government. If the market is working efficiently, those managers will be responding to the people themselves, their consumers and investors. After all, no corporate management in the world, no matter how powerful, can make consumers buy Edsels or switch to New Coke or invest in a company with poor prospects. In countries where the government makes the decisions about what corporations will sell, where they will be located, and what the conditions of employment will be, there are few choices left to consumers and employees.

The premise of the capitalist system is that we will let any company that wants to make toothpaste try it. If that means that a dozen different brands are on the shelf, it is evidence that the market is providing a broad variety of consumers exactly what they need. This does not mean that we all get our first choice. Someone whose heart's desire is pizza-flavored toothpaste is unlikely to find it under this system. But it beats a system where one person in the government gets to decide that pizza-flavored toothpaste will be the only option available. Allowing the market (the consumers) to decide how many varieties of toothpaste will be available and giving the market (the investors) the ability to respond when corporate management does poorly is more likely to result in total wealth maximization than giving that authority to the government or any of the other alternatives.

This all supposes, however, that the market is indeed efficient, which has not always been the case, even under capitalist systems.

Inefficiency leads to abuse of corporate power, made possible by impediments to market-based accountability.

Governance should focus on performance and competitiveness. Its objective must therefore be to minimize the "agency costs" inherent in any system where the people who provide the capital hire someone else to manage their property. Owner and manager will always have different interests, and at least some of the time those interests will conflict. A well-governed corporation is one in which the interests are aligned to as great a degree as possible, providing optimal efficiency and profitability.

Therefore, the most important task for the corporate governance system is ensuring a balance between the freedom to maximize wealth (power) and the limits of doing so without imposing disproportionate costs on others (accountability). In this sense, corporate governance must both protect corporations from society and society from corporations.

The indispensable link between the corporate constituents is the creation of a credible structure (with incentives and disincentives) that enables people with overlapping but not entirely congruent interests to have a sufficient level of confidence in each other and the viability of the enterprise as a whole. That structure, of course, will vary with the relationships and the circumstances.

**The Corporate Era**

As we discussed in Chapter 2, America's founding fathers were profoundly aware of the abuses of power and the importance of making sure that all power – private as well as public – drew its legitimacy from a system of checks and balances. The fight for independence was a fight over the right to representation, to ensure that the actions of the legislature reflected the priorities of the community which they affected. The earliest documents of our country's history reflected these concerns and the commitment that all power, public and private, would be grounded in accountability.

In early American history, the government attempted to limit corporate power and activity by requiring the approval of each charter, but this was unworkable. By the end of the nineteenth century, the government focused instead on assuring the competitiveness of the corporate environment. The theory – beginning with Adam Smith – continues to be that a truly competitive marketplace will insure socially desirable results. In the 20th century, United States government has focused on specific problems like product safety, the adverse impact of corporations on the environment, health hazards in the workplace, and discrimination in employment. While the earliest regulatory agencies of the federal government focused on economic regulation, from the 1960s on the focus shifted to health and safety. Transportation and telecommunications were increasingly deregulated to enable them to compete. To the extent that the federal government's involvement goes beyond health and safety issues, tax policy, and criminal standards, it tends toward disclosure requirements (in aid of consumer and investor knowledge and confidence, and therefore market efficiency), and works through independent private organizations – the New York Stock Exchange, the National Association of Securities Dealers, the Financial Accounting Standards Board, among others – to encourage self-regulation whenever possible.

In just over two centuries, the American corporation has gone from an enterprise strictly limited by the state in both its scope and duration to a perpetual entity that has been held by the Supreme Court to be a "person" with Constitutionally protected powers of speech. Yet many observers remain concerned that the centralization of vast power inherently threatens the freedom of individuals. "The large private corporation fits oddly into Democratic theory. Indeed, it does not fit."[1]

If that is true domestically, it is even more true in the global context. The world now boasts a total of 37,000 trans-national companies that control about a third of all private sector assets, and enjoy worldwide sales of about $5.5 trillion – slightly less than America's GDP last year.[2] Now, with multinational corporations larger in assets and population than many countries, we have no clear answer to the question – to whom are those who control these great enterprises accountable?

In theory, the owners, the holders of equity securities, and the government, representing the society as a whole, play that role. The basic framework for ensuring that accountability is established by the legislature of the company's domicile. But the company's managers can choose virtually any place for domicile no matter where the corporation actually resides or operates. An international "race to the bottom" is the result of competition for fees and taxes associated with corporate domicile, so that any attempt at accountability through chartering restraints on corporate power will ultimately be diluted to meaninglessness.

## The Limits of Government in a Global Economy

The "race to the bottom," now on a global scale, has left us with a system that may have gone too far in giving corporate managers power without proportionate responsibility. In addition to specific cases of abuse, the overall inability of the market to respond adequately to performance failures and of the government to respond adequately to violations of law force us to question whether the current structure provides enough of a balance to protect society against abuses of corporate power.

Consider the classic externality of environmental pollution. We would not want environmental rules that effectively prohibit manufacturing any more than we would want environmental rules (or absence of rules) that permit corporate managers to emit effluents into the air and water without regard to the cost to the community. We try to design environmental rules (and, we hope, all rules) based on the most reliable cost-benefit analysis. We recognize that combustion engines are responsible for much of the damage to the air, but we do not consider for a moment the possibility of prohibiting cars and trucks, because we recognize the value they add to our society. So, we negotiate at the margin, requiring fuel and auto manufacturers to eliminate the use of especially harmful substances, like lead, and reduce other kinds of emissions to carefully calibrated levels, and we create incentives for development of alternatives. In a few areas, like the Food and Drug Act's notorious Delany clause, we do not have the luxury of a cost-benefit analysis, and we end up banning one substance (like cyclamates), only to find a decade later that the substance that replaced it was even more hazardous.

But corporations have become so effective at influencing political and regulatory decision making that the result has been too many occasions when the cost-benefit analyses used to underlie legislative and regulatory standards have been based more on political costs than economic costs. The record of the automobile companies with regard to emissions and airbags is just one example. The political process is too dependent on money to make it possible for the government to be the ultimate guardian of accountability.

The failed experiments with Communism in the post–World War II era reflect the conclusion that state ownership and control over business does not best serve the public interest or promote corporate vitality. With all of the capitalist system's failures, its commitment to competition enabled it to outperform Communism. Any number of former Soviet republics and Czechoslovakia have distributed "ownership vouchers" to their citizens as a means of transition to private ownership. Countries that have been capitalist have become even more so with privatization of formerly public enterprises. France, Italy, and the United Kingdom have distributed the state's equity in various enterprises through underwriters to private investors. In Germany, the bellwether company Daimler-Benz has broken out of the fifty-year Government/Hausbank control structure by listing its shares on the New York Stock Exchange in an effort to get access to the most cost effective world capital markets. Japan retains its government sanctioned *kereitsu* arrangement, but top business leaders there say that the need for change is urgent.[3] Surprisingly, in Britain, no attention was given to the governance issues raised by the Thatcher-era privatization.[4]

The shift was more a move away from government control than a move to a private, ownership-based corporate system. There may not have been a universal conclusion that private ownership was good, but there was a universal conviction that any alternative was better than ownership by the state. In Eastern Europe and especially in the former Soviet Union, the inefficiencies of the bureaucratic state permeated the production and service sector.

Twenty years ago, I waited alongside my colleague Simon Chilowich, who exported farm implements to the Soviet Union, in the Moscow Industry Park for an inspection visit by Brezhnev. I looked over the various combines, bailers, plows, and other implements and noted that there was a plastic envelope containing a wheel attached to each piece of equipment. The wheel did not accord in size to any of the other wheels, so it did not seem suitable as a spare. Finally, I asked Simon what the extra wheel was for. He roared with the laughter of a Pole whose family had done business with Russia for over two hundred years and said: "Finally, my friend, you have learned something about Russian business. Those wheels are for the Russian tractors. Their tractor plant does not make a front wheel, so they buy our attachments to make the whole thing work." I asked, "Why doesn't somebody do something about it? Why don't you tell Brezhnev yourself when he comes by?" Simon placed the index finger of his right hand to his right temple in the universal sign of a pistol and compressed the middle finger indicating that he would be shot. The importation of the spare wheel without which Soviet tractors could not be operated exemplified the system of control in which information could not be circulated at the risk of death.[5]

If it is not economic to have the state own the corporations, it is not much better to have the corporations own the state. In some countries, like Italy and Japan, the interconnection between government and large corporations has been so pervasive that it raises questions about the legitimacy of both. Are the corporations really profitable and competitive, or are they being subsidized by the taxpayers? Is the government simply an agent for maintaining a corporation/business oligarchy in wealth and power?

Even France, with its great pride in its education and technology, seems to be evolving away from *dirrigisme.* Its enormous unemployment levels cast doubt on the efficacy of even the most intelligent centrally directed economic systems; nor is its government/business relationship immune from the corruption more usually associated with Italy.

The only answer is a system of governance that originates from within the corporation itself and that includes the participation of an informed and effectively manifested broad class of "owners." As documented throughout this book, especially in the discussions of ineffective boards and shareholders, that system is not yet in place.

## Pension Plan Capitalism Based on a Federal Law of Ownership

Within the category of institutional investors, the largest group, public and private pension funds, are the best suited to playing that "legendary" supervisory role. As we discuss in Chapter 2, the other institutions have a short-term perspective (money market funds) or conflicts of interest (banks, insurance companies, and other entities who rely on corporations for business). Pension funds have a perspective so long term it is almost perpetual, with an average of 30 years from the date an employee puts the first dollar in to the date he or she takes the first dollar out. By that time, a whole new generation of employees is paying in. Pension funds and the professionals who manage them have conflicts of interest, too. But the strict fiduciary standards that apply to them should ensure that all aspects of the portfolio, including shareholder rights, are exercised, in the words of ERISA,[6] "for the exclusive benefit of (pension) plan participants," so that all conflicts must be resolved in favor of the beneficial holders.

The funded pension systems in the United States, both public and private, have created a class of long-term owners whose interests are congruent with those of society. To a certain extent, the competition between companies and industries has created a collective choice problem in dealing with issues that are of value to the group as a whole, but uneconomic as an individual choice.

Fields like vocational education, energy conservation, occupational health and safety, and environmental sensitivity fit in this category. This is an agenda that can be addressed only by government in conjunction with a "universal shareholder."

The pension plan participants want not only retirement income security but also the security of living their retirement years in a country that is economically strong and socially safe, comfortable, and just.[7] They are the quintessential long-term owner. There are approximately one hundred million Americans who have interests in public and private pension systems. This means that 40 percent of the entire population has an interest in enjoying retirement years in a society that is clean, safe, internationally confident, and stable. Because pension funds hold shares in literally every public company and every industry, they also constitute a new class of "universal owners." But they are also absentee owners. We must therefore focus on how these "new owners" can function as the core of an international system of governance.[8]

Pension funds have mushroomed in size not so much because of a sense of obligation to workers as because of government subsidy. The "tax cost" of pensions is in excess of $50 billion per year and is, after defense, the largest item on the United States budget. Because pension funds are "paid for" in substantial part by public funds, it is appropriate for the government to define broadly how pension fund trustees should function in their capacity as owners of the country's industrial establishment. While pension funds (with some 30 percent of the total – 20 percent private, 10 percent public) are the largest single institutional investor, other trusteed funds subject to federal government oversight – mutual funds (SEC) and bank trusts (FDIC, Comptroller, Federal Reserve) – are so substantial that today a majority of the equity capital in the country is held by trustees, whose obligation and authority is defined by federal regulators.

The development of a governance system based on increasingly active shareholders does not require any changes in law. The institutional investors are already covered by federal standards; even the state-authorized pension funds must meet at least some of the fiduciary standards of ERISA in order to qualify for tax-exempt status. The October 1992 amendments to the Securities and Exchange Commission's proxy rules lessened the restrictions on institutional investors who want to communicate with each other about proxy issues. The Department of Justice has ruled that institutional shareholders can collaborate with respect to their ownership rights in portfolio companies, without violating anti-trust standards.[9] All that is required is for the institutions – particularly the private pensions subject to ERISA to recognize that activism is in their long-term best interest.

Having the responsibilities of legal (trustee) ownership of 55.8 percent[10] of the 1000 largest United States corporations susceptible of definition by the DOL, the SEC and the various bank regulators give rise to the prospect of a Federal Law of Ownership. Coordinated action by the relevant agencies, probably following the lead of the DOL, can reinstate the long missing legal basis for our system of governance.

But it is important to remember that pension funds and other institutional investors have their own limitations. They are as susceptible of bureaucratic failings as the companies in which they invest. It would be folly simply to substitute one bureaucracy for another. Public pension plans have the further liability of having a "political" agenda, whereby they might use their ownership power to advance non-commercial objectives. The trustees of private pension plans are appointed by managements. The "fundamental contradiction" of ERISA, permitting corporations to oversee trusts for their employees' benefit, has contributed to the situation in which private trustees have been virtually silent in their responsibility as owners. On one hand, as a corporate manager, the pension fiduciary would tend to favor provisions that, on the other hand, as a shareholder, he or she might find unduly protective of management. And this could be so as a general matter or more specifically; he or she could even be a board member of the company whose equity securities are being held by the pension fund.

This is one reason that the exclusion of shareholders from "ordinary business" decisions of their portfolio companies is so important. To go back to the themes of this book, shareholders are clearly not the group with the best information to make these decisions. Beyond that, the "Federal Law of Ownership" will never work unless the crippling problems of "collective action" and conflict of interest are effectively addressed. The first has been addressed to some extent. The problem is that trustee holding as much as 1 percent of a large company has a very large investment in terms of dollars, but a very small one in evaluating the prospect of expending all of the resources of an activist initiative in exchange for only a pro rata share of the benefits. The collective choice problem is gradually being ameliorated as ownership is understood as a responsibility in addition to being a right (see, for example,

Interpretive Bulletin 94–1, issued by the Department of Labor). This means that judicious exercise of ownership is not only an appropriate action (and expense) for a trustee exercising "care, skill, prudence, and diligence; it is a requirement." The SEC's 1992 amendments to the rules governing communication between shareholders help to make collective action economic, and therefore legitimate.

But the second remains a problem. Fiduciaries under ERISA (as well as the Securities & Banking Regulations) have many conflicting interests, as is inevitable in a pluralist economy. The question is how these conflicts are resolved in the context of exercising ownership responsibility for portfolio companies. At present, too often the "ownership" responsibilities to beneficiarial holders are subordinated to the commercial conflicts of the trustees.

> Plan sponsors, in addition to the DOL, need to be more active to ensure the integrity of pension funds. In some cases, achieving this goal may require plan sponsors to retain voting responsibility for the shares in the plan's portfolio. Plan sponsors who delegate such decisions to outside managers should monitor closely how voting decisions are made to ensure that they are not tainted by conflicts of interest.
>
> Investment managers, too, need to play a greater role in the debate on the fiduciary duty under ERISA. While investment managers and other institutional investors were among the first to question the effect of antitakeover measures on the value of the shareholders' investment, it is equally clear that money managers, as a group, have been reluctant to confront publicly the problem of conflicts of interest.[11]

ERISA trustees operate today in a climate of seriously conflicted interest. How does an ESOP trustee, with other important business relationships with the company, resolve those conflicts? How poor does the company's performance have to be, how egregious do the proposed anti-shareholder proxy items need to be, before the ESOP trustee must vote against the same management that hires (and fires) him?

The government must set the standard for interpreting and enforcing the "exclusive benefit" rule of ERISA to provide guidance for private sector fiduciaries. At some point, DOL will have to be explicit in requiring ERISA trustees to act for the "exclusive benefit of" and "solely" in the interest of plan participants for the purposes of this kind of monitoring. ESOP fiduciaries will not necessarily be foreclosed from other commercial relationships with the plan sponsor; they will simply have to bear the burden of proving that they are acting free of conflict of interest. This may spur the creation of special purpose fiduciary institutions in the future.

## Structure for an Ownership-Based System of Governance

Once we understand that the existence of a class of long-term – essentially permanent – shareholders provides a stable financial infrastructure, we can create a system that benefits from their stability and uses them as a foundation. Knowing that the largest group of investors will be permanent "citizens" of the corporation makes it possible for one or more "owners" to undertake primary responsibility for monitoring a particular corporation. It must be clear to all parties that monitoring is an essential but strictly limited endeavor. Just as there are agency costs in having directors or managers make decisions best left to the shareholders, there are agency costs in having shareholders make decisions that are best left to managers or directors. Shareholders should monitor the director nomination and evaluation process, the executive and director compensation plans, and overall performance and structure. They should not monitor ordinary business decisions. Even if they had the right to do so, and even if they had the information to do so, the very fact of their diversified holdings would make it impossible. They cannot give Ford business advice when they are equally interested in the productivity of all of its competitors and suppliers.

In the context of these limitations, there are several possible models for organizing monitoring structures. The first is some structure for large investors to use to share information and resources and develop policies. The Council of Institutional Investors (CII), and the Committee on Investment of Employee Benefits Assets (CIEBA) of the Financial Executives Institute are two examples. CII has already shown that its members can combine forces to develop lists of poorly performing companies that can benefit from some shareholder feedback. Its impact has been so effective that an investment strategy based solely on CII-listed companies placed third in a national competition. Some of the CII members have set up group meetings with CEOs and directors. They could take this one step further by developing a systematic approach to "assign" problem companies to one or two member institutions, which would take the lead and report back to the group.

Another model was proposed by George W. Dent in a recent law review article. "The proxy system is the key to management control; giving shareholders control of the proxy system, therefore, is both a necessary and a sufficient condition for uniting ownership and control. However, collective action problems prevent coordination among all the shareholders, so control must vest in some subset of shareholders. Hence the law should grant exclusive access to the corporate treasury for proxy solicitation to a committee of the ten or twenty largest shareholders of the firm. The largest shareholders should comprise this committee because they are the most knowledgeable, have the greatest stake in the firm, and therefore should be the most diligent in improving corporate performance."[12]

A third approach is to use the ESOP structure (addressing the conflict of interest issues described earlier) as the basis for effective ownership involvement.

> Employees with stock in an ESOP have the right to vote on major issues and, in some cases, even for the board of directors. This is more voting rights than they have when they own stock through any other pension or benefit plan or through a mutual fund. In a normal pension or benefit plan, the trustees buy and sell stock and vote the shares without ever consulting the employees who are the beneficial owners of those shares. With an ESOP, the employees also have the benefit of a trustee who is bound to provide them with unbiased information, information that may be at odds with the information provided by the company's managers. The employees also have a representative at the annual meeting who is bound by law to look out only for their best financial interests.
>
> Of course, the proper role of the ESOP trustee must be explained to the employees, along with the employees' role in voting their shares and receiving information from the trustee. If this process is properly explained, everyone should feel confident that their interests are being looked out for and that they are better off than they would be without the ESOP trustee.[13]

Still another possibility is suggested by Allen Sykes:

> Each of the [most prominent] investment institutions would become "relationship investors" in say 8 of the top 100 companies. Each such company would then have 5 relationship investors whose combined shareholding would be say 15 percent to 20 percent (8 percent–10 percent in the biggest companies), i.e., enough for influence but not dominance. Each institution would appoint a capable busi-

nessman (*not* an institutional manager) as a non-executive or as I shall call them henceforth, a "shareholder director." These directors, *on behalf of all shareholders* to whom they would be responsible at shareholder meetings, would discharge the monitoring and remuneration functions, i.e., hold executive directors (senior managers) fully accountable.[14]

A variant of this approach is a proposal Robert Monks developed for the the 1992 Exxon Annual Meeting, which would have created a "shareholder advisory committee" (see page 284). This was designed as a mechanism for shareholder involvement that would minimize the "free rider" problem and the difficulty and expense of communicating with other shareholders. The Exxon proposal makes it possible for *any* shareholder (or group of shareholders) having a threshold economic interest to submit a competitive proposal to be elected as the shareholder representative. The elected shareholder is entitled to (i) compensation for costs up to a limit; (ii) compensation for time expended; and (iii) liberal access to the company's proxy statement thus enabling economical communication with the shareholders. This proposal enables suitable shareholder groups to make competitive proposals based on their qualifications and records. If they are "elected" by the shareholders, they can be paid an amount sufficient to compensate for their effort. This will remove some of the "free rider" inhibitions that account for the dearth of shareholder activism by those seemingly most qualified. It should engender the growth of an "ownership" profession alongside of the various other specialties found useful in managing money.

Like other shareholder initiatives, the agenda for these "shareholder committees" should stay away from "ordinary business" and focus on an overall (and process-based) "mission statement" for the board of directors, with specific governance and performance goals for the enterprise and benchmarks by which to measure their accomplishments.

Those who can best decide what directors should do are those who will be most affected by their actions; that is, the shareholders. They now have little reason to ponder the question because they play no role in the selection of directors. Only when shareholders control the board will they start to figure out how much time outside directors should devote to their positions, how actively they should participate in corporate planning, how to handle executive compensation, takeover defenses, and all the other problems that have long plagued corporate governance.[15]

The advantage of this approach is that it makes it possible to ensure that the company (and the shareholders) have the appropriate energy and expertise on the board at all times, even though the company's needs are constantly changing. The other advantage is that the expenses are covered by the company. Because of the free rider and collective choice problems, there must be a way to compensate those shareholders who act on behalf of shareholders as a group; the corporate treasury is the appropriate source for funding these activities.

CII has also considered the possibility of establishing a clearinghouse for director candidates, like the United Kingdom's Pro-NED. This would address a key failure of the current system, the self-perpetuating nature of the board selection system.

## Finding Directors

The board chairperson bears primary responsibility for defining the board's priorities and overseeing the board's effectiveness. This is precisely the area where they do have fewest conflicts of interest of anyone in the governance process. If some structure enables shareholders to become effective monitors, and therefore have the best access to information as well, their primary duty should be to identify the best possible board chairpersons (and possibly other director candidates) for portfolio companies.

If the chairperson is to be the CEO, the shareholders should put special focus on designating a "lead director," independent vice-chair, or other liaison for the outside directors. The costs of the search, including use of search firms, should be borne by the company (possibly, after limits have been established), but the effort should be staffed and the offer extended by the lead shareholders. The same process should be used to find the Chairperson, if it is a different person from the CEO. In either case, the lead shareholders can also establish criteria and approve the process for selecting the other board candidates. These should include a meaningful investment in the company's common stock, the ability and willingness to devote the requisite time, as well as professional experience and expertise in a relevant area. "Lead directors" and separate Chairpersons should have compensation that reflects the time and attention the positions deserve.

What is critical is that directors owe their job to the shareholder – no matter how large their personal investment; it is of almost equal importance that their job security, their reputation, and their professional advancement will be at risk in their performance of the directorial responsibility. There must be someone to whom a director is meaningfully accountable for his or her stewardship, and there is no better choice for that role than those to whom he or she is accountable as a fiduciary.

### Ownership Stock and Trading Stock

There is another possible approach to giving ownership interests the optimal structure for effective monitoring, and that is an equity structure that reflects the different needs and abilities of the different classes of investor. This would give institutional shareholders who want it the interest and the ability to monitor corporate performance.

United States shareholders currently enjoy an enviable package of rights, including the right to the residual benefits of the enterprise; the right to limit liability to the amount of their investment; the right to immediate and inexpensive transferability; and, among all the constituents having to do with the corporation, the exclusive right to the franchise of control. These rights accompany all shares, even though different kinds of shareholders assign them different levels of value. Individuals and some institutions, for instance, value liquidity and the capacity to exchange their holdings for cash at any time. These shareholders see stock like betting slips on a horse race. They have no interest in the underlying venture and view share ownership merely as an efficient means of gambling. The house take is small and performance seems relatively free of being rigged. Liquidity is not important to pension plans and "index funds." As "permanent owners,"[16] they have no alternative but to become involved in the governance of portfolio companies. On the other hand, shareholder monitoring could involve unacceptable costs and constraints for individuals and mutual funds.

We can recognize this fact by offering a variety of instruments to today's owners, rather than continuing to treat demonstrably different interests as if they were the same. For example, we could have "ownership shares," which give up some liquidity in return for greater ownership rights, and "trading shares," which give up some ownership rights in favor of liquidity. Another approach, suggested once by Dean LeBaron, is to let ownership rights trade separately. But that creates another set of agency costs, and one that is more difficult to solve.

As participants in the heated exchange over the proposed amendments to the NYSE's long-time "one share, one vote" rule, we have testified that the problem is not in different classes of stock but in making sure that all classes are presented to the market on an equal basis, and not through coercive exchange offers.[17] The history of abuse and coercion requires careful planning to make sure that: (1) all holders should be free to choose whether they want to be "ownership" or "trading" shareholders; (2) the constraints on each should be publicly disclosed; (3) shareholders should determine any restrictions – like the number of holders, or percentage of total equity – that might apply to the new "ownership class;" and (4) the holders of the "ownership" shares must recognize their fiduciary obligation to the other shareholders.

It will be difficult, though probably not impossible, for fiduciaries, especially pension fiduciaries, to hold any other class of common stock than "ownership." Index funds and defined benefit plans have no need for liquidity and a fiduciary obligation to function in some way as owner. "In such funds, the investments are often held on a long-term basis and the prudent exercise of proxy voting rights or other forms of corporate monitoring or communication may be the only method available for attempting to enhance the value of the portfolio."[18] But there are other species of investors, with other time horizons, who will find the "trading" shares have attractive risk/reward alternatives for equity participation. The DOL's rulings suggest that ERISA plans will presumptively hold "ownership shares."[19] Bank regulators might conclude the same about conventional trusts; the SEC probably would permit mutual funds to include either class in accordance with the representations in the prospectus.

A category of common stock that rewards investors' willingness to make a long-term commitment makes sense. Consider the analogous situation of Warren Buffett who has been successful in persuading company managements to create new classes of security for his investment, usually convertible preferred stock assuring him a current return superior to that available to the common shareholder together with participation in equity growth at American Express, Champion Paper, USAir, Salomon Brothers, and others.

Harvard Professor Michael Porter wrote the synthesis paper for the Council on Competitiveness project analyzing the national system of capital allocation. One of his conclusions was that the United States should enable a new ownership structure with interests aligned closely to those of the corporation itself. "These long-term owners would commit to maintaining ownership for an extended period, and to becoming fully informed about the company. In return for a long-term ownership commitment, however, must come a restructuring of the role of owners in governance. Long-term owners must have insider status, full access to information, influence with management, and seats on the board."[20] For pension funds, this represents a long-overdue recognition of the unique value of their capital investment. Having virtually no need for liquidity, their investments in common stock have been reduced in value by the costs of maintaining a marketplace for those who do.

The need for such a class of investors does not mean that this should be the only class of common stock. If this model were adopted, trading markets would be maintained in both classes of equity security with appropriate arrangements to ensure the commitments of "long-term" holders.

## Measuring Performance

As discussed in chapters 1 and 4, the limits of the available vocabulary and performance measurements limit the accountability of corporate management. After all, they can only be effectively held accountable to the extent that their performance can be quantitatively described in a language which is accessible and comprehensible to all parties. Generally Accepted Accounting Principles (GAAP) have been thought of as a workable language of accountability because they are seemingly precise and because they are intended to measure the business or commercial aspects of an enterprise. The principal attraction of GAAP is not that it contains the most appropriate – or even an appropriate – measure of performance, but that it has the weight of history, consistency, wide acceptance, and the illusion of precision. Even that is hard to hold on to, however, as shown by the pattern over the last half dozen years of "restructuring charges," which remove any semblance of consistency in valuation. Any new management can take advantage of the opportunity to write down the past and thus "hard wire" profits for as long as possible in the future. "IBM's earnings plunged in 1989, Akers gave up on the year in early December, announcing he was going to cut ten thousand jobs and taking a big write-off. He made sure that write-off was big enough to give him a cushion going into 1990 – some securities analysts estimated that the write-off let him take in 1989 above $1 billion of expenses that he otherwise would have had to account for in 1990."[21] Even bringing in an outside accounting firm does not solve the problem. GAAP values equipment and real property, but does not value the skills and relationships of its employees. Consistent with GAAP, companies have enhanced their own balance sheets by imposing the costs on government, consumers, and the community.

GAAP have value, but they are not up to the task we set for them, and they have failed to provide a genuinely informative and reliable standard for evaluating performance. Former New York State Controller Ned Regan suggested that companies be judged periodically by a special audit process. But that does not solve the agency cost problem; it just adds another layer. What, then, are the ingredients necessary for a new language of performance that can support some standard for corporate accountability?

> One of the basic problems is that management has no way to judge by what criteria outside shareholders value and appraise performance – the stock market is surely the least reliable judge or, at best, only one judge and one that is subject to so many other influences that it is practically impossible to disentangle what, of the stock market appraisal, reflects the company's performance and what reflects caprice, affects the whims of securities analysts, short-term fashions and the general level of the economy and of the market rather than the performance of the company itself.[22]

The only entities who can provide appropriate normative performance standards for corporate performance are long-term owners. Informed and involved owners can require the board to create an incentive and accountability system within the enterprise that rewards compliance with law, and with whatever less clearly defined social norms may appear appropriate. The permanent owners are uniquely able to evaluate whether an option being considered will optimize the value of the enterprise in the long run. Again, this does not mean that they should make "ordinary business" decisions. It means that they should determine the standards to be used to evaluate the performance of the company – and its board. For example, who is in the best position to evaluate the performance of the company and the board when the management has violated the law? GAAP and stock price do not do a good job. But the fiduciaries who manage money for the people who invest in, work at, buy from and sell to, and live near the company can. Here again, they have the best access to information (the long-term value of community standards as codified in law, the long-term cost of violating criminal or regulatory provisions), and the fewest conflicts of interest.

## Watching the Watchers – Preventing a New Bureaucracy

> I remember speaking to one of the principal authors of ERISA, Senator Jacob Javits, and asking him what he had in mind when he placed "control" of corporate America in the hands of ERISA trustees. Jack mused and replied: "Bob, no one who knows me will accuse me of modesty, but I must confess to you that we never anticipated this."[23]

What was unanticipated was the "success" of ERISA in providing an incentive for voluntary retirement savings, the iron logic of compound interest and exemption from taxation, and a long bull market. Suddenly, the law of trusts that was intended to define conduct for an infinitesimally small portion of the GNP of 18th century Britain was the informing energy underlying legal owner-ship of the nation's industry. No one understood what they were doing; no one could anticipate the consequences.

The rules for trusteeship were not devised with their twenty-first century role in mind. Trustees are severely penalized for improper investment and are not allowed an incentive reward for what they do well. Trustees are, first and foremost, risk averse. Trustees are most comfortable taking action to avoid the possibility of liability. That may be fine for a small segment of the market, but it is strange at best for the dominant shareholder in a capitalist economy whose prosperity depends on the intelligent assumption of risk.

Shareholder monitoring, including shareholder activism, is an investment decision. If shareholders are able to spend less in per-suading a company to revise its pay plans to more closely tie pay and performance than they will make as a result of improving the incentives, they have made an investment decision. If the returns from this initiative are greater than returns from selling the stock or other kinds of investment decisions, then it is a good investment decision.

This is reflected in the 1994 DOL interpretive bulletin requiring trustees to consider activism as a value adding or preserving ele-ment in their fiduciary responsibilities as investor. Whether ERISA trustees will ultimately become effective monitors depends on two factors – the DOL's willingness and capacity to enforce its regula-tion and, more importantly, the conclusion by corporate management that an ownership-based governance system is ultimately in their best interest. Given the alternatives of government regulation, limiting activism to public pension funds (with possible political agendas), or a completely ownerless system, they are likely to conclude that it is.

But in addition to their other seeming disqualifications, pension trustees have no particular expertise as "owners," much less as monitors of the performance of corporate managers and directors. The statute plainly authorizes the hiring of experts and even the delegation of fiduciary duties. Trustees normally designate expert economists, program traders, stock pickers, actuaries, etc. As soon as "ownership" becomes widely recognized as an essential component of an ERISA manager's exercise of "prudence," specialized firms will develop, and competition will ensure that they prove their worth. The creation of a "market" for ownership managers is likely to solve problems of conflict of interest and collective action. The market approach will also minimize the risk of creating a new level of bureaucracy and agency costs.

No enabling legislation is necessary. As noted above, pension funds can create new institutions by requiring that service providers serve only pension funds or furnish other satisfactory proof of lack of conflict of interest. A firm offering "ownership services" to pension funds will not be distracted by the temptation of selling products to managements. This elimination of conflict of interest assures responsible, independent, skillful, and prudent exercise of ownership responsibility. PWBA could issue an opinion granting a "safe harbor" for pensions only institutions, so that they will be preemptively considered "prudent" and free from conflict of interest problems, with a rebuttable presumption for other institutions.

## Conclusion

> ". . . (T)here are no successful systems of corporate governance, past or present, without committed and knowledgeable long term shareholders, managements with the preconditions and incentives for long term performance, and with such managements being properly accountable to their shareholders . . ."[24]

Both for reasons of power legitimacy and business competitiveness, a "real" governance system for large corporations is desirable. Both law and theory suggest that accountability to ownership is the optimum structure. "Pension Fund Capitalism" will permit the emergence of "ownership shareholders" with an incentive to be informed and active in monitoring corporations in which they invest.

Nothing meaningful will occur, however, unless the three most affected parties conclude that it is in their self-interest for the changes to take place. The government must explicitly adopt the policy that commercial competitiveness is a national priority and that an effective governance system is a necessary precondition for such success. Government can view a system in which its guidance significantly provides a framework within which institutional owners effectuate the oversight necessary for legitimacy and competitiveness as one that affords adequate protection against the threats of excessive corporate power for the citizens. Institutional investors need a government drawn "bright line" delineating the limits of permissible conflict of interest in acting as an ERISA fiduciary. Conflict has been so rife over the last twenty years that government's acquiescence has created the impression that the "exclusive benefit" rule prescribed by ERISA will not be enforced. So long as government takes this attitude, it is folly to expect commercial enterprises voluntarily to complicate their lives and diminish their profits. A PWBA directive might encourage the creation of new ERISA specific fiduciary ownership institutions – there is so much money available for management services that the market will take care of the rest.

Most importantly, management of the great American corporations – the leadership of the Business Round Table – will need to adopt the notion that "creative tension" between themselves and their owners is a preferable system of government that other alternatives, including a continuation of the present that might be styled "phony governance." There have been indications that the necessary statesmanship can be forthcoming; there have been contrary indications particularly in the area of executive compensation and the willingness to go to the extreme of pushing the government into accounting in order to protect options. Ultimately, what will work is the market. Companies having effective governance perform better, are valued more highly in the market, have a lower cost of capital – and the cycle goes on. Daimler-Benz, in listing on the NYSE, demonstrates that the exchange providing the highest standards of governance makes available capital on the most favorable rates. This – in a capitalist system – is the ultimate reality.

*EXXON PROPOSAL*

*RESOLVED: To adopt the following new by-law:*

*Article IIIA*

COMMITTEE OF SHAREHOLDER REPRESENTATIVES

1.  *The corporation shall have a committee of shareholder representatives consisting of three members. The committee shall review the management of the business and affairs of the corporation by the board of directors and shall advise the board of its views and the views of shareholders which are expressed to the committee. The committee may, at the expense of the corporation, engage expert assistance and incur other expenses in a reasonable amount not to exceed in any fiscal year $.01 multiplied by the number of common shares outstanding at the beginning of the year. The committee shall be given the opportunity to have included in the corporation's proxy statement used in its annual election of directors a report of not more than 2,500 words on the committee's activities during the year, its evaluation of the management of the corporation by the directors, and its recommendations on any matters proposed for action by shareholders.*
2.  *The members of the committee shall be elected by the shareholders by plurality vote at their annual meeting. Elections of members shall be conducted in the same manner as elections of directors. Each member shall be paid a fee equal to half the average fee paid to nonemployee directors, shall be reimbursed for reasonable travel and other out-of-pocket expenses incurred in serving as a member, and shall be entitled to indemnification and advancement of expenses as would a director.*
3.  *The corporation shall include in its proxy materials used in the election of directors nominations of and nominating statements for members of the committee submitted by any shareholder or group of shareholders (other than a fiduciary appointed by or under authority of the directors) which has owned beneficially, within the meaning of section 13(d) of the Securities Exchange Act of 1934, at least $10 million in market value of common stock of the corporation continuously for the three-year period prior to the nomination. Nominations must be received by the corporation not less than ninety nor more than 180 days before the annual meeting of shareholders. The corporation's proxy materials shall*

*include biographical and other information regarding the nominee required to be included for nominees for director and shall also include a nominating statement of not more than 500 words submitted at the time of nomination by the nominating shareholder or group of shareholders.*

*4. Nothing herein shall restrict the power of the directors to manage the business and affairs of the corporation.*

*5. This Article IIIA shall not be altered or repealed without approval of shareholders.*

## ACCOMPANYING STATEMENT

*The proposed by-law would establish a three-member committee of shareholder representatives which would review and oversee the actions of the board of directors in managing the business and affairs of Exxon. We believe such a committee could be an effective mechanism for shareholders to communicate their views to the board and would serve a useful advisory function at relatively little cost.*

## NOTES

1. Lindbloom, Charles E., *Politics and Markets: The World's Political Economic Systems* (Basic Books, 1977), p. 356.
2. *The Economist,* 7/30/94, p. 57.
3. Makihara, B. Minoru, CEO of Mitsubishi Corporation in a speech at Suffolk University, 4/29/94. There is concern that "corpocracy – control of the state by business – exists in modern Japan. Consider the following fictionalized account by author Tom Clancy, *Debt of Honor* (Putnam, 1994), at p. 120: "Japan was not a democracy in any real sense, rather like America in the late Nineteenth Century, the government was in fact, if not in law, a kind of official shield for the nation's business. The country was really run by a relative handful of businessmen – the number was under thirty, or even under twenty, depending on how you reckoned it – and despite the fact that those executives and their corporations appeared to be cutthroat competitors, in reality they were all associates, allied in every possible way, co-directorships, banking partnerships, all manner of inter-corporate cooperation agreements. Rare was the parliamentarian who would not listen with the greatest care to a representative of the zaibatsu."
4. Private letter to the author from Allen Sykes.
5. Conversation with Robert Monks.
6. ERISA, Section 404(a)(a)(A).

7. See, however, *Politics and Public Pension Funds* by Roberta Romano, Manhattan Institute, June 1994 – "public pension funds may be free of some of the particular types of conflicts which afflict private funds, but they are subject to many other, mostly political, which make activism on their part of dubious value."

8. France, in particular, has had great difficulty accommodating the goals of both privatization and of protecting what are thought to be industries vital to the national industry. The pattern of insuring "control" over publicly held companies through the issuance of special shares – the "noyaux durs" (the functional equivalent of the "golden share" in the UK) – to safe affiliates was rudely jolted when Swedish Volvo withdrew from a much acclaimed merger with Renault. At the end of the day, the Swedish interests were not prepared to cede "control" of the merged enterprise to a "nominee" of the French government. The French are now in the process of trying to create a funded pension system. "Because of the lack of big institutional investors and the stable long-term shareholders they represent, French industry has been forced to seek alternatives. One such has been a relatively high reliance on bank loans and direct equity investment by banks. Another has been the creation of complex systems of cross-shareholdings. The pattern of cross-shareholdings is also open to criticism . . . 'The system can reduce the rigor of shareholder discipline'. . ." *Financial Times,* "Grey on Top, Thinning Below," 7/27/94, at p. 11.

9. See – Rule, Charles F. – Letter to Institutional Shareholder Services (ISS).

10. The Brancato Report, Vol. I, Edition 3, September 1994, p. 3.

11. The Department of Labor's Enforcement of the Employee Retirement Income Security Act (ERISA), a report prepared by the Subcommittee on Oversight of Government Management of the Committee on Governmental Affairs, United States Senate, April 1986, p. 70.

12. Dent, George W., Jr., "Towards Unifying Ownership and Control in the Public Corporation," 5 *Wisconsin Law Review* (1989), p. 881, 907.

13. McWhirter, Darien A., *Sharing Ownership* (John Wiley & Sons, Inc. 1993). See also, *Ownership and Control: Rethinking Corporate Governance for the Twenty-first Century* (Brookings, 1995).

14. Sykes, *ibid.* at p. 15.

15. Dent, George W., Jr. "Toward Unifying Ownership and Control in the Public Corporation," 1989 *Wisconsin L. Rev.,* pp. 881, 914, 915.

16. ERISA requires investment managers to diversity to the maximum extent practical – unless to do so is clearly harmful to the fund. Public pension plans can escape the vulnerability of "back door socialism" best through indexing.

17. Testimony of Robert A.G. Monks, Securities and Exchange Commission, December 17, 1986.
18. DOL Interpretive Bulletin, *op. cit. supra,* at fn. #30.
19. Several analyses estimate the level of "management fees" for ERISA plans at 1/2 percent of capital. This suggests that up to $15 billion is currently being paid. Charles Ellis and Wilshire Associates have suggested that the results of stock management have been zero value added. In view of the large sums available and the problematic benefit of other forms of "management," it seems not unreasonable to require trustees to expend reasonably on being informed and active shareholders. This appears to be the recommendation of the DOL in its 7/28/94 statement.
20. Porter, Michael E., "Capital Choices: Changing the Way American Invest in Industry," *Council on Competitiveness,* 1992, p. 92.
21. Paul Carroll, *Big Blues, The Unmaking of IBM* (Orion, 1993) at p. 222.
22. Letter from Peter F. Drucker to Robert Monks, 6/17/93. Peter Drucker, along with former New York State Controller Ned Regan, has advocated periodic business audits by expert outside parties to provide perspective in evaluating a company's performance. My own view is that professionals belong inevitably to the person paying them (or, at least the person most likely to pay the largest bills in the intermediate run). There are few professional service organizations in the United States who did not provide corroboration of this – harsh seeming – judgment in connection with "fairness opinions" during the 1980s.
23. Conversation with Robert A.G. Monks (1984).
24. Sykes, Allen, for the October 1994 (No 2.4) edition of *Corporate Governance,* an International Review.

# 6

# Re-Empowering the Board:
# A Proposed Agenda for Action
# By Hugh Parker

The preceding chapters of this book describe the evolution of the corporation as the basic wealth-generating engine in our modern capitalist system; the concept and nature of ownership and control of corporations; the evolution and role of the board of directors as the interface between the corporation and its owners; the role of management in adding value to the corporation by maximizing its performance in the marketplace; and how corporate governance has taken different forms in countries other than the United States. Chapter 6 concludes that the present relationship between shareholders and managements needs to be changed fundamentally to ensure greater accountability by the latter to the former, and suggests some specific steps toward doing so.

This chapter will carry that line of reasoning one stage further to propose an "agenda for action." It addresses three questions: first, is there a demonstrable correlation between the quality of "governance" in a corporate boardroom and the performance of the company in the marketplace? Second, what are the underlying reasons for the present unsatisfactory state of governance in American companies? And third, what steps can be taken, and by whom, to enhance the effectiveness of all American boards of directors?

## CORPORATE GOVERNANCE AND
## CORPORATE PERFORMANCE

Frederick Winslow Taylor (1856–1915) was the American industrial engineer who is generally credited with having been "the father of scientific management." From his work and that of other pioneers in this new field there has during the 20th century developed a whole new profession: the profession of management. Like the older professions of law, medicine, and the ministry, management today is a well-developed profession in its own right with its own language, literature, academic institutions, theories, and techniques. (This is not to say of course that people were not managing things long before Frederick Taylor. The design and construction of the Great Pyramid of Cheops 5,000 years ago, to take an example, was a managerial achievement that even Jack Welch might be proud to include in his résumé.) But what Taylor started was the systematic analysis of the production process, and the organization of all the basic means of production – human effort, materials, power, and finance – to create products with maximum efficiency. The first management consultants were in fact called "efficiency engineers."

Management skills and techniques are today applied to virtually every kind of human activity, not just the production of material objects like those (steel, textiles, machine tools) with which Frederick Taylor was concerned. Now it is taken for granted that the owners of any institution – whether it is a business, a factory, a law firm, a university or a hospital – expect it to be well managed. And that means that those responsible for that result, the managers at every level from the CEO down, will be judged and rewarded on the measurement of their performance.

Thus, the very idea of improving the effectiveness of management is predicated on the assumption that managerial performance can be measured in some meaningful way. Much of what is taught at business schools, much of what guides the decisions and actions of managers at every level, and much of what is discussed in boardrooms has to do with various measures of performance: unit costs, fixed and variable overheads, shares of market, profit margins, cash flow, and a wide range of financial ratios such as EPS, ROA, ROCE, etc. So the modern concept of management as a professional discipline with measurable performance criteria has been evolving for approximately 100 years. But what about the performance of that other much talked-about element called "corporate governance" – i.e., the board of directors – with which corporate performance is presumed to be correlated?

Whereas the systematic development and application of improved management practices has been going on now for 100 years, the term "corporate governance" has been in use for not much more than ten. Before that it was referred to, if at all, as "effective boardroom management" but even that term, and the idea that it represents, dates back no more than 20 years. Professor Myles Mace at the Harvard Business School was a pioneer in this country, while Sir Adrian Cadbury and I were among the first to consider the subject of boardroom effectiveness in the United Kingdom during the early 1970s.

So all the current concern about the quality of corporate governance is of comparatively recent origin. Two of the best books on the subject – *Pawns and Potentates* by Jay Lorsch, and *Power and Accountability* by Robert Monks and Nell Minow – were published in 1989 and 1991, respectively. Implicit in both, though not conclusively proven in either, is the premise that more effective governance – i.e., a more effective board of directors – must in time lead to better corporate performance. Monks and Minow do assert that "the value of a company with involved shareholders is greater than the value of one without" and the success of their LENS investment fund supports that claim. Moreover, logic and common sense argue that a company with a strong and competent board of directors must over time outperform a comparable company without such a board. The main role of the board is generally seen as that of a *monitor* of the CEO. But a good board can also act as a valuable *mentor* to the CEO, i.e., as a "wise and trusted counselor" (Webster) to whom he can turn for advice and support. Nowadays the perceived quality of a board, and of its relationship with the CEO, can actually be reflected in the share price – as recently shown at W.R. Grace and Morrison Knudson.

In addition to such indirect evidence of a causal relationship between the quality of a company's board and the actual performance and value of that company, there is plenty of direct evidence to show that a weak or ineffectual board will sooner or later allow even a good company to lose its way, to make fatal strategic misjudgments, to be poorly managed, and ultimately even to fail or be taken over. How else to explain the recent debacles at such supposedly well-managed corporate icons as American Express, Eastman Kodak, General Motors, IBM and Westinghouse, to name only a few of the better known. None of these companies was the victim of some unforeseeable and unavoidable cataclysm; all were the victims of a cultural trend that has for decades been allowing a growing and dangerous imbalance to develop between all-powerful and self-perpetuating CEOs and what can be described as disempowered boards of directors.

## THE PRESENT STATE OF U.S. CORPORATE GOVERNANCE

One of the cornerstones underpinning the strength of our national economy is the democratic system of government that has evolved in this country in the two centuries since adoption of our unique Constitution and Bill of Rights. These provide the legal foundation on which our present system of national and state government is based. One of its central doctrines, which has relevance to corporate governance, is the clear separation of powers into the legislative, executive, and judicial branches which establishes the principle of "checks and balances" that ensures a safe and continuing state of balance among them.

Because of its relevance to corporate governance, it is worth a look at how this principle is worded in the Constitution. Article I says that "all legislative powers shall be vested in a Congress of the United States, which shall consist of a Senate and a House of Representatives." Article II says that "the executive power shall be vested in a President of the United States (who shall be) Commander-in-Chief of the Army and Navy of the United States, and of the State Militias." Article III says that "the judicial power shall be vested in one Supreme Court." The clear intention of the Founding Fathers was to create a system of checks and balances that would make it safe for the electorate, through the elected Congress, to vest such large powers in one individual combining the titles of President, Chief Executive, and Commander-in-Chief of the Armed Forces.

Today there are some American companies that are larger and more powerful in terms of financial resources, economic influence, and global reach than the entire United States of America 200 years ago, or indeed of many sovereign nations today. Yet they all have one thing in common: these great corporations, and these United States, are governed by fallible human beings with all the virtues and vices of human nature. The great difference between them – and it is a crucial difference – is that their forms of governance have evolved in very different ways. Our system of national governance is the result of a rigorous and never-ending debate among the three branches and the electorate who put them in office, a political process of constant challenge and response among them that has been going on for more than 200 years.

Corporate governance, on the other hand, has evolved more through a process of natural selection among its officers in a climate of non-intervention and benign neglect on the part of corporate owners (shareholders) who have been either unwilling or unable to assert the legal powers vested in their boards of directors. As Jay Lorsch and Robert Monks/Nell Minow demonstrate in their books cited earlier, and Monks and Minow do again in this one, many American CEOs are today, in effect, accountable to no higher authority because no *effective* higher authority exists. Their boards of directors, which are supposed in theory and in law to fill that role, have allowed themselves to be marginalized and rendered ineffectual; in other words, they have been disempowered. And this dangerous condition is not confined to just a few American public company boards; it is in varying degrees the accepted norm in most of them.

## RE-EMPOWERING THE BOARD OF DIRECTORS

"Power tends to corrupt; absolute power corrupts absolutely."
Lord Acton

"Whenever an institution malfunctions as consistently as boards of directors have in nearly every major fiasco of the last forty or fifty years, it is futile to blame men. It is the institution that malfunctions."
Peter Drucker

Partly as a result of some well-publicized "major fiascos" in the higher echelons of corporate America, like the five high-profile companies mentioned earlier, and partly as the result of persistent initiatives by Robert Monks and other shareholder activists, some steps have been taken in recent years by some companies to obviate some of the more egregious boardroom malpractices. But many of these – e.g., the 1994 "General Motors Board Guidelines on Significant Governance Issues" that will be referred to later – have been largely procedural or cosmetic changes aimed at improving the perception of boards' effectiveness rather than attacking the problem at its root. So what is the real problem?

The Romans made an important distinction between *autoritas* (authority) and *potestas* (power) and that distinction is still valid, although today these two terms are often though mistakenly used interchangeably. The real problem is that in most American companies today there is a huge imbalance between the actual *power* of the CEO and his or her management on the one hand, and the nominal *authority* on the other hand of the board by which he is officially appointed and to which he is legally accountable. The practical result of this imbalance is that the typical American CEO today is vested with executive authority that is equivalent to that of the President of the United States, but without the countervailing restraints of an independently elected Congress. And in the absence of such countervailing restraints, the CEO's delegated authority can become absolute power, and the board's authority – vested in it by statute and bylaws – becomes effectively powerless. That is the root of the problem that must be addressed.

If this central problem is to be addressed effectively – that is, with any realistic chance of success – then the first question must be: who has the will and the power to do so? Close study of the extensive literature that now exists on the subject of corporate governance leads to the inescapable conclusion that the only agency that can take on this daunting initiative is comprised of the major institutional investors acting in concert. There are of course legal, regulatory, economic, and even philosophical obstacles standing in the way of such investors taking this kind of initiative. But the stakes are so high that ways must be found to overcome these obstacles.

The authors of this book take a long-term view of this problem. They propose actions that are aimed at making changes in the present practices of corporate governance that will require five years or more to take effect. But the essential first step on the long road to re-empowering American boards of directors is that the institutional investors now controlling 55 percent of corporate equity must declare their full commitment to that goal. Without that commitment no significant progress can be achieved – ever. With that commitment, however, it is possible to contemplate a process or campaign by which boards of directors can take back their legitimate power, the power that they have over the years ceded by default to ambitious and strong-willed CEOs, and thus re-establish a healthier balance between them.

Before undertaking the design of a campaign or program of change to reverse the process of board disempowerment that has been going on for decades – a process that was greatly accelerated by the "financial re-structuring" frenzy of the 1980s – it is necessary to analyze and understand in some detail the specific factors that have caused that disempowerment. This is necessary because such a complex problem must be attacked holistically if it is to be resolved at all. Picking at its component parts – e.g., by simply increasing the ratio of outsider to officer directors, or creating new oversight committees – will not be enough. The long-term objective of this campaign is nothing less than a fundamental reform of boardroom attitudes and practices that will have the effect of leveling the playing field on which they engage their CEOs.

## WHY U.S. BOARDS ARE SYSTEMICALLY INEFFECTUAL

In spite of all the attention focused in recent years on the quality of corporate governance – i.e., on the effectiveness (or not) of public company boards of directors – and in spite of some steps taken to improve them, it is safe to say that American boards today are still only marginally more effective than they were ten years ago. On a scale of 1 to 10, they may collectively have moved from, say 2 or 3 to maybe 4 or 5. So there is plenty of scope for significant further improvement. In other words, the challenge and objective is to achieve an order-of-magnitude improvement by making all boards as professionally competent and effective in their trusteeship role as the management for which they are responsible are supposed to be in their managerial role. Merely continuing the present process of gradual marginal improvement is not an adequate or acceptable objective.

What specifically are the underlying reasons for this systemic weakness of boards of directors? There are several:

*Reason #1:* Boards of directors on both sides of the Atlantic have almost never fully and effectively performed the basic trustee role for which they are legally accountable to the shareholders by whom they are theoretically "elected." This is equally true in the United Kingdom where "the board" was invented in the early 19th century, and in the United States where the UK model was adapted and adopted later in that century. By tradition and long habit, boards of directors in both countries have always been more or less honorary and powerless bodies of which little effective action has either been wanted or expected. Board meetings have typically consisted (and still do) largely of routine rituals through which they are led by chairmen and CEOs equipped with information, knowledge, and staff support that ensure that they can and generally do control the agenda absolutely. In short, while boards may have the legal authority, CEOs have the effective power.

*Reason #2:* For obvious reasons this traditional imbalance suits most CEOs perfectly. The very title "Chief Executive Officer" confers on that officer near-absolute authority and power, especially when it is combined with the title of Chairman. Few if any of these corporate Masters of the Universe are going voluntarily to hand any part of these powers back to their boards, and attempts by some boards to regain some of these powers have so far only succeeded in crisis situations – e.g., by the General Motors board in 1993. But even then, instead of consolidating their newly regained power, the aroused GM board formulated a set of "guidelines" that are largely symbolic. Although clearly intended to give the impression that the new GM board is firmly in control, these guidelines are worded so tentatively and flexibly (see later) that the old imbalance of real power between the board and the CEO/ Chairman remains virtually unchanged. If such guidelines are to have real effect the board must, in Emerson's words, "speak in words as hard as cannonballs" – and then be prepared to back them by appropriate action, if necessary in a showdown even by firing the Chief Executive.

*Reason #3:* Combining the offices of board Chairman and CEO in one person virtually guarantees that the board will be ineffectual. A board can only be as effective as its Chairman wants it to be or is capable of making it. A strong and effective board can only be so under the leadership of a strong and independent Chairman, and that is a combination that few CEOs are likely to welcome.

There are few absolute rules about effective corporate governance, but one of these – and perhaps the most crucial one – is the imperative of separating the roles of Chairman and CEO. It is not an option as the GM guideline #1 seems to suggest in saying that "The Board should be free to make this choice in any way that seems best for the Company at a given point in time. The Board does not have a policy, one way or the other, on whether or not the role of CEO and Chairman should be separate . . ." An independent Chairman must when necessary be able to look his CEO in the eye and say "my board and I do not agree on this issue with you and your management." This clearly will never happen if the two offices are combined. It is worth noting that today 85 percent of UK companies have separated these offices, but less than 20 percent of US companies have so far done so.

In spite of their own guideline #1 referred to above, it is interesting to note that the GM board members have in fact separated these two offices between John F. Smith, Jr. as CEO and John G. Smale as chairman, and, according to a long article by long-time observer of boards Judith H. Dobrzynski in the *New York Times* (July 9, 1995), the arrangement is working well. It remains to be seen, of course, whether they will decide to continue the split when one or both of the present incumbents retires from office.

*Reason #4:* Most US boards are simply too big. In 1994, 80 percent of the Fortune 500 companies had boards with 12 or more members, and 40 percent had 15 or more. But the GM Guideline #14 has this to say about board size: "The Board presently has 14 members. It is the sense of the Board that a size of 15 is about right. However, the Board would be willing to go to a somewhat larger size to accommodate the availability of an outstanding candidate or candidates."

The reasons for these high boardroom numbers seem to be: (a) a total misunderstanding of what a board is supposed to do; (b) a belief that a lot of distinguished names and titles will impress investors; (c) a desire by the CEO to include as many fellow-CEOs and old friends as possible; and (d) pressures to make a board look fully "representative." A fifth unspoken and often perhaps subconscious motive may be the realization by politically astute CEOs that the larger the board the less effective it can be. It can be argued that beyond a total of say 7 or 8 members a board's effectiveness tends to become inversely proportional to its size.

*Reason #5:* Too many outsider and supposedly independent directors are simply not qualified to do the job properly. They often lack the relevant experience, the character and the basic skills to perform the exacting role of directors to the high professional standards required in today's environment. But even worse, although they are legally elected by the shareholders, in practice they are almost always selected and nominated by the CEO with the passive concurrence of the board and shareholders. So the wrong people get on corporate boards for the wrong reasons, and their independence is a myth.

*Reason #6:* Most outsider directors lack the motivation and/or the time to do the job right. Annual directors' fees tend to cluster in the $40,000 to $50,000 range. For an active CEO earning $500,000 or more elsewhere this is too little to justify more than a day or two per month, but for an academic or retired admiral with an income of $75,000 it is too much to put at risk by being too independent. But neither class of directors has any really compelling stake in the long-term future of the company (other perhaps than a few stock options), and so are largely motivated by loyalty to the CEO who appointed them, which may not always be in the best interest of the shareholders.

*Reason #7:* All directors have less knowledge and information about the company and the issues with which they must deal than the CEO whom they are supposed to monitor and judge, and they are entirely dependent on him for what they do have. It is safe to say that all outsider directors have less information than they need to fulfill their duties properly, and only find out about key strategic and policy issues when things go seriously wrong, by which time it is too late for anything but crisis management and damage limitation. The *New York Times* story on the GM board reports that Smale "unequivocally supports the separate chairman concept," quoting him as saying that "it is very difficult to logically defend any other format." According to Smith, having an outsider as chairman "allows directors to decide what they want to look at, and to demand what they want to see in terms of performance . . . It sets the priorities of the organization. It makes us get the attention of people right down to the plant floor." Dobrzynski concludes that

> To some extent, the withholding of information from the GM board by previous management is what got the car maker into such deep trouble in the first place. Through the 1980's and early 1990's, G.M. kept spiraling down – multi-billion dollar losses, closing plants, cutting jobs and eventually floating stock to help cover operating costs. But the board did nothing and G.M.'s then-chairman and CEO, Roger B. Smith, liked it that way. He gave directors as little information as possible, several have complained privately.

## TOWARD A TRULY INDEPENDENT AND ACCOUNTABLE BOARD

Corporate governance has evolved in different ways in each of the major OECD countries, and several of these are described in chapter 5: Japan, Germany, France, and the United Kingdom. The governance system that has evolved in each of these countries naturally reflects the history, culture, economics, social structure, and legal system of that country. One of these variables is what might be called the degree of shareholder primacy in each country which varies in each from quite high in the United Kingdom, to moderate in Germany, to low in France, to virtually nil in Japan.

From the point of view of the United States, where shareholder primacy is higher than in any other developed country, the experience of boardroom evolution in the United Kingdom is the most relevant. A brief look at the UK experience may be instructive.

Until the early 1970s two totally different boardroom models co-existed in the United Kingdom: that of the holding banks and insurance companies, and that of the industrial companies. In the former, boards of 40–50 directors were the norm, and these consisted entirely of outsider or non-executive directors. In the industrial companies, on the other hand, the boards were typically much smaller (10 to 20) but consisted entirely of insider or "executive" directors. Since then, however, these two models have tended to converge so that typical boards in both sectors today are much smaller with a substantial and growing proportion of non-executive members. Also increasingly, the offices of Chairman and CEO have been separated: this is now the case in more than 85 percent of companies and is expected to approach 100 percent by the end of the century. On this important point the United Kingdom leads the United States.

The aim of these changes in the UK context has been to make public company boards more independent of the traditionally all-powerful Chairman, and more responsive and accountable to their increasingly activist institutional shareholders (which hold an even higher portion of the total UK equity than do their US counterparts). Some of these changes were originally triggered by the shocking failures of such respected companies as Burmah Oil and Rolls Royce in the early 1970s, and have been accelerated more recently by such corporate shipwrecks as BCCI, Brent Walker, Maxwell Communications, and Polly Peck.

Both the American experience outlined earlier, and the UK experience cited here, reflect growing pressure from shareholders – which nowadays means institutional investors – to make the boards of their portfolio companies more independent of their CEOs and management, and more responsive and accountable to their shareholders. This in a nutshell is what the current interest in corporate governance is all about.

Although it is stating the obvious, a truly independent and accountable board requires two essential ingredients: the unquestioned leadership of a strong and independent Chairman and a hard core of truly independent outsider/non-executive directors. The former, as argued earlier, absolutely requires the separation of the offices of Chairman and CEO, and this can be done whenever the shareholders decide to do it. The latter will be more difficult to achieve, and will take more time.

One approach to the problem of finding enough independent directors to fill a growing need was the joint initiative taken about 15 years ago by the Bank of England and other institutions in the City of London to establish a new agency called PRO NED (an acronym for *PRO*motion of *N*on *E*xecutive *D*irectors). The stated aim of PRO NED was to encourage the appointment of more and better non-executive directors to public company boards which at that time (1979) typically had no such outsiders at all, or only one or two – and these were usually "token NXDs." (The PRO NED initiative did achieve some results, but for various reasons these fell short of the expectations of its founders and it has now been discontinued as a free-standing agency).

What can be done in this country to achieve what PRO NED was originally intended to do – namely, to increase the proportion of properly qualified and truly independent directors to public company boards? One idea that seems worth exploring is to "professionalize" the board of directors. This is by no means a new idea, but it may be one whose time has finally come. The idea of "professional" directors has been considered from time to time by various academics and others interested in improved governance, but perhaps most comprehensively and persuasively by Professors Ronald Gilson and Reinier Kraakman in their 1990 paper titled "Reinventing the Outside Director: An Agenda for Institutional Investors." This chapter therefore concludes with an elaboration and further discussion of their basic thesis that it is now time for the chairmen and directors of American public companies to become as professionally competent in their governance role as the professional CEOs and senior executives who are accountable to them have for many years been in their managerial roles.

## PROPOSALS TO PROFESSIONALIZE
## THE BOARD OF DIRECTORS

Practitioners of all the traditional professions – accounting, law, medicine, the ministry – are required to be formally qualified. This means that they must have completed an approved course of study or training, have passed certain examinations and tests, and have achieved standards of competence that satisfy the relevant authorities governing their professions. Such competence is typically recognized by the granting of a license to practice, a diploma, or certificate of competence. The same applies to other less traditional occupations such as management and management consulting, nursing, teaching, law enforcement, and the like.

It seems odd, if not downright perverse, that no such qualifications are required of individuals who are appointed as directors to the boards of public companies. In that capacity such directors are arguably responsible – in theory, at least – for the efficient management of companies which in aggregate determine the health of the national economy, and ultimately therefore the wealth and strength of the nation itself. So common sense suggests that it is now time to consider ways to professionalize these boards of directors.

What are the defining characteristics of the new-model "professional director" to bring about this transformation of the boardroom? Reflecting the reasons cited earlier for the systemic weaknesses of today's boards, he or she should: (a) fully understand the real legal powers, duties, and liabilities of the board and all its members; (b) be prepared to commit the time and effort necessary to fulfill these duties to a high professional standard; (c) be well led by a strong and independent Chairman, and also serve in some cases as such a Chairman himself; (d) be fully qualified for this professional role in terms of relevant prior experience, personal character, and appropriate training; (e) be strongly motivated to perform this role effectively; and (f) have access to and be able to understand all the information necessary to participate in and contribute to all board discussions, debates, and decisions. This set of criteria may seem at first sight to set unrealistically high standards, but nothing less will be required to achieve an order-of-magnitude improvement in boardroom performance. To elaborate briefly on each:

*Understanding the Board's true role:* The point was made earlier that, by tradition and long habit, few if any boards and their directors have ever (except in a few cases of acute crisis as, recently, at GM) fully lived up to their legal obligations. This may more often have been through ignorance rather than through willful negligence. Such low standards have however become the accepted norm, tolerated by shareholders and not discouraged by strong-willed CEO/Chairmen. Orientation courses for directors have recently been offered by several US and UK universities, but with as yet unknown results. In Australia, the Institute of Company Directors will require would-be board members to take a course – and pass an exam – in order to be eligible to serve.

*Time and commitment:* One of the most widely voiced criticisms of outsider directors has been their tendency to take on too many such directorships and to devote too little time and attention to each. Examples are cited of CEOs of major companies who also hold half a dozen or more part-time directorships on other boards often chaired by fellow-CEOs. How, it can be asked, can they possibly do justice to all? The answer is that they can't and don't. But this practice too has become accepted as the norm, and one not likely to be changed by the very CEOs who like it that way. In their suggested profile of the new professional directors, Professors Gilson and Kraakman recommend that a full-time professional's portfolio should consist of no more than six boards, but it can be argued that even that is too many. Robert Monks, for one, suggests a limit of three.

*The independent Chairman:* If there is one lesson to be learned by American boards from recent British experience it is the emergence in the UK of the part-time non-executive chairman which represents a sort of middle ground between two extremes in the balance of boardroom power that have occurred in the United Kingdom since World War II. These are worth a closer look since they may suggest a similar development in this country.

Up until WW II and continuing into the 1960s, the boards of most UK public companies were dominated by powerful chairmen: the very title of Chairman carried with it great authority and real power, in some cases because these chairmen were also the founders of these companies – e.g., Sir Eric Bowater (Bowater), Sir Allen Clark (Plessey), Sir Jules Thorn (Thorn Electrical), Sir Alfred Mond (ICI), and Lord Leverhulme (Unilever). In the case of the banks and insurance companies it was easy for the Chairman to dominate a board which by its sheer size (40 to 50) and composition (members of the nobility, retired field marshalls, major clients, friends of the Chairman) was not much more than a quarterly luncheon club fulfilling an essentially decorative role. In the industrial companies, on the other hand, the Chairman could easily dominate a board consisting entirely of executive or employee directors who, outside the boardroom, were his subordinates.

Some time in the late 1960s a new force entered the UK scene: the American headhunters. These quickly created a marketplace for the managerial talent that the growing activities of also largely American management consultants revealed to be in very short supply. These conditions led to the introduction of other American practices: escalating compensation, stock options, and – most significant in this context – the new title of Chief Executive Officer which soon began to displace the traditional British title of Group Managing Director. And so, in the space of a few years, the once all-powerful Chairman had been reduced to a virtual figurehead and his place taken by the all-powerful American-style CEO.

Some of the corporate shipwrecks mentioned earlier raised serious questions about the effectiveness of public company boards in general, and these in turn led to the appointment in 1991 of Sir Adrian Cadbury's Committee on the Financial Aspects of Corporate Governance. In 1992 this Committee published its "Code of Best Practice" which says, among other things, that "There should be a clearly accepted division of responsibilities at the head of a company which will ensure a balance of power and authority, and that no one individual has unfettered powers of decision." While this Code stops just short of recommending the separation of Chairman and CEO it goes on to say "Where the

Chairman is also the Chief Executive, it is essential that there should be a strong and independent element on the board, with a recognized senior member. The board should include non-executive directors of sufficient caliber and number for their views to carry sufficient weight in the board's decisions."

This Code has now been adopted by the London Stock Exchange, and companies listed on the exchange are now required to state in their annual reports the extent to which they have complied with each of the Code's provisions, and non-compliance must be explained, The growing practice in UK companies of separating the roles of Chairman and Chief Executive – already adopted in 85 percent of them – is already restoring a more even balance between them. It is time for that practice to be adopted in this country. As this happens, as it surely will, there will also emerge a class of professional chairmen who will be recognized as being just as important as professional CEOs, as seems now to be the case at General Motors.

The most common objection to this separation of roles is that it is "divisive"; that it will divide and lead to indecision and political infighting in the board; that this in turn will undermine the authority of the CEO; and that this will weaken the leadership of the company itself. This view fails to understand that there are two quite different roles: managing the board of directors, and managing the company. The Chairman is responsible for the former and his jurisdiction is limited to the boardroom. The CEO bears the full responsibility for managing the company with the commensurate authority and powers to do so delegated to him by the board to which he is accountable.

*Qualifications for directors:* What kind of people make effective directors? Professors Gilson and Kraakman suggest (understandably) that academics are ideally suited to the role, and they also include senior partners in accounting and management consulting firms. There is no question that people drawn from those sources can be excellent directors, but they usually lack one important qualification: the insights and credibility gained from the experience of having actually managed a company themselves.

There is, however, another and potentially very rich source of outstanding candidates that does not yet seem to have been identified or systematically tapped. These are the respected CEOs of successful companies who are approaching retirement and who for a variety of reasons may be considering one last career change before they decide to retire fully, a change that would offer an interesting and worthwhile challenge to cap a successful career as an executive manger. Such a candidate might look something like this:

He (or she) has completed the successful turnaround or rejuvenation of an ailing public company, or perhaps the leadership of a smaller private company or MBO to the point of going public. Either way, he has demonstrated the skills and personal character required to be a good director, and moreover has a strong personal balance sheet to show for it. At the age of, say, 55 he has proven himself in the real world and is considering a move into an equally interesting but less intensely pressured occupation. To such a person the prospect of three or four challenging directorships could be an attractive alternative to simply continuing on for another 7 or 8 years as CEO in the same company. By doing so such people would, as the British phrase goes, become "poachers turned gamekeepers," and it is this experience that gives them the edge as directors over most academics and consultants.

Candidates from this particular source already have most of the proven qualities to be effective directors, but could be made even more so by a short and intensive course in corporate governance and practical directorship. A modest step in that direction has been taken in the United States and the United Kingdom, as mentioned earlier. The National Association of Corporate Directors has announced that it is convening a "Blue Ribbon" commission to make recommendations on director "certification," possibly along the lines of the Australian example mentioned above.

*Information for directors:* The point was made earlier that outsider directors in virtually all US companies today are simply not in possession of all the information they should have to discharge their trusteeship obligations fully. This deficiency of information is perhaps the underlying cause of many of the recent corporate debacles referred to earlier. In post mortem analyses of these "major fiascos," to use Peter Drucker's phrase, the inevitable question is "what was the board doing when all these things were going wrong? Didn't the directors know what was happening?" to which the answer usually is that they did not – or, if they did, they were unwilling or unable to do anything about it.

There are of course many reasons for this, not the least being the limited role that their CEOs typically expect or want them to play – and indeed the limited role that such directors themselves expect or want to play. A commitment of one or two days per month (not to mention the compensation for that commitment which will be referred to later) does not allow for much time and attention to absorb great quantities of information. In short, the inadequate information typically made available to directors is a direct reflection of their limited time commitment.

Another and more fundamental problem is the qualitative deficiency of the information received. Some boards are supplied with daunting quantities of information, but much of this may be of marginal use to the director in gaining a real understanding of the company's *real* situation, and of the *real* issues that the board should be addressing. What most outsider directors get is a selective digest of what the CEO and officers already know and are willing to pass on to the outside directors. But a professional director of the quality, experience and motivation proposed here will intuitively know what he or she needs to do the job right, and will request and if necessary demand it.

It has been suggested that a special staff resource should be made available by the company specifically to serve the outside directors. Such a resource would be dedicated to satisfying their needs and requests for information. It is said that "knowledge is power" and the truth of that axiom can be observed in every boardroom, especially in its negative sense: the lack of knowledge is lack of power.

*Compensation of directors:* The traditional and present form of payment to outsider directors can be described as nominal payment for nominal service: they don't get paid very much for not doing very much. Total annual fees typically amount to around $40,000 which, for the reasons explained earlier, is too little to motivate some directors to be really effective while at the same time being too much to motivate others to be really independent. Another drawback to this fee arrangement is that, however modest these fees may be, they are still paid by the company; so to that extent the outsider director is really an employee of the company and thus ultimately of the CEO. In short, the present system of payment in the form of annual and attendance fees is inherently demotivating and counterproductive.

Two statements by Robert Monks point the way toward a more motivating and effective system of director compensation. In a *Wall Street Journal* article, Monks explained why he would not support management's nominations to the Westinghouse board at a forthcoming shareholders meeting, then added that "I own 132,200 Westinghouse shares, which may not be a lot, but it is more than the total number of shares now owned by all the other directors put together." And in another article Monks made the self-evident observation that "nothing makes a director think and act like a shareholder more than being a shareholder."

Under the earlier heading of "Qualifications for Directors" it is suggested that the best candidates for professional directorships should not only have had the real-world experience of actually having managed a company themselves, but also have a strong personal balance sheet to show for it. This is a key factor in the line of reasoning, started by Monks's observations, that leads to the proposal that outsider directors should have a substantial financial stake in the company to be eligible for appointment to the board. Again, this is by no means a new idea, but so far it does not seem to have been seriously tested. The time may now be right to do so.

A typical professional director of the kind envisaged here might, around the age of 55 or so, decide that he or she has had enough of being a CEO, and – having built up enough capital in doing so – would now like to do something equally challenging but different. One option is of course to do more directorships at $40,000 each, spend half his time serving on those boards and the other half playing golf or whatever.

A different option, and a potentially more interesting one, would be to select just two or three companies with boards on which his experience and special skills would enable him to make a real impact over the period of, say, 10 years during which he intends to remain actively involved in business. However, instead of being paid the usual fees for this service, he would invest a substantial amount of his own money – in the order, say, of one or two million dollars – and thus become the "involved shareholder" referred to earlier by Robert Monks as the best way to add value to a company. In that capacity he is in a strong position to influence the performance of the company and the value of his shares – a sort of mini–Warren Buffet.

With the kind of money being paid to successful CEOs nowadays there should be a plentiful supply of such people with which to "seed" a number of boards that need and could benefit from the contributions that a hard core (three or four) of such investor/directors could make. Experience has shown that such a core can effectively influence a board even if they do not have a numerical majority: weight is more important than numbers since few board issues are ever put to a vote. Legally, they would of course have exactly the same authority and obligations as every other director;

the only difference being the way in which they are compensated – i.e., as professional "investor/directors" rather than the traditional fee-earning directors.

The attractions of such a campaign to bring highly motivated professional directors into underperforming boardrooms are obvious: First, it requires little or no changes in existing laws, bylaws, and regulations. Second, it can be started on a small scale – initially perhaps half a dozen such directors introduced onto two or three carefully selected boards – and then, if successful, gradually extended. And third, it can be tried at no expense to the company, nor to the shareholders who stand to gain if it is successful. What such a campaign does require, however, is the will and resources to test and experiment with it over a long enough period of time to prove that it can really work.

# 7
# International Governance

## THE GLOBAL PICTURE

The main varieties of capitalism have always differed in significant respects. In America, for instance, shareholders have a comparatively big say in the running of the enterprises they own; workers, who are for the most part only weakly unionized, have much less influence. In many European countries, shareholders have less say and workers more. In Germany, for example, the representatives of unions serve on supervisory boards; the companies' principal bankers also have plenty of clout in the strategic decisions of management. On this spectrum, Japanese capitalism lies even further away from the American variety. Until recently shareholders in Japan played virtually no role except to provide capital; managers have been left alone to tune the companies as they see fit – namely for the benefit of employees of allied companies, as much as for shareholders.[1]

There is no ideal model of capitalist structure; different forms will be appropriate in different countries at different times. Indeed, it is by granting individual companies the flexibility to change that capitalism as a whole has advanced. But with flexibility comes accountability. Those who exercise the power to direct a given enterprise must be meaningfully accountable to some entity or persons outside the enterprise. This can be the shareholders, as in the theoretical Anglo-American model; a supervisory board, including stakeholder representation such as employees, as in the German or continental model; or a clearly understood national culture, as in the case of Japan.

It is a mistake to attempt to impose one country's corporate governance system on another's. There are the usual problems associated with transplants. But comparative corporate governance – involving, as it does, different cultural and political assumptions, vocabularies, and systems – raises some additional questions. First, we must ask whether the other systems actually work better. Are German or Japanese companies more competitive than American companies? Some commentators suggest that they are, and that this is a part of a natural evolutionary arc.

But even as different nations and cultures seek optimal methods of corporate organization, so current trends seem to indicate that governance practices will increasingly converge. A 1992 research paper by Oxford Analytica, an English consulting group, identified possible developments in corporate governance in the seven leading industrialized countries (G7) over the next decade. The paper concluded that a major force for such confluence, or homogenization, will be the increasing globalization of capital. As trade barriers fall, markets expand and automate, and information flows improve, it will be as easy for a US pension fund to invest in, say, Switzerland or Japan, as for it to invest in US markets. Currently, US institutions hold a total of $140 billion in non-US equities.[2] By the same token, some 21 percent of US stock purchases were made by foreign buyers in the mid- to late-1980s.[3]

Oxford Analytica predicts that such a fluid, worldwide capital market will have immense effects on governance. As asset managers seek to invest abroad, they will be attracted by those markets with the most open, shareholder-friendly governance structures. For instance, an investor might be repelled from investing in Japan by the consistently low dividend yield offered by Japanese companies, or because of the all but nonexistent recourse Japanese shareholders have for voicing their concerns. Or an investor might think twice about investing in Germany because financial disclosure laws there are so lax. In every instance, investors are likely to favor markets where disclosure of financial and other information is well established and where there are clear avenues of protest should managerial decisions be made that might not be in the shareholders' best interest.

Thus, good governance will be an important factor in the competition for global capital. Companies from around the world will offer strong shareholder relations as a way of attracting money. This trend, combined with the globalizing effects of the 117–nation General Agreement on Tariffs and Trade, signed in 1993,[4] should cause a confluence of different governance practices over the next decade. Elsewhere, we have discussed in depth how US institutions may increasingly behave more like members of a Japanese *keiretsu* or a German *Hausbank* in forming long-term relationships with the corporations in which they are invested. By the same token, many of the characteristics that define governance in the United States may find favor abroad. In many of the countries discussed below we find evidence of US-style shareholder activism, including demands for a greater say in the operation of the company, for improved disclosure of financial results, or for reforms to improve the independence of boards of directors.

## JAPAN

As Japan rebuilt its economy in the years following World War II, it developed a unique corporate governance structure. Some of the notable features of this structure are listed below.[5]

- Powerful government intervention, dominated by the Japanese Ministry of Finance (MOF). MOF has maintained strong regulatory control of all Japan's business, supervising every aspect of industrial activity including capital flows.
- A pattern of cross-shareholdings by affiliated companies, often including customers and suppliers. There is often a dominant shareholder, such as a "main" bank or a *keiretsu* partner. (The *keiretsu* system roughly translates to what in the West would be called "relationship investing." For a description of the *keiretsu* in action, see the T. Boone Pickens case in point).
- The existence of very close relationships between the corporate and government sectors, that has often bordered on corruption. (Witness the recent political upheaval in Japan, and the disgrace of the Liberal Democratic Party, or LDP.)
- Corporate priorities are focused on growth and market share, not shareholder returns (except through share price appreciation).
- An all but nonexistent market for corporate control with minimal takeover activity.

While this system has proved its worth in Japan's spectacular economic success, we shall see later that many aspects of the structure are weakening or even collapsing.

### Case in Point: T. Boone Pickens and Koito Manufacturing Co.

In 1989, Texan corporate raider and shareholder advocate T. Boone Pickens paid nearly $800 million for 19 percent of Koito Manufacturing Co., an auto parts manufacturer. Pickens's purchase made him Koito's largest single shareholder. However, an interlocking shareholder group made up of friendly banks, other companies, and customers owned 62 percent of Koito. The key member of this *keiretsu* was Toyota Motor Corp., Koito's largest customer.

Pickens argued that his stake entitled him to some special recognition, notably board seats. Toyota, he argued, held a 19 percent stake and had three such seats. In an hour-long meeting with Koito officials in April 1989, Pickens insisted that his holding justified similar representation on the board. He also demanded that Koito pay larger dividends, though American-size dividends are rare in Japan.

Pickens's demands were summarily dismissed. Koito and Toyota asserted that Pickens was merely after a greenmail buyout of his holding, and was not interested in the long-term health of the company. Pickens vociferously denied that charge, saying that Koito (with 1988 earnings of $26 million on sales of $815 million) had tremendous unrealized value that he wished to exploit. Pickens told the *Washington Post:* "We consider ourselves to be a long-term shareholder in Koito. . . . All we want to do is to work with the Koito management." The media suggested a third motive: that Pickens was gearing up to compete for the governorship of Texas, and that the Japanese episode was a way to raise his profile.

In June 1989, Pickens attended the Koito annual shareholders' meeting in Japan. The meeting lasted three hours – an unheard of length for a Japanese shareholder gathering – and ended with the 20 nominated directors being elected and Pickens staging a noisy walkout. Pickens told reporters: "I'm beginning to wonder if the reason I'm denied this right [to seats on the board] is because I'm not Japanese." Pickens raised the same point in Senate testimony one month later.

The next year, Pickens sued Koito for failing to disclose its tax return to him. Under Japanese law, shareholders owning 10 percent or more of a company can demand access to certain proprietary information. Koito argued in court that Pickens's motivation was that he was still hoping for a greenmail payment. As such, his request was not valid. The court dismissed Pickens's application.

Recently, some US institutions have attempted to improve their relations with Japanese companies, though it has not been easy. For instance, 1992 was the first year that US institutions received English language meeting notices and meeting agendas.

CalPERS has taken to voting Japanese proxies the last few years. However, in 1993, several Japanese companies contended that they did not receive any "no" votes on issues relating to dividends and board size, when a number of US institutions had clearly voted "no." It turned out that Japanese banks never forwarded the US votes to the companies, as required. CalPERS general counsel, Rich Koppes, called the oversight "very disturbing."

## GERMANY

Germany has a governance system that resembles the Japanese structure in some respects, yet is very different in others. For a full description of German governance, we will turn once again to the experts.

All public limited companies and private limited companies with more than 500 employees are required by law to have a supervisory board *(Aufsichtsrat)* and an executive board *(Vorstand)*. A "workers council" must be consulted on hiring, firing, and other workplace issues.

### Signs of Change

There are many signs that elements of the German system will change over the coming years. As Germany struggles under a severe recession (exacerbated by the costs of integrating East Germany into the republic), there is increasing criticism of Germany's closed-door system of management, and an ever more urgent need to look beyond Germany for new capital. These forces are likely to have a far-reaching effect on German governance:

- German banks are reconsidering their stakes in German companies.
- German and foreign shareholders are challenging the German practice of voting rights restrictions.
- Generally lenient financial disclosure requirements in Germany may be about to change. In order to bolster Frankfurt as an international financial center, for example, the German federal government proposed legislation . . . debated in the Bundestag in the autumn of 1992. Included in the "Finanzplatz Deutschland" package is a proposal for a new federal supervisory agency for the securities industry and proposed legislation outlawing insider trading.

German institutions are likely to improve their standards of financial disclosure. The giant insurance firm, Allianz, revealed the extent of its corporate holdings in the autumn of 1993. The disclosure prompted the following comment from the *Financial Times.*

Allianz's decision to disclose its holdings of 10 percent or more in financial and industrial companies is a milestone in the history of the Munich based insurer. The significance of the move lies in what was disclosed – large stakes in 11 German financial and industrial companies and five foreign ones – and because the disclosure was made at all. . . . German corporations are increasingly keen to engage in investor relations activities. . . . These developments show a decisive, if not all-pervasive, shift in the attitude of the management of big German companies to minority shareholders – predominantly the foreign institutional investors whose interest have not tended to be paramount in German corporate decision making.[7]

While many have praised Germany's two-tier structure as a more efficient means of holding management accountable,[8] there is no guarantee that it provides a foolproof check against mismanagement. Indeed, the recent trend to appoint an outgoing CEO as chairman of the supervisory board calls into question the extent of the supervisors' independence from management. A recent episode at Metallgesellschaft, a metals and mining group, showed that the German structure is as susceptible of abuse as the Anglo-American board structure.

## Case in Point: Metallgesellschaft

Metallgesellschaft is Germany's fourteenth largest industrial company, with a turnover of around $15 billion. Metallgesellschaft shareholders include some of the biggest names in German finance – Deutsche Bank, Dresdner Bank, and Allianz Insurance. They, along with other large shareholders, owned 60 percent of the company's shares. True to the German system, these large shareholders were represented on the supervisory board. The chairman of the board was Ronaldo Schmitz, the head of Deutsche Bank's corporate finance department. His fellow members of the board had equally strong credentials – Gerhard Liener, chief financial officer at Daimler-Benz, and Bernhard Walter, a director of Dresdner Bank.[9]

It was these people – the very cream of the German industrial elite – who were responsible for supervising the management of Metallgesellschaft. Yet, in December 1993, the company's management revealed that Metallgesellschaft was close to collapse. The cause was a series of huge losses run up by MG Corp., the company's US trading subsidiary.[10] The losses required Metallgesellschaft bankers to arrange a $2.15 billion rescue package.

While the management team was fired within two weeks of the losses coming to the notice of the supervisory board, larger questions remain for the German governance system. Most importantly: who supervises the supervisory board?

Germany, too, has its own nascent shareholder rights movement, the *Deutsche Schutzvereinigung für Wertpapierbesitz e.V.* (DSW), founded over 40 years ago. Its membership is composed largely of individual investors, many of whom choose to exercise their votes via the DSW.[11] Oxford Analytica discusses DSW's aims:

> The DSW has also campaigned for higher dividends and more transparent accounting methods. These two issues are closely linked, as the former would be easier to accept if the latter were improved so that the amount of retained profits could be seen. Thus far, management's position has been little affected by shareholder activism, however, which has not had anything like the significance in Germany which it has had in the United States.[12]

The DSW is also active in submitting a wide range of proposals and counterproposals at German annual meetings.[13] The German corporate governance system allows for two types of direct shareholder action on the agenda of the annual meeting: the counterproposal and the shareholder proposal. The counterproposal must state (a) the shareholder's intention to object to a proposal of the supervisory board or the management board; and (b) the shareholder's request that other shareholders vote with him against the proposal. Sometimes, the counterproposal presents an alternative proposal (such as an alternative allocation of net income or an alternative nominee to the supervisory board). While there is no minimum ownership requirement for the submission of a counterproposal, a shareholder must hold at least five percent of the total share capital or shares with a total nominal value of at least DM1 million ($666,666) in order to submit a shareholder proposal requesting a vote on an item not already on the agenda.

The DSW has been effective in focusing attention on corporate governance issues by submitting both proposals and counterproposals. A shareholder proposal submitted at the December 1992 annual meeting of the energy conglomerate RWE called for the abolition of shares with enhanced voting rights. The proposal won the support of US institutional investors, including CalPERS. A PERS representative attended the RWE meeting and made a speech saying it was naive for German companies to maintain voting restrictions and still expect to retain access to international capital markets. The proposal also won the support of a wide range of German shareholders.

A shareholder counterproposal at the April 1993 Hoechst AG annual meeting questioned the accountability of the supervisory board. Less than 1 percent of voting shareholders supported the proposal, though it became a major media event and raised the issue of accountability in Germany.

As of late 1993, DSW is most concerned about the role of German banks in exercising votes at general meetings. The DSW contends that banks are often unwilling to cast votes against management due to their dual role as lenders as well as equity holders in many German companies. As a result, the DSW is advising its members not only to support proposals and counterproposals calling for improved corporate governance, but also to be represented at the meeting by the DSW in order to ensure that the votes are actually cast as instructed.

## FRANCE

The defining characteristic of the French governance system is the absence of a diverse investment community. Rather, the state, banks, and corporate management hold the controlling interests in the French governance structure. In this respect, the French system departs from the Anglo-American model; though it also departs significantly from the German model.

### French Ownership

Companies in France are controlled by the state, management, or by families. The top 50 industrial, commercial, and service companies of France break down as follows:

- 12 state controlled;
- 17 management controlled;
- 14 family controlled and managed;
- 3 family controlled (but with outside management);
- 4 subsidiaries.

In no other modern industrialized country, save Japan, does the state play as powerful a role as it does in France. This is, in part, due to the long French tradition of encouraging the nation's finest minds into the civil service, via the educational system of the *Grandes Ecoles.* Since World War II, when the state stepped in to rebuild France's shattered economy, the French intellectual elite – represented by both civil servants and industrial managers – has been intimately involved in the formation of industry. So important did the civil service become in the creation of business that private groups, seeking to compete, recruited the same *Grandes Ecoles/*

civil-servant types who were familiar with the corridors of government power.[14]

Thus serving industry and serving the state has become almost one and the same thing in France. The managers who run the largest companies, the bankers who provide them with capital, and the government officials who oversee them, are all drawn from the same educational background and all share the same goal of keeping French industry in French hands.

The state's strong role in the economy, known as *dirigisme*, is perhaps the main factor affecting governance in France. Though the state is becoming less *dirigiste*, it has been active in forcing mergers and restructurings in state-owned industries for policy purposes, and keeping key industries firmly under government control. The results have been mixed. While France has enjoyed some notable successes (nuclear power, aerospace) it has not been without failures (computers, consumer electronics). The government has substantial holdings in cars, steel, insurance, and banking and has a monopoly in most public utilities, rail, coal, tobacco, radio, and television.

The French state's motivation is to keep what it perceives as key industries in French hands. Traditionally, this was achieved simply by keeping such industries nationalized. However, as nationalized companies became increasingly uncompetitive, the Jacques Chirac government of 1986–8 engaged on a privatization drive, similar to that of Margaret Thatcher's government in the United Kingdom. To protect fledgling private companies from takeover, they were left with a *noyeau dur* (hard core) of management-friendly shareholders. These hard core holding groups (generally close to Chirac's party) could not sell their controlling blocks for a period of five years without the company's approval. One example is the Banque Nationale de Paris (BNP), which was privatized in December 1993. Despite overwhelming interest from individual shareholders, who quickly bought up the shares reserved for them in tiny allotments, no fewer than 16 friendly institutional shareholders own 30 percent of BNP's shares. Half of those shares are held by Union des Assurances de Paris (UAP), a state-owned insurer. The result is that BNP is virtually immune from takeover.

The state protects industry in other ways. For instance, any non-EC company buying a fifth of the capital of a French firm needs clearance from the government. Even in non-state-owned companies, the government plays a powerful role. There is a tangled web of relationships among directors, managers, and the government.

In private companies, directors and executives shuttle back and forth between the private and public sector. Many of the top people in the finance ministry move across to jobs in state-owned and private companies alike. The French call this *pantouflage* – literally, "putting on one's slippers." In 1992, *pantouflage* became so common that the government had to introduce new rules to stem the tide of people leaving the civil service.

The state's control over private companies also extends indirectly through the banking system. France's financial institutions (banks and insurance companies) are leading providers of capital to French industry, and now account for one-twentieth of the Bourse's capitalization. However, many of the banks are state owned, or heavily state influenced – for instance, even the largest private banks are usually run by ex-government officials. Banks are informed, long-term shareholders who have played a strong role in protecting French companies from takeover.

Thus, the state asserts a good deal of influence over private, or recently privatized, companies. But by the same token state-owned companies can sometimes display a powerful independence from the government. For instance, in 1988, Finance Minister Pierre Beregovoy attempted to takeover the recently privatized Société Générale from the *noyeau dur* of shareholders that controlled it. The raid was financed mainly by the state-owned Caisse des Depots et Consignations, the largest state deposit institution. However, the President-Directeur-General (PDG) of state-owned UAP refused to support Beregovoy's raid, despite the fact that he was a government-appointed manager and a one-time senior government official from the same party as Beregovoy.[15] In such situations it is hard to see where the line between public and private sectors is drawn.

France has developed a complex system of cross-sharing, not unlike the Japanese *keiretsu*. The *verrouillage* system, in which shares are "parked" with friendly companies, accounts for an estimated two-thirds of the shares traded on the Bourse. By other mechanisms, companies can effectively hold their own shares. This system plays a strong role in defeating unsolicited takeovers.

## UNITED KINGDOM

While the UK system closely resembles that of the United States, there are a few notable differences. For instance, in contrast to the United States, a majority of boards in the United Kingdom have a non-executive chairman. However, many boards have a majority of inside directors – only 42 percent of all directors are outsiders, and 9 percent of the largest UK companies have no outside directors at all.[16]

Also, institutional investors in the United Kingdom hold a larger stake in domestic equities than do their US counterparts. In the United Kingdom, 67 percent of equity is held by UK institutions[17]; the comparable figure for the United States is 46.8 percent.[18]

UK institutions have generally exerted their influence in behind-the-scenes discussions with management, rather than becoming involved in the high-profile proxy fights that have occurred in the United States. The chief executive of the insurance giant, Legal & General, estimates that his company schedules 500 meetings annually with the managements of portfolio companies.[19] British institutions successfully lobbied the management of Barclays Bank to appoint a separate CEO and chairman in 1993, and played a powerful role in the June 1992 ouster of Robert Horton, chairman and CEO of British Petroleum. Increasingly, British institutions are associating themselves with more high-profile battles with management.

## Case in Point: Hanson Plc

In 1993, institutional investors in both the United States and the United Kingdom joined to oppose changes in the corporate bylaws of the British industrial conglomerate, Hanson Plc. The changes would have required shareholders to muster a 10 percent shareholder vote to nominate a director, and 5 percent to amend ordinary resolutions. Hanson sought the changes to make shareholder meetings more orderly.

The result was a barrage of criticism from the National Association of Pension Funds and the Pensions and Investments Research Consultants in the United Kingdom, and from the State of Wisconsin Investment Board and the Florida State Board of Investments in the United States. Hanson, expressing surprise at the force of the protest, withdrew the changes.

Such activism has been prompted in part by the long, deep recession that struck the United Kingdom in 1990 and partly by a series of high-profile corporate disasters (most notably the collapse of Asil Nadir's Polly Peck International, Robert Maxwell's MGN/Pergamon empire, and the Bank of Credit and Commerce International), which raised the issue of corporate accountability both in the public mind and in the House of Commons. Corporate Britain is currently undergoing a period of self-analysis to see how to avoid expensive corporate disasters in the future.

- *The Cadbury Committee* In December 1992, a Committee on the Financial Aspects of Corporate Governance, chaired by Sir Adrian Cadbury, published its "Code of Best Practice," aimed at the directors of UK companies. The code calls for a strong independent element on the board in the form of independent directors, the need to make executive directors more accountable to shareholders, and the need to establish effective audit, compensation, and nomination committees.

  Cadbury's "Statement of Best Practice" recommends that "There should be a clearly accepted division of responsibilities at the head of a company, which will ensure a balance of power and authority, such that no one individual has unfettered powers of decision. Where the chairman is also the chief executive, it is essential that there should be a strong and independent element on the board, with a recognized senior member. The board should include non-executive directors of sufficient calibre and number for their views to carry sufficient weight in the board's decisions."[20]

  As a requirement of the London Stock Exchange, listed companies will have to state in their annual reports how they comply with the code's recommendation, and in the areas where they do not comply, they must explain why. However, there is no penalty for failing to adopt the code. In this field, as in most cases, the City of London has chosen to follow the path of self-regulation.
- *The Goode Report* Following death of Robert Maxwell, and the collapse of his media and communications empire, in the winter of 1991, it was discovered that Maxwell had stolen $700 million from his employees' pension fund to finance his increasingly shaky operation. Parliament commissioned a study on how the law might be improved to prevent such crimes occurring again. The report, chaired by Oxford University Professor Roy Goode, published its 2,000 page findings in the fall of 1993. Goode recommended a new pensions act, run by a pension regulator, to smooth out the confused variety of laws and regulations that currently govern the operation of pension funds. He also proposed that plan participants be allowed to elect at least one-third of the plan's trustees. Finally, Goode proposed that pension funds be required to meet minimum solvency standards.[21] (Such a rule would prevent the kinds of problems developing in the United

States, such as General Motors' $17 billion pension fund short-
fall. See chapter 2.)

## Case in Point: British Petroleum

New standards of governance appear to have taken hold at some
of the UK's largest companies. In June 1992, British Petroleum
forced the resignation of CEO and Chairman Bob Horton. Following Horton's ouster, the company pledged to:

- establish a nominating committee made up solely of outside directors;
- separate the roles of chairman and chief executive;
- endorse the Cadbury Committee's Code of Best Practice.

In the annual report following the changes, the company's chairman,
Lord Asburton, explained the changes:

> In June, in a new departure for BP, the board decided to split the
> functions of the chairman and chief executive.
>
> By way of very brief explanation, I, as part-time chairman, am
> responsible for the management of board affairs and am closely
> in touch with the development of strategy. David Simon, the
> group chief executive, and his six fellow executive managing
> directors, are responsible for formulating strategy for the board
> as a whole to consider, as well as for the conduct of BP's day-
> to-day business. Already, after only eight months of the new
> arrangement, I believe the management of BP's affairs is benefiting
> from the splitting of the two roles.
>
> The past year has seen much debate in the United Kingdom
> about the duties of company directors, both executive and non-
> executive, and about the structure and functioning of boards.
> This culminated in the publication of the Cadbury Report on
> corporate governance. BP was among the many leading compa-
> nies and other organizations that contributed to the deliberations
> of the Cadbury Committee and we believe that we already sub-
> stantially comply with its recommendations.

### Privatization

When Margaret Thatcher became Prime Minister in 1979, the
British economy was still heavily managed by the government. All
utilities, as well as heavy industries such as steel and coal production, were state owned. Thatcher committed her Conservative
government to privatizing many of these industries. Over the next
decade, companies such as British Telecom and British Gas were

sold off to the public, as were the entire water and power generating industries.

But the government retained an interest, by means of a "golden share." This was a share that, while minimal in value, held a controlling vote of the stock. Thus could the government provide against rapid takeovers of the fledgling companies.

### Activism in the United Kingdom

There are many groups dedicated to improving the accountability of corporations to their owners. They include:

- *PRO NED,* dedicated to the Promotion of Non-Executive Directors. The group publishes a best-practice guide for outside directors.
- *National Association of Pension Funds.* In 1992, NAPF launched a proxy advisory service to help pension fund trustees and their investment managers to identify controversial proxy issues. NAPF's membership represents 57 percent of the UK equity market.
- *Pension and Investment Research Consultants.* This group encourages institutional activism, and campaigns against anti-shareholder moves by corporate management.

## THE EUROPEAN COMMUNITY: THE GOAL OF "HARMONIZATION"

The three countries discussed above – Germany, France, and the United Kingdom – have very different governance structures and practices. Yet all three are members of the EC. This has raised some difficult questions for the Community's policy makers in Brussels.

We argued earlier that the most powerful force affecting governance over the next decade will be the globalization of capital. There are, however, countervailing trends. For example, the globalization of the markets raises the specter of a worldwide "race to the bottom," with countries competing to provide the most accommodating possible domiciles for corporate managers (who select the company's domicile) in order to get the benefits of the registration fees, legal business, and tax revenues. This recalls the role that Delaware plays in American corporate law.

This problem has been addressed in depth by the nations that belong to the European Community (EC). As noted by one scholar, "The formation of a single European market in 1992 has raised again the difficult issue of the 'race to the bottom' – more elegantly termed the 'lowest common denominator,' or, more fearsomely, the prospect of 'regulatory meltdown.' "[22] A second academic describes the trend as "regulatory arbitrage":

> Securities firms will migrate from one jurisdiction to another to avoid markets subject to relatively more stringent rules governing disclosure, manipulative conduct, and other regulations protective of investors. No investment firm wants to end up "in some oasis of regulatory purity" while its competitors operate under more liberal rules.[23]

One example was the debate over the EC directive on cross-border mergers, approved in late 1989 by EC member states. One observer noted that a major barrier to passage was the "fear by those member states requiring employee participation in corporate management that interstate mergers will be used to circumvent such requirements."[24] For this reason, among others, the EC rules apply to only the very largest transactions.

One difference between the EC and the American "Delaware factor" is a matter of timing. Bringing together economies that have been established over centuries is very different from the long-term American commitment to freedom of interstate commerce. Before the EC, each European state was free to exclude corporations of any other state from doing business. Furthermore, if it did allow a foreign corporation to do business, it could impose its own regulations and taxes.

The EC's approach has been "harmonization," rather than standardization. The rules which are adopted focus on ends and leave the member states a great deal of flexibility on means. The Treaty establishing the European Economic Community notes that: "A directive shall be binding, as to the result to be achieved, upon each Member State to which it is addressed, but shall leave the national authorities the choice of form and methods."[25]

One issue that has attracted fierce controversy is that of employee ownership. It is important to recognize that the so-called "Fifth Company Law Directive (Employee Participation in Corporate Governance)" was proposed to the EC in 1972, most recently revised in 1983, and still has little prospect of being adopted. The fact that it has languished so long, even after redrafting, is indicative of the obstacles to attempts to "harmonize" the corporate law of different jurisdictions.

The Fifth Directive proposal can be seen as an effort to prevent an international "race to the bottom" by establishing some minimum standards. The proposal's most controversial provision is based on the German and French models, requiring a dual board system, with two-thirds of the supervisory board selected by shareholders and one-third by employees. The 1983 redraft allowed one board, but required employee participation through one of three available options. The Directive also includes core shareholder rights based on the American model. As described by one scholar, these include:

> compulsory annual and special meetings of shareholders; notices, agendas, and proxy voting at meetings; the availability of corporate information to shareholders; majority voting on resolutions; the content of minutes; and shareholder adoption of audited financial statements. In addition, the Directive would create a private cause of action to minority shareholders for damages sustained by the company as a result of breach of duties by members of either board. No similar remedy is provided to employees.[26]

A proposed Directive on Takeover Bids, proposed in 1988, also contains some protection for shareholders. It would require equal treatment of all shareholders, and would impose substantive rules on the amount of time a tender offer must remain open, the disclosures that must accompany it, and so on. And it would require each member state to designate a competent authority to oversee compliance with these rules.

Beyond the debate and delay, there are other obstacles to meaningful "harmonization" in the EC. Opposition from the Eurosecurities industry resulted in significant loopholes. Disclosure is still inadequate.

> Conspicuously absent is regulation of business conduct. . . . No rules have been proposed to prohibit numerous types of manipulative practices relating to both the distribution and trading of securities. . . . Lastly, the EC has developed no institutional mechanism to assure the coordination and enforcement of the regulatory system it has created. While regulatory disparities among the Member States continue to abate, virtually nothing has been proposed to harmonize enforcement. The directives generally provide for cooperation among competent authorities, but they mandate little else.[27]

Another approach to "harmonization" was provided when EC leaders concluded that enterprises should be enabled to form

"Community corporations" that would not be viewed as "nationals" of any particular member, nor subject to idiosyncrasies of national laws.

As the EC has tried to harmonize the disparate corporate laws of the member nations, so a Europe-wide shareholder rights organization has developed. There is an organization called the European Shareholders' Group that functions as an umbrella group for the many shareholder associations that already exist in the European Community. The group's aim is to improve contact among national associations and also to undertake investor advocacy work with the EC.

## AUSTRALIA

Australia has a system similar to those in the United States and the United Kingdom. Directors are appointed by shareholders for two or three years, depending on the company's articles.

Most boards have a majority of outsiders, but as in the United States and the United Kingdom, this is no guarantee of genuine independence. This is an area where Australia's nascent shareholder movement is focusing its attention.

On the regulatory side, the Australian government is undertaking a set of reforms to improve disclosure of financial information and to update accounting rules. This follows several financial debacles in the late 1980s, including the collapse of a number of the country's largest financial conglomerates. In response, the Australian federal government founded the Australian Securities Commission in 1991 (a body similar to the Securities and Exchange Commission in the United States), revised corporate law to supersede state law, and revised accounting standards.

Institutional ownership in Australia is significant. Most of the large financial institutions own an average of between 2 and 10 percent of most of Australia's largest corporations, and there is a sizable concentration of assets among just a few of the country's largest institutions. At most corporations, the largest institutional holder has board representation.

Corporate pension funds have not been active shareholders in the past. However, in the last few years the Australian government has encouraged most firms to make pension fund contributions. These assets will be managed both by existing institutions and by in-house corporate pension managers, and the size of such assets is expected to grow significantly through the 1990s. It is still uncertain what role they will assume in the governance of the companies they own.

Labor unions are powerful in Australia. Indeed, long-time Prime Minister Bob Hawke was a union leader before entering national politics. Labor-affiliated directors are found at most government-related companies, as well as at a few of the larger corporations. For example, the Commonwealth Bank, where 30 percent of the capital was recently privatized in a public sale, includes labor representatives among its directors.

There are two main shareholder groups in Australia. The Australian Shareholders' Association promotes the interests of individual shareholders, while the Australian Investment Managers Group represents institutional money managers. As these two groups grow in size and mission, they are finding their corporate critics.

The Stock Exchange of Australia (ASX), like the New York Stock Exchange, creates governance standards via listing requirements. For instance, the ASX writes rules governing employee and executive stock-option plans. In 1992, the ASX, supported by the Australian Shareholders Association, opposed a stock option plan at the John Fairfax Group, a large Australian publisher. Ultimately, the company dropped the option plan.

Governance in Australia appears to be informal, and a little "behind the scenes." Although Australian boards have been under pressure to raise the number of outside directors at boards, and to form independent nominating and compensation committees, Australian directors are highly management friendly. As one ISS analyst observes: "Essentially, the system was, and continues to be, an old-boy network."[28]

Despite the clubbiness, however, relations between management and the investment community are strong. Australia seems to have established a system of "relationship investing" much more fully than have either of its closest counterparts, the United States and the United Kingdom. The closeness comes as a result of the comparatively large size of the Australian institutions relative to their market. Like their largest counterparts in other countries, Australian institutions are unable to follow the Wall Street Walk.

As a result, Australian institutions are known as large, long-term investors. As such their influence is recognized by management. In the words of the ISS analyst: "These long-term commitments and the influence that even a mid-sized insurance company or bank can have on the share price of a company mean that [institutions] are treated very well by companies."[29]

Another result of the close relationship between companies and their largest investors is that agreements and decisions tend to be made in private, and not in the public forum of the annual meeting. Resolutions may be sponsored by shareholders representing 5 percent of the company's shares, or by a group of at least 100 holders whose average holding is no less than A$200. While resolutions are common, their success is not, since the largest shareholders don't tend to support them – they have no need of such a public approach.

For example, in October 1992, the chairman and four other directors resigned from the board of Westpac, Australia's largest bank. Their resignations came in the wake of long-term underperformance and a number of other scandals including alleged insider trading. The five directors apparently resigned under pressure from institutional shareholders, who threatened not to support the incumbent board in the event of a proxy contest. This is typical of the "closed door" activism that occurs in Australia.

## Case in Point: News Corp.

In October 1993, Rupert Murdoch, the founder and controlling shareholder of News Corp. told shareholders gathered for the company's annual meeting that he planned to issue "super voting stock." The plan, conditional on the approval of Australian securities regulators, would allow Murdoch to issue equity to partners without diluting his stake. In other words, Murdoch could form strategic alliances via large issues of shares while maintaining his 30 percent block of stock.

Less than two months later, Murdoch withdrew the plan, mostly due to opposition from Australian institutions as well as the Australian stock exchange. The institutions controlled 40 percent of News Corp.'s stock, and feared that the plan would allow Murdoch to maintain his controlling stake in the company without having to pay for it.

News Corp.'s shares improved 8.4 percent on the announcement that Murdoch was withdrawing the plan.

Shann Turnbull, an Australian expert in corporate governance with strong credentials as an academic, investor, and a corporate manager, argues that "most corporations in the English-speaking world are inherently corrupt because their unitary board structures concentrate conflicts of interest and corporate power." He recommends a dual board structure, with a corporate "senate" to oversee the regular board. The corporate senate has no more than three members, elected on the basis of one vote per shareholder (instead of one vote per share). It has no pro-active power of any kind. Instead, it has veto power over any activity where the board has a conflict of interests, and even that can be overridden by a vote of 75 percent of the shares.[30]

## NOTES

1. Clive Crook, "The Future of Capitalism," *The Economist,* Sept. 11, 1993, p. 52.
2. This estimate quoted in Leslie Wayne, "Exporting Shareholder Activism," *New York Times,* July 16, 1993, p. D1.
3. According to the Securities Industry Association, cited in the *Wall Street Journal,* Aug. 10, 1993, these levels began to fluctuate widely after the crash of Oct. 1987, but are now stabilizing at close to their former levels.
4. On Dec. 15, 1993, 117 nations signed the General Agreement on Tariffs and Trade in Geneva, Switzerland, a multinational trade agreement that will break down trade barriers among signatory nations. Although each country's participation must be approved by its own national legislature, the prognosis is good for this historic development.
5. See Bruce Babcock, "The Seeds of Change in Japan," *The Corporate Governance Advisor,* 1, 8, Dec. 1993.
7. David Waller, "Allianz disclosure helps clear fog," *Financial Times,* Oct. 8, 1993, p. 22.
8. The Anglo-American world has seen many proposals that would, in essence, replicate the Germany two-tier system. See Shann Turnbull's discussion of corporate "senates" on page 316, or the shareholder advisory committee, or the proposal submitted to Exxon by one of the authors of this book, Robert A.G. Monks on page 168. Both models provide for a "supervisory" council to oversee the board. Other proposals, such of those of the Cadbury Commission in the United Kingdom (see page 303) or the Lipton/Lorsch "lead director" proposal (see page 221) have also been criticized for undermining the unitary structure.
9. David Waller, "A Bashing at Metall," *Financial Times,* Jan. 18, 1994, p. 10.
10. Id.
11. Geoffrey Mazullo and Thomas Zinzi, "Shareholder Activism in Europe," *ISSue Alert,* VIII, 9, November 1993, p. 5.
12. Oxford Analytica, supra, p. 82.
13. This section on the DSW has been reproduced, by kind permission of Institutional Shareholder Services, Washington, DC, from Geoffrey

Mazullo and Thomas Zinzi, "Shareholder Activism in Europe," supra, p. 5.

14. Oxford Analytica, supra, p. 96.
15. Id., p. 103.
16. Oxford Analytica, supra, p. 62.
17. Institutional Shareholder Services, "Proxy Voting Guidelines: United Kingdom," 1993, p. 7.
18. Leslie Scism, "Institutional Share of US Equities Slips," *Wall Street Journal,* Dec. 8, 1993, p. C1.
19. Oxford Analytica, supra, p. 64.
20. Report of the Committee on The Financial Aspects of Corporate Governance, The Code of Best Practice, Dec. 1, 1992, parts 1.2, 1.3.
21. Editorial, "Goode in Parts," *The Economist,* Oct. 2–8, 1993, p. 84.
22. David Charney, "Competition among Jurisdictions in Formulating Corporate Law Rules: An American Perspective on the 'Race to the Bottom' in the European Communities," *Harvard International Law Journal,* 32, 2, Spring 1991, p. 423.
23. Manning Gilbert Warren III, "Global Harmonization of Securities Laws: The Achievements of the European Communities," *Harvard International Law Journal,* 31, 1, Winter 1990, p. 189.
24. Id., p. 204.
25. "Completing the Internal Market: White Paper from the Commission to the European Council 310," June 14, 1985, art. 189.
26. Warren, supra, p. 203.
27. Id., p. 231.
28. Bruce Babcock, "Proxy Voting Guidelines: Australia," Institutional Shareholder Services, Washington, DC, 1993.
29. Id.
30. Shann Turnbull, "Improving Corporate Structure and Ethics: A Case for Corporate 'Senates,'" *Director's Monthly,* 17, 5, May 1993, pp. 1–4.

# INDEX